NB * Notes at back.

CM01603530

TOURING IN SOUTH AFRICA

WILLIE & SANDRA OLIVIER

Struik Publishers
(a division of New Holland Publishing (South Africa) (Pty) Ltd)
London • Cape Town • Sydney • Auckland

Garfield House
86–88 Edgware Road
W2 2EA London
United Kingdom
www.newhollandpublishers.com

Cornelis Struik House
80 McKenzie Street
Cape Town 8001
South Africa
www.struik.co.za

14 Aquatic Drive
Frenchs Forest, NSW 2086
Australia

218 Lake Road
Northcote, Auckland
New Zealand

New Holland Publishing is a member of the Johnnic Publishing Group

Copyright © in published edition 2001: Struik Publishers
Copyright © in text 2001: Willie and Sandra Olivier
Copyright © in maps 2001: Struik Publishers
Copyright © in photographs 2001: as listed below

10 9 8 7 6 5 4 3 2 1

Publishing manager: Annlerie van Rooyen
Design director: Janice Evans
Managing editor: Lesley Hay-Whitton
Designer: Michelle Ludek
Editor: Alfred leMaitre
Project co-ordinator: Glynne Newlands
Cartographer: John Hall
Indexer: Mary Lennox
Proofreader: Gill Gordon

Reproduction by Hirt & Carter Cape (Pty) Ltd
Printed and bound by Craft Print (Pte) Ltd

ISBN 1 86872 388 7

All rights reserved. No part of this publication may be reproduced, stored in a retrieval system, or transmitted, in any form or by any means, electronic, mechanical, photocopying, recording or otherwise, without the prior written permission of the copyright owner/s.

AFS=Athol Franz Studio; BAC=Brandon Amron-Coetzee; BER=Bloemendal Estate Restaurant; BR=Brendan Ryan; CL=C Lanz; CLB=Colour Library; CW=Chanan Weiss; DA=D Allen; DB=David Bristow; DDP=Dennis & de la Harpe Photography; DJ=Di Jones; DP=D Pinnock; DR=David Rogers; DS=David Steele; DvdO=Dorothee von den Osten; ET=Erhardt Thiel; FK=Fanie Kloppers; GA=Getaway; GD=Gerhard Dreyer; GI=Gallo Images; GS=G Scoble; HdP=Herman du Plessis; HP=Herman Potgeiter; HvH=Hein von Hörsten; IvN=Izak van Niekerk; JF=J Fox; JJ=Jeremy Jowell; JL=Jason Lauré; JM=Jackie Murray; KY=Keith Young; LE=Leopard Enterprises; LH=Leonard Hoffmann; LvH=Lanz von Hörsten; ML=Mark Lewis; MS=Mark Skinner; NJD=Nigel Dennis; PA=Photo Access; PP=Peter Pickford; PR=Photo Royal; PS=Philip Schedler; RD=R Daly; RdlH=Roger de la Harpe; RdT=Richard du Toit; RH=Rod Haestier; SA=Shaen Adey; SIL=Struik Image Library; SL=Steve Lunderstadt; WK=Walter Knirr; WL=Wicus Leeuwner; WT=Warwick Tarboton

Front cover: (top) WK, (centre top) HvH/SIL, (centre bottom) RdT/GI, (centre main) LvH/SIL; back cover: NJD/DDP; title page: WK; 4: LvH/SIL; 5: DR; 8: (top left) Monex, (top right) ET/SIL, (bottom) WK; 9: (top & centre top left) SA/SIL, (centre, top right) KY/SIL, (centre, bottom left)WK, (centre bottom right) HvH/SIL, (bottom) LH/SIL; 10: (1) SA/SIL, (2) WK; 11: (3) SA/SIL, (4) WK/SIL; 12: (1) SA/SIL, (2) CLB/SIL; 13: (3 & 4) SA/SIL, (5) ET/SIL; 14: (1) BER, (2) SA/SIL, (3) WK; 15: (4) WK, (5) SA; 16: (all) SA/SIL; 17: (5) WK, (6) ET/SIL; 18: (1) MS/SIL, (2) WK, (3) SA/SIL; 19: (4) SA/SIL, (5) LvH/SIL; 21: (1) HvH, (2) HdP, (3 & 4) HvH/SIL; 22: LvH/SIL; 23: (2) WK, (3) LvH/SIL; 24: (1) KY/SIL, (2) KY, (3) WK; 25: HvH/SIL; 26: (1) DS/PA, (2) WK; 27: (3 & 4) HvH/SIL; 28: (top, both) SA/SIL, (bottom) LvH/SIL; 29: (top left & right) SA/SIL, (centre) HvH/SIL, (bottom left) SA/SIL, (bottom right) PP/SIL; 30: (1) ET/SIL, (2) LvH/SIL; 31: (3) LvH/SIL, (4) KY/PA; 32: (1, 3 & 4) SA/SIL, (2) Greater Hermanus Association for Commerce & Tourism, (5) HP/GI; 33: (6) KY/SIL, (7) HvH/SIL; 34: (1) GA/CL/PA, (2) SA/SIL; 35: (3) HvH/SIL, (4) KY, (5) SA/SIL; 36: (1) LvH/SIL, (2) SA/SIL, (3) HvH/SIL; 37: (4) SA/SIL, (5) The Photo Workshop; 38: (1) ET/SIL, (2) DS/PA; 39: (3 & 4) LvH/SIL, (5) WK; 40: (top) SA/SIL, (bottom) WK/SIL; 41: (top) JF, (centre above left) FK/LP, (top right) ET/SIL, (centre below left and right) SA/SIL, (bottom) KY/SIL; 42: (1) GA/GS/PA, (2 & 3) BAC; 43: (4) HvH/SIL, (5) GA/GS/PA; 44: (1) ET/SIL, (2) SA/SIL, (3) GA/DS/PA; 45: (4) WK/SIL, (4) SA/SIL; 46: SA/SIL; 47: (2) DS/PA, (3) JF, (4) SA/SIL, (5) GA/CL/PA; 48: (1) WL, (2 & 3) IvN; 49: NJD/SIL; 50: JJ; 51: (top left) GD/SIL, (top right & centre) SA/SIL, (bottom left) NJD/SIL, (bottom centre & right) GD/SIL; 52: (1, 3 & 4) GD/SIL, (2) NJD/SIL; 53: (5) CLB, (6) WK/SIL; 54: (1) JJ, (2) GA/RD/PA, (3) HvH/SIL; 55: (4) DR, (5) WK, (6) HvH/SIL; 56: (1 & 2) DR, (3) DS/PA; 57: (4) WK, (5) WK/SIL; 58: (all) GD/SIL; 59: (5) GD/SIL, (6) WK; 60: SA/SIL; 61: (2) KY/SIL, (3–5) GD/SIL; 62: (1) GD/SIL, (2) PP/SIL; 63: (3) WK, (4) GA/DS/PA, (5 & 6) GD/SIL; 64: (1) WK, (2) JJ; 65: (3 & 4) GD/SIL; 66: (both) WK; 67: (top left) HvH/SIL, (top right) SA/SIL, (centre left) PP/SIL, (centre right) HvH/SIL, (bottom) WK; 68: KY; 69: (2 & 4) WK, (3) KY/SIL; 70: (1–3) HvH/SIL, (4) GA/CL/PA; 71: (5) WK, (6) HvH/SIL; 72: (1 & 2) HvH/SIL; 73: (3) HvH/SIL, (4) WK; 74: (1) PS, (2) HvH/SIL, (3) WK; 75: (4 & 5) WK; 76: (1) LvH/SIL; (2 & 3) HvH/SIL; 77: WK/SIL; 78: (1) NJD/SIL, (2) HvH/SIL; 79: (3 & 4) WK/SIL, (5) PP/SIL; 80: HvH/SIL; 81: (2 & 3) HvH/SIL; 82: (1 & 2) DR; 83: (3) HvH/SIL, (4) DR; 84: HvH/SIL; 85: (2 & 5) DR, (3) WK, (4) KY; 86: (1) JF/PA, (2) GA/JF/PA; 87: (3 & 4) WK, (5) JF; 88: (top left) GA/DB/PA, (top right) DR, (bottom) CLB/SIL; 89: (top left & right) SA/SIL, (centre) WK/SIL, (bottom left) RdlH/DDP, (bottom centre) GA/CL/PA, (bottom right) NJD/SIL; 90: (1) LH/SIL, (2) WK; 91: (3) WK/SIL, (4) WK; 92: (1) RH/GI, (2) SA/SIL, (3) DR, (4) LvH/SIL; 93: LvH/SIL; 94: (1) KY/SIL, (2) WK, (3) SA/SIL; 95: (4) SA/SIL, (5) RdlH/SIL; 96: 1) WK, (2) NJD/SIL; 97: (3) RdlH/SIL, (4) DR, (5) SA/SIL; 98: (1) HvH/SIL, (2) RdlH/SIL; 99: WK/SIL; 100: (top left & right) SA/SIL, (bottom) CLB/SIL; 101: (top left) RdlH/SIL, (top right) SA/SIL, (centre and bottom left) LH/SIL, (bottom right) NJD/SIL; 102: RdlH/DDP; 103: (2 & 4) WK, (3) RdlH/SIL; 104: (1) RdlH/SIL, (2) SA/SIL; 105: (3) RdlH/SIL, (4) SA/SIL; 106: (1 & 3) SA/SIL, (2) RdlH/SIL; 107: (4 & 6) NJD/SIL, (5) PP/SIL; 108: NJD/SIL; 109: (2) SA/SIL, (3 & 4) RdlH/SIL; 110: (top left) NJD/SIL, (top right) JF, (bottom) WK/SIL; 111: (top and centre) JF, (bottom) KY; 112: KY/SIL; 113: (2) KY, (3), WK/SIL, (4) HvH/SIL; 114: (1) GA/DP/PA, (2 & 3) GA/DR/PA; 115: (4) PR/PA, (5) GA/JF/PA, (6) DS/PA, (7) JF; 117: (1) GA/DR/PA, (2) DJ/GI, (3) DR; 118: (1) JF, (2) RdlH/SIL; 119: (3) WK/SIL; (4) WT/GI; 120: (top) JM/SIL, (bottom) SA/SIL; 121: (top left & right) ML/SIL, (centre & bottom left) WK/SIL, (bottom right) DvdO; 122: SA; 123: (2) SA/SIL, (3 & 4) WK/SIL; 124: (1) WK, (2) SA/SIL; 125: (3 & 4) SA/SIL; 126: (1) WK, (2) SA/SIL; 127: (3) SA/SIL, (4 & 5) WK; 128: (1) SA/SIL, (2) LvH/SIL; 129: (3 & 4) WK/SIL; 131: AFS; 132: (1) GA/ DP/PA, (2) GA/DB/PA; 133: (3) JF, (4 & 6) GA/DB/PA, (5) GA/JF/PA; 134: (top) LH/ SIL, (bottom) DA/DP; 135: (top left & right) LvH/SIL, (centre left) CLB/SIL, (centre right) WK/SIL, (bottom) SA/SIL; 136: (1) RdlH/SIL, (2) CLB/SIL; 137: (3) WK, (4) RdlH/SIL; 138: (1) SA, (2 & 3) WK; 139: (4 & 5) WK, (6) WK/SIL; 140: DS/PA; 141: (2 & 4) WK, (3) WK/SIL; 142: (1) DA/PA, (2) SA/GI; 143: (3) DA/PA, (4) JL/GI; 144: (top) NJD/SIL, (bottom) SA; 145: (all) NJD/SIL; 146–150: (all) LvH/ SIL; 151: (2) SA, (3) WK, (4) NJD/SIL; 152: (1) LvH/SIL, (2) WK/SIL; 153: (all) LvH/SIL; 154: GA/DR/PA; 155: (all) WK; 156: HvH/SIL; 157: (all) WK; 158: (top left & right) NJD/SIL, (bottom) DS/PA; 159: (top left) LH/SIL, (top right) CW, (centre) LvH/SIL, (bottom) NJD/SIL; 160: (1 & 2) WK; 161: (3 & 4) WK; 162: (1) SL, (2) RdlH/GI, (3) BR/GI; 163: (4) BR/GI, (5) SL; 164 & 165: (all) WK; 166: (1) WK/SIL, (2) WK; 167: (3) DR, (4) PL/PA; 168: (1 & 2) LvH/SIL, (3) HvH/SIL; 169: (4) DS/PA, (5) HvH/SIL; 170: (1 & 2) GD/SIL, (3) HvH/SIL; 171: (4) KY, (5) GD/SIL.

CONTENTS

BIBLIOGRAPHY

The following sources were consulted and will prove useful if you wish to obtain more detailed information.

- Ackhurst, J., Irwin, D. and Irwin, P. 1992. *A Field Guide to the Natal Drakensberg.* Grahamstown: Rhodes University.
- Ambrose, D. 1976. *The Guide to Lesotho.* Johannesburg: Winchester Press.
- Apps, P. (Ed) 1996. *Smithers' Mammals of Southern Africa – A Field Guide.* Johannesburg: Southern Book Publishers.
- Cameron, T. and Spies, S. B. 1986. *An Illustrated History of South Africa.* Johannesburg: Jonathan Ball.
- Chittenden, H. 1992. *Top Birding Spots in Southern Africa.* Johannesburg: Southern Book Publishers.
- Coombe, E. and Slingsby, P. 2000. *Beard Shaver's Bush – Place Names in the Cape.* Cape Town: Authors.
- Deacon, H. J. and Deacon, J. 1999. *Human Beginnings in South Africa – Uncovering the Secrets of the Stone Age.* Cape Town: David Philip.
- Derwent, S. 1999. *Guide to Cultural Tourism in South Africa.* Cape Town: Struik Publishers.
- Erasmus, B. J. P. 1995. *On Route in South Africa.* Johannesburg: Jonathan Ball.
- Hobson, T. and Collins, J. 1997. *South Africa's Winelands – A Visitor's Guide.* Cape Town: Struik Publishers.
- Hughes, D., Hands, P. and Kench, J. 1992. *South African Wine.* Cape Town: Struik.
- Laband, J. P. C. and Thompson, P. S. 1983. *Field Guide to the War in Zululand and the Defence of Natal 1879.* Pietermaritzburg: University of Natal Press.
- Leigh, M. 1986. *Touring in South Africa.* Cape Town: C Struik.
- Lewis-Williams, D. and Blundell, G. 1998. *Fragile Heritage – A Rock Art Fieldguide.* Johannesburg: Witwatersrand University Press.
- Lubke, R. A., Gess, F. W. and Bruton, M. N. 1988. A *Field Guide to the Eastern Cape Coast.* Grahamstown: Grahamstown Centre of the Wildlife Society of Southern Africa.
- Mackay, M. 1996. *The Knysna Elephants and their Forest Home.* Knysna: Wildlife and Environment Society Knysna Centre.
- Maclean, G. L. 1993. *Roberts' Birds of Southern Africa.* Cape Town: John Voelcker Bird Book Fund.
- Mountain, E. D. 1968. *Geology of Southern Africa.* Cape Town: Books of Africa.
- Nimmo, A. 1976. *The Knysna Story.* Cape Town: Juta & Company.
- Oberholster, J. J. 1972. *The Historical Monuments of South Africa.* Cape Town: National Monuments Council.
- Olivier, W. and Olivier, S. 1996. *Exploring the Natural Wonders of South Africa.* Cape Town: Struik.
- Olivier, W. and Olivier, S. 1995. *Hiking Trails of Southern Africa.* Johannesburg: Southern Book Publishers.
- Olivier, W. and Olivier, S. 1998. *Overland Through Southern Africa.* Cape Town: Struik.
- Pakenham, T. 1979. *The Boer War.* Johannesburg: Jonathan Ball Paperbacks.
- Picton-Seymour, D. 1989. *Historical Buildings in South Africa.* Cape Town: Struikhof.
- Raper, P. E. 1987. *Dictionary of Southern African Place Names.* Johannesburg: Lowry Publishers.
- Raper, P. E. 1972. S*treekname in Suid-Afrika en Suidwes.* Cape Town: Tafelberg.
- Rosenthal, E. 1970. *Gold! Gold! Gold! – The Johannesburg Gold Rush.* Johannesburg: AD. Donker.
- Saunders, C. (Advisory Editor). 1994. *An Illustrated Dictionary of South African History.* Sandton: Ibis Books and Editorial Services.
- Scott, A. 1995. T*he Overberg Explorer – A guide for environment-oriented travel in Cape Overberg.* Cape Overberg Tourism Association.
- Simons, P. B. 1987. *A Concise Guide to Cape Dutch Houses.* Cape Town: C Struik.
- Smalberger, J. M. 1975. *A History of Copper Mining in Namaqualand.* Cape Town: C Struik.
- Torlage, G. and Watt, S. 1999. *A Guide to the Anglo-Boer War Sites of KwaZulu-Natal.* Randburg: Ravan Press.
- Viljoen, M. J. and Reimold, W. U. 1999. *An Introduction to South Africa's Geological and Mining Heritage.* Randburg: Mintek.

INTRODUCTION

South Africa has justly been described as a 'world in one country'. From the precipitous peaks of the Ukhahlamba (KwaZulu-Natal Drakensberg) and the unspoilt beaches of the Maputaland coast, to the fynbos paradise of the Western Cape and the unrivalled game-viewing offered by the Kruger National Park – this beautiful land presents the visitor with an ever-changing kaleidoscope.

No less impressive is the cultural diversity, ranging from the stately Cape Dutch manor houses and the colourful Malay inhabitants of the Bo-Kaap, to the spine-chilling dances of the Zulu and the striking geometric patterns characteristic of Ndebele homesteads.

For those seeking adventure, there is an abundance of hiking trails, easy walks, mountain bike trails, scuba-diving sites and adrenaline-pumping action such as bungi jumping and abseiling.

With all this in mind, *Touring in South Africa* has been designed to enable travellers to see and experience the country's most outstanding tourist attractions. While some of the routes are well known, others take travellers to byways, well off the busy highways. We have attempted to integrate many different elements, such as scenery, history, wildlife and culture, into each tour.

Given the dynamic nature of tourism in South Africa and the number of tourist attractions, it has not been possible to give mention or to provide a description of all of them. There is, however, sufficient information to whet any traveller's appetite to start planning a trip.

An indication of the total distance of each route is provided as a guide when planning a tour. Most of the tours can be completed in a day but, to avoid rushing, it is advisable to consider spending a night, or more, along the way. A number of the longer tours (400 km and more) will, however, require at least one overnight stop. Allowance has been made for side trips and game-viewing in parks and nature reserves. Distances on maps and distances measured on odometers vary considerably and thus should be treated as an estimate only.

Detailed route directions have been sacrificed to provide more information on what there is to see and do. In addition, South Africa's road network is constantly expanding and it is, therefore, advisable to obtain an up-to-date road atlas, or the excellent maps published by the Automobile Association of South Africa, before embarking on your journey. Information on accommodation has been restricted mainly to national parks and other conservation areas for the same reason.

This implies that travellers will still need to do a fair bit of planning themselves – looking at maps and distances, contacting information bureaux for information about accommodation, finding out when attractions are open, and so on. But it has always been our attitude that planning is, after all, half the fun of going on a holiday!

Finally, we'd like to thank the many publicity associations and individuals who helped us with information. A special word of thanks to Annlerie van Rooyen of Struik who commissioned us, Alfred leMaitre for his meticulous editing, Lesley Hay-Whitton, the managing editor, Glynne Newlands, who co-ordinated the project, Michelle Ludek, the designer, and John Hall, the cartographer.

Willie and Sandra Olivier

FRONT COVER: (TOP) LONG STREET ARCHITECTURE, CAPE TOWN; (TOP LEFT) XHOSA WOMAN; (BOTTOM LEFT) LION CUBS; (RIGHT) RIVIERSONDEREND; BACK COVER: ADDO ELEPHANT NATIONAL PARK; P. 1: PRINCE ALFRED PASS IN THE BAVIAANSKLOOF; P. 4: RICHTERSVELD SCENIC; P. 5: DRAKENSBERG HORSE RIDERS.

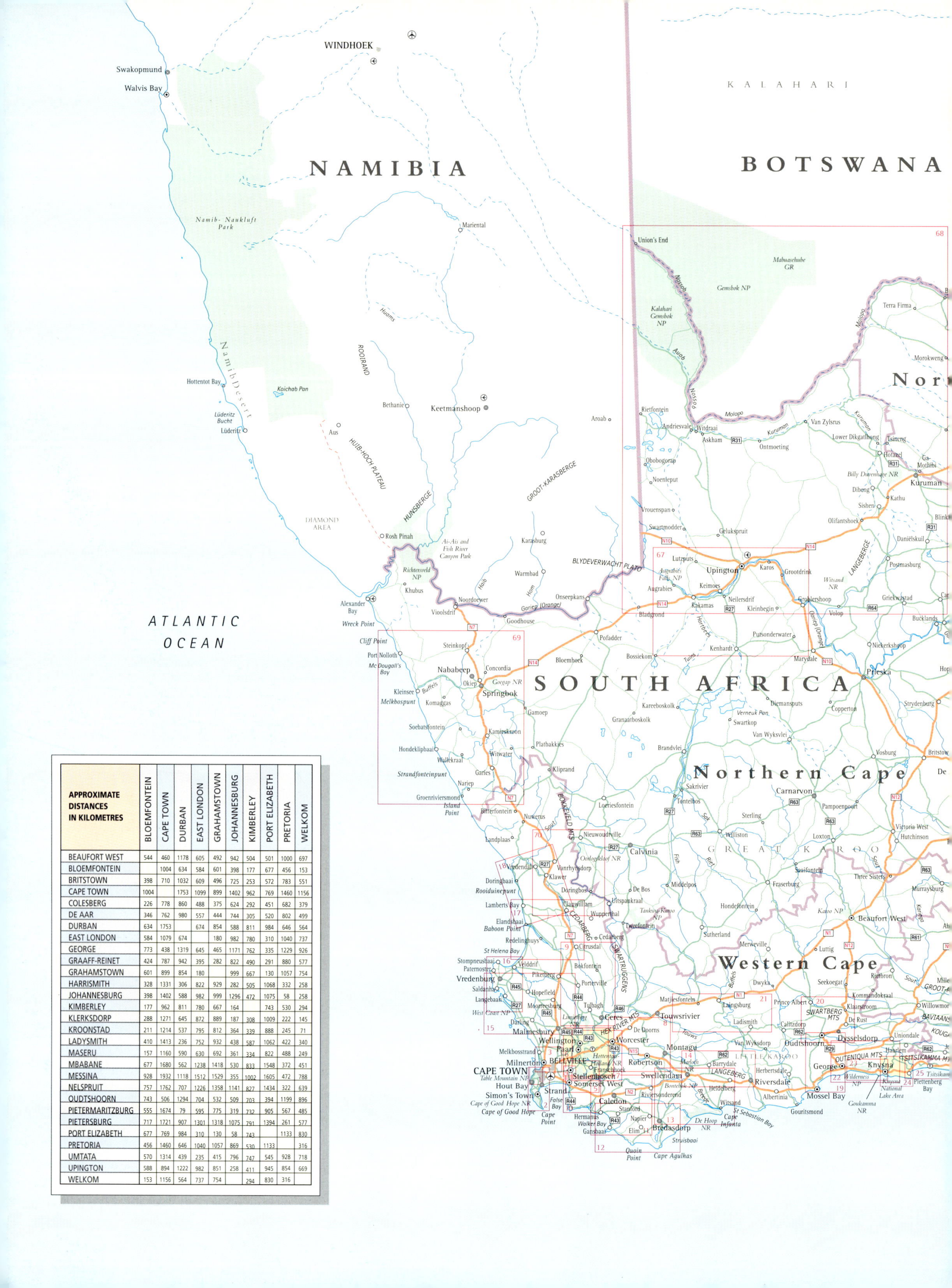

APPROXIMATE DISTANCES IN KILOMETRES	BLOEMFONTEIN	CAPE TOWN	DURBAN	EAST LONDON	GRAHAMSTOWN	JOHANNESBURG	KIMBERLEY	PORT ELIZABETH	PRETORIA	WELKOM
BEAUFORT WEST	544	460	1178	605	492	942	504	501	1000	697
BLOEMFONTEIN		1004	634	584	601	398	177	677	456	153
BRITSTOWN	398	710	1032	609	496	725	253	572	783	551
CAPE TOWN	1004		1753	1099	899	1402	962	769	1460	1156
COLESBERG	226	778	860	488	375	624	292	451	682	379
DE AAR	346	762	980	557	444	744	305	520	802	499
DURBAN	634	1753		674	854	588	811	984	646	564
EAST LONDON	584	1079	674		180	982	780	310	1040	737
GEORGE	773	438	1319	645	465	1171	762	335	1229	926
GRAAFF-REINET	424	787	942	395	282	822	490	291	880	577
GRAHAMSTOWN	601	899	854	180		999	667	130	1057	754
HARRISMITH	328	1331	306	822	929	282	505	1068	332	258
JOHANNESBURG	398	1402	588	982	999	1296	472	1075	58	258
KIMBERLEY	177	962	811	780	667	164		743	530	294
KLERKSDORP	288	1271	645	872	889	187	308	1009	222	145
KROONSTAD	211	1214	537	795	812	364	339	888	245	71
LADYSMITH	410	1413	236	752	932	438	587	1062	422	340
MASERU	157	1160	590	630	692	361	334	822	488	249
MBABANE	677	1680	562	1238	1418	530	833	1548	372	451
MESSINA	928	1932	1118	1512	1529	355	1002	1605	472	788
NELSPRUIT	757	1762	707	1226	1358	1141	827	1434	322	639
OUDTSHOORN	743	506	1294	704	532	509	703	394	1199	896
PIETERMARITZBURG	555	1674	79	595	775	319	732	905	567	485
PIETERSBURG	717	1721	907	1301	1318	1075	791	1394	261	577
PORT ELIZABETH	677	769	984	310	130	58	743		1133	830
PRETORIA	456	1460	646	1040	1057	869	530	1133		316
UMTATA	570	1314	439	235	415	796	747	545	928	718
UPINGTON	588	894	1222	982	851	258	411	945	854	669
WELKOM	153	1156	564	737	754		294	830	316	

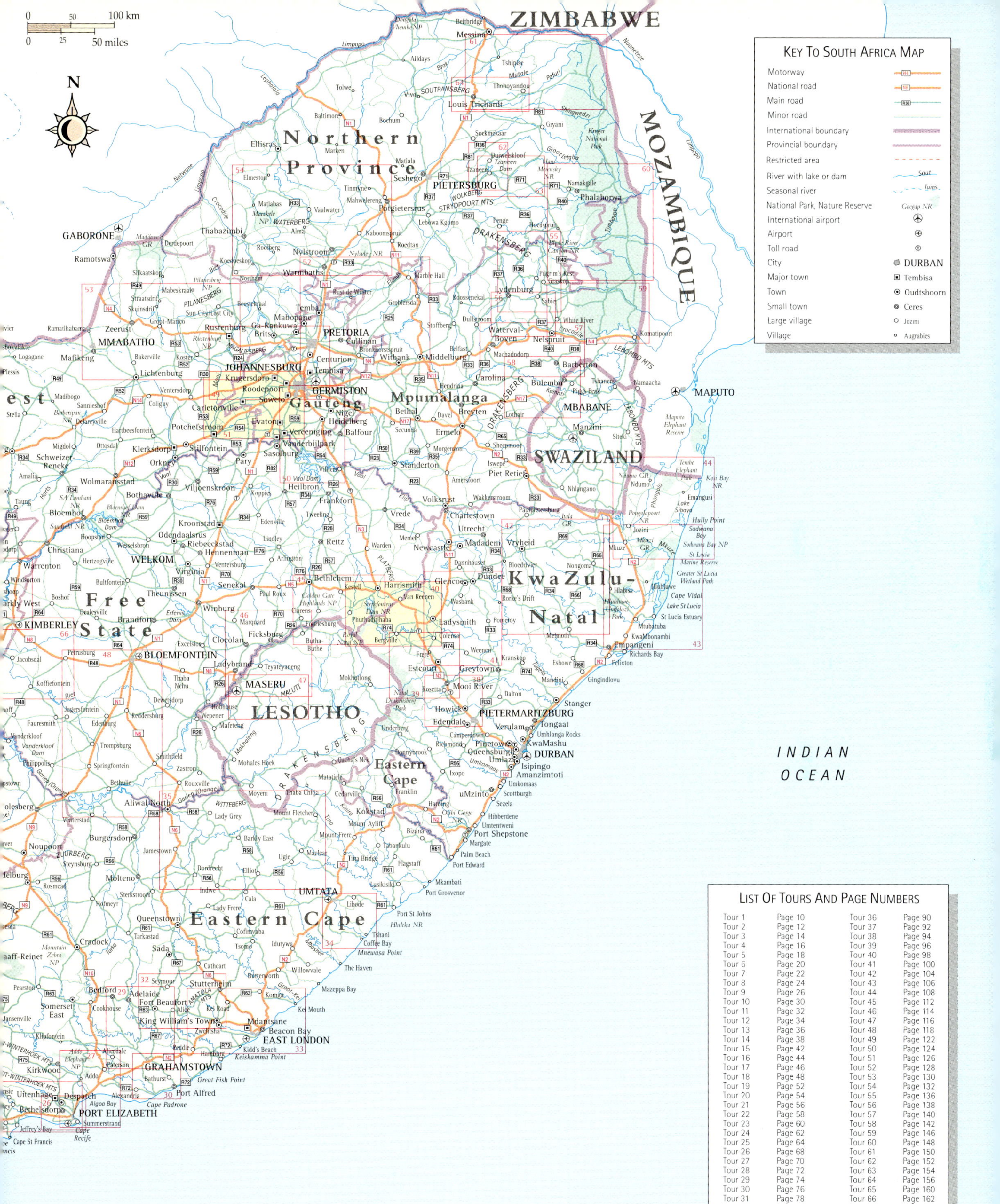

Key To South Africa Map

- Motorway
- National road
- Main road
- Minor road
- International boundary
- Provincial boundary
- Restricted area
- River with lake or dam
- Seasonal river
- National Park, Nature Reserve
- International airport
- Airport
- Toll road
- City — DURBAN
- Major town — Tembisa
- Town — Oudtshoorn
- Small town — Ceres
- Large village — Jozini
- Village — Augrabies

List Of Tours And Page Numbers

THIS PAGE FAR LEFT: RATANGA JUNCTION (P.14); LEFT: TABLE MOUNTAIN DASSIE (P.10); BELOW: TABLE MOUNTAIN PANORAMA (P.10). **OPPOSITE** TOP: CAPE MINSTRELS (P.10); CENTRE LEFT: HOUT BAY HARBOUR (P.11): CENTRE RIGHT: ST JAMES BEACH HUTS (P.13); BOTTOM LEFT: BO-KAAP HOMES (P.10); BOTTOM RIGHT: STELLENBOSCH VINEYARDS (P.16); BOTTOM: PINCUSHION PROTEA (P.11).

CAPE PENINSULA & BOLAND

WESTERN CAPE

1

1

75 KM

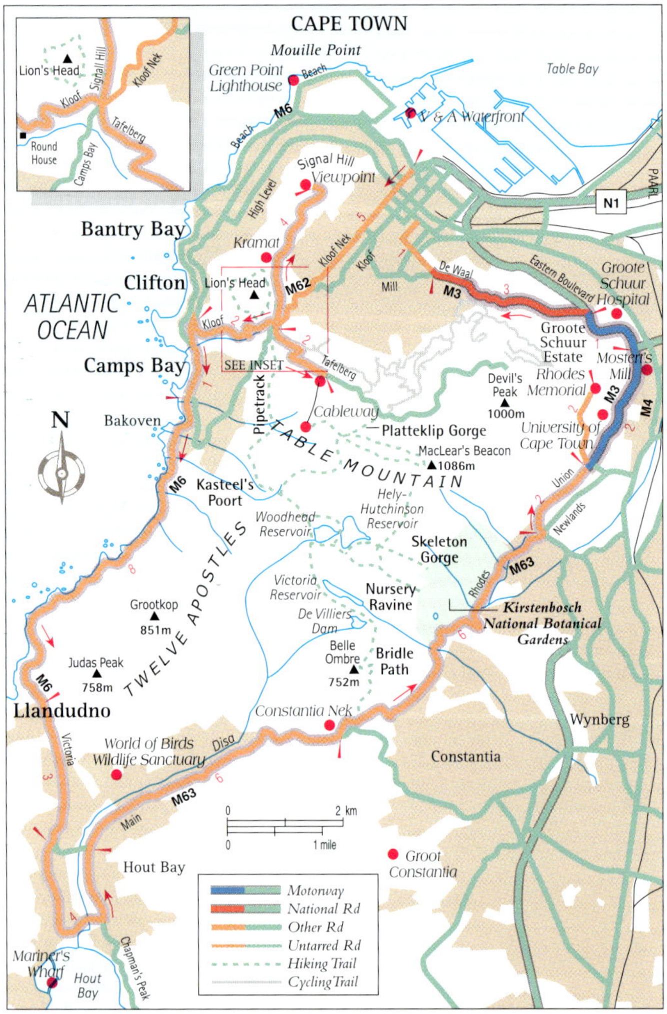

CAPE TOWN developed around the refreshment station established at the foot of Table Mountain by the Dutch East India Company in 1652. Among the city's numerous historic treasures are the pentagonal Castle (built between 1666 and 1679) and the Cultural History Museum, erected in 1679 as slave quarters, and subsequently serving as government offices and a supreme court. The nearby Company's Garden ① was established in 1652 to supply passing ships of the Dutch East India Company with fresh produce, and between 1692 and 1783 it was developed into a world-famous botanical garden. Along the oak-lined Government Avenue stand the South African National Gallery, the South African Museum and Bertram House, an early-19th-century red brick Georgian house with an outstanding collection of English furniture. The Old Town House (1755) on Greenmarket Square houses a world-renowned collection of paintings by Dutch and Flemish masters. Koopmans De Wet House, with its neoclassical façade, has a fine collection of old Cape furniture, Chinese and Japanese ceramics and Dutch delftware. Not far away, in the area formerly known as the Malay Quarter, the Bo-Kaap Museum portrays the richness of Cape Malay culture, while the District Six Museum chronicles the forced removal of 60 000 people from District Six to the Cape Flats from 1966 to 1982.

2

TABLE MOUNTAIN, together with Lion's Head and Signal Hill to the west, and Devil's Peak to the east, is one of the best-known natural landmarks in the world. It is home to a rich diversity of fynbos flora, and among its 1 470 plant species are proteas, ericas, reeds, the exquisite red disa (*Disa uniflora*) and a profusion of other flowering plants. Declared a national monument in 1957, Table Mountain ② forms part of the Cape Peninsula National Park, which was proclaimed in May 1998. The park stretches from Signal Hill to Cape Point, and is expected to cover about 30 000 ha once sections of state land and privately owned property have been incorporated. The mountain can be ascended along several walking routes, but this is best done with a guide if you are unfamiliar with the routes. The mountain's highest point, Maclear's Beacon, towers 1 086 m above the Mother City.

CABLEWAY More than 13 million people have made the journey to the top of Table Mountain by cable car ② since the cableway was officially opened in October 1929. In October 1997, a major upgrade was completed, and two large cable cars, each capable of carrying 65 people at a time, now make the five-minute journey to the summit. During the trip, the car floor rotates through 360 degrees, providing passengers with a superb view of the city. The summit offers spectacular views of the city, the sweep of Table Bay, Robben Island and the Table Mountain chain.

LION'S HEAD Rising steeply to a height of 669 m immediately to the northwest of Kloof Nek, Lion's Head is an erosional relic of sandstone underlain by more resistant granite. The soil derived from the weathered granite is favoured by the silver tree (*Leucadendron argenteum*), a member of the protea family. The largest remaining natural population of this species can be seen on the southeastern slopes of Lion's Head. The name of the conical peak is thought to come from its resemblance to the head of a lion – with Signal Hill forming the rump. Lion's Head offers an ideal vantage point; in 1673, a signalling post was set up on its summit, and watchers would fire a small cannon to notify the Castle of any approaching ships.

SIGNAL HILL, originally named Leeuwenbil (Lion's Rump) by the early Dutch settlers, but after the second British occupation of the Cape in 1806, it replaced Lion's Head as a signalling station and became known as Signal Hill. Every day except Sunday, in a city tradition dating back to 1902, the Noon Gun is fired from the Lion Battery, established on the northeastern slopes of Signal Hill in 1891. Between Lion's Head and Signal Hill is one of several Muslim kramats, or shrines, which form the 'circle of Islam' around the Cape Peninsula. According to a 275-year-old Malay prophecy, those living within the circle will be safe from fire, famine, plague, earthquakes and tidal waves. From the parking area at the end of Signal Hill, there are fine vistas over Cape Town, Table Bay, Green Point and the city's northern suburbs.

CAMPS BAY ④ Kloof Road winds down into the Glen and passes the Round House (once the hunting lodge of British Governor Lord Charles Somerset) before reaching the fashionable suburb of Camps Bay, with its palm-lined beach, tidal pool and lively atmosphere. The Twelve Apostles and Table Mountain's ravines and buttresses form an impressive backdrop.

HOUT BAY, with its picturesque harbour setting guarded by The Sentinel, is a charming seaside village. Centred around the hull of a 1940s trawler at the harbour front, Mariner's Wharf has a fish market, seafood bistro, restaurant, wine shop and several curio shops. At the World of Birds, the largest bird park in Africa, visitors can get close-up views of over 3 000 birds of 450 indigenous and exotic species, as well as a variety of small mammals. Set on 4 ha of land in the Hout Bay valley, the park has over 100 landscaped walk-through aviaries. Popular excursions from Hout Bay include a launch cruise to Duiker Island, home to a Cape fur seal colony, and a sunset cruise to Cape Town.

KIRSTENBOSCH NATIONAL BOTANICAL GARDEN ③ Covering 528 ha of natural and landscaped gardens, Kirstenbosch ranks among the world's most famous botanical gardens and has over 4 500 plant species. The cultivated garden covers 36 ha, and among its attractions are the Fragrance Garden, Cycad Amphitheatre, the Dell – with its massive tree ferns – Colonel Bird's Bath and the Fynbos Walk. The Conservatory houses a fascinating collection of plants from seven of southern Africa's arid regions in natural settings around an enormous baobab tree, which forms the focal point of the Conservatory. There are also collections of ferns, alpine flora and bulbs. The Summer Sunset Concerts held in the late afternoon on Sundays between December and March are an extremely popular annual event.

RHODES MEMORIAL This imposing memorial to Cecil John Rhodes (mining magnate and former prime minister of the Cape Colony), was designed by Sir Herbert Baker and is based on the Greek temple at Segesta, Sicily. The equestrian sculpture by GF Watts portrays 'Physical Energy'; behind it, eight bronze lions guard the steps leading up to the colonnaded temple, with its bust of Rhodes.

UNIVERSITY OF CAPE TOWN Built on the lower slopes of Devil's Peak, the University of Cape Town has its origins in the South African College, which was founded in 1829. After the college was granted university status in 1928, it was decided to relocate from the top end of the Company's Garden to the present site on Rhodes' Estate. Dominating the university grounds is Jameson Hall, with its classical portico, while the original dressed-sandstone buildings are spread out below.

MOSTERT'S MILL, a distinctive landmark on the route to and from Cape Town's southern suburbs, was one of several private mills built in the 18th century for grinding wheat. In Holland, such mills were known as *bovenkruiper*, or 'overshot' mills. The date 1796 on one of the beams suggests that the windmill was probably built by Dirk Gysbert van Reenen, who owned the farm Welgelegen at the time. The mill later came into Sybrand Mostert's possession, a son-in-law of Van Reenen, and became known as Mostert's Mill.

GROOTE SCHUUR HOSPITAL This large, well-known hospital was officially opened in 1938, six years after the foundation stone was laid. Groote Schuur Hospital became world famous on 3 December 1967, when a medical team led by Dr Chris Barnard performed the world's first heart transplant on a critically ill patient, Louis Waskansky. The story of this medical breakthrough, and subsequent heart transplants, is told in the hospital's Transplant Museum. Groote Schuur serves as the medical school of the nearby University of Cape Town.

3

4

1

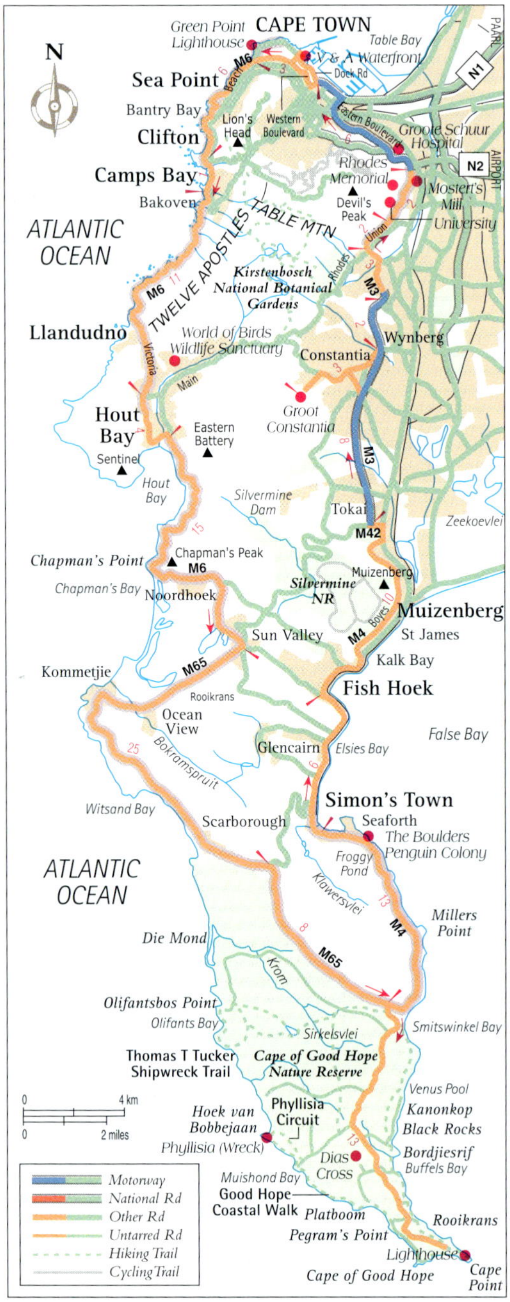

2

170 KM

2

CAPE TOWN See Tour 1, page 10.

GREEN POINT The most conspicuous feature of Green Point is the 20-m-high red-and-white lighthouse ① that for over 175 years has warned ships against hazards along the coast. Designed and built by German builder, Herman Schutte, the Green Point Lighthouse (often incorrectly called Mouille Point Lighthouse) is the oldest solidly constructed navigational aid along South Africa's coast. It became operational in 1824 and automated in 1961.

SEA POINT is one of Cape Town's most sought-after residential and holidaying areas, and its Beach Road is dubbed the 'Platinum Mile'. Lion's Head forms an impressive backdrop to the many high-rise luxury apartments, while Sea Point Promenade ① extends for 4 km along the seaward side of the road. The promenade is popular with joggers, residents walking their dogs and sundown strollers.

SEA POINT CONTACT At this notable geological site can be seen the intrusion of a large mass of granite into the older sedimentary shales of the Malmesbury Group, dating back about 550 to 600 million years. What makes the site remarkable is the nature of the contact: instead of being sharply defined, the granite and shales are extensively mixed in a wide belt. The contact became famous after Charles Darwin visited the site in 1836, and is indicated by a National Monuments Council plaque.

CLIFTON Famed for its four small beaches nestling among granite outcrops, Clifton is popular with sun-worshippers, despite the frigid water. It is also one of the city's most fashionable suburbs, with luxurious apartments and penthouses hugging the mountain slopes. Originally known as Schoenmakersgat, after a shoemaker who lived in a cave, it was later renamed Clifton-on-Sea after a resort in the United Kingdom. Still later it came to be known simply as Clifton.

CAMPS BAY See Tour 1, page 11.

HOUT BAY See Tour 1, page 11.

CHAPMAN'S PEAK DRIVE, one of the world's most spectacular coastal drives, was built between 1915 and 1922 when the road was cut into the precipitous cliffs that soar for over 500 m above the coast. The road engineers exploited the weakness in the rock by following the contact between the 550 to 600-million-year-old Cape Granite and the overlying sedimentary rock of the Table Mountain Group. Its highest point is 160 m above the sea. Chapman's Peak Drive was closed to traffic in 1999 due to rock falls, but is scheduled to reopen in 2002. In the meantime, the route to the Cape of Good Hope Nature Reserve detours from Hout Bay via Constantia Nek, along Ou Kaapse Weg to Kommetjie and Scarborough.

CAPE OF GOOD HOPE NATURE RESERVE Situated at the southern tip of the Cape Peninsula, the Cape of Good Hope section of the Cape Peninsula National Park covers 7 750 ha of fynbos vegetation and dramatic coastal scenery. The area can be explored by car along a network of tar roads, or on foot on one of the seven trails that meander through fynbos, with its over 1 100 plant species. Animals to be seen include Cape Point's famous baboons, bontebok, grey rhebok, eland and red hartebeest, and over 250 bird species have been recorded in the reserve. There are also several good spots for whale-watching and angling, while the coast offers excellent snorkelling and swimming opportunities.

CAPE POINT Sheer coastal cliffs rise nearly 200 m above the Atlantic Ocean, creating a spectacular vantage point over False Bay to the east and the Cape of Good Hope, the southernmost tip of the peninsula. Ranked amongst the highest sea cliffs in the world, Cape Point was described in 1579 by British navigator, Sir Francis Drake as '... the fairest cape and the most stately thing we saw in the whole circumference of the globe'. If you are feeling energetic, you can walk from the car park up to the old lighthouse ④, built on the 249-m-high Da Gama Peak in 1859. Or take the funicular railway to the viewpoint and stroll back down to the parking area.

BOULDERS is a picturesque bathing spot with beaches of white sand nestling among grey granite outcrops. It is home to one of only two land-based breeding colonies of the endangered African penguin ② (*Spheniscus demersus*, previously known as the jackass penguin) along the South African coast. From two pairs that bred in 1985, the population has grown to over 950 breeding pairs. Visitors can get excellent close-up views from a board-walk and viewing platform at Foxy Beach. At Boulders Beach, where swimming is permitted, penguins sometimes come ashore and waddle comically past sunbathers.

SIMON'S TOWN Named after the Dutch governor Simon van der Stel, Simon's Town has a rich maritime history dating back to 1743 when it became the official anchorage for ships of the Dutch East India Company. To protect the bay against attack by foreign fleets, the company built the Zoutman Battery on the northern outskirts of the settlement in 1793. Simon's Town served as the Southern Atlantic base of the Royal Navy between 1814 and 1957, when it was transferred to the South African Navy. Ramble down the Historic Mile, which has 21 buildings dating back more than 150 years, or visit Jubilee Square with its monument to Able Seaman Just Nuisance – one of the few dogs to attain naval rank! Other attractions include Simon's Town Museum, the South African Naval Museum, Warrior Toy Museum and Martello Tower, built in 1796 as part of the British fortification of Simon's Bay.

FISH HOEK features a magnificent sweep of sandy beach and opportunities for swimming and snorkelling off Jager Walk. From August to December, the walkway is a good vantage point for whale-watching. For many years, Fish Hoek enjoyed the status of being one of the only 'dry' towns in South Africa.

KALK BAY owes its name to the 17th-century lime kilns in which crushed sea shells were burned to make lime. The picturesque fishing harbour was built in 1913 to protect boats against the gales that often lash False Bay. The harbour is a hive of activity when boats return with catches of Cape delicacies such as snoek, geelbek and yellowtail.

ST JAMES, with its colourful wooden changing rooms, tidal pool and sandy beach, is a popular family beach. It was named after the St James Church, which was demolished in 1900 to make way for a railway station after the original platform, built 17 years earlier, became inadequate.

MUIZENBERG, with its wide sweeping beach, offers safe swimming and is a popular destination with holiday-makers and surfers. It has variously served as a cattle post (established in the 1670s by the Dutch East India Company at nearby Sandvlei), a winter anchorage for company ships and a military outpost. In the 1740s, the fort became known as Muijsenberg after Wynand Muijs, the sergeant in charge. Among its cultural treasures is the Natale Labia Museum, a beautiful dressed-stone mansion built in the 1930s for Prince Natale Labia and Princess Ida Labia. It now serves as a satellite museum of the South African National Gallery. De Post Huys, built in 1673 by the Dutch East India Company as a signal house and a small fort, is one of the oldest European-built houses in South Africa. Also of interest is Rhodes' Cottage, an unassuming thatched home where Cecil John Rhodes died in 1902.

GROOT CONSTANTIA forms part of the farm granted to Governor Simon van der Stel in 1685. He named his farm Constantia and planted the estate's first vineyards. After his death in 1712, the farm was divided into three. Groot Constantia changed hands several times until it was bought by Hendrik Cloete in 1778, and remained in the Cloete family for over a century. During this time the estate's wines became world-famous. Its focal point is the magnificent U-shaped Cape Dutch manor house ⑤ with its unusually high gable; the house is now a museum portraying life at Constantia from the 17th century on. At the rear of the manor house is the Cloete Cellar, dating back to 1791, with its magnificent sculptured pediment by Anton Anreith.

VICTORIA & ALFRED WATERFRONT Centred around the Victoria and Alfred basins of Cape Town's harbour, the Waterfront ③ is one of South Africa's top tourist attraction. Its huge variety of attractions, activities, speciality shops and restaurants, all within the setting of a working harbour, include the Two Oceans Aquarium, Telkom Exploratorium and IMAX Cinema in the BMW Pavilion. Visitors can take a cruise around the harbour, a longer boat trip in Table Bay or a helicopter flip over the city. Art and craft enthusiasts should visit the Waterfront Craft Market and Red Shed Craft Workshop. The Waterfront is also the embarkation point for tours of Robben Island; now a museum and nature reserve, it was declared a World Heritage Site by UNESCO in 1999.

3

4

5

1 

3

145 KM

 2

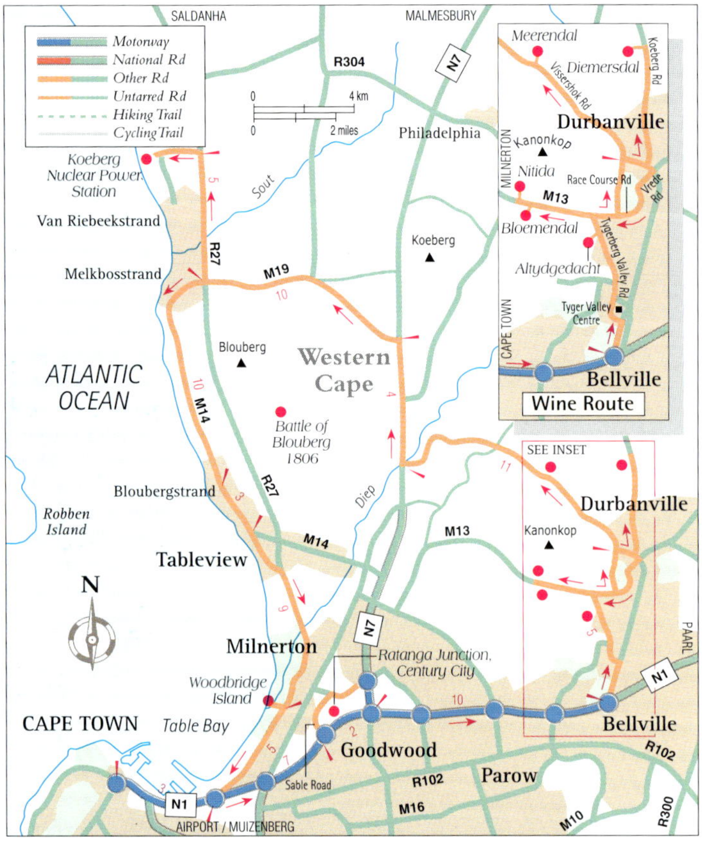

3 

CAPE TOWN See Tour 1, page 10.

RATANGA JUNCTION Covering 20 ha, Ratanga Junction is Africa's first entertainment theme park. While some of the more than 30 rides are suitable for families with children, the most heart-stopping ones are not for the faint-hearted. The Cobra ⑤ speeds along at 100 km an hour on a suspended looping coaster, while Monkey Falls is one of the highest log flumes in the world. Other rides for the wild at heart include the Diamond Devil Run (a run-away train), the Congo Queen (a swinging boat ride) and a wild white-water raft ride down Crocodile Gorge. There is a variety of theme restaurants, as well as live entertainment. Adjoining Ratanga Junction is Canal Walk ③, a giant shopping mall featuring cinemas, restaurants, live entertainment and the MTN Science Centre, and which together with Ratanga Junction, forms part of the Century City complex.

DURBANVILLE WINE ROUTE Situated in one of the coolest wine-growing areas in South Africa, the Durbanville Wine Route enjoys one of the best climates for the production of wine in South Africa. Although wines have been produced by farms in the Durbanville area since the days of the Dutch East India Company, it was not until 1990 that the Durbanville Wine Trust was established to promote the region and its wines. Nestling on the slopes of the Tygerberg Hills, Durbanville is one of South Africa's smallest wine routes. It consists of seven estates and 11 farms producing high-quality grapes for other wineries and cellars.

ALTYDGEDACHT Originally named De Tygerbergen, this farm on the slopes of the Tygerberg Hills was granted in 1689 to Elsie van Suurwaarde, the wife of an official of the Dutch East India Company. It was renamed Altydgedacht in 1826. One of the oldest wine farms in the Cape, the estate has been producing wine under its own label since 1985. A variety of excellent red and white wines are produced, among them merlot, shiraz, pinotage and sauvignon blanc.

BLOEMENDAL lies between Kanonkop and the Tygerberg Hills and enjoys superb views over the Peninsula and Table Mountain ①. The south-facing slopes of Kanonkop are planted mainly under white grape varieties, while the north-facing slopes of the Tygerberg Hills are ideally suited to reds ②. The estate has been producing wines under its own label since 1987, and is renowned for its bottle-fermented dry sparkling wine and port. Wines bottled under the estate's label include sauvignon blanc, semillon, merlot and cabernet sauvignon.

NITIDA CELLARS is named after waboom trees (*Protea nitida*) which once grew in profusion on the slopes of Kanonkop. The cellar lies on the farm Maasspruit, bought in 1990 by Bernhard and Peta Veller, and produced its first wine, a sauvignon blanc, in 1995. The range includes pinotage, cabernet sauvignon, shiraz, chardonnay and sauvignon blanc.

DURBANVILLE is a popular northern suburbs residential area with a country atmosphere. Originally named Pampoenkraal (Pumpkin Corral), the settlement was later renamed D'Urban after the Cape governor, Sir Benjamin D'Urban. To avoid confusion with Durban in KwaZulu-Natal, the name was later changed to Durbanville. Attractions include the Durbanville Rose Garden and Onze Molen, one of only two existing windmills in Cape Town. The Oude Meester art collection and ceramics by South African artists are displayed in Rust-en-Vrede, a beautiful Cape Dutch mansion dating back to 1850.

DIEMERSDAL dates back to 1698 when it was granted to Hendrik Sneewind, and owes its name to a Captain Diemer, who married Sneewind's widow. In the 1920s, the farm switched from wheat to wine, and the estate has a long-standing reputation for its excellent red wines. However, until 1986 the farm sold all its production in bulk to the KWV, and the first wine to be bottled under the Diemersdal label was a 1987 vintage dry red. Wines bottled under the Diemersdal label include cabernet sauvignon, pinotage, shiraz and sauvignon blanc.

MEERENDAL was granted to Jan Meerland in 1702, and 14 years later vineyards were already established. The focal point of the estate is its gracious Cape Dutch manor house. When the estate was acquired by the Starke family in 1929 it was a wheat farm, but in the 1940s the focus changed to wine farming and a range of red wine varietals was planted. The first wines bottled under Meerendal's own name were the 1969 pinotage and shiraz, and now include cabernet sauvignon, merlot, a red blend and some whites. The wines are matured and bottled on the estate.

KOEBERG NUCLEAR POWER STATION, operated by the electricity utility, Eskom, is the only nuclear plant in Africa. Based on the pressurised water reactor (PWR) design, construction began in 1976 and Koeberg I came on stream in 1984. Koeberg II was synchronised to the electricity grid the following year, and the two reactors can generate a maximum of 1 840 MW. Koeberg's most conspicuous features are the two dome-shaped structures housing the nuclear reactors. The reactors, which use enriched uranium dioxide for fuel, heat pressurised water; in a separate system, the water is transformed into steam, which drives the turbines in each unit. The turbines in turn drive the two generators with an output of 921 MW each. An area of 3 000 ha to the north of the power station has been set aside as the Koeberg Nature Reserve to protect the strandveld flora and fauna. Visitors can explore the reserve via one of three day-walks.

MELKBOSSTRAND takes its name from the milkwood trees (*Sideroxylon inerme*) growing along the coastal dunes north of the town. It has long been a favourite summer holiday destination with Swartland farmers, and is the venue for the annual Beach Festival on 2 January when traditional *boeresport* competitions like *toutrek* (tug-of-war) are held. The sandy beaches are popular with sunbathers and surfers.

BLOUBERGSTRAND is renowned for its classic view of Table Mountain ④, and its beaches draw many sunbathers, surfers, windsurfers and anglers. The town owes its name to a nearby hill which appears blue when viewed from vessels approaching Table Bay, and was originally named Blaauwberg (Blue Mountain) by the Dutch. In 1806, when the Cape was occupied by Britain for the second time, the Battle of Blaauwberg was fought here. After a skirmish between the 6 654-strong British force under Major-General Sir David Baird and a 2 000-strong force commanded by the Governor, Lieutenant-General Jan Janssens, the defenders withdrew and the colony surrendered. Bloubergstrand has several well-known restaurants with superb views across Table Bay to Table Mountain and the city, making it an ideal place to enjoy sundowners or dinner before returning to Cape Town.

MILNERTON was named after Sir Alfred Milner, Governor of the Cape Colony between 1897 and 1901. The historic wooden bridge to Woodbridge Island was built by British troops in 1901 to defend the coast against possible attacks by Boer guerrilla forces during the South African War. It is still used as a pedestrian crossing over the Rietvlei estuary. The 21-m-high Milnerton Lighthouse, built in 1960, is a local landmark and is one of only a few cylindrical lighthouses along the South African coast.

4

5

1

2

4

50 KM

3

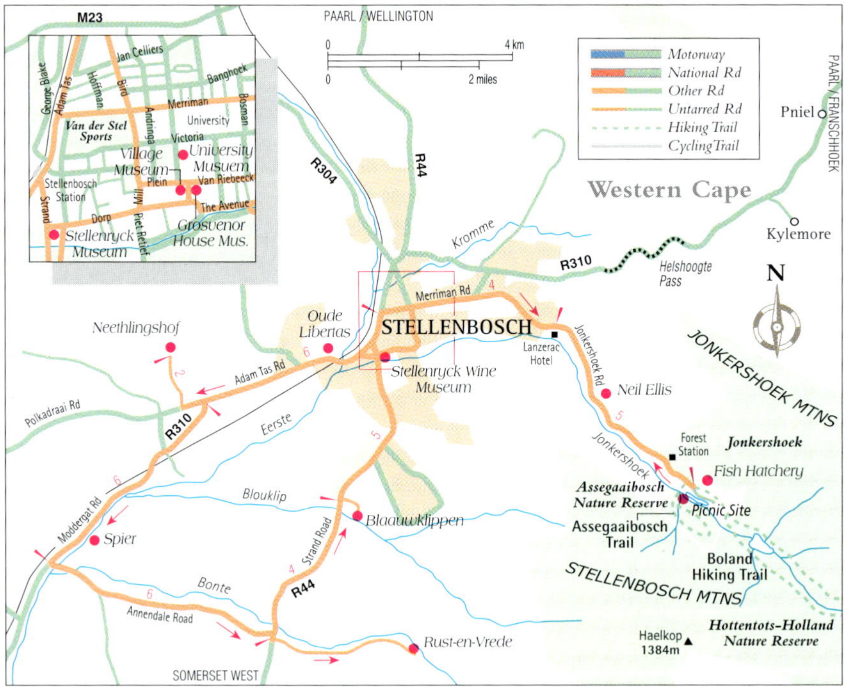

4

STELLENBOSCH, with its oak-lined streets, water furrows and beautifully preserved historic buildings, is the centre of the country's best-known wine-producing area ② and an important university town. South Africa's second-oldest town, Stellenbosch was founded in 1679 and named after the Dutch governor, Simon van der Stel. In addition to its numerous splendid Cape Dutch buildings, the town also has fine examples of Cape Georgian and Victorian houses. The cultural heritage of Stellenbosch can only be truly appreciated by taking a stroll down Dorp Street, which has one of the longest rows of historic buildings in the country. Well worth a visit is the Stellenbosch Village Museum, comprising four buildings from different periods of the town's history. Art-lovers should not miss Oom Samie se Winkel ① and the Rembrandt van Rijn Art Museum in the historic Libertas Parva homestead. The nearby cellar is now known as the Stellenryk Wine Museum.

STELLENBOSCH WINE ROUTE Founded in April 1971, the Stellenbosch Wine Route was the first of its kind in South Africa. It offers visitors an opportunity to sample the region's famous wines, while enjoying the superb scenery. With Stellenbosch as the central point, the 41 cellars (estates, cellars and co-operative wineries) are linked by the four major roads leading into town. Stellenbosch and the surrounding winelands also boast numerous fine restaurants, where visitors can enjoy traditional Cape fare such as smoorsnoek, bredies and koeksisters.

BLAAUWKLIPPEN, on the lower slopes of the Stellenbosch Mountains, dates back to 1690 when the farm was awarded to Gerrit Visser, a Dutch craftsman. Dominating the estate is the gracious H-shaped Cape Dutch manor house built in 1789 with florid gables. With some 16 grape varieties under cultivation, Blaauwklippen ③ produces a wide range of white and red wines. The estate's museum has an interesting collection of antique Cape furniture, kitchen utensils and coaches. Blaauwklippen is well-known for its Coachman's lunches which can be enjoyed on the estate between October and April, when coach rides are also offered.

RUST-EN-VREDE dates back to 1694 when the farm Bonterivier was granted to a stock farmer, Willem van der Wêreld. The complex of historic buildings – built, uniquely, in a straight line – comprises the Jonkershuis (1780), the wine cellar (1790) and the Cape Dutch manor house (1825). The farm was acquired by former Springbok rugby player Jannie Engelbrecht in 1978, and is one of the few Stellenbosch wineries specialising exclusively in red wines. The estate was one of the first to mature its entire production in French Nevers oak barrels. Cabernet sauvignon, merlot, shiraz and the flagship Rust-En-Vrede Estate Wine (the only blended wine) are bottled under the estate's label. The original cellar is used for barrel ageing the red wines, while the modern underground cellar is used for bottle maturation.

SPIER Dating back to 1692, Spier offers visitors a combination of wine tasting, historic buildings, restaurants ④, picnics, art and culture. Among the historic buildings are the old wine cellar (1776), the Jonkershuis (1778) and the slave quarters (1812), which accommodates a restaurant. The buildings on the estate have a total of 21 gables – a unique feature of Cape Dutch architecture – making Spier the largest collection of gables on a single site. The outstanding collection of paintings, antiques and porcelain in the manor house provides a picture of life on a Stellenbosch wine farm in the 1700s. Between November and March, Spier's open-air theatre is the setting for a music festival featuring classical music concerts and performances of opera, jazz and dance. Spier Wine Centre offers an impressive range of wines from various wineries and also holds tastings. Visitors can sample the estate's own Four Spears wines in the cellar situated across the Eerste River.

NEETHLINGSHOF After passing through the imposing entrance gates, visitors drive along a kilometre-long avenue of soaring pine trees to the estate's historic H-shaped manor house, dating back to 1814. The farm was granted to Barend Lubbe in 1692, and was originally known as Wolwedans. It was renamed Neethlingshof after it came into the possession of Johannes Henoch Neethling in 1816. The estate has been planted under 17 varieties of grapes and produced its first wines under the Neethlingshof label in 1971. Today, it produces a wide range of white and red wines, all bearing the distinctive label of the pine avenue. The Lord Neethling (the nickname of the flamboyant Johannes Neethling) restaurant offers traditional South African dishes and international cuisine, while light lunches can be enjoyed at the Palm Terrace.

OUDE LIBERTAS is the headquarters of South Africa's largest wine company, the Stellenbosch Farmers' Winery (SFW), which markets and distributes Chateau Libertas and the well-known Zonnebloem, Nederburg and Lanzerac ranges of wine. The Oude Libertas centre consists of a wine-tasting and conference centre with tours and sales, a restaurant and the Oude Libertas Amphitheatre ⑥. Built in 1977 on the slopes of the Pappegaaiberg, the 430-seat open-air amphitheatre resembles the Greek theatres of Athens and Epidauros. During the summer season (December to March), the amphitheatre provides the setting for a variety of cultural events ranging from music and dance performances to light-hearted comedy. Especially popular are the Sunday evening twilight concerts.

LANZERAC ⑤ is situated on the farm Schoongezicht, which was granted to Isaq Schrijver in 1692. Built in 1830, the U-shaped Cape Dutch manor house features a neoclassical front gable with well-defined mouldings, pediment and pilasters, while the wine cellar dates back to 1815. Under winemaker Angus Buchanan, who bought the farm in 1947, Lanzerac won numerous awards, including the prestigious champion red wine trophy for eight consecutive years. The farm was bought in 1958 by David Rawdon, who converted it into one of the country's best-known hotels, which it remains to this day. In 1988, Lanzerac changed hands again, and three years later it was bought by the well-known Cape businessman, Christo Wiese. Lanzerac Rosé and Lanzerac Pinotage are produced by Distell, while all other wines in the Lanzerac range are grown, made and bottled on the estate. The range includes cabernet sauvignon, merlot and chardonnay, as well as five wines sold under the De Forellen label.

NEIL ELLIS WINES This cellar, located in the picturesque Jonkershoek Valley, has established an international reputation for its vineyard selection wines. Winemaker Neil Ellis, former cellarmaster at Groot Constantia and Zevenwacht, uses only high-quality grapes from vineyards where specific varieties grow in optimum conditions. Given the emphasis on quality, the Neil Ellis wines are produced in small quantities. Wines under the Neil Ellis label include chardonnay, sauvignon blanc, shiraz and cabernet sauvignon, with a second tier range produced under the Inglewood label.

THE JONKERSHOEK VALLEY Nestling between the rugged Jonkershoek Mountains and the Stellenbosch Mountains, the Jonkershoek Valley is one of the Western Cape's most beautiful spots. Towering more than 1 300 m above the valley floor are the jagged peaks of the 1 494 and 1 504-m-high Twin Peaks. The valley was named after a German ensign, Jan Andriessen, who was the first colonist to settle in the upper valley. At the time ensigns were referred to as 'jonkers', and he became known as Jan de Jonker. Visitors can explore the Jonkershoek Plantation by following a circular drive, walk to First Waterfall, or try their hand at fishing for trout in the Jonkershoek Dam. The adjoining Assegaaibosch Nature Reserve covers 204 ha of mainly fynbos vegetation and can be explored along a 2-km walk. Shady picnic places are provided on the banks of the Eerste River. Trout are bred at the Jonkershoek Fish Hatchery, and an experimental breeding programme is under way to rear several threatened indigenous fish species.

5

6

1

5

140 KM

2

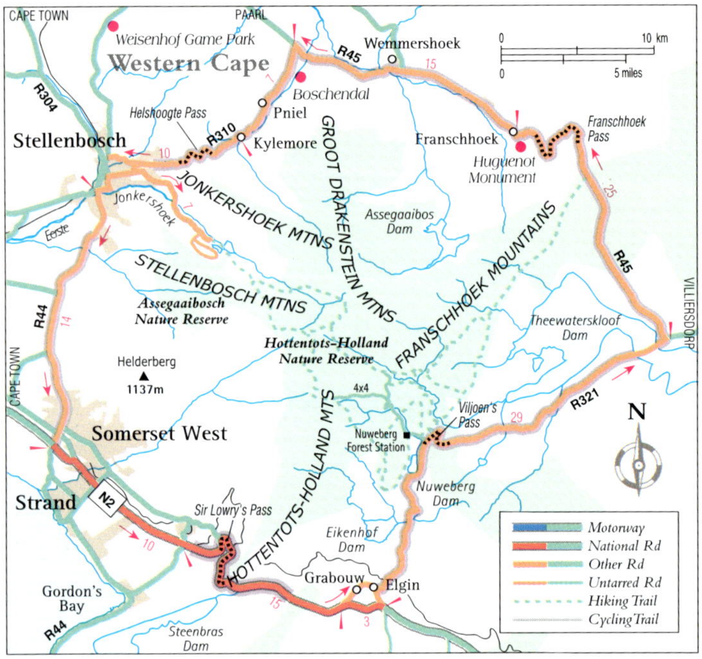

3

STELLENBOSCH See Tour 4, page 16.

SIR LOWRY'S PASS The route into the Cape interior across the Hottentots Holland Mountains initially followed a game trail known to the Khoikhoi as the Gantouw, a name meaning 'elands' path'. The route, about 2 km northeast of the summit of Sir Lowry's Pass, followed a steep, narrow kloof; the deep ruts carved by the thousands of wagons that crossed the mountain can still be seen in the rocks. At nearby Kanonkop, the Dutch East India Company sited two cannons to signal the arrival of ships in Table Bay and to warn of impending Khoikhoi attack. The Gantouw was replaced in 1828 by a new route named in honour of Sir Lowry Cole, the Cape Governor at the time. At the top of the pass there is a splendid view over False Bay.

HOTTENTOTS HOLLAND MOUNTAINS The name Hottentots Holland was originally given to the mountainous area between False Bay and the Palmiet River, but in time the whole mountain range came to be known by that name. An entry in Jan van Riebeeck's diary for 6 June 1657 states that the name was given to the area by the Khoikhoi, who called it their Holland, or fatherland. The Hottentots Holland Nature Reserve covers 42 000 ha and provides protection to some 1 300 species of mountain fynbos. The reserve stretches from Sir Lowry's Pass in the south to the Franschhoek Pass in the north and from the Stellenbosch Mountains in the west to the Groenland Mountains in the east. There are several day walks and overnight trails along which the reserve can be explored.

GRABOUW ② is the centre of one of the country's most important apple-producing regions, and is also a major producer of pears, plums and nectarines. Situated on the banks of the Palmiet River in a sheltered valley between the Hottentots Holland and the Groenland mountains, the town developed around a trading store opened by Wilhelm Langschmidt in 1856. He named it Grabau, after his birthplace in Germany.

ELGIN When the railway reached Grabouw in 1902, the station had to be built on more level ground as the gradient above the village was too steep. Land was made available on the farm Glen Elgin (named in honour of the 9th Earl of Elgin, the Colonial Secretary at the time) and the station was named Elgin. In time, the name was also used to refer to the whole valley. The first apples were planted in the area in 1905 by Sir Antonie Viljoen, and today Elgin is famous world-wide for its Granny Smith, Golden Delicious and Starking apples. The story of the apple industry is told in the Elgin Apple Museum (open daily during summer), one of only two apple museums in the world. Several local farm stalls tempt travellers to buy fresh fruit and vegetables, as well as homemade farm produce.

VILJOEN'S PASS After meandering through a mosaic of apple and deciduous fruit orchards, the route reaches Viljoen's Pass. The original pass wound along the mountain slopes east of the river, but was replaced in the early 1900s by a route cutting through the Groenland Mountains along a gorge carved by the Palmiet River. The name of the pass honours local apple pioneer Sir Antonie Viljoen.

THEEWATERSKLOOF DAM was built along the course of the Riviersonderend in the 1970s, primarily for irrigation, but also to provide water for domestic use to the Cape Town metropolitan area, Stellenbosch and

Paarl. Covering an area of approximately 52 km², it is the seventh largest dam in South Africa and has a capacity of 483 million m³. It is linked to the Assegaaibos Dam on the Berg River by a 11,7-km-long tunnel, and by a 20-km-long tunnel to the Jonkershoek Dam. During the dry summer months, water is pumped from Theewaterskloof through the tunnels into the two dams, and in winter excess water is pumped into Theewaterskloof. The large dam is a popular destination with water-sport enthusiasts.

FRANSCHHOEK PASS The original route over the Franschhoek Mountains followed the tracks of the San and migratory herds of game – hence the original name of Elephant Pass. It was not until the completion of the Cats Path in 1819 that wagons could make the journey over the mountains. Building of the present pass began in 1823 on the instructions of Lord Charles Somerset and was completed two years later. From the 750-m-high summit there are splendid vistas over the Franschhoek Valley ⑤.

FRANSCHHOEK was established in 1688 when 207 French Huguenots, who had fled France because of religious persecution, arrived at the Cape. The French origins of the town still persist in the surnames of many residents and the distinctly French names of many of the farms in the fertile valley. A prominent landmark on the eastern outskirts of the town is the Huguenot Monument ③; the three arches symbolise the Trinity, while the figure of a woman, with the Bible in her right hand and a broken chain in her left, represents freedom of religious belief. The nearby Huguenot Memorial Museum houses exhibits on the history of the Huguenots, and is also a research, information and education centre. Franschhoek is famous for its many fine restaurants offering Cape Huguenot, French, traditional South African and Malay cuisine.

FRANSCHHOEK WINE ROUTE The Huguenots brought with them their extensive knowledge and skills of winemaking, and the fertile Franschhoek Valley ① became one of the earliest wine-producing regions in the Cape. In 1885, the vineyards were ravaged by an outbreak of phylloxera, and many farmers planted fruit trees instead. Almost a century later, new vineyards were planted and the valley has once again established itself as an important wine-producing region. Owing to the variations in climate, soil conditions and the location of the farms, the area produces an unusually large variety of wines. The Vignerons de Franschhoek, an association of over 20 wine farms, was formed in 1984 to promote their wines and the valley. Among the well-known wine farms are Boschendal, La Motte, Mont Rochelle, Augusta Wines, Dieu Donné, L'Ormarins and Cabrière Estate.

BOSCHENDAL – with its magnificent setting in the Groot Drakenstein Valley and impressive Cape Dutch manor house – is one of the most famous wine farms in the Cape. The farm dates back to 1685 when it was granted to a French Huguenot, while the U-shaped manor house was completed in 1812. Since the release of the first wines under the Boschendal label in 1976 the estate has established a strong reputation for its white wines, but in recent years more red varietals have been planted. The museum in the manor house boasts antiques from the 17th and 18th centuries and has a priceless collection of Ming porcelain and Dutch East India Company glassware. Boschendal ④ is famous for its French-style picnics, which can be enjoyed under the fragrant pine trees between November and April.

PNIEL, located at the foot of the Simonsberg along the Dwars River, is a picturesque village set among oak trees, vineyards and orchards. Founded in 1843 as a mission station by the Dutch Reformed Church, the mission was named after the place where Jacob struggled with God (Genesis 32:30).

HELSHOOGTE At the head of the Banhoek Valley, the Helshoogte Pass winds up to the saddle between the Simonsberg and the Jonkershoek Mountains. Built in 1854 to link Stellenbosch and Franschhoek, Helshoogte means 'hell's heights'. The name is thought to come from the difficulties encountered by ox wagons in negotiating the precipitous route, as well as from the fearsome reputation of the Banhoek Valley, which was believed to be haunted. In the early Settler days, numerous lion and leopard roamed the area, prompting travellers to name it Ban(g)hoek, or 'scary corner'.

4

5

CAPE BRANDY CELLARS

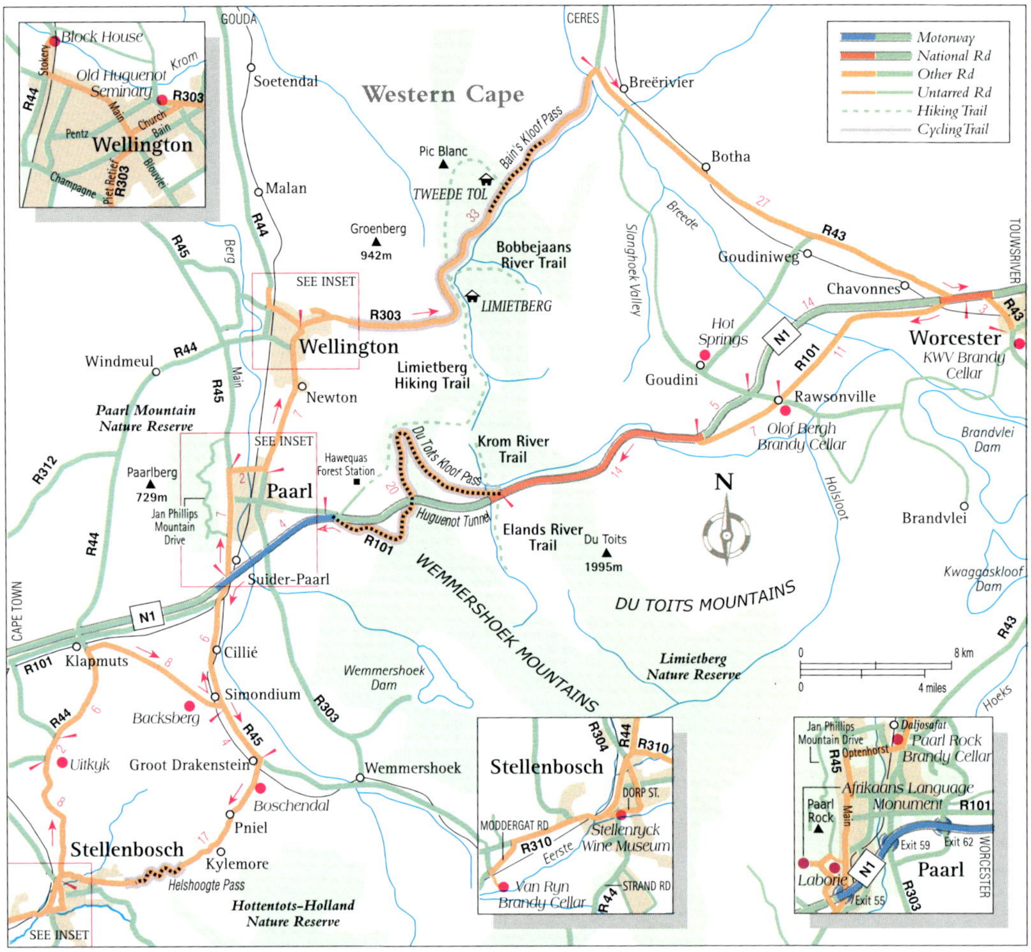

6

235 KM

BACKSBERG Set on the northeastern slopes of the Simonsberg, Backsberg was originally known as Babylonstoren. Since 1916, it has been in the hands of the Back family, after whom the farm was renamed. Renowned for its excellent wines, the Backsberg range includes seven white, a rosé and seven red wines. Owner Michael Back also produces an estate brandy – named after his father, Sydney – that is similar to the cognacs of France, but with its own distinctive character. Wine from the estate's chenin blanc grapes is distilled in a computer-controlled pot still imported from Cognac in 1991. It is then matured for three years in French Limousin oak barrels before it is released and sold under the Sydney Back Estate Brandy label.

BRANDY ROUTE In 1997, 325 years after the first brandy was distilled in South Africa, the South African Brandy Foundation launched the Brandy Route, the first of its kind in South Africa. Stretching from Stellenbosch through Paarl and Wellington to Worcester, it gives visitors an opportunity to learn about the many sides of the brandy industry, such as the different varieties of brandies and the various production methods. South Africa is the fifth largest producer of brandy in the world, and brandy represents 65 per cent of all South African spirits. Average annual production amounts to over 57 million litres, and there are about 50 brandy trademarks in the country. There are currently nine cellars on the Brandy Route, seven of which are described in this tour.

STELLENBOSCH, with its extensive vineyards, is a natural starting point on the Brandy Route. See also Tour 4, page 16.

VAN RYN CELLARS The Van Ryn Brandy Cellar ② at Vlottenburg is the oldest working brandy cellar in the country, and was the first to open its doors to visitors. The cellar is named after a Dutch immigrant, Jan van Ryn, who arrived at the Cape in 1845 and established the cellar. On a guided tour, visitors will find out all about the production of brandy. The tour includes a visit to the distillation pot stills, maturation cellars and the cooperage – one of only two working cooperages on the Brandy Route. Here, visitors can see how the maturation barrels are made from French oak in the traditional manner.

UITKYK, on the slopes of the Simonsberg, has as its most outstanding feature the magnificent neoclassical manor house attributed to the French architect, Louis-Michel Thibault. Completed in 1788, its urban design in a country setting makes it unique among the historic buildings of Stellenbosch. Uitkyk's history goes back to 1712, when the farm was granted to Jan Oberholzer, but its winemaking potential was only realised in the 1930s. The estate produces two white wines (chardonnay and sauvignon blanc) and two reds – the full-bodied flagship wine, Carlonet (cabernet sauvignon) and a cabernet sauvignon and shiraz blend. All Uitkyk wines are marketed by the Bergkelder. The estate recently introduced a fine 10-year-old estate brandy to the market.

PAARL See Tour 7, page 22.

LABORIE Set among vineyards on the lower slopes of Paarl Mountain, historic Laborie estate dates back to 1691. The focal point of the estate is the H-shaped manor house ③, which was built in the late 1700s. The estate was bought by the KWV in 1972, and has since been redeveloped into one of the country's leading wine estates. Its first wines were introduced to the public in 1982, and today its celebrated range includes two white, one blanc de noir, four red and one fortified wine, as well as a sparkling wine made in the tradition of the Champagne region of France. Laborie launched its first brandy, the Laborie Estate Alembic Brandy, in late 1997. It is made from sauvignon blanc grapes and double-distilled in an 18th-century copper pot still. Visitors can explore the lower slopes of Paarl Mountain by following a one-hour walking trail through the vineyards. The Laborie Restaurant is well known for its excellent traditional dishes.

PAARL ROCK BRANDY CELLAR Overlooked by the natural landmark for which it is named, this cellar dates back to 1856, when it was established by the De Villiers brothers. This is the only cellar in South Africa where brandy is still made by hand according to the De Villiers family tradition. The cellar uses wines mainly from the Paarl region, and its brandies undergo a double distillation process in traditional Woudberg copper pot stills before maturation in imported French oak vats. After maturation, the brandy is blended in accordance with the brothers' original recipe.

WELLINGTON See Tour 7, page 23.

BAIN'S KLOOF See Tour 7, page 23.

WORCESTER See Tour 7, page 23.

KWV BRANDY CELLAR This is the largest brandy distillery of its kind in the world under one roof. The cellar ① accommodates 120 copper Woudberg pot stills for the distillation of the famed KWV range of brandies, such as KWV Ten and Twenty Year Old. In addition to producing its own range of brandies, the KWV supplies domestic wholesalers with over 50 per cent of the brandies sold on the local market. The Worcester cellar is one of only two cellars on the Brandy Route where visitors can watch coopers making barrels (the other being the Van Ryn cellar). The tour includes an audio-visual presentation and tours of the distillation room and maturation cellars, and ends with a brandy tasting.

OLOF BERGH SOLERA BRANDY CELLAR Situated in the fertile Breede River Valley near Rawsonville, the Olof Bergh Cellar uses 22 Woudberg copper pot stills, similar to those used in the Cognac region of France, for the distillation of high-quality colombard wines. The cellar's brandy is distilled exclusively from grapes grown in the surrounding region. Interestingly, it is the only brandy cellar in South Africa to use the Solera method of maturation and blending. Initially developed by the sherry-makers in Spain, the brandy flows through layers of maturation barrels from the top to the bottom, depending on the degree of maturation desired.

DU TOIT'S KLOOF PASS For many years after the first farmers settled in the Berg River valley, the route across the Hawekwas and Klein Drakenstein mountains was nothing more than a game track. Although efforts to improve the pass were made as early as 1842, it was not until 1949 that Du Toit's Kloof Pass was completed. By the 1980s, increasing traffic volumes on the busy N1 highway running through the pass necessitated the construction of the nearly 4 km-long Huguenot Tunnel. Begun at the end of 1984 and opened in March 1988, the tunnel cuts 11 km off the distance travelled along the old route. Motorists now have the option of travelling along the old pass ④, which affords beautiful vistas of the Berg River valley, or taking the shorter route through the toll tunnel.

1

2

3

4

7
225 KM

1

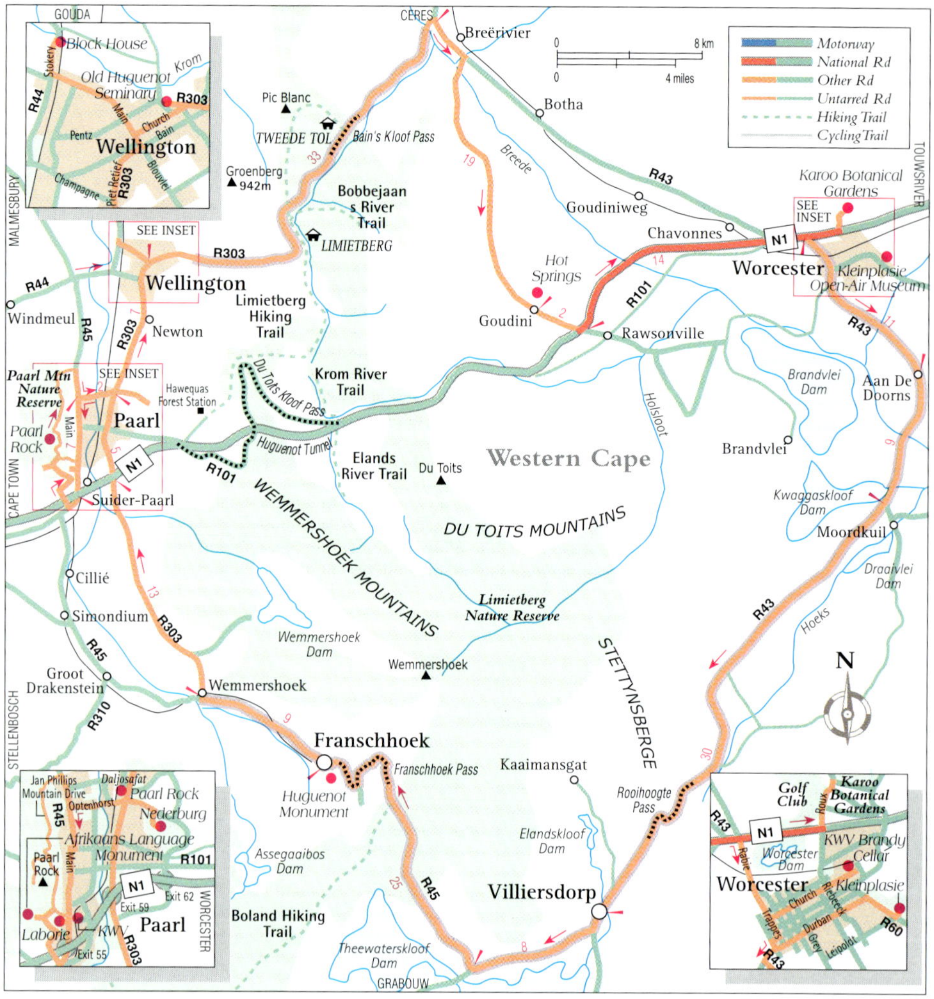

PAARL When the Dutch *fiskaal* (revenue collector), Abraham Gabbema, and his party first saw the granite domes that dominate the Berg River valley glistening like gems in the rising sun in October 1657, he named them the 'Paarl' and the 'Diamant' (Pearl and Diamond). In 1687, Governor Simon van der Stel awarded the first farms in the valley, and in the following year several Huguenots settled here. Paarl Mountain lies within the Paarl Mountain Nature Reserve ①, accessible along the 11-km-long Jan Phillips Mountain Drive. The mountain originated some 550 million years ago when granite intruded into the rocks of the Malmesbury Group. Over millions of years the softer, overlying rock was eroded, exposing the more resistant granite outcrops. The Afrikaans language had its formal origins in Paarl in 1875, with the foundation of the Society of True Afrikaaners. The Afrikaans Language Monument on the southern slopes of Paarl Mountain was unveiled in 1975 to commemorate the birth and development of the Afrikaans language in Paarl a century earlier. To appreciate Paarl's wealth of historic buildings, take a walk down Main Road. Starting at the Strooidak Kerk (Thatched Roof Church), dating back to 1805, the walk takes visitors past Zeederberg Square (surrounded by several historic buildings) to the Afrikaans Language Museum. The only language museum in the world, it focuses on the history of Afrikaans. The walk ends at the Oude Pastorie Museum, built as a parsonage in 1786. The graceful U-shaped manor house, with its pedimented gable, contains a fine collection of antique Cape furniture, silverware and copper.

KWV The KWV (Ko-operatiewe Wijnbouers Vereniging van Zuid-Afrika), founded in 1918, produces a wide range of internationally renowned wines, port, sherries, brandies and liqueurs. It also supplies local brandy wholesalers with over half their annual requirements. The 22-ha cellar complex is the largest of its kind in the world. A highlight of the cellar tour is the Cathedral Cellar, with its dome-shaped roof, slightly tinted windows and enormous 1 200-litre red wine vats decorated with carvings depicting the Cape's winemaking industry. The tour also includes a visit to the Sherry Cellar, where sherry has been produced since 1937 in accordance with the methods of the Spanish bodegas. Here visitors can see the world's five largest vats under one roof. After operating as a co-operative for nearly 80 years, the KWV was converted to a group of companies in December 1997.

NEDERBURG is one of South Africa's best-known wine cellars, and its wines have received over 1 000 international and national awards. The farm was awarded to Philippus Wolvaart in 1791, and named after the Commissioner-General of the Dutch East India Company, Sebastiaan Nederburg. The beautiful H-shaped Cape Dutch manor house, with its magnificent gable, was completed in 1800. After a succession of owners, Nederburg was acquired by Johann Graue in 1937, and under the talented winemaker Günter Brözel the estate's wines became famous. The extensive range includes red and white wines. sparkling and champagne-style wines and a range of late harvest and dessert wines. Since 1975, the estate has hosted the annual Nederburg Wine Auction, one of the top five wine auctions in the world. Over 1 600 guests and participants attend the event, and annual sales exceed R6 million. Between November and February, visitors can enjoy picnics on the estate grounds.

DAL JOSAFAT, meaning 'Valley of Josafat' was named after the biblical Josaphat, the 'place of judgement' in Joel 3. The first farms in the fertile valley were awarded in 1692, and the area was settled mainly by Huguenots. The valley is noted for its beautifully preserved 18th-century buildings – Roggeland, Non Pareille, Goede Rust, Schoongezicht and Vlakkeland. Dal Josafat is closely associated with the development of the Afrikaans language, as the Society of True Afrikaaners had its origins in the area. SJ du Toit, founder and leader of the first Afrikaans Language Movement, and his brother, DF du Toit, another founder member of the society, were born on the farm Kleinbosch. In 1880, the farm was bought by another prominent campaigner for the Afrikaans language, Petrus Jacobus Malherbe, the eldest son of Gideon Malherbe and the society's printer.

WELLINGTON lies in a picturesque valley originally known as Limiet Valley, regarded by the early Dutch settlers as the boundary or limit of the settlement at the Cape. The town was once famous for its wagon-making industry and became known as Wagenmakersvallei (wagon makers' valley) before it was renamed Wellington in 1840. It is the centre of the country's dried fruit industry and one of the most important centres for growing grafted vines. The twelve cellars on the Wellington Wine Route include Bovlei, Wamakersvallei, Wellington, Jacaranda, Welvanpas, Cape Wine Cellars and Hildenbrand Wine and Olive Estate, and produce a wide variety of white and red wines. Wellington is also well known for its educational institutions, among them Huguenot College and Boland College. Noteworthy buildings include the Dutch Reformed Church (1840), and the various buildings of the old Huguenot Seminary. Just north of the town is a blockhouse, built to guard the railway bridge over the Kromme River, a tributary of the Breede, against Boer guerrilla attacks during the South African War.

BAIN'S KLOOF PASS is named after master road builder, Andrew Geddes Bain, who began building the pass in 1849 with convict labour and completed it four years later. The vantage point just below the summit affords motorists spectacular views of the Berg River valley; a little further on, just south of Bain's Kloof village, lie the graves of 11 convicts who died during the construction of the pass. From here the scenic pass follows the winding course of the valley ② carved by the Wit River between the Limietberg and the Slanghoek mountains. Large sections of the road had to be blasted out of solid rock; one large outcrop, Dacres Pulpit, was left hanging over the road. In some places the road had to be supported by 12-m-high dry-stone retaining walls.

SLANGHOEK VALLEY Bounded by the rugged Slanghoek Mountains in the west, Badsberg to the east and Kleinberg to the north, the Slanghoek Valley is famous for its spectacular mountain scenery. The fertile valley is also noted for the production of quality wines, especially chenin blanc, colombard, sauvignon blanc and chardonnay.

GOUDINI SPA is centred around thermal springs that bubble to the surface at a temperature of 41°C. The resort comprises indoor and outdoor thermal pools, a jacuzzi-spa complex, conference centre and a variety of recreational facilities. Accommodation consists of rondavels and flats, and there is also a restaurant and a shop.

WORCESTER Situated amid rugged mountain scenery on the banks of the Breede River, Worcester is the 'Capital of the Breede River Valley'. About 25 per cent of the area under vineyards in the country lies in the Worcester region, making it one of South Africa's most important wine-producing areas. It is especially noted for its dry and semi-sweet white wines, dessert wines and brandy. The Kleinplasie Open-Air Museum depicts the lifestyles of the early Cape pioneer farmers. The museum comprises 26 buildings and structures representative of agricultural industries in the Western Cape between 1690 and 1900. Daily demonstrations of traditional home industries and activities (witblits distilling, candle making and tobacco rolling) are given. The town of Worcester is also a well-known education centre, and the Nuwe Hoop Centre for the Hearing Impaired, the Institute for the Blind and the Institute for the Deaf are located here.

VILLIERSDORP ③ is the centre of a productive farming area where nectarines, peaches, pears, apples, apricots are grown and wine is produced. Founded in 1843 by Pieter de Villiers, of French Huguenot stock, the town has retained its rural character and atmosphere. Among the town's historic buildings are several Victorian-era cottages, Oude Radyn (1844), Oude Huis (1852) and St Augustine's Anglican Church (1858). A variety of fynbos species can be seen in Villiersdorp Wild Flower Garden and Nature Reserve on the slopes of Aasvoël mountain.

THEEWATERSKLOOF DAM See Tour 5, page 18.

FRANSCHHOEK See Tour 5, page 19.

2

3

1

2

8
305 KM

3

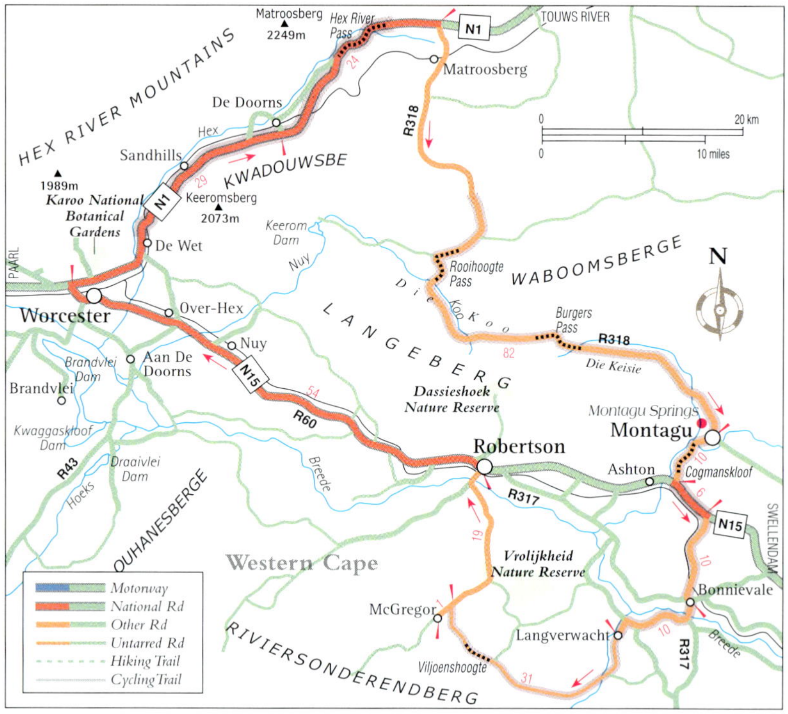

MONTAGU Formerly known as Agter Cogmanskloof, Montagu ① lies between the Keisie and the Kinga rivers which join at the western end of the town. Founded in 1851, the town was named after Sir John Montagu, Colonial Secretary at the Cape from 1843 to 1853. The town's name is synonymous with muscadel grapes, soft fruit (apricots, peaches and nectarines) and hot springs. Montagu is regarded as one of the best-preserved late Victorian agricultural villages in the Cape, and a variety of architectural styles can be seen along Long Street, the oldest part of town. Among Montagu's historic buildings are the old Mission Church, built in 1907 in Cape Gothic style, and the Cape Dutch Joubert House, dating to 1853. Both buildings now form part of the Montagu Museum, which tells the history of the town and its people. The hot mineral springs at the entrance to Badskloof have a temperature of 43° C at their source. The springs have attracted visitors for over two centuries and the modern complex comprises six outdoor and two indoor pools, three spa baths, a hotel, self-catering apartments and restaurants.

COGMANS KLOOF, carved by the Cogmans River, is a spectacular gorge with magnificent contorted rock strata, some of which have been thrust almost vertically. In the 19th century, Cogmans Kloof provided the only access to Montagu from the west, and involved a challenging, often hazardous journey during which the river had to be forded eight times. Construction of a new pass began in 1869, but the road was only opened after the completion of the tunnel through Kalkoenkrans in 1877. With a height of 5 m, the 16-m-long tunnel is one of the outstanding features of the pass built by the renowned road builder, Thomas Bain (son of Andrew Geddes Bain). Perched on top of Kalkoenkrans is a stone fort built by the British in 1899 to deny access through the kloof to Boer forces during the South African War.

BONNIEVALE, on the northern banks of the Breede River, lies amid a patchwork of peach and apricot orchards and vineyards. In the early 1900s many of the farms in the area concentrated on ostrich farming. But following the collapse of the industry in 1914 the farmers switched to wine and dairy farming; soon six cheese factories operated in the valley. Boesmanrivierse Co-operative cheese factory, established in 1926, has grown into the largest cheese factory in South Africa; its products are sold under the Parmalat label. The factory produces Gouda and Cheddar cheese, as well as milk powder and butter.

McGREGOR Founded in 1861 in a scenic valley surrounded by mountains, McGregor is a picturesque, tranquil village of whitewashed thatched cottages ②. The town was originally named Lady Grey after the wife of the Cape Governor, Sir George Grey, but in 1903 it was renamed after Reverend A McGregor to avoid confusion with Lady Grey in the Eastern Cape. With its neat grid plan, orchards and beautifully preserved historic houses, McGregor is regarded as one of the best examples of a mid-19th century village in the Western Cape. Among its variety of architectural styles are whitewashed cottages with low-pitched thatched roofs and plain end-gables and Georgian-style double-storey houses with flat roofs. It is the start and finish of the popular Boesmanskloof Hiking Trail. The 14-km-long route meanders through the Riviersonderend Mountains between Greyton and Die Galg, 14 km northeast of Greyton.

VROLIJKHEID NATURE RESERVE was proclaimed in 1957 and for some years housed a predator control research and hound training centre. In the late 1980s the research centre was closed down and the 1 872-ha reserve was developed to protect the succulent vegetation of the Karroid Broken Veld and its fauna. The reserve is especially attractive between August and October, when fields of gazanias and other species come into full bloom. From 1987 to the early 1990s, Vrolijkheid was the centre of the Quagga Breeding Project, which aimed to revive the extinct quagga (a zebra-like mammal) through selective breeding. The animals have since been relocated to several new host sites. Visitors can explore the reserve along the 3-km Heron Trail or take the 19-km Rooikat Trail, which requires a full day to complete.

ROBERTSON Lying below the Langeberg in the Breede River valley, Robertson is surrounded by vineyards and orchards, while the streets of the town are lined by numerous fine Cape Dutch, Victorian and Georgian houses and cottages. Robertson was established in 1853, and among its historic buildings are the 'Pink Church' (1859), the Powder House – once used to store gunpowder – and Druid's Lodge (1860), a long rectangular house which is now occupied by the town's museum. Robertson enjoys a high reputation for its wines, roses and thoroughbred horses, and is also an important producer of apricots ③, peaches and nectarines. With its lime-rich soil and dry climate, the Robertson Valley is one of the Western Cape's largest wine-producing regions under irrigation. It enjoys acclaim for its excellent dessert wines, and also produces outstanding whites (notably chardonnay, sauvignon blanc and colombard). The Robertson Valley Wine Route, embracing the Ashton, Bonnievale, McGregor and Robertson districts, comprises 24 wineries open to the public. The 865-ha Dassieshoek Nature Reserve lies on the northern outskirts of the town on the slopes of the Langeberg and preserves a tract of montane fynbos.

WORCESTER See Tour 7, page 23.

THE KAROO NATIONAL BOTANICAL GARDEN The focus of the Karoo Garden, on the northern outskirts of Worcester, is the conservation of the succulent flora of the Karoo. The garden provides protection to about 400 plant species occurring naturally in the 114-ha flora reserve. About 10 ha of the garden has been developed for the cultivation of Karoo plants from the arid summer and winter rainfall areas, as well as the flora of other arid areas, such as the Richtersveld, Knersvlakte and Namib Desert. In addition to the 400 species occurring naturally, some 6 000 other arid-adapted species have been established.

HEX RIVER VALLEY Bounded by the Hex River and the Quadu mountains, the 22-km-long Hex River valley ④ is a beguiling mixture of vineyards, orchards and dams. One of the most scenic valleys in South Africa, the Hex River is especially attractive in autumn, when the vineyards are transformed by a kaleidoscope of autumn hues. In winter, snow often mantles the peaks, which are dominated by the Matroosberg (2 250 m). Planted with over eight million vines on 3 500 ha under irrigation, the Hex River valley is the largest producer of export table grapes in southern Africa. Over 50 per cent of the country's export table grapes, mainly Barlinka, are produced here. The town of De Doorns owes its name to the many thorn bushes that grew here when stock farmers first settled the valley. For visitors travelling by train, the scenery is no less spectacular. To eliminate the many tight curves of the original railway line, a new one – featuring four new tunnels totalling 16 km in length – was brought into service in 1989.

DIE KOO AND DIE KEISIE Apples, peaches and wheat are the main agricultural products of the fertile Koo valley, nestling between the Waboomberge and the Langeberg. Named after the Koo River, a Khoi name which has been interpreted to mean 'cold' or 'an edible plant', the name is used for a well-known brand of canned fruit, jams and vegetables. To the east of Die Koo lies Die Keisie, a valley which owes its name to the Keisie River, a Khoikhoi name translated as 'ugly'.

4

1

9
280 KM

2

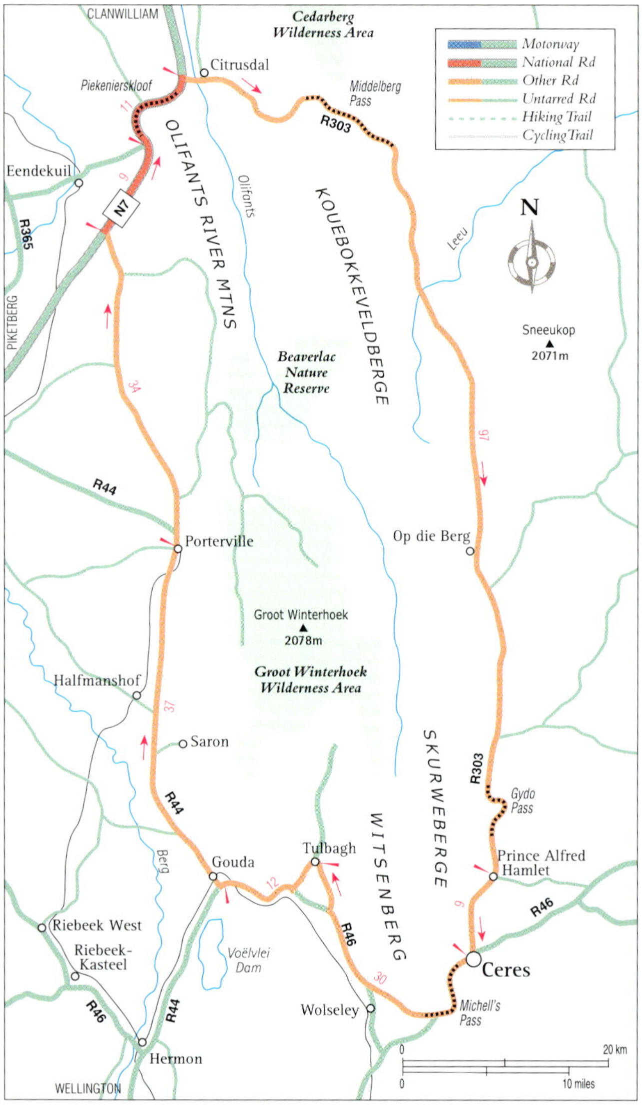

TULBAGH lies in a secluded valley that was originally named Het Land van Waveren by Governor Willem Adriaan van der Stel after the influential Van Waveren family of Amsterdam. The town was proclaimed in 1804, and was named after the former Dutch Governor, Ryk Tulbagh. Enclosed by mountains on three sides, the valley is a mosaic of orchards, vineyards, wheat fields and fynbos-clad mountain slopes. The town is famous for the many magnificent Cape Dutch and Victorian buildings lining Church Street, which stretches between the old Dutch Reformed Church ② and its parsonage. On the night of 29 September 1969, Tulbagh was struck by an earthquake measuring 6,4 on the Richter scale. As a result of the quake, 23 buildings had to be completely restored. The Old Dutch Reformed Church, built in 1743 to a cruciform design, is the focal point of the Oude Kerk Volksmuseum. The church, along with three annexes in Church Street, has displays of old furniture and porcelain, as well as material on the 1969 earthquake and local geology. Other noteworthy buildings include the old Drostdy (1806), Mon Bijou (1812), the Dutch Reformed Parsonage (1769) and Ballotina, with its unusual gable.

PADDAGANG is situated on the west side of Tulbagh's Church Street, against the backdrop of mountains. A verdant lawn leads up to a Cape Dutch building ① dating back to 1809, when it was built as a residence. In 1821 it became one of the the country's first tap-houses (a combination of bar and retail outlet for wine), a purpose it served until such establishments were prohibited due to the disturbances created by drunken soldiers and sailors. After careful restoration, Paddagang was opened in 1974 as a restaurant and wine house. The name means 'frog passage', and is said to refer to an early irrigation canal much favoured by frogs. In the restaurant, visitors can enjoy traditional Cape fare such as waterblommetjie bredie, venison pie and sweet potatoes, accompanied by local wines. A fine range of wines with innovative frog themes is produced under the Paddagang label.

TULBAGH WINELANDS The Tulbagh area is especially suited to white cultivars such as weisser riesling, cape riesling, chenin blanc, sauvignon blanc and chardonnay. The Tulbagh wine route comprises nine wineries, with the Drostdy Winesr and Twee Jonge Gezellen, Theuniskraal and Lemberg estates among the best-known names.

GOUDA The name of this small town immediately brings to mind the famous Dutch cheese, but the name is in fact of Khoikhoi origin, and is variously said to mean 'antelope', 'honey path' or 'honey defile'. Originally known as Porterville Road, Gouda served as a railhead for Porterville until the branch line from Hermon was built in 1929. Voëlvlei Dam, 6 km to the south, plays an important role in the supply of water to Cape Town and in controlling and augmenting the flow of the Berg River. Built in 1952, the dam has a capacity of 16 million m³, and behind the 17,7-m-high dam wall lies an 8-km-long lake.

PORTERVILLE, at the foot of the Olifants River Mountains, is an agricultural centre for the surrounding farms, which concentrate on wheat and wine. Wine production is focused mainly on white varietals such as chardonnay, colombard, sauvignon blanc and chenin blanc, and the town falls within the Swartland wine region. Porterville was laid out on the farm Pomona, which was subdivided into plots in 1863. Its name honours William Porter, the popular Attorney-General of the Cape Colony from 1839 to 1866. The scenic Dasklip Pass, linking the Swartland with the plateau below the Groot Winterhoek mountains, is a popular hang-gliding site.

PIEKENIERSKLOOF PASS The formidable barrier presented by the Olifants River Mountains, originally known as the Groote Clooff (Large Kloof), was first crossed on 7 December 1660 by a Dutch soldier, Jan Danckaert. In 1675, a band of Khoikhoi raiders escaped across the mountains because the pursuing commandos were weighed down by their heavy pikes. Following a report to the Council of Policy in 1739, a military post was set up to defend Swartland farmers against Khoisan attacks and the name Piekenierskloof (*piekenier* means a guard armed with a pike) became established. It was not until 1857 that Thomas Bain began building a road through the pass. Completed the following year, it was named Grey's Pass, after the British Governor, Sir George Grey. When the new pass was built higher up the mountain slopes, it was given its original name.

CITRUSDAL See Tour 17, page 46.

GYDO PASS, between the Skurweberg and Gydoberg, was built in 1848 by Andrew Geddes Bain to link the Cold and the Warm Bokkeveld. 'Gydo' is of Khoikhoi origin and is said to mean 'steep pass', or 'milkbush poort' after a species of euphorbia. From the summit, travellers can enjoy fine views of the Hex River Mountains and the Warm Bokkeveld.

PRINCE ALFRED HAMLET, at the foot of the Gydo Pass, is the centre of an important deciduous fruit farming area. Established in 1861 as a fruit-packing centre on the farm Wagensboomrivier, it was named after Queen Victoria's son, Alfred, first Duke of Edinburgh, who visited the Cape in 1867.

CERES Following the completion of Michell's Pass, the site for a village was laid out at the eastern entrance of the pass, and the first 20 plots were sold by public auction on 21 July 1849. Situated in a fertile basin on the banks of the Dwars River and surrounded by the Skurweberg mountains, the settlement was named after the Roman goddess of agriculture in recognition of the fertility of the land. Farmers initially concentrated on wheat production, but gradually began switching to fruit farming. The completion of the railway line between Ceres and Wolseley in 1912 provided a tremendous boost to the fruit industry, and Ceres is today one of the biggest deciduous fruit-producing districts in the country. The area is especially known for its pears, but also produces large quantities of other fruits such as apples, peaches, apricots, plums and cherries. Given the abundance of fruit, it is not surprising that about 80 per cent of South Africa's fruit juices are packed in Ceres. In recent years, the district has also become a major producer of potatoes, and accounts for 40 per cent of the total production in South Africa. In winter, snow often falls in Ceres ④, attracting large numbers of visitors.

MICHELL'S PASS When the explorer Henry Lichtenstein travelled along the first road through the Skurweberg ravine in 1803, he described it as 'one of the worst and most dangerous roads in the Colony'. Construction of the new pass was begun in 1846 by 200 convicts under the direction of Andrew Geddes Bain, and the 9-km road was officially opened on 1 December 1848. It was named after Major Charles Michell, the Surveyor-General at the time. A tollhouse ③ was built and passing wagons were charged a toll of three pence a wheel. Following the discovery of diamonds near Kimberley in 1870, Ceres became an important stop-over on the northward route to the diamond fields, and heavily laden wagons made their way across the pass.

WOLSELEY Lying in a beautiful valley of the Breede River, Wolseley is surrounded by the Waaihoek, Witsen and Watervals mountains. The town was established in 1875 and named in 1910 after Sir Garnet Wolseley, the British Governor of Natal. Fruit, vegetable, wheat, dairy and stock farming are practised in the area. Of historical interest are two blockhouses built during the South African War to protect the bridges along the railway line south of the town. The Jan Danckaert Museum, named after the early Dutch explorer, depicts the town's history through photographic displays and other museum pieces.

3

4

SONO BOOTH
BIENTANG'S CAVE
ENVIRONMENTAL CENTRE
INDOOR DISPLAYS
MUSEUM OFFICE
LEMOEN HATCHERY

FROM THE BOLAND TO THE OVERBERG

OPPOSITE TOP LEFT: ARNISTON CHILDREN (P.35); TOP RIGHT: HERMANUS OLD HARBOUR SIGNS (P.32); BOTTOM: HELDERBERG NATURE RESERVE (P.30); **THIS PAGE** TOP LEFT: DE HOOP CYCLISTS (P.36); TOP RIGHT: DRIED FISH, ARNISTON (P.35); ABOVE: WHEATFIELDS, CALEDON (P.33); BOTTOM LEFT: BETTY'S BAY FYNBOS (P.31); BOTTOM RIGHT: AFRICAN BLACK OYSTERCATCHER, DE MOND NATURE RESERVE (P.35).

1

10

145 KM

2

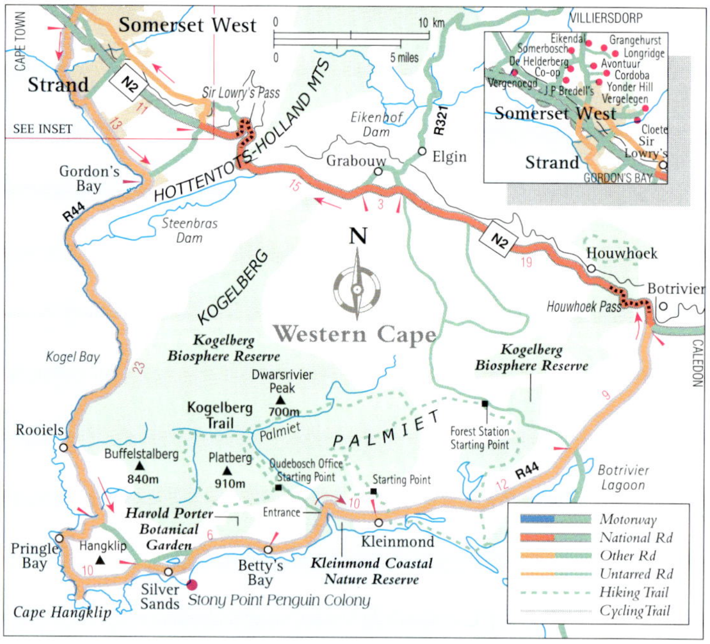

SOMERSET WEST Nestling on the slopes of the Helderberg, Somerset West was founded in 1822 on part of the historic farm, Vergelegen ②. Originally named Somerset, after Lord Charles Somerset, Governor of the Cape from 1814 to 1826, the name was later changed to Somerset West to avoid confusion with the town of Somerset East in the Eastern Cape. Other wineries in the Somerset West region include Avontuur, Meerlust and Eikendal. On the edge of Somerset West lies the Helderberg Nature Reserve, which covers 245 ha of unspoilt fynbos vegetation. The reserve is criss-crossed by a network of walking trails and offers good birding opportunities.

HELDERBERG WINE ROUTE The Helderberg wine region owes its name to the majestic Helderberg Mountain, which dominates the scenery between Stellenbosch and Somerset West. The region is especially noted for its superb red wines and ports, but also produces outstanding sauvignon blanc and chardonnay wines. This tour allows sufficient time to visit some of the 21 wine farms, cellars and co-ops on the Helderberg Wine Route. Among the well-known wineries are historic Vergelegen – granted to Governor Willem Adriaan van der Stel in 1700 – with its magnificent Cape Dutch manor house and avenue of camphor trees, JP Bredell Wines (renowned for its red and port-style wines), Vergenoegd, Longridge and Yonder Hill.

STRAND ③ has been sought-after since the mid-1800s, when it was the traditional summer holiday resort for farmers from the Stellenbosch area. Situated on the north-eastern shore of False Bay, the 5 km-long expanse of white sandy beach offers safe swimming, making it popular with families, sunbathers and surfers.

GORDON'S BAY The picturesque harbour town of Gordon's Bay ① lies in a secluded cove on the eastern shore of False Bay. From the slopes high above the town an enormous anchor, made of whitewashed rocks, overlooks the luxury waterfront developments that now line the bay. Main Beach and Bikini Beach, next to the harbour, offer safe swimming and are packed with sunbathers during the summer months. Candidate officers of the South African Navy are trained at the South African Naval College on the eastern side of the harbour.

KOGELBERG BIOSPHERE RESERVE lies at the southern end of the Hottentots Holland Mountains, in the heart of the Cape Floral Kingdom. Characterised by high mountain peaks and deep river valleys, the reserve comprises a core area of 18 000 ha and several smaller fragments. Kogelberg is internationally renowned for its diversity of fynbos plants, and is home to some 1 600 species, including 150 endemics. Among its rare botanical treasures are the endangered marsh rose (*Orothamnus zeyheri*) and the greatest concentration of Mimetes species in the Cape. Visitors can experience the wilderness atmosphere and spectacular scenery along several day walks and an overnight trail. Kogelberg was declared southern Africa's first biosphere reserve in 1998.

ROOIELS ④, with its small sandy beach, takes its name from the farm granted to Abraham Louw in 1839 and the river of that name. It refers to the red alder (*Cunonia capensis*), a riverine tree occurring in the area.

PRINGLE BAY is a beautiful sandy inlet lying between the mouth of the Buffels River and a small rocky headland named The Point.

Its name honours Rear-Admiral Thomas Pringle, commander of British naval forces at the Cape from 1796 to 1798. In the early 1800s, the bay was earmarked as a port to enable farmers to ship their produce across False Bay to Simon's Town rather than negotiating the arduous Gantouw Pass over the Hottentots Holland Mountains. Over the years, the bay's remote location attracted its fair share of deserters and runaway slaves, and a cave just north of the Buffels River still bears the name Drostersgat (Deserters' Cave).

HANGKLIP, at the southern extremity of the Hottentots Holland Mountains, marks the eastern end of False Bay. Originally named *Punta Espinosa* (Thorny Point) by early Portuguese navigators, the 454-m-high mountain was later renamed *Cabo Falso* (False Cape) as it was sometimes mistaken for Cape Point during bad weather conditions. To the Dutch, it resembled a hanging lip, and so they called it Hanglip (which later became Hangklip). During World War II, Hangklip was the site of a radar station built to keep a watch for German vessels.

BETTY'S BAY is a pleasant coastal resort and angling spot established in the 1930s. At Stony Point, the western extremity of the bay, visitors can get close-up views of a colony of African penguins (*Spheniscus demersus*), one of only three mainland colonies in Africa. The first penguins started breeding here in 1982, and within eight years the breeding population had increased to just over 100 pairs. Nearby can be seen the remains of the Southern Cross Whaling Station, which operated between 1907 and 1928. Relics include part of the jetty, the ramp used to winch carcasses ashore and the remains of the *Balena*, one of the last whaling vessels.

HAROLD PORTER BOTANICAL GARDEN Covering 188 ha, this beautiful gardens lies against a backdrop of high mountains and incorporates two beautiful forested kloofs with waterfalls: Disa Gorge and Leopard's Kloof. The garden was named after the original owner of the land, who bequeathed it to the National Botanical Gardens of South Africa when he died in 1957. The garden focuses on the conservation and cultivation of the flora of the winter rainfall area. A network of footpaths meander through the 5 ha of cultivated gardens, with their lawns, tranquil ponds and collections of various plant families, as well as the natural fynbos on the mountain slopes. The walk to the waterfall in Disa Gorge is highly recommended, especially from late December to mid-January when the red disas are in bloom.

KLEINMOND Bounded by the Palmietberge to the north and the Atlantic Ocean to the south, Kleinmond nestles along the rocky coastline between the Palmiet Lagoon in the west and the Kleinmond Lagoon in the east. It has been a popular holiday destination ever since farmers from Elgin began using Kleinmond as their annual summer holiday retreat almost a century ago. Covering 355 ha, the Kleinmond Coastal Nature Reserve extends from the coast, with its strandveld vegetation, to the fynbos-covered mountain slopes north of the town, and provides protection to more than 1 000 plant species. The reserve adjoins the Kogelberg Biosphere Reserve and is criss-crossed by a network of trails. Kleinmond Lagoon offers safe swimming and canoeing, while the sandy beach off Sandown Bay can be accessed via a footbridge.

HOUWHOEK PASS In the early days of travel, crossing the Houwhoek Mountains, which separate the Elgin Valley from the rolling hills beyond the Bot River, presented a formidable obstacle. Houwhoek means 'hold corner', and probably came from the need to hold back, or slow down, the ox wagons when negotiating the steep descent. The original pass was completed in 1831. At the summit of the pass is the Houw Hoek Inn, established in 1834 on the site of an old tollgate, and the oldest inn in the country. Most of the ground floor dates back to 1779, while the upper storey was added in 1860.

GRABOUW/ELGIN See Tour 5, page 18.

STEENBRAS DAM was commissioned in the early 1920s after the reservoirs on Table Mountain could no longer meet the growing water demands of Cape Town. Since its completion, the dam wall has been raised twice to increase the dam's capacity. Covering 380 ha when full, the water backs up to 8 km behind the 36-m-high dam wall. Steenbras is one of only two pumped storage power stations in South Africa, with a maximum capacity of 400 MW. When demand for electricity is low, water is pumped from a lower reservoir for storage in the dam. When demand rises, the water is released to generate electricity.

SIR LOWRY'S PASS See Tour 5, page 18.

3

4

1

2

11
310 KM

3

4

5

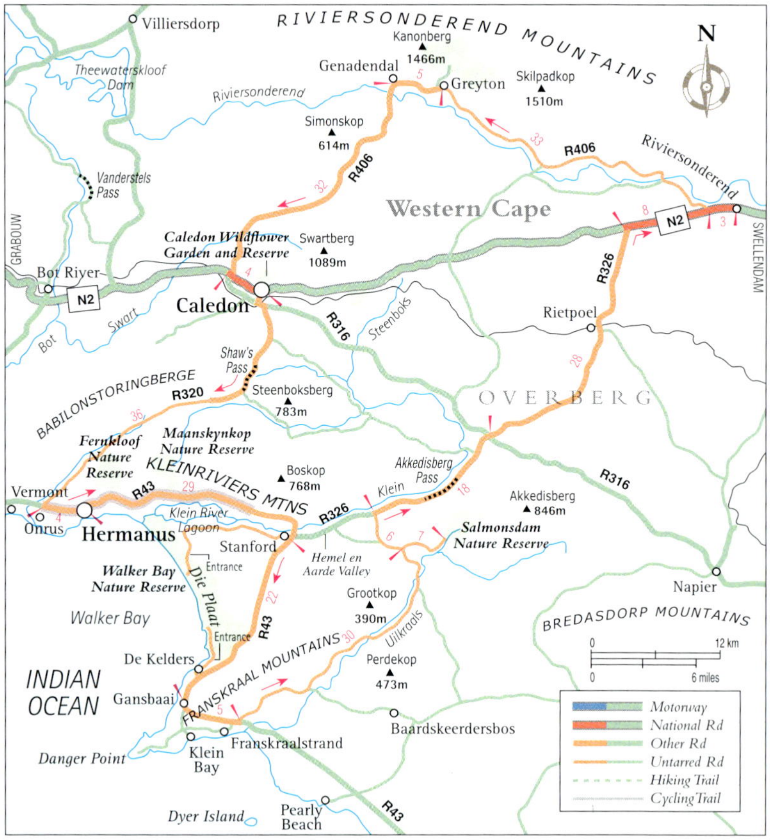

HERMANUS is the heart of the popular Whale Route, and the town's 12-km-long Cliff Path offers one of the best shore-based whale-watching spots ① in the world. The southern right whales arrive in Walker Bay in June/July to calve and remain until November. Visitors are kept up to date about the latest whale sightings by the town's Whale Crier ②, the only one of his kind in the world. The coastline around Hermanus is characterised by numerous sheltered coves and bays, which are ideal for swimming and sunbathing. Grotto Beach, at the town's eastern end, features a magnificent sandy beach. On the hills above the town, visitors can enjoy walking among the fynbos flora in the Fernkloof Nature Reserve, which has 40 km of hiking trails. Not to be missed is a visit to the craftmarket ③ and the old stone harbour ④ with its interesting museum, where you can listen to whale sounds transmitted from a sonar buoy offshore.

STANFORD Built along the banks of the Klein River, Stanford's Victorian buildings, smallholdings and water furrows lend the village a charming, rural air. Facing the central market square is a cluster of Edwardian houses built in 1920–23. Also of interest are the thatched Anglican chapel, the first school built from local stone around 1890 and the original farmhouse of Captain (later Sir) Robert Stanford. After retiring from the British Army in 1838, Stanford bought the farm Kleinrivier and exported his produce by boat from Stanford's Cove, 2 km north of Gansbaai. When the village was laid out in 1857, it was named after Stanford.

WALKER BAY NATURE RESERVE The main section of the Walker Bay Nature Reserve covers 1 000 ha of lowland coastal fynbos and dunes between the Klein River estuary and Die Kelders. It is bounded in the west by Walker Bay and incorporates 17 km of white sandy beaches and rocky limestone outcrops. Excavations at Klipgat Cave, near the southern boundary of the reserve, have provided important archaeological records of Middle Stone Age occupation (between 85 000 and 65 000 years ago), as well as occupation by Later Stone Age people some 20 000 years ago. Recreational activities include day walks, angling and picnicking.

DE KELDERS This small resort town owes its name to the nearby limestone caves, one of which has a series of natural freshwater pools fed by seepage from a spring. Among its early visitors was Lady Anne Barnard, who bathed in the pools during a visit in 1798. The rocky coastline provides ideal vantage points for whale-watching, and is also popular with anglers.

GANSBAAI Situated in a protected cove on the eastern side of Walker Bay, Gansbaai ⑤ is a busy fishing village with two harbours, a cannery and a fishmeal factory. It is also popular with angling, diving and boating enthusiasts, while the 7-km Duiwelsgat Hiking Trail offers magnificent views over Walker Bay. The narrow channel between Dyer Island and Geyser Island, 7,5 km off the Gansbaai coast, has one of the largest concentrations of great white sharks in the world. Gansbaai is the centre of several shark-viewing and cage-diving operations; the months between April and October are generally the best for shark-viewing.

SALMONSDAM NATURE RESERVE This small reserve lies in a basin at the foot of the Paardenberg mountains and covers 834 ha of unspoilt mountain fynbos. Visitors can explore the forested ravines, caves, waterfalls and interesting rock formations along three-day walks from one to two hours' duration or take the Mountain Drive to the viewpoint at Ravenshill. Among the mammals occurring here are bontebok, grey rhebok, klipspringer and common duiker, while more than 120 bird species have been recorded. The area and the reserve were named after Captain Robert Salmond, the commander of HMS *Birkenhead*, which ran aground off Danger Point in the early hours of 26 February 1852. There is, however, no large dam as the name might suggest, only a small one made of earth.

RIVIERSONDEREND is the centre for the surrounding wheat farming region, an area well known for its colonies of blue cranes, South Africa's national bird. The town owes its name to what was known as the Rivier Zonder End ('river without end'), a tributary of the Breede River. The river's name refers to the difficulties encountered by early explorers in tracing it to its source.

GREYTON Established in a fertile valley at the foot of the Riviersonderend mountains in 1854, Greyton has retained much of its rural charm: thatched cottages amid beautiful gardens, oak-lined streets and 'leiwater' canals. Among its many fine buildings ⑥ are the Moravian Church, Greyton Lodge (the original buildings date back to 1876) and the Post House, which formed part of the original homestead on Weltevreden, the farm on which the village was laid out. In the 1890s, the building housed Greyton's first post office, hence the name. An area of 2 200 ha to the northeast of the town has been set aside as a municipal nature reserve, and can be explored along a network of walks and trails ranging in duration from 30 minutes to three hours. The 14-km-long Boesmanskloof Hiking Trail between Greyton and McGregor is a popular day trail.

GENADENDAL was founded by missionary George Schmidt in 1738 to minister to the Khoi people. Originally known as Baviaanskloof, the name was changed to Genadendal (Valley of Grace) in 1806. The first Moravian mission station in South Africa, the village is centred around the historic Church Square, dominated by the mission church built in 1891. All the buildings around the square were declared national monuments in 1980, and among these are the first church (1795), old mill (1796), church bell (1798) and several school buildings. The history of the mission station is depicted in the Mission Museum, housed in a building (built in 1838) which served as the first teachers' training college in South Africa. Just south of the town is the Beinbrecht Bridge, completed in 1820 under the guidance of the Moravian missionary JD Beinbrecht. The original bridge was supported by five massive stone pillars, three to four metres in height and measuring 3,6 m in diameter at the base. After a flood in 1822, the height of the pillars was increased by two metres. The 25,3-km-long Genadendal Hiking Trail winds through the Riviersonderend Mountains, and takes two days to complete.

CALEDON is the centre of an agricultural area ⑦ noted for its production of wheat, onions, wool and barley, the latter processed into malt for the beer industry. The town is home to the largest malt producer in the country, with an annual output of around 140 000 tonnes. Caledon originally developed around a hot spring (38° C at source) that has attracted visitors since the 17th century and now forms part of a major casino development. The Caledon Museum, housed in a Victorian building, takes as its the theme the Victorian era (1837–1901). Among the town's historic buildings are the Anglican Church (1855) and the beautiful Victorian houses along Mill Street. The Caledon Wildflower Garden and Reserve covers 56 ha of landscaped indigenous gardens, water features and lawns, as well as 158 ha of natural fynbos vegetation on the slopes of the Swartberg. Caledon is famous for its wild flower show, held in September each year. First staged in 1892, the event is the largest of its kind in South Africa, with over 600 fynbos species on display.

HEMEL-EN-AARDE VALLEY Bounded by the Onrus Mountains and the western outlier of the Kleinsrivier Mountains, this beautiful valley lies in the folds of the course carved by the Onrus River. It was in this valley, with its cool maritime climate, that Timothy Hamilton Russell established Africa's southernmost vineyard in 1976. Since then, Bouchard Finlayson, Whalehaven and Cape Bay Wines have also established themselves in the valley.

6

7

1 

 2

12

345 KM

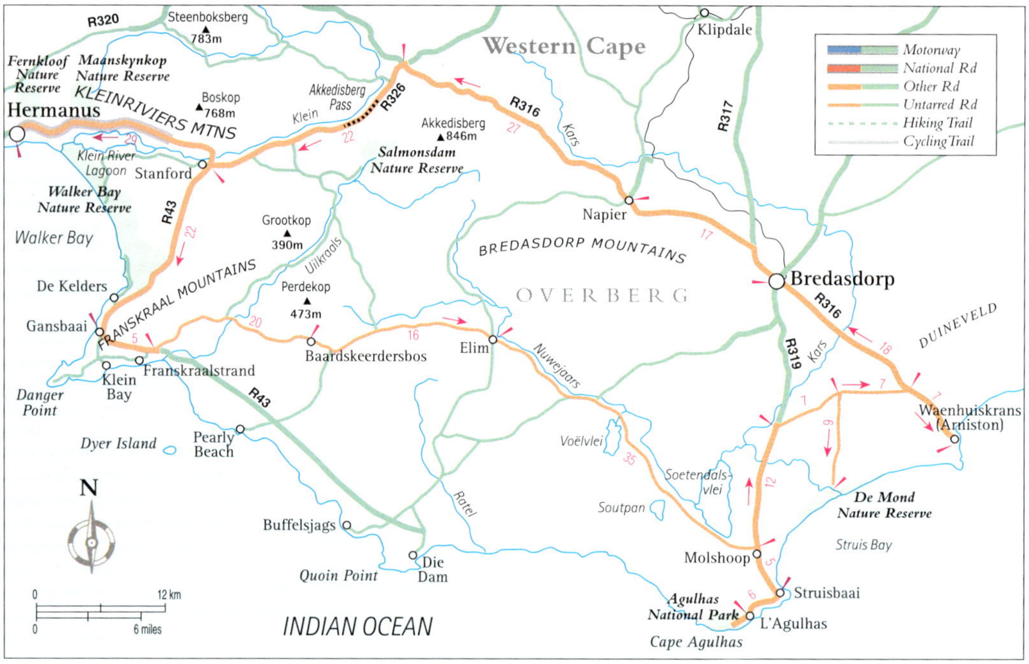

CAPE AGULHAS The early Portuguese navigators named Africa's southernmost tip Cabo das Agulhas, or Cape of Needles, after noticing that their compass needles showed little magnetic deviation and pointed almost due north when passing this point ③. The dangers of this treacherous coastline prompted the construction of a beacon to warn mariners to stay clear. The original Agulhas lighthouse, commissioned on 1 March 1849, stood 27 m in height and was built from limestone in the style of the ancient Pharos lighthouse at Alexandria, Egypt. After 117 years' service, it was replaced by a new lighthouse commissioned in 1966. Appropriately, the old lighthouse ④ has served as the Cape Agulhas Lighthouse Museum since 1994. The only one of its kind in Africa, the museum provides an account of the development of lighthouses through the ages and the history of the Cape Agulhas Lighthouse in particular. Also on display are lenses, lanterns, gas burners and foghorns. About 1 km west of the lighthouse, the southernmost tip of Africa (34° 49' 58" south and 20° 00' 12" east) is marked by a cairn and plaque. L'Aghulhas is the southernmost town in Africa, and is a popular holiday destination, especially during the summer months.

HERMANUS From Hermanus to Gansbaai this tour follows the same route through Stanford, De Kelders and Gansbaai as the one described in Tour 11, page 32.

BAARDSKEERDERSBOS is a quaint village with an intriguing name, which is literally translated as 'beard shaver's bush'. It was in fact named after a ten-legged arthropod known in English as a solifuge. The descriptive Afrikaans name, *baardskeerder*, refers to the mandibles of these spider-like creatures, which are reminiscent of the clippers used by barbers to cut hair and shave beards.

ELIM This picturesque mission village, with its rows of whitewashed thatched houses, was founded in 1824 by the Moravian Church. It was named after the biblical oasis, with its 12 springs and 70 palm trees, where the Israelites made their second stop after crossing the Red Sea (Exodus 15:27). The mission station and houses are exceptionally well preserved, and the entire village has been declared a national monument. All the roads in the village lead to the gabled, thatched church, which features an 18th-century clock acquired in 1914 from a church in Herenhut, Germany, from where the Moravian missionaries originally came. The clock faces on both sides of the gable are connected by a rod and operate from a single set of works. Also of interest is the slave monument, the only monument in South Africa to commemorate the freeing of the slaves in 1834. The old water mill ① at the bottom of the church grounds dates back to 1838, and is the biggest wooden water wheel in the country. At the Old Mill Tea Room, visitors can sample Elim's famous *mosbolletjies* (dough leavened with a ferment of must) and biscuits baked with stone-ground flour from the mill.

STRUISBAAI Originally a fishing village, Struisbaai has become a popular coastal resort and angling destination. The modest cottages at Hotagterklip serve as a reminder of the community's humble beginnings. The cottages, built about 90 years ago, feature thatched roofs, simple end gables and lime-washed walls. Struisbaai's main attraction is its 14-km-long beach, said to be the longest continuous stretch of sandy beach in South Africa, which offers safe swimming.

AGULHAS NATIONAL PARK This national park was proclaimed in 1999, primarily to protect the rich diversity of fynbos plant species occurring on the Agulhas Plain, the unique system of wetlands and their associated fauna, the scenic coastline and the rich cultural heritage of the area. The Agulhas Plain has approximately 2 000 species of indigenous plants, including 100 endemics. The initial core of the park includes Africa's southernmost point and the 97-ha area around the lighthouse. Planners envisage the enlargement of the park to 20 000 ha, stretching from near Quoin Point in the west to Agulhas in the east, and including the Soetanysberg and associated wetland habitats. This will be done by purchasing key properties and acquiring state-owned land, and by managing part of the park on a contractual basis. Plans for the future include an environmental education centre, an upgraded museum and interpretive centre and a network of nature trails.

DE MOND NATURE RESERVE The focal point of this reserve ②, which stretches for approximately 9 km along the coast between Struisbaai and Waenhuiskrans, is the mouth of the Heuningnes River. Covering 954 ha of shifting sand dunes, dune and limestone fynbos, salt marshes and tidal flats, the reserve offers good birding possibilities. It is one of only two known breeding sites of the endangered Damara tern (*Sterna balaenerum*) enjoying protection in South Africa. The rare black oystercatcher (*Haematopus moquini*), South Africa's second most threatened coastal bird, can also be seen here. Picnic facilities are provided, and visitors can explore the reserve along the 7-km-long Sterna Trail.

WAENHUISKRANS ⑤ is named after the enormous cave carved by the sea into the cliffs near the village. Large enough to hold several ox wagons, the name is translated as 'coach-house cliff'. The popular seaside village is also widely known as Arniston after the British troopship *Arniston*, which ran aground in Marcus Bay on 30 May 1815, with the loss of 372 lives. The picturesque village of Kassiesbaai is characterised by its thatched cottages with whitewashed walls and kitchen chimneys, which are typical of the fishing villages built along the Cape coast in the early 1900s. The entire village of 84 cottages has been declared a national monument.

BREDASDORP, the centre of the surrounding wheat and sheep farming district, was established in 1838 by Michiel van Breda. The highlight for visitors is the Shipwreck Museum, which houses a fascinating display of figureheads, cannons, coins, porcelain, ships' bells and other artefacts recovered from the many vessels wrecked along the Overberg coast. The adjacent old coach house contains an interesting collection of Cape carts, a Scotch cart (a two-wheel tip cart drawn by horses or oxen), two horse-drawn hearses and an old fire engine. The Old Parsonage is a typical strandveld house, and has been furnished with articles salvaged along the coast. The Audrey Blignault Room, at the tourism bureau, is dedicated to the Afrikaans author, who was born in Bredasdorp. The bureau also has an interesting display on the Foot of Africa Marathon, the continent's southernmost marathon. South of Bredasdorp, the 800-ha Heuningberg Nature Reserve provides protection to over 300 plant species, including eight of the 14 genera of the protea family, a rich diversity of ericas, buchu and geophytes. Among the over 36 endemics to be seen are the Bredasdorp lily (*Cyrtanthus guthrieae*) and a pincushion(*Leucospermum heterophyllum*). There are many short walks, as well as two longer routes of 2,5 and 3 hours, respectively.

NAPIER Lying at the foot of the Soetmuis and Bredasdorp hills, amid the rolling wheat and barley fields of the Overberg, Napier has retained an old-world charm. The town developed around the Dutch Reformed Church, built in 1838 after a dispute over where the church should be built. The dispute was not resolved, resulting in two churches: one in Napier, the other in Bredasdorp. Napier's has a beautiful teak wood interior. The adjacent Feeshuis 150, one of the oldest buildings in the village, served as slave quarters and later as wine cellars in the 19th century. A number of artists have settled in Napier, and their studios and workshops can be visited by following the Napier Village Route.

3

4

5

1

13
310 KM

2

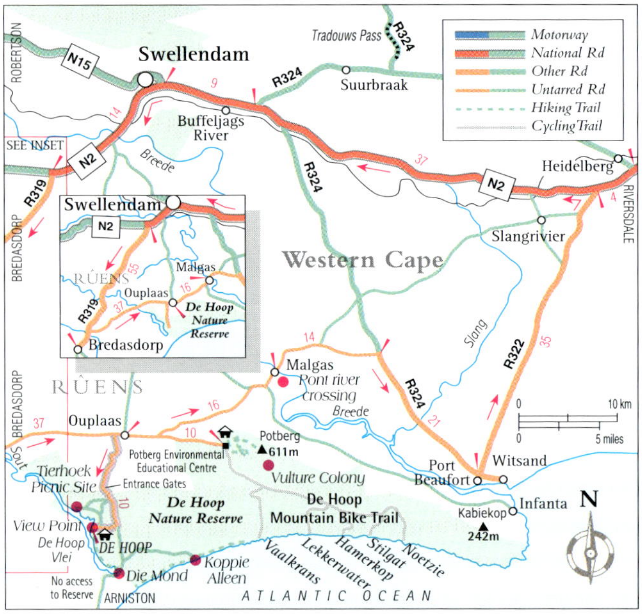

3

SWELLENDAM, at the foot of the Langeberg Mountains, is the third-oldest town in South Africa. Established in 1743 as a magisterial district, Swellendam briefly enjoyed the status of a republic when the local burghers revolted against the maladministration of the Dutch East India Company on 17 June 1795. The republic was short-lived, though, as three months later the first British occupation of the Cape began.

The town is renowned for its many well-preserved Cape Dutch and Georgian buildings, among them the Drostdy (magistrate's court) ③, the only 18th-century drostdy still in existence. The stately building forms the focal point of a museum complex consisting of the Ambagswerf (tradesmen's yard), the old gaol, Mayville with its Victorian rose garden and Zanddrif, an 18th-century farmhouse (now a restaurant). Several day walks, ranging from easy one-hour rambles to a strenuous full-day hike, range over the mountain slopes of the Marloth Nature Reserve just north of the town. Swellendam is the centre of the world's largest youngberry-producing area, as well as the surrounding wheat, fruit, sheep and dairy farms.

RÛENS This Afrikaans name, meaning 'ridges', refers to the typically undulating landscape traversed by the road between Swellendam and Bredasdorp. Also referred to as the Ruggens, or Ruggensveld, the region extends from the Riviersonderend Mountains southwards to the Duineveld along the coast, and from the Houwhoek Pass eastwards to beyond Bredasdorp. It owes its undulating nature to the incision of numerous rivers and streams through the limestone overlying the ancient rocks of the Malmesbury Group.

BREDASDORP See Tour 12, page 35.

DE HOOP NATURE RESERVE Covering 36 000 ha, the De Hoop Nature Reserve features a variety of habitats: large tracts of coastal fynbos, shifting sand dunes, the scenic De Hoop Vlei and 45 km of unspoilt coastline. The reserve lies in an area with some 1 500 species of fynbos ②, including 50 species that are endemic to De Hoop. Fauna include the largest bontebok population in the country, Cape mountain zebra, eland, grey rhebok, steenbok, common duiker, Cape grysbok and ostrich. Birders flock to the 15-km-long De Hoop Vlei, a wetland of international importance for migratory birds. Of the 260 bird species recorded, 97 are waterbirds, among them 12 waterfowl species and 13 species of migrant waders such as little stints, curlew sandpipers and ruffs. The coast is the habitat of the African black oystercatcher and the Damara tern. In addition to a short circular drive for vehicles near the office complex, there are also picnic sites and day walks, as well as a mountain bike route ④. The waters off De Hoop have the largest concentration of southern right whales along the South African coast and the reserve offers superb vantage points for viewing these majestic creatures. Self-catering cottages are available, but visitors must provide their own bedding and kitchen utensils. A campsite is also available.

POTBERG Rising over 400 m above the coastal plain in the north-eastern corner of the De Hoop Nature Reserve, Potberg is an inselberg (island mountain) of sandstones and quartzites. The mountain cliffs are home to the last breeding colony of the Cape vulture (*Gyps coprotheres*) in the Western Cape; with the active co-operation of local farmers, the colony has increased from a mere 45 in 1986 to 107 adult birds in 2000. The mountain has at least 12 endemic plant species, among them a small ground protea (*Protea denticulata*), the *potbergensis* subspecies of Protea aurea and a wild tea bush (*Aspalathus* *potbergensis*). Facilities for day visitors include an interpretation centre, picnic sites and two day walks. The Klipspringer Trail is a 5-km circular route, while the Potberg Trail is a 4-km route to the summit of the mountain from where there are fine views over the Breede River valley and the reserve. The Potberg environmental education centre is used by organised groups, especially schools.

MALGAS During the period 1757 to 1894, several pont crossings were in operation on the Breede River. The crossing at Malgas, a small settlement on the western bank of the river, came into use in 1830. When the original wooden pont eventually sank, it was replaced with a steel one which was washed away in the great flood of 1906. The current pont ①, introduced in 1914, is the only remaining hand-driven pont in South Africa. In addition to serving as a pont crossing, Malgas became a busy inland port during the mid-1800s, when it was a terminus for the trading firm of Barry and Nephews. Instead of using the arduous overland trek, goods were brought from the Cape by sea to Port Beaufort at the mouth of the Breede River. After negotiating the sandbanks at the mouth of the river, the vessels steamed the 48 km upstream to Malgas where cargo was offloaded and products destined for the Cape taken on board.

PORT BEAUFORT Established in 1817 as a point of communication with the interior, Port Beaufort was named after the Earl of Beaufort, father of Lord Charles Somerset, on whose instructions the estuary was surveyed. Under the trading firm of Barry and Nephews, established in the early 1820s, Port Beaufort developed into a thriving settlement, with a shop, warehouses and approximately 20 houses. On 26 September 1859, the firm's specially built steamer, *Kadie*, steamed up the Breede River to Malgas on her maiden voyage. Over the next six years, she successfully completed 120 trips, until becoming stranded on rocks along the river bank on 17 November 1865. Soon afterwards, the company's fortunes began to decline, and after it ceased operations in 1882 the once-thriving port sank into obscurity. The small thatched church built in 1849 by Thomas Barry serves as a reminder of Port Beaufort's prosperous days.

WITSAND ⑤, at the mouth of the Breede River, is renowned for its excellent fishing, and offers opportunities for both surf angling and fishing in the estuary. It also offers a wide range of water sports in the sea and on the river, while the long sandy beach has safe swimming.

HEIDELBERG Established on the banks of the Duivenhoks River below the Langeberg, Heidelberg is the centre for the surrounding wheat and sheep farms. The town developed around a church established in 1855 to serve the farming community living in the area between Swellendam and Riversdale, and was named after the German city where the catechisms were originally drawn up.

BUFFELJAGSRIVIER is a small settlement and railway station named after the Buffeljags River, which was known by that name as early as 1676. The Afrikaans name means 'buffalo hunt river', as it was a noted spot for hunting buffalo.

4

5

14
265 KM

1

2

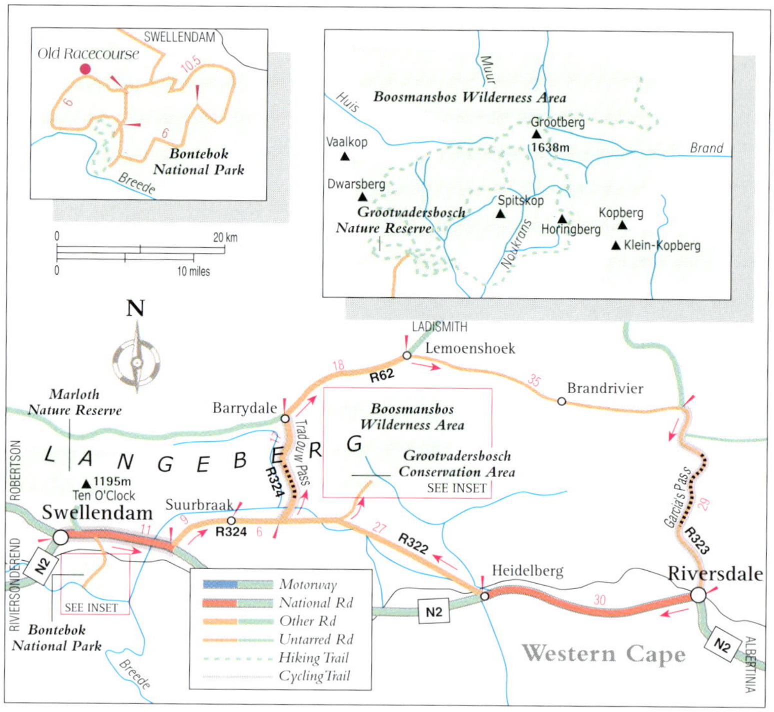

SWELLENDAM See Tour 13, page 36.

OUDE POST on the farm Rietvallei was established around 1734 to protect farmers against stock theft by Khoikhoi raiders and to prevent illegal cattle-trading. It consisted of a small fort manned by seven soldiers under the supervision of a *post houder* (post holder). Situated on the road into the interior, the outpost became a popular stopping place with travellers, among them the Swedish botanist Carl Thunberg, Governor Joachim van Plettenberg and Lady Anne Barnard.

SUURBRAAK The history of Suurbraak dates back to 1812, when the London Missionary Society founded a mission station at an Attaqua Khoikhoi settlement known as Xairu. The Khoikhoi name, meaning 'beautiful', was later changed to Suurbraak, a reference to the sour fallow land used as the village square. Situated at the foot of the Langeberg range, the tranquil village is shaded by stately oak trees, and orchards and vegetable gardens are spread along the main street. Many of the houses ② are the original dwellings built by converts of the missionaries, and, unique among the mission stations of the Cape, there are a number of double-storey houses. Be sure to visit the Suurbraak (square) which is surrounded by beautifully restored houses and the old mission church dating back to around 1835. Suurbraak is famed for its handmade chairs, and the craft shop offers fine embroidery and local crafts.

LANGEBERG, meaning 'long mountain', is an apt name for this range, which forms a natural barrier nearly 400 km long between the coastal plains and the Breede River valley to the south and the Little Karoo to the north. Stretching from the Hex River Mountains to the Outeniqua Mountains, the Langeberg reaches its greatest elevation (1 710 m) at Misty Point near Swellendam. The range ⑤ has a rich diversity of ericas, proteas, reeds, rushes, orchids and other flowering plants, and the slopes are particularly attractive in spring when they are covered in masses of pink ericas.

TRADOUW PASS Before the Tradouw Pass was built, the Khoikhoi used two routes between De Oude Post (where they traded) and their settlement north of the Langeberg. The men used a longer, more difficult route, while the women used the easier route known as the Tradouw, a name translated as 'women's path'. The building of the pass started in 1868, under the direction of the famed road engineer, Thomas Bain. At one stage, as many as 300 convicts worked as labourers on the pass. After various delays the pass was opened in 1873. The historic bridge over the Gats River, built of Burmese teak by Bain after the original bridge was washed away, can still be seen. Known as Letty's Bridge, it was named after Aletta Catherina van Reenen, the wife of John Barry, a nephew of trader Joseph Barry. When the new pass was built in the mid-1960s, the sections of Bain's pass that were not incorporated into the new route were put to use as viewpoints. From these, travellers can enjoy the magnificent scenery of the Tradouw Pass, with its lichen-encrusted cliffs, deeply folded rock strata, cascades and wild flowers.

BARRYDALE Nestling below the northern slopes of the Langeberg at the top of the Tradouw Pass, Barrydale lies in a lush green valley contrasting sharply with the sparsely vegetated plains of the Little Karoo. The fertile valley is a productive farming area noted for its dried fruit (especially apricots and prunes), pears and apples, as well as wine. The town developed around the church built here after the completion of the Tradouw Pass and was named in honour of the Barry family, who played a significant role in the economy of the Overberg between the 1820s and the late 1860s.

GARCIA'S PASS is named after a former Civil Commissioner of Riversdale, AH Garcia, who in the 1860s saw the necessity for a direct route between Riversdale and the Little Karoo. After surveying a route, Garcia used convict labour to built a footpath over the mountain. Following appeals by the residents of Riversdale for a proper road, the Cape Parliament approved the construction of a pass in 1872. The route was surveyed the following year by Thomas Bain, and convicts were put to work to build the pass. Progress was slow, however, and it was not until 31 December 1877 that the pass was opened to traffic. A tollhouse was built at the summit of the pass, and tolls were collected until the end of 1918. The tollhouse, a national monument, now serves as a starting point of two hiking trails traversing the Langeberg Mountains. Dominating the scenery to the west of the pass is the well-known peak, Sleeping Beauty, the outline of which resembles a sleeping woman.

RIVERSDALE The pleasant town of Riversdale was established on the farm Doornkraal in 1838 as an agricultural centre for the surrounding farms. It was named after Harry Rivers, Commissioner and Resident Magistrate of Swellendam from 1834 to 1841. Art-lovers should be sure to visit the Julius Gordon Africana Centre in Versveld House, a magnificent residence built in the Georgian style. The centre houses a fine collection of South African paintings, including the second-largest collection of paintings by Thomas Bowler, as well as works by Jan Volschenk, Gregoire Boonzaaier, Pieter Wenning and Irma Stern. Among the collection of antiques are stinkwood chairs, old clocks, china and a horse-drawn hearse. Other attractions are Jurisch Park, which includes a section for exotic plants, and the indigenous Van Riebeeck Park, noted for its variety of aloes. Among the town's historic buildings are St Matthew's Church (1856) and the Old Prison (1859).

HEIDELBERG See Tour 13, page 37.

GROOTVADERSBOSCH NATURE RESERVE ③, 22 km northwest of Heidelberg, covers some 250 ha of magnificent indigenous forest of yellowwood, stinkwood and red alder. Visitors can explore the reserve along a network of trails ranging in length from 2 km to 10 km. The Grootvadersbosch forest is the largest tract of indigenous forest west of the Knysna forests. Noteworthy among the nearly 200 bird species recorded in the reserve to date are the Knysna woodpecker, Narina trogon, forest buzzard and Victorin's warbler. The forest offers excellent birding opportunities, and a canopy-level bird hide is a delight to birders.

3

4

BONTEBOK NATIONAL PARK This small but delightful national park was proclaimed in 1961 to save the bontebok (*Damaliscus dorcas dorcas*) ①, a species restricted to the coastal plains of the southwestern Cape, from extinction. The park was originally established in the Bredasdorp area in 1931, with a nucleus of only 17 animals. However, it proved to be too small and unsuitable, necessitating a move to a larger site. The population grew rapidly in the new park (which has a carrying capacity of around 200 bontebok), and so animals have had to be moved to other nature reserves and private land. Today, the total population stands at between 2 000 and 3 000. In addition to bontebok, visitors can also see red hartebeest, Cape mountain zebra, springbok, grey rhebok, grey duiker, steenbok and Cape grysbok. Among the over 190 bird species found here are Stanley's bustard, blue crane and Cape sugarbird. Picnic facilities are available for day visitors on the banks of the Breede River ④ and swimming is possible in the river in the vicinity of the rest camp. There are two short circular trails, starting and ending at the rest camp.

5

THIS PAGE LEFT: CLUB MYKONOS, WEST COAST (P.44); BELOW: CHURCHHAVEN ON LANGEBAAN LAGOON (P.44); **OPPOSITE** TOP: VERLORENVLEI (P.47); CENTRE TOP LEFT: WEST COAST STRAND-LOPER (P.44); CENTRE TOP RIGHT: PATERNOSTER COTTAGE (P.45); CENTRE BOTTOM LEFT: FISHING BOATS, PATERNOSTER (P.45); CENTRE BOTTOM RIGHT: PENGUINS, MELKBOSSTRAND (P.15); BOTTOM: CAPE GANNETS (P.46).

SWARTLAND AND WEST COAST

WESTERN CAPE

1

15

245 KM

2

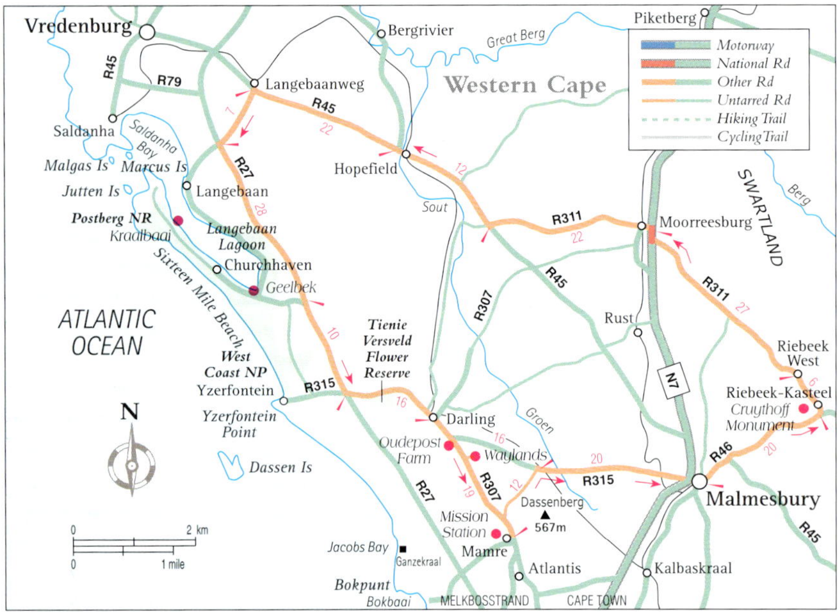

3

SWARTLAND This well-known wheat-producing area is centred around the town of Malmesbury, and stretches from Philadelphia in the south to Piketberg in the north. In the east, the Swartland is bounded by the Winterhoek Mountains, Heuningberg and the Olifants River Mountains, while the dunes of the West Coast and the Groen Kloof River form its western boundary. The region is characterised by its gently undulating hills and rolling wheatfields, which account for about 20 per cent of the country's wheat production. Although the Dutch name 'het Zwartland', which means 'the black country', was first used in 1701, there are several interpretations of its origin. One of the more plausible is that the name refers to the colour of the once-plentiful renoster bush (*Elytropappus rhinocerotis*), which is black when wet. The main centres of the Swartland are Malmesbury, Mooreesburg, Piketberg and Porterville, as well as the Riebeeck Valley. The Swartland Wine Route consists of several estates, co-operatives and cellars and one private cellar.

DARLING Once little more than a dot on the map (except during the spring flower season), Darling has become a fashionable country retirement *dorp* (village). It is also home to several artists, including satirist Pieter-Dirk Uys who has converted the Darling Station into a mini-theatre and restaurant called Evita se Perron ②. Founded on the farm Langfontein in 1853, the town's name honours British Governor Charles Henry Darling. Darling is aptly known as the 'Flower of the West Coast' because the surrounding farmlands are transformed into a kaleidoscope of colours when the spring flowers burst into bloom ③. The floral wealth of Darling lies mainly in its bulbous flowers, with species like chinkerinchee, ixias and heliophila, and the best season is usually between August and mid-October. The town is famous for its wild flower show (in the third week of September) which has been held since 1917. During the flower season, several flower reserves on local farms are open to the public, among them Oudepost, Waylands, Slangkop and Contreberg. A section of the Darling Museum depicts the region's butter-making industry and has a fascinating collection of wooden butter-washing machines, old butter churns and farming implements.

MAMRE is a picturesque mission settlement, with neat rows of whitewashed hipped-roof cottages, each with its own little garden, and stately oak trees. Originally named Groenekloof, a military outpost known as De Kleine Post was established in the lush green valley in 1701. The outpost later served as a trading station until it was closed in 1791. In 1808, the Moravian Church founded its second mission station in the country here, renaming it 46 years later after the biblical Mamre (Genesis 13:18), which means 'fatness'. In time, the mission station became an important educational centre, and members of the community were trained in various skills. Among its architectural treasures are Long House, a farmhouse which served as barracks for the garrison between 1701 and 1791, the Parsonage (1701) and the mission church (1814), with its Cape Dutch gable. Other historic buildings include the school, bakery, packing shed, stables and the water mill (1844), which now serves as a museum. Two of South Africa's most threatened vegetation types, West Coast renosterveld and sand plain fynbos, are protected in the Mamre Nature Garden, established on land owned by the community.

MALMESBURY is the principal town of the Swartland. Settlement of the area by the Dutch dates back to the early 1700s, when the first farms were awarded. After the Dutch

Reformed Church was established in 1745, the town became known as Zwartlandkerk. It was renamed in 1829 by Sir Lowry Cole in honour of his father-in-law, the first Earl of Malmesbury. In addition to wheat, the Malmesbury area ④ is also noted for wine, sheep and dairy farming. Of historical interest are the Neo-Gothic Dutch Reformed Church, dating back to the early 1860s, the old Jewish synagogue of 1911 (now a museum depicting the development of the town and the history of bread and baking) and the Masonic Lodge (1866).

CRUYTHOFF MONUMENT This monument at the foot of the Kasteelberg recalls the trading expedition led by Corporal Pieter Cruythoff in 1661 to barter with the Khoikhoi for cattle needed to supply the ships of the Dutch East India Company. One of the expedition members, Pieter Meerhof, ascended the mountain on 3 February 1661 and named it 'Riebeeck Casteel' in honour of Jan Van Riebeeck, commander of the settlement at the Cape.

RIEBEECK-KASTEEL ⑤ It seems incongruous to have two 'Riebeecks' a mere 4 km apart, and that this state of affairs should have come about through religious dissent. Until the 1850s, the communities of Riebeeck-Kasteel and Riebeeck-West fell under the Dutch Reformed Church at Malmesbury. Following a decision in 1854 to establish a congregation in the Kasteel Valley, a dispute arose between the two communities over the location of the church, eventually resulting in two independent congregations. The cornerstone of the Oude Kerk was laid in 1855, and in time the town developed around the church. Another building of interest is the Royal Hotel ①.

RIEBEECK WEST Situated on the eastern slopes of the Kasteelberg, Riebeeck West lies in a farming area noted for its peaches, nectarines and wines. It is also an important producer of the country's cement requirements. Two of South Africa's former prime ministers were born on farms close to each other. DF Malan, who led the National Party government into power in 1948, was born on the farm Allesverloren (now well-known for producing port-style wines) between Riebeeck-Kasteel and Riebeeck West. About 3 km northwest of Riebeeck West, a signpost indicates the turnoff to Bovenplaas, where Jan Smuts was born in 1870. Smuts was Prime Minister of South Africa from 1919 to 1922 and again from 1939 to 1948. The original farmhouse, school room, poultry house, coach house, dairy and stables have been restored by the owners of the farm, cement company PPC. An interesting collection of photographs is displayed in one of the outbuildings.

MOORREESBURG The importance of wheat to the town of Moorreesburg is reflected in the Wheat Industry Museum – one of only three such museums in the world. The museum focuses on the history and development of the wheat industry, and activities such as harvesting and milling are portrayed in dioramas. There is also an interesting collection of sowing and harvesting machinery. The Dirkie Uys Art Gallery houses a collection of paintings by noted South African painters, such as Jacob Pierneef, Gregoire Boonzaaier and Maggie Laubscher. Originally known as Hooikraal after the farm awarded to Tobias Lochner in 1839, the town developed around the Dutch Reformed Church which was built after the farming community decided in 1863 to found a congregation independent of Malmesbury.

HOPEFIELD Situated in the Sandveld, a region bounded by the Olifants River in the north, the Berg River in the south and the Olifants River Mountains in the east, Hopefield is a popular destination during the spring flower season. The season usually stretches from mid-August to the end of September, and during the last weekend of August the town hosts the annual Hopefield Flower Show. Of interest in the town is a replica of a wattle-and-daub cottage (*hartebeeshuisie*) typical of those built in the area by pioneer cattle farmers. The information office has an interesting collection of fossils and stone tools from nearby Elandsfontein, an archaeological site of major importance. Among the displays is a cast of part of the Saldanha skull, from an early human being dating back to the Middle Pleistocene (780 000 to 125 000 years ago).

4

5

1

16
240 KM

2

3

Saldanha is an important export terminal for iron ore, which is transported from Sishen in the Northern Cape along an 860-km-long railway line. The ore tipper station in the harbour has a capacity of 8 000 tonnes an hour. Just outside the town is Saldanha Steel, a R7-billion steel mill, which has a capacity of 100 000 tonnes of hot-rolled steel coil a month.

LANGEBAAN The history of Langebaan is closely related to that of nearby Saldanha. Founded around 1870, the name Langebaan is translated as 'long track' or 'long course'. The origin of the name is somewhat obscure, with no fewer than four explanations. In 1909 a whaling operation was established at Donkergat, northwest of Langebaan, across Saldanha Bay. Following the demise of the industry in the 1930s, fishing became an important economic activity. Langebaan is a popular resort town, Club Mykonos and the Strandloper restaurants being two of its attractions. Langebaan Lagoon ③ and Saldanha Bay offer a variety of watersports.

WEST COAST NATIONAL PARK Centred around the Langebaan Lagoon, the West Coast National Park covers 30 000 ha of wetlands, strandveld and unspoilt coastline. The 5 600 ha lagoon ranks as a wetland of international importance and supports up to 50 000 waterbirds at times – regularly, there may be as many as 30 000 migrant waders present. For birding enthusiasts, there are two bird hides overlooking the lagoon and one in the salt marshes. Nearly 250 000 coastal seabirds are attracted to the five islands in Saldanha Bay. Malgas Island is one of only six breeding colonies of the Cape gannet (*Morus capensis*), with up to 20 000 breeding pairs, while the Saldanha-Langebaan area supports 12 per cent of the world population of the African black oystercatcher (*Haematopus moquini*). Marcus Island, in turn, is home to the largest African penguin (*Spheniscus demersus*) colony in the world.

The Postberg section of the park is famed for its magnificent display of spring flowers, especially its gousblomme, a collective name for several species of the genera Gazania and Arctotis. This section

SALDANHA ② has a long, interesting maritime history dating back to 1601 when Dutch sailor Joris van Spilenberg sailed past the bay. Mistaking it for Aguada de Saldanha ('the watering place of Saldanha', after the Portuguese admiral António de Saldanha) – the early Portuguese name for Table Bay – he recorded the name Saldanha in his logbook, while the bay originally named Aguada de Saldanha was renamed Table Bay. In 1670 French warships sailed into the bay, attacked the Dutch outpost on Schaapen Island and hoisted the French flag. Eleven years later, four Dutch cargo ships lying at anchor in the bay fell into the hands of an English fleet, and in 1799 the Dutch admiral Engelbertus Lucas surrendered his fleet of 14 vessels to the British. During World War II, the bay was used as a staging point for Allied convoys and became an important naval base for South Africa.

of the park is open only during the flower season (August and September). The lagoon is popular with a variety of watersport enthusiasts, and most watersports are permitted in the multifunctional zone at its northern end. The focal point of the park headquarters at Geelbek is the Cape Dutch manor house dating back to 1860. The Geelbek Gold Fields Environmental Centre offers a range of courses for educational groups.

WEST COAST FOSSIL PARK The fossil-rich area of Langebaanweg is internationally known for its wealth of fossils of extinct animals, dating back between seven and five million years. At this time, the shoreline extended to Langebaanweg which was situated at the mouth of an early Berg River, and the prevailing warm and moist climatic conditions supported lush vegetation. Fossil bones of over 300 species of vertebrate and invertebrate animals have been unearthed to date; among them are mammals such as a bear, sabre-toothed cats, three-toed horses and short-necked giraffes, as well as fish, birds and reptiles. The site was mined for phosphates until 1995, and a 14-ha area was declared a national monument in 1996. Since the park is still being developed, visits are currently by appointment only, but guided tours will be conducted on a regular basis once the park is fully operational. Tours last about two hours; during the winter months, when excavations are carried out, visitors can view the process of uncovering the fossils. A number of interesting fossils, including a cast of the Saldanha skull, is displayed in a small, fascinating information centre, which also includes information on the rehabilitation of the phosphate mine.

VELDDRIF Situated about 6 km upstream from the mouth of the Berg River, Velddrif has been an important fishing centre for over a century. The town is especially known for its *bokkoms*, a typical West Coast delicacy. Harders (mullet) caught in nets in the Berg River estuary are salted and then dried in bunches, an activity that can be seen at the drying sites upstream from the town. The lower Berg River is an important wetland for waterbirds, which constitute just over half of the 250 bird species recorded to date. At times, over 20 000 birds are attracted to the estuary and its floodplains.

ST HELENA BAY ④ was named after the mother of Roman emperor Constantine the Great by the Portuguese navigator Vasco da Gama, who landed here on 7 November 1497. A monument was erected just east of Stompneus Bay in 1969 to commemorate the 500th anniversary of Da Gama's birth, while the Vasco da Gama Nautical Museum at Shelley Point depicts his voyage around the Cape of Good Hope in search of a sea route to India. St Helena Bay is the centre of the country's fishing industry and is also noted for its catches of rock lobster and snoek.

PATERNOSTER ⑤, a typical West Coast seaside village with small whitewashed fisherman's cottages, is known for its crayfish ①. The Latin name means 'Our Father', and it is generally assumed that the village was named after the prayers said by shipwrecked Catholic sailors. The earlier name, St Martin's Paternoster, was used on maps until 1693.

CAPE COLUMBINE NATURE RESERVE This scenic reserve, with its rocky bays and granite boulders, covers 263 ha of sandveld vegetation and is especially attractive in spring. Dominating the reserve is the Cape Columbine Lighthouse, which has been in operation since 1936. Built on an outcrop known as Castle Rock, the lighthouse features an unusual square tower instead of the more conventional tapered round tower. The picturesque Tieties Bay, immortalised by the Afrikaans writer Pieter Pieterse, is a popular summer holiday destination.

VREDENBURG is the centre of a prosperous wheat and wool farming area. It was laid out in 1883 near the site of a freshwater spring that gave rise to constant quarrels between two neighbouring farmers. In 1875 a church was built, and, as the church often had to settle disputes, it was decided to rename the village Vredenburg ('town of peace'). In 1975 the municipalities of Saldanha and Vredenburg were amalgamated, and since then St Helena Bay, Paternoster, Jacobsbaai and Stompneus Bay have been incorporated into the West Coast Peninsula area, at one time South Africa's largest municipality.

4

5

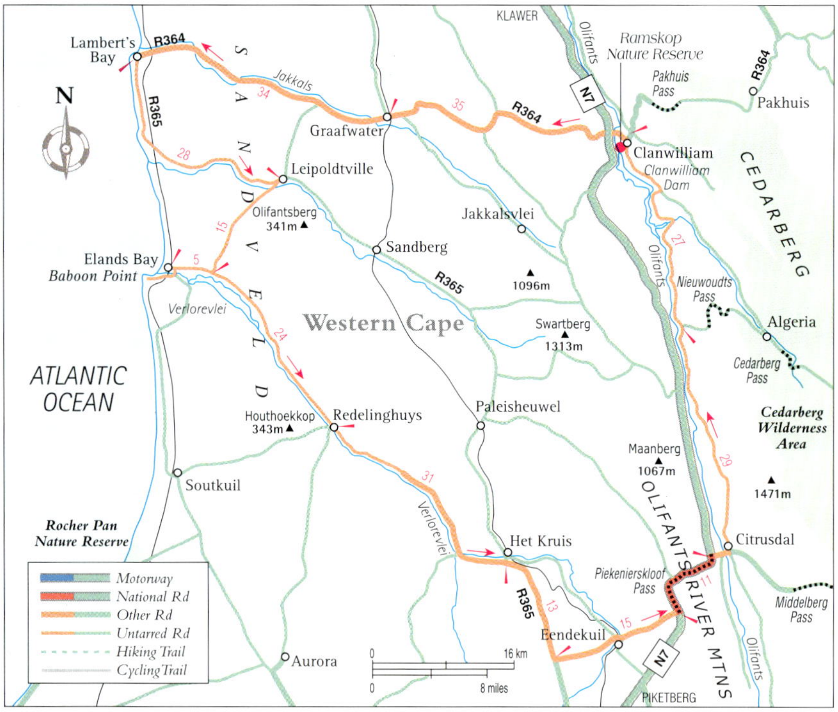

17

300 KM

1

CITRUSDAL Situated along the upper reaches of the Olifants River Valley, Citrusdal is bounded in the west by the Olifants River mountains and by the Cedarberg range to the east. The area was first explored in 1660 by the Dutch soldier Jan Danckaert and farmers began settling in the fertile valley in 1725. Citrusdal is the centre of the country's third-largest citrus-producing area, and accounts for about 14 per cent of the total crop. It is especially noted for its navel and Valencia oranges, grown by about 200 farmers in the area. The valley also has a tradition of winemaking going back more than two centuries, and produces a wide range of red and white wines, as well as dessert wines and wine for brandy.

Citrusdal is also known for its hot springs, The Baths, located 18 km south of the town. A military post was established at the hot spring in 1739, and thatched bathing huts were built for visitors. The water emerging at the surface has a temperature of 43 °C and contains potassium, sodium, chloride and magnesium. Accommodation ranges from fully equipped chalets and flats to campsites, while amenities include hot and cold swimming pools, spa baths and a range of recreational activities. In recent years, Citrusdal has become popular with skydivers and outdoor enthusiasts.

RAMSKOP NATURE RESERVE This 70-ha nature reserve on the banks of the Clanwilliam Dam is especially attractive in August and September, when the wildflowers burst into bloom. Within the reserve is the Clanwilliam Wildflower Garden ②, a 7,5-ha landscaped garden where over 200 species of plants are cultivated. Visitors can view the garden and the reserve along a 1,5-km circular wildflower trail, which leads to a viewpoint affording splendid views over the dam, the rugged Cedar Mountains and the Olifants River Valley.

CLANWILLIAM is synonymous with rooibos tea, the Cedarberg Wilderness Area and *velskoene* (handmade leather shoes). The town is the centre of a region where farmers cultivate the indigenous rooibos (*Aspalathus linearis*), the leaves of which are used to make a healthy, caffeine-free tea. Set against the backdrop of the rugged crags and buttresses of the Cedarberg's Krakadouw peaks, Clanwilliam lies between the Olifants and Jan Dissels rivers. Initially named Jan Dissels Valley, it was renamed in 1814 after the Earl of Clanwilliam, the father-in-law of Governor Sir John Cradock. The town's annual wild flower show is held towards the end of winter in the old Dutch Reformed Church (1864). About 360 species of flora are displayed and there are also concerts and a street carnival. Other historical attractions include the St John's Anglican Church, a beautiful dressed-stone building dating back to 1866, and the old gaol, with its simple Georgian façade. Built in 1808 as detention barracks for the British garrison stationed here, the building was later converted into a civilian gaol and now serves as the town's museum and information centre. At Clanwilliam Dam, the water backs up as much as 22 km behind the dam wall. The dam is popular with watersport enthusiasts and is rated as one of the best spots for water-skiing in the Western Cape.

GRAAFWATER owes its name to the fact that water could only be obtained here by digging wells or drilling boreholes. The settlement was established after the railway line between Cape Town and Bitterfontein was built in 1910. After good winter rains, the sandveld to the south of Graafwater is transformed into a colourful tapestry of spring flowers. Among the flowering splendours are the yellow rapuis (*Euryops*), a variety of daisies, sporrie (*Heliophyla*), mesembs or vygies and viooltjies (*Lachenalia*).

LAMBERT'S BAY Also known as the Rock Lobster Capital of South Africa, Lambert's Bay is a picturesque fishing village ①. It is known for its open-air seafood restaurants and thousands of seabirds. Just offshore, Bird Island is home to between 4 000 and 6 000 breeding pairs of Cape gannet (*Morus capensis*) ④. The island was connected to the mainland by means of a breakwater in 1959. Bird Island is one of only six breeding colonies of the Cape gannet in the world, while large numbers of Cape cormorants (*Phalacrocorax capensis*) and a small population of African (Jackass) penguins (*Spheniscus demersus*) also breed on the island. Close-up views of the gannets can be had from a hide which has one-way reflective glass at ground level and an open viewing window on the first floor. Other facilities include a small theatre where visitors can watch an educational video, a pool with captive penguins, an aquarium, a small museum devoted to the guano industry and a coffee shop.

ELANDS BAY Like most other West Coast towns, Elands Bay originated as a fishing village, and gradually developed to the north of the harbour. Overlooked by the Bobbejaansberg to the south, and with white sand dunes forming an impressive backdrop to the east, Elands Bay is a pretty village which depends largely on the crayfish (or rock lobster) industry for its economic well-being. The long stretch of beach, with its fast and powerful left-breaking waves, ranks among the best surfing spots in the country. An abundance of seafood and its spring flowers ⑤ are other attraction for visitors who flock to this resort.

VERLORENVLEI ③ With a length of about 13,5 km and a width of 1,4 km, Verlorenvlei is one of the largest natural wetlands along the West Coast and one of the few coastal freshwater lakes in South Africa. Although connected to the sea via a narrow channel, the vlei only overflows into the sea during the rainy winter months. Extensive reedbeds fringe the vlei, which has a bird list of over 189 species. Among these are white pelican, greater and lesser flamingo, a variety of duck species and marsh harrier. The name Verlorenvlei is derived from Verloren Valleij ('lost valley'), the name of the farm granted to a Dutch settler in 1723. One possible explanation for the name is that it refers to the farm's isolated location. Another possibility is that it refers to the way in which the water loses itself among the reeds.

REDELINGHUYS, situated at the head of the Verlorenvlei, was founded in 1866 and named after JN Redelinghuys, who donated part of his farm, Wittedrift, to the Dutch Reformed Church. A condition of the land grant was that no liquor was to be sold. The little village was established here in 1906.

PIEKENIERSKLOOF PASS See Tour 9, page 27.

2

3

4

5

1

18

280 KM

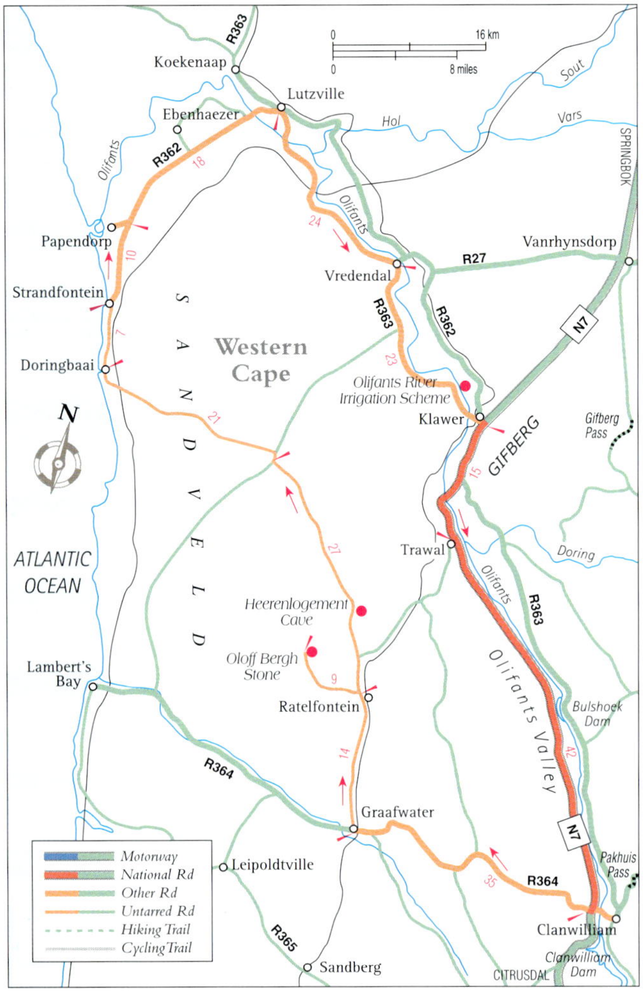

2

3

CLANWILLIAM See Tour 17, page 46.

GRAAFWATER See Tour 17, page 46.

OLOF BERGH SPRING In the early days of travel, the spring at Klipfontein Mountain was an important landmark for travellers heading into Namaqualand. It owes its name to Dutch ensign Olof Bergh ① who rested here on 9 November 1682 during his expedition to Namaqualand in search of copper. Numerous other travellers to the region stopped here, including Governor Simon van der Stel (1685), J Starrenburg (1705) and Ensign IT Rhenius (1721). Bergh and Rhenius are among those who inscribed their names on the rock above the spring.

HEERENLOGEMENT Brought to the attention of travellers after Olof Bergh described it in 1682, the Heerenlogement Cave became another important landmark for travellers and explorers bound for Namaqualand. The Dutch name means 'gentlemen's lodging', and among those who slept in the overhang were Governor Simon van der Stel (1685), Kaie Jesse Slotsbo (1712), Ensign IT Rhenius (1721), the Swedish botanist Carl Thunberg (1774) and the French traveller François le Vaillant (1783). Several well-known travellers also visited the cave during the 19th century, among them Captain James Alexander and Andrew Geddes Bain (1854). Many of these people carved their names on the walls of the overhang; during a survey carried out in 1940, a total of 174 names and initials were recorded.

OLD IRON FORT Lying on the lower slopes of the Heerenlogement Mountain, this fort was one of a series of small bastions erected by the British Army in the Northern Cape during the South African War (1899–1902). Built to prevent incursions by Boer forces into the Cape Colony, the line of defence stretched from Lambert's Bay to Noupoort via Williston. It originally stood on a farm between Graafwater and Lambert's Bay, but was dismantled and re-erected here after the war.

DORINGBAAI ② originally served as a harbour from where goods were transported to Vanrhynsdorp by camel. In recent years this small village, with its rocky coastline, has developed around the rock lobster processing factory, while offshore marine diamond mining has become another important economic activity.

STRANDFONTEIN ④ is the northernmost of the West Coast holiday settlements. The Afrikaans name means 'beach fountain', a reference to a spring that surfaces near the beach. Strandfontein is a popular summer holiday destination for West Coast farmers.

PAPENDORP Close to its mouth, an island splits the Olifants River estuary into two arms that rejoin before entering the sea. Situated on the southern bank of the estuary is Papendorp, named after the missionary who founded the settlement. Fishing ③ plays an important role in the economic life of the small community, while salt is still collected in the traditional way from pans in the area. At high tide, flat-bottomed boats can reach Lutzville, which lies 30 km upstream. In years gone by, fishermen used the river as a means of getting to Lutzville to sell their fish.

The ruins of the house built for Katherine Fryer by her husband, Richard, tell a poignant story. The couple came to South Africa from Ireland in 1820, and were among the 350 Irish immigrants who were settled in the Clanwilliam area. Most of these settlers later left for the Eastern Cape, but Richard Fryer sought out a piece of land that somehow resembled Ireland to comfort the homesick Katherine.

EBENHAEZER was established in 1831 along the banks of the Olifants River by one of the founders of Wupperthal mission, Baron Theobald von Wurmb of the Rhenish Missionary Society (RMS). It was named after the biblical Ebenhaezer (1 Samuel 7:12) which means 'stone of help'. In those early days, the river was navigable for 50 km upstream from its mouth and fresh water and supplies were ferried to the mission by boat. Following an agreement between the RMS and the Dutch Reformed Mission Church in 1932, the mission was taken over by the latter. Ebenhaezer lies at the end of the Olifants River Irrigation Canal, which was extended in 1978 when a dam was built to store the canal's surplus water, which otherwise would have flowed back into the Olifants River. Water from the dam is used for the irrigation of lucerne, coriander and beans.

VLERMUISKLIP Until 1945, Lutzville was known as Vlermuisklip, a name derived from the original Dutch name Vleermuisklip ('bat stone'), for a rocky overhang that was inhabited by bats. On 15 December 1661, the Dutch explorer Pieter Everaerts stayed here during his expedition to find the legendary kingdom of Monomotapa. Following his visit, Vleermuisklip became a landmark for travellers heading to Namaqualand. Among those who camped here were Pieter van Meerhof and Governor Simon van der Stel.

LUTZVILLE The farming village of Lutzville was established in 1923 and named after Johan Lutz, an irrigation engineer responsible for the surveying of irrigable land in the Olifants River Valley. The Lutzville Vineyards, on the road to Koekenaap, is among the largest co-operatives in South Africa and is renowned for its wines bottled under the Fleermuisklip label. The area also produce raisins, sultanas and currants, while beans and tomatoes are grown for the canning industry. The Sishen-Saldanha railway bridge over the Olifants River, which can be seen en route to Vredendal, is a major landmark. The 1 035-m-long bridge was built in 1976 by sliding the 23 prefabricated spans, each weighing 610 tonnes, from the construction site forward on Teflon-coated plates using hydraulic jacks. The bridge is supported by 22 pillars, the highest of which is 52,5 m, with each pillar extending 45 m into the riverbed.

VREDENDAL is an important agricultural centre for the wine and vegetable farms along the lower Olifants River Valley. Originally known as Bakkeley Plaats, after an altercation between the Dutch and the Khoikhoi in 1668, the name was changed to Vreedensdaal, ('vale of peace') following the conclusion of a peace treaty. The Vredendal Winery is one of the largest co-operatives in the country and processes over 70 000 tons of grapes annually. Among its well-known wines is a blend of chardonnay and sauvignon blanc called Goiya Kgeisje, a San name pronounced 'Hoya-hey-see' (connected with a loud click), and meaning 'first wine'. Although primarily a white wine area, the cellar produces an excellent ruby cabernet. A wide range of wines is produced by Spruitdrift Winery, 5 km from the town. Vredendal also has one of the world's most modern grape-juice concentrate plants. Other crops grown in the fertile alluvial soil include potatoes, tomatoes, onions, pumpkins, watermelons and sweet melons.

THE OLIFANTS IRRIGATION SCHEME Although the irrigation potential of the Olifants River was recognised as early as 1832, the Olifants River irrigation district was only proclaimed in 1911. The scheme consists of the Bulshoek Dam, the Clanwilliam Dam and a 321-km network of canals. The main canal is 261 km long, while the total length of the 11 branch canals is 60 km. The Bulshoek Dam, 25 km north of Clanwilliam, and some of the canals were completed in 1924, but soon proved to be inadequate. Construction of the Clanwilliam Dam began in 1932, and was completed three years later.

KLAWER lies at the foot of the Matsikamma Mountains on the banks of the Olifants River. The settlement developed around the railway station serving the Olifants River Valley and takes its name from the Afrikaans word for wood sorrel, common here, especially after rains. The Klawer Winery produces mainly white wine and dessert wine.

4

OPPOSITE BEACON ISLE, PLETTENBERG BAY (P.62); **THIS PAGE** ABOVE: MOSSEL BAY HARBOUR (P. 52); TOP RIGHT: BROEKIE-LACE, PRINCE ALBERT (P.55); RIGHT: OUTENIQUA CHOO-TJOE, GARDEN ROUTE (P.62); BELOW: PIED KINGFISHER, WILDERNESS (P.60); BOTTOM LEFT: WILDERNESS ANGLER (P.60); BOTTOM RIGHT: PANSY SHELL, PLETTENBERG BAY (P.62).

1

2

19
220 KM

3

4

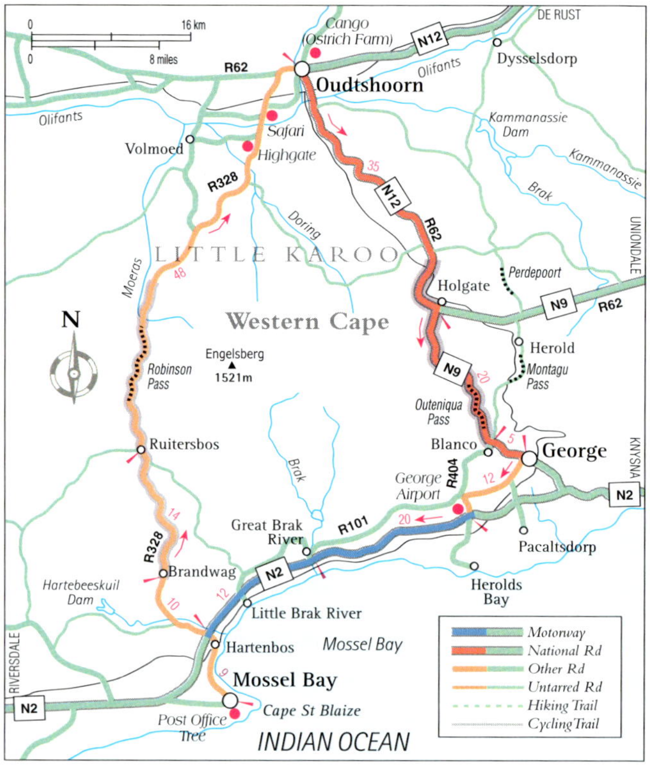

MOSSEL BAY ③ In 1488, Bartholomeu Dias anchored in the bay, which was later named Aguada de São Bras (the watering place of Saint Bras), after he became the first Portuguese navigator to round the Cape of Storms. The Bartholomeu Dias Museum Complex comprises several museums and places of interest, among them the Maritime Museum which has as its main attraction a life-size replica of Dias' caravel. The complex also includes the Culture Museum, which depicts the town's history from the earliest times, and the Shell Museum, with its large collection of sea shells. Well known is the historic Post Office Tree ①, a milkwood tree where a Portuguese naval officer, Pedro de Ataide, left a letter in a shoe, or iron pot, when his ship put in here on the voyage back to Portugal from the east in 1500. The letter was found the following year by a naval officer sailing to the east. In time, the milkwood tree was increasingly used as a 'post office' by passing sailors. The Point, also known as Cape St Blaize, features a large wave-cut cave that was inhabited between 100 000 and 70 000 years ago by nomadic Khoi people who exploited the coastal resources. The Cape St Blaize Lighthouse above the cave has been a beacon to ships since it was commissioned in 1864.

ROBINSON PASS ④ After a relatively easy journey across the coastal plains east of Houwhoek, early travellers were forced to cross the Outeniqua Mountains near present-day Mossel Bay to avoid the almost impenetrable Knysna and Tsitikamma forests, with their precipitous ravines. The earliest route across the mountains was along the Attaquas Kloof, named after a chief of the Hessequa Khoikhoi. Originally an elephant track, the route was first explored by the Dutch ensign Isaq Schrijver who penetrated through the kloof to reach the Olifants River valley in January 1689.

For over a century, the route remained the gateway to the Little Karoo, and among the numerous explorers who passed this way were Hermanus Hubner (1736), August Beutler (1752), Captain Robert Gordon and William Paterson (1777). When Thomas Bain was commissioned to build a new pass linking Mossel Bay and Oudtshoorn, he decided to follow the easier gradients of the mountain slopes in the Ruitersbos area, some 8 km east of Attaquas Kloof. Construction of the pass began in 1867, and when it was completed two years later it was named after Mr M Robinson, the Chief Inspector of Public Works and Commissioner of Roads at the time.

LITTLE KAROO Stretching from Worcester in the west to Uniondale, the Little Karoo lies in a narrow valley bounded in the south by the Langeberg and Outeniqua mountain ranges. In the north, the Witteberge and Swartberg ranges separate the Little Karoo from the Great Karoo. Although a semi-arid region, the numerous river valleys have been blessed with fertile alluvial soil. This, together with the dry climate and sunny weather, creates ideal conditions for the cultivation of various crops such as grapes, apricots, lucerne, tobacco and wheat.

OSTRICH FARMS The ostrich industry of the Little Karoo had its beginnings in the hunting of wild ostriches for their feathers. By 1838 over 250 kg of feathers were being exported, and the increasing demand resulted in the domestication of ostriches around the 1850s. By 1861 the export of ostrich feathers had increased to 1 553 kg, and twenty years later the number of birds stood at around 100 000. Between 1900 and 1914 the industry experienced an unprecedented boom. At the height of the boom years, the number of ostriches ② reached more than 750 000 and wealthy farmers built palatial homes, dubbed 'feather palaces', in Art Nouveau and neo-Cape Dutch styles.

The industry collapsed upon the outbreak of World War I, but subsequently recovered. However, the market for ostrich feathers never regained its former peak. Today, the ostrich industry comprises about 400 farms. In addition to feathers, the birds provide fresh meat and biltong, while ostrich leather handbags and shoes are much sought after. Visitors can learn more about these fascinating birds on guided tours offered by Oudtshoorn's famed ostrich farms, which include Hoopers Highgate, Safari and Cango.

OUDTSHOORN Once known as the Ostrich Feather Capital of the World, Oudtshoorn has a rich cultural heritage. Many of its fine sandstone buildings ⑤ date back to the feather boom period, including the old Boys High School (1907) – with its 27,5-m-high clock tower – now known as the CP Nel Museum, and the Le Roux Dorpshuis, a fine Edwardian art nouveau-style 'feather palace' with a circular tower and intricate iron railings. Other historic buildings include the Gothic-style Dutch Reformed Church (1879), Pinehurst and the Prince Vincent and Company building of 1914. Also of interest is Arbeidsgenot, the house of the well-known Afrikaans lawyer, writer, poet and politician, CJ Langenhoven. A longtime campaigner for the Afrikaans language, Langenhoven wrote the words of *Die Stem* (the sole national anthem of South Africa until 1994) and was also the author of some 40 books (see Tour 21, page 57). In March/April each year, Oudtshoorn is host to the popular Klein Karoo National Arts Festival, which attracts upwards of 100 000 people for a week-long celebration of Afrikaans artistic expression.

OUTENIQUA PASS This pass across the Outeniqua Mountains was built between 1943 and 1951 to replace the winding Montagu Pass, built between 1844 and 1847 (see Tour 22, page 59), and to provide a more direct and faster route between George and Oudtshoorn. Italian prisoners of war were used as labourers during its construction. After following the valley carved by the Klip River between Waboomskraalberg to the west and Camferskloofberg, the road descends in a series of sweeping bends along the eastern slopes of Geelhoutboomberg. A viewpoint on the left-hand side of the road provides expansive vistas over the Cradock Pass (built in 1812) and the Montagu Pass (built in 1844).

GEORGE Laid out on the coastal plain below the Outeniqua Mountains, George is a picturesque town with streets lined by majestic oak trees planted soon after it was founded in 1811. The town was named in honour of the then reigning monarch, George III. Situated in the heart of the Garden Route, George is popular with outdoor enthusiasts who are attracted to the numerous hiking trails and walks in the nearby forests and mountains. Places of interest along the 1,5-km-long historical walking tour include the George Museum, housed in the Drostdy building. The main theme of the museum is the region's timber industry, but it also has an important collection of vintage gramophones and musical instruments. Also to be seen along the walk is the King Edward VII Library (the best example of Edwardian architecture in the town), the old slave tree, St Mark's Anglican Cathedral (1850) and the historic Dutch Reformed Church (1842) ⑥. The George Timber Route meanders from the George Museum past several tree species, furniture manufacturers and the Dutch Reformed Church (1842), with its magnificent yellowwood ceiling and handcarved stinkwood pulpit. An interesting collection of railway equipment, coaches and locomotives, as well as a replica of an old station, can be seen at the Outeniqua Railway Museum.

5

6

20
230 KM

1

2

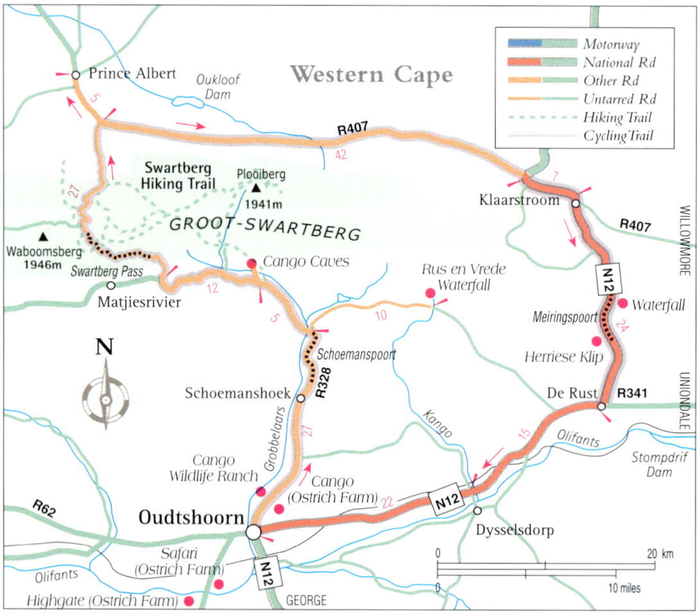

3

OUDTSHOORN See Tour 19, page 53.

CANGO WILDLIFE RANCH Originally established as the first crocodile show farm in South Africa, the Cango Wildlife Ranch is also famous as a breeding centre for cheetah ①. Visitors can view lion, cheetah, leopard and jaguar from the Cat Walk, an elevated walkway that leads through enclosures resembling the animals' natural habitats. The reptile park has a variety of local and exotic snakes, while the crocodile breeding centre has over 400 crocodile and a large population of American alligator. Regular guided tours are conducted to give visitors a better understanding of these much-maligned reptiles. Among the unusual animals here are emu (the Australian relative to the ostrich), capybara (the largest rodent in the world), pygmy hippo, wild dog and racoon. Visitors can take a trip around the ranch aboard a mini-train, and there is a mini-farmyard and play park for children.

SCHOEMANSPOORT, an 18-km-long defile carved by the Grobbelaars River through the foothills of the Swartberg, links the Cango Valley with the fertile Olifants River valley. The road initially makes its way past smallholdings with ostriches, lucerne fields and tobacco-drying sheds, and then meanders through the scenic poort. A pleasant detour is a drive to the Rus-en-Vrede Waterfall, which cascades 61 m into a pool hidden in a lush forested kloof.

CANGO CAVES ④ The magnificent caves in the southern foothills of the Swartberg range were formed over millions of years by rainwater seeping through fissures in the limestone. The water gradually dissolved the limestone, forming an extensive network of subterranean caverns and tunnels. When the acidic oxygen in the rainwater comes into contact with the calcium carbonate in the limestone, a crystalline solution is formed, which hardens and eventually accumulates as stalagmites, stalactites and flowstones. From the entrance, a flight of stairs descends to Van Zyl's Hall, an enormous cavern that is 107 m long, 54 m at its widest and up to 17 m in height. Other well-known formations include the 10-m-high Cleopatra's Needle – with an estimated age of 150 000 years – the Organ Pipes, the Ballerina and the Frozen Waterfall. Visitors can choose from a 30-minute scenic tour, 60-minute standard tour or 90-minute adventure tour, all of which are conducted at regular intervals daily. The adventure tour snakes along narrow passages and tunnels with appropriate names like Lumbago Walk, Devil's Chimney and the Letter Box.

SWARTBERG Rising to a height of some 2 326 m, the Swartberg range stretches for 200 km from near Matjiesfontein in the west to Willowmore in the east, where it merges with the Baviaanskloof Mountains. Its western outlier, the Klein Swartberg, is separated from the Groot Swartberg by the Seven Weeks Poort (see Tour 21, page 57). Among the outstanding features of the range are the spectacularly twisted and contorted greyish-white and reddish-brown sandstone strata, formed some 150 million years ago when the Cape Folded Mountains were pushed up by immense forces in the earth's crust.

SWARTBERG PASS ⑤ Of the numerous passes built by Thomas Bain, the Swartberg Pass is widely regarded as one of his masterpieces. The steep gradients provided the brilliant road engineer with a formidable challenge; after carrying out a survey in 1879, Bain wrote to the Chief Inspector of Public Works that he had to try four different lines before he succeeded in finding the correct one. Work started on the Prince Albert side of the mountains in 1881, but construction ground to a halt just over a year later when road-builder John Tassie was declared insolvent. Construction of the pass resumed in November 1883, when Bain took over the work. Using between 200 and 240 convict labourers, Bain built sweeping zigzag curves and dry-packed stone retaining walls to support the road where the slopes were too steep to excavate. The pass, the last to be built by Bain, was completed in 1886 at a cost of £14 500, excluding the cost of the convict labour. Some 19 signposts indicating places of historic interest have been erected along the route, among these the ruins of the Blikstasie (Old Jail) where the convicts slept at night and the site of the Old Toll House, which came into service on 5 May 1888.

PRINCE ALBERT Lying on the northern foothills of the Swartberg range, Prince Albert ② is a picturesque farming village with an old-world charm. It is renowned for its variety of well-preserved architectural styles, and for its 'Prince Albert gables', which date from 1840–60. This unique gable features the outlines of the 'holbol' gable with a narrow pediment, while horizontal mouldings connect the outlines of the gables. Other building styles include Karoo houses, with their symmetrical façades and flat roofs, as well as Victorian and Georgian-style buildings. Also of interest is the historic water mill built in the 1850s. It is the only remaining one of five built in the Prince Albert area during the 19th century. The Fransie Pienaar Museum depicts the natural and cultural history of the area, and has an interesting display on the brief but frantic gold rush which took place following the discovery of alluvial gold in the area in 1890.

Prince Albert was laid out in 1842 on the farm De Queekvaleij which was granted to Zacharias de Beer as a loan farm on 12 February 1762. Originally named Albertsburg, it was renamed after the husband of Queen Victoria in 1845. The arid area is ideal sheep farming country, but Prince Albert is also known for its apricots and figs, as well as for its olives, which are fêted at the annual olive festival held in May.

MEIRINGSPOORT One of the two original links between the Little Karoo and the Great Karoo, the spectacular poort carved by the Groot River through the Swartberg created a natural passage ideally suited to a road link. Building of the road started in August 1856 and the official opening took place on 3 March 1858. It was named after Petrus Meiring, a prominent farmer who had campaigned vigorously for the construction of the road to facilitate commerce between the wool farmers of the Great Karoo and the traders in Oudtshoorn, George and Knysna. Because of the narrowness of the poort, the road had to cross the river numerous times; Langstraat, the longest section without a river crossing, measured 2,4 km. The road was frequently washed away by the river, and after the floods of 1885 it was rebuilt by Thomas Bain. Each of the drifts (crossings) was named after a particular feature or event. One of these, Ontploffingsdrif (Explosion Drift), recalls an incident when a wagon carrying dynamite exploded. Perskeboomdrif (Peach Tree Drift) was named after the peach trees that once grew at the ford.

Among the points of interest along the route is the 60-m-high waterfall ③ which cascades down a steep cliff face into a 9-m-deep pool, and Herrie se Klip, where the well-known Afrikaans writer, CJ Langenhoven, chiselled the name of his imaginary elephant, Herrie, into the rock. Although Bain eliminated some of the crossings, the tarred road built between 1966 and 1971 still crosses the Groot River no fewer than 25 times.

DE RUST, a typical Karoo village with beautiful Victorian houses ⑥, lies at the southern entrance of Meiringspoort. Established in 1900, the village owes its name to the farm De Rust (Dutch for 'the resting place'), which was acquired in 1822 by Petrus Meiring – for whom the route through the Swartberg was named. The Mons Ruber Estate is celebrated for its white dessert wines (jerepigo), port and witblits, while Domein Doornkraal produces a wide range of red and white wines and a sparkling wine bottled under the label *Tickled Pink*.

4

5

6

1

21
360 KM

2

3

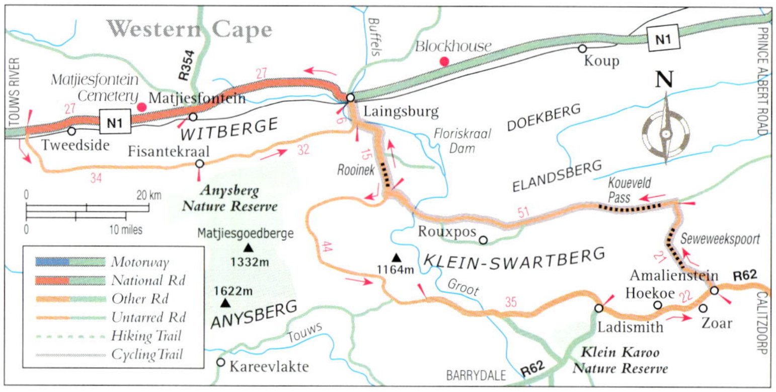

MATJIESFONTEIN ② is a charming Victorian village that was developed around a railway halt in the Karoo by a Scotsman, Jimmy Logan. In the early days of rail travel in South Africa, trains did not have dining carriages, and in 1844 Logan obtained the concession to open a refreshment room at Matjiesfontein. Within a few years, Logan's village had become a popular health and holiday resort, as well as the headquarters of his business enterprises. Famous visitors to Matjiesfontein included Cecil John Rhodes, Lord Randolph Churchill (father of Winston Churchill) and the author Olive Schreiner, who lived for some time in a cottage now known as Olive Schreiner Cottage. During the South African War, 10 000 British troops and 20 000 horses were quartered in a military camp established on the outskirts of the village. Matjiesfontein's famous hotel ①, with its towers and ornate cast ironwork, was built during the early stages of the war. The hotel served as a military hospital, while the central turret became a lookout post. Among the many other fine Victorian buildings lining the main street are the Masonic Hotel (now the Losieshuis), Post Office, Village Office and the Laird's Arms, a Victorian country pub.

After Logan's death in 1920, the village sank into obscurity, and declined even further when the new national road, built at the end of World War II, bypassed the village. In 1968, however, the entire village was bought by the well-known hotelier David Rawdon, and after careful restoration the Lord Milner Hotel was reopened two years later. The Marie Rawdon Museum contains a fine collection of Victorian and Edwardian domestic articles and furniture, as well as a collection of costumes and dresses.

MATJIESFONTEIN CEMETERY lies a few kilometres to the west of the village against a hillside dominated by an obelisk erected in memory of Major-General Andrew Wauchope, the Commander of the Highland Brigade at the Battle of Magersfontein, which took place on 11 December 1899. Wauchope was killed in the early stages of the battle (see Tour 66, page 162) and was buried the following day in the Modder River cemetery near Magersfontein. At Jimmy Logan's request, Wauchope's remains were exhumed for reinterment at the Matjiesfontein cemetery. Also buried here are Jimmy Logan, his wife Emma, their son and George Lohmann, one of England's greatest cricketers.

TWEEDSIDE The cast-iron entrance gates and avenue of eucalyptus trees mark the location of the farm bought by Jimmy Logan in the early 1880s. The enterprising Logan sank numerous boreholes, planted pine and eucalyptus trees and established extensive orchards, which supplied fresh fruit to the markets in Kimberley, then abuzz with diamond fever. Tweedside even had its own private railway siding.

WITBERGE To the unsuspecting traveller, the valley bounded by the Witberge to the north and Suurkloof se Berg to the south is surprisingly lush, in sharp contrast to the arid Karoo plains. With an abundance of runoff from the mountains after rain, the fertile valley is a patchwork of waving wheatlands, fields of lupins and orchards. In spring, the uncultivated land is covered in a profusion of daisies and mesembs (vygies).

KLEIN SWARTBERGE This range forms the western extremity of the Swartberg range, and merges with the Anysberg to the southwest and the Matjiesgoed Mountains to the west, while the Elandsberg lies to the north. Seven Weeks Peak (2 326 m) is the highest point in the Swartberg range, but the dominant feature is without doubt the twin peaks of Toorkop (also spelt Towerkop), which rise 2 203 m above sea level. The name means 'magic hill', and is said to have been given because the mountain changes its shape when viewed from different angles. Legend also has it that the two peaks were created when a witch struck the summit, splitting it in two. Endemic to the range is the Ladismith protea (*Protea aristata*), which has magnificent crimson flowers in summer.

LADISMITH, at the southern foot of the Klein Swartberge, was established in 1852 on the farm Elandsvlei. It was initially named Lady Smith after Lady Juana Smith, the wife of the Cape governor, Sir Harry Smith. In 1879, however, the name was changed to Ladismith to avoid confusion with Ladysmith in Natal, founded in 1850. The town is a centre for the district's ostrich industry, and wine, fruit and lucerne are also produced. Ladismith is also famous for its dairy products, named after the peak which overlooks the town. In addition to the historic Dutch Reformed Church, dating back to 1873, there are numerous beautiful Victorian-style dwellings in the town.

HOEKOE is the name of the valley where the renowned Afrikaans author, poet and politician, CJ Langenhoven, was born in 1873. A man of exceptional qualities, he wrote numerous literary works and was a vigorous campaigner for the promotion of the Afrikaans language. In 1914 he entered politics, serving in the Cape Provincial Council and the House of Assembly before being elected as a senator in 1920. In 1918, he wrote the words of *Die Stem*, South Africa's national anthem from 1957 to 1994. He died in his house, Arbeidsgenot, in Oudtshoorn in 1932 (see Tour 19, page 53).

ZOAR is a picturesque mission station set amid lush green irrigated gardens. Founded on the farm Elandsfontein by the South African Missionary Society (SAMS) in 1817, the settlement was named after the biblical Zoar on the Red Sea (Genesis 14:2–8). Its history is closely linked with nearby Amalienstein, dating back to 1833, when the Berlin Missionary Society took over control of the mission station at the request of the SAMS. As a result of dissatisfaction among some members of the congregation over, among other things, the introduction of candles and the crucifix, responsibility for Zoar returned to the SAMS in 1843.

AMALIENSTEIN ③ The focal point of this small mission station is the beautiful Lutheran church, painted in the traditional mustard, blue and rust colours of the early Lutheran Church. The Amalienstein mission was established by the Berlin Missionary Society and its name honours Amalie von Stein, who donated the money to purchase the land. Water from a nearby stream is used for irrigation, and a variety of crops, such as grapes, peaches, nectarines and plums, are cultivated.

SEVEN WEEKS POORT, with its spectacular folded and warped layers of sandstone ④, ranks among South Africa's most spectacular routes. The course carved by the Seven Weeks River through the Swartberg ⑤ forms a natural link between the Little Karoo town of Ladismith and the Great Karoo. A route through the narrow poort was constructed as early as 1862, but the road was frequently washed away, prompting the decision to build the Swartberg Pass. Various explanations as to the origin of the name range from a stock thief who hid in the poort for seven weeks to a corruption of the surname of Louis Zerwick (Zerwick se poort), an early missionary at Amalienstein.

4

5

1

22
255 KM

2

3

4

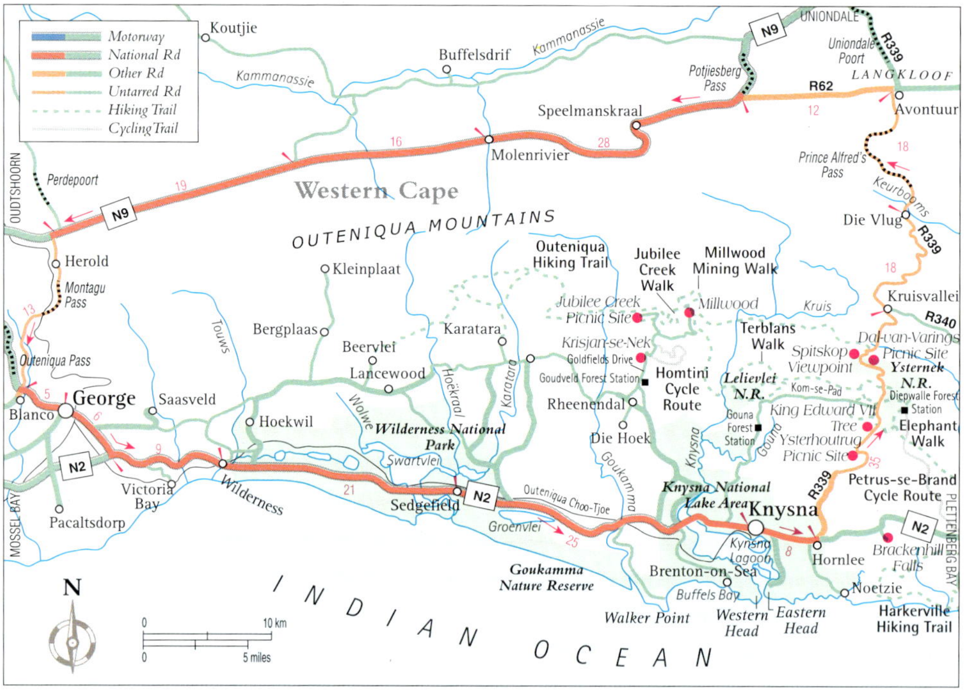

KNYSNA ⑥ lies on the banks of a tranquil lagoon, guarded at its mouth by The Heads, and overlooked to the north by the Outeniqua Mountains. Surrounded by lush indigenous forests of yellowwood, stinkwood, Cape beech and red alder, its history is closely linked to the exploitation of the forests and to George Rex, a legendary figure who bought the farm Melkhoutkraal in 1804 and established himself as a timber merchant. One of the most popular coastal resort towns along the Garden Route, Knysna offers visitors a wide range of water sports (in the lagoon and the sea) and adventure activities. Those in search of a more relaxed holiday can explore the lagoon aboard a houseboat, or on a tour boat ①. The lagoon is home to the endangered Knysna seahorse (*Hippocampus capensis*) as well as many of the over 230 bird species recorded in the area to date. It is also famous for its fresh oysters. Places of interest include Millwood House ② and ③, dating back to the region's short-lived 1870s gold rush and now a museum; George Rex's grave; and the Angling Museum. Numerous arts and crafts galleries, gift shops, farm stalls ⑤ and furniture factories abound.

PRINCE ALFRED'S PASS By the mid-1850s Knysna was becoming an important port and the need arose for a route through the Knysna forests and across the Outeniqua Mountains into the interior. The route was surveyed by Andrew Geddes Bain in 1856, but construction only began in 1863, and it took Thomas Bain four years to complete the pass. It was named after Prince Alfred, Duke of Edinburgh, who visited the Cape Colony in 1867. During his visit to Knysna, the prince took part in an elephant hunt in which several elephants were wounded and two killed.

YSTERHOUTRUG This ridge in the forest owes its name to the ironwood (*Olea capensis* spp. *macrocarpa*), which was mainly used for railway sleepers and as heavy-duty structural timber. Until 1949, Ysterhoutrug was the northern terminal of a 35-km-long railway line built by the South Western Railway Company in 1904–07 to transport timber to Knysna.

KING EDWARD VII TREE This forest giant is the largest of several enormous Outeniqua yellowwoods (*Podocarpus falcatus*) ④ growing in the Knysna forests. With a crown spread of 24 m and a circumference of 6 m, it towers 39 m above the forest floor. Originally known as Templeman's Tree, after the woodcutter who bought it, the tree was never felled because it was simply too big to handle. It was renamed after King Edward VII when a delegation of the British Parliamentary Association was treated to a lunch at the tree in 1924. Its age is estimated at 650 years.

YSTERNEK NATURE RESERVE is one of several fynbos 'islands' surrounded by the Knysna forest. The origin of these islands was initially attributed to the activities of early woodcutters, hunters or the Khoikhoi. More recent research, however, has suggested that at least some of these 'islands' are remnants of what used to be a far more extensive fynbos area, and which have been isolated by the expanding forest. The reserve was established to provide protection to an area of mountain fynbos and the surrounding indigenous forest. It was in the vicinity of Ysternek that Thomas Bain established his first construction camp.

VALLEY OF FERNS This fairy-tale patch of forest lies within the Ysternek Nature Reserve amidst a section of wet forest consisting of red and white alders, stinkwood, Cape beech and Cape holly. Shaded by the dense tree canopy, the well-watered valley supports a lush grove of forest tree ferns (*Alsophila capensis*) up to 4 m tall.

SPITZKOP rises to a height of 933 m above the indigenous forests of yellowwood, stinkwood, white stinkwood, knobwood and candlewood. At an altitude of 830 m, the viewpoint offers expansive views to the north of the Outeniqua Mountains. To the south lie the forests and Knysna Lagoon, while the view to the east extends beyond Plettenberg Bay.

DE VLUGT The remote farming settlement of De Vlugt became a bustling community after Thomas Bain moved his construction camp here in 1863. Bain's camp consisted of a stone house built for his family, accommodation for the convicts and a chapel, also used as a school. From De Vlugt Bain embarked on the most challenging section of Prince Alfred's Pass, much of which had to be cut into steep slopes, with deep river gorges dictating the building of numerous bridges.

AVONTUUR The first farm in the area was granted to Matthys Zondagh in 1765, and although the name Avontuur was already in use by 1778, the exact origins of the Afrikaans name, translated as 'adventure', are not known. The settlement lies at the western end of the 610-mm narrow-gauge railway line which served the farms in the Langkloof, a region famous for its apples, until it was discontinued in 1993 due to economic reasons.

LANGKLOOF was originally named Terra das Trovoadas (Land of the Thunder) by the Portuguese. The first European to explore the area was a Dutch sergeant, Isaq Schrijver, who travelled along the valley in 1689 and named it Langkloof, meaning 'long ravine'. Lying parallel to the coast, the Langkloof stretches from Herold eastwards for 160 km to just beyond Joubertinia. The valley, which ranges in width from 8 km to 16 km, is bounded in the north by the Kamanassie Mountains and by the Tsitsikamma Mountains to the south.

HEROLD, a small farming settlement at the northern end of the Montagu Pass, was named after TJ Herold, the Dutch Reformed minister at George from 1812 to 1823. Hops make up the area's most important agricultural crop.

MONTAGU PASS Until the completion of the Outeniqua Pass in 1951, the Montagu Pass was the most direct route between George and the Little Karoo. In 1844, about 250 convicts began building the pass under the supervision of the Australian road engineer, Henry Fancourt White. Completed in 1847, the pass was only opened in 1849 and was named after the Colonial Secretary, John Montagu. Signposts along the route indicate places of interest; among them are the ruins of the hotel at North Station, the site of the old smithy, the magnificent arched stone bridge across the Keur River and the tollhouse. Many of the bends were named after a particular feature or incident.

BLANCO, at the foot of the Montagu Pass, was established as a construction camp during the building of the pass. In addition to the quarters for the convict labourers, storerooms and houses were built for the artisans and supervisors engaged to work on the pass. Originally named White's Village, after road engineer Henry Fancourt White, the name was later changed at his request to Blanco. Much to the chagrin of the inhabitants of George, the village flourished after the opening of the pass, as traffic bypassed George. The historic Fancourt manor house, which White built for himself, is now the focal point of one of South Africa's premier golfing and leisure destinations.

GEORGE See Tour 19, page 53.

5

6

23
190 KM

1 

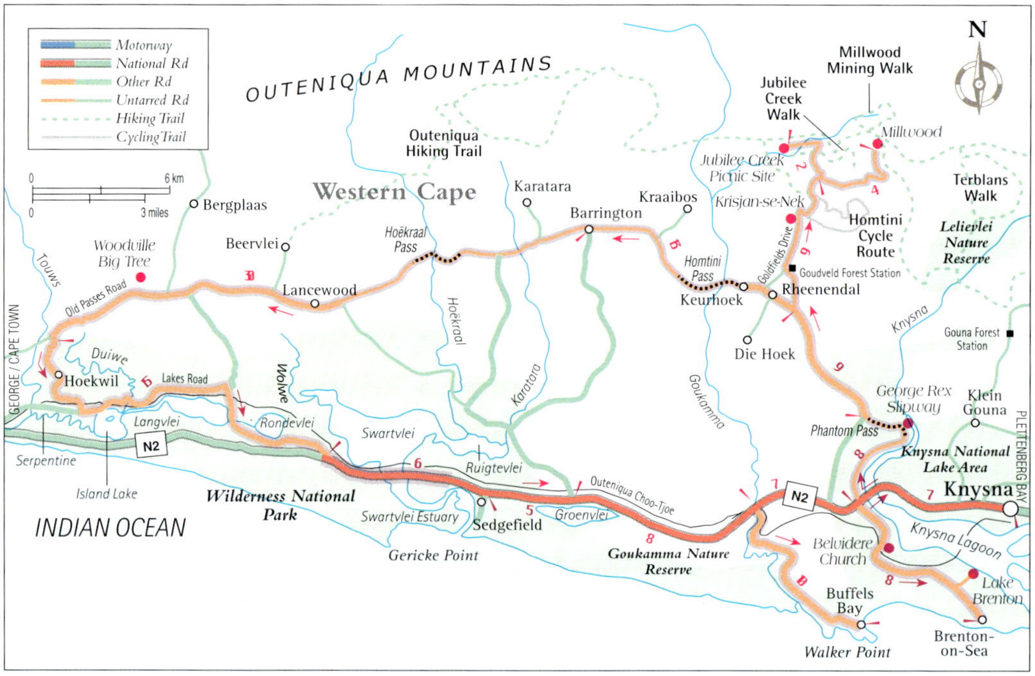

KNYSNA See Tour 22, page 58.

MILLWOOD sprung up after a gold nugget was discovered in the Karatara River in 1876. The discovery of reef gold in 1886 and the proclamation of the Millwood goldfields the following year caused a rush of miners and fortune-seekers. At the height of the gold rush, the population of the goldfields stood at 400 permanent residents, with 600 diggers living mainly in tents. Over 40 syndicates mined 27 reefs, and Millwood grew to a sizeable village of 75 buildings, including a government office, six hotels, a bank and a post office. The village also had three newspapers, the *Millwood Sluice Box*, *Millwood Eaglet* and the *Millwood Critic*. However, the reefs were uneconomical to mine, and gold fever soon died down. Many miners left Millwood following the discovery of gold on the Witwatersrand in 1886. By the early 1890s most of the syndicates were bankrupt, and by 1893 Millwood's population had declined to a mere 74 people and the forest soon reclaimed the land. All that remains of Millwood today are Monk's Store (now a museum), abandoned mining shafts, the old cemetery and the street names. The Mining Museum ② at the Bendigo Mine has several pieces of old mining machinery on display, including a five-stamp battery and a 1901 Ransomes Jeffries and Sims steam engine.

JUBILEE CREEK lies in a sylvan setting of magnificent indigenous forests and a murmuring, dark-brown stream. Named in honour of the golden jubilee of Queen Victoria, the area was once the scene of frantic gold-mining activity. A reminder of this era is the old alluvial gold diggings about 200 m from the start of the Jubilee Creek Walk, an easy 4-km walk starting from the picnic site. The area also provided the setting for Dalene Matthee's book, *Circles in the Forest* (1984).

PASSES ROAD Construction of a road link between Knysna and George began from George in 1868 under Adam de Schmidt and the engineer Thomas Bain, but it was not until 1883 that the entire route was completed. Until the opening of the N2 in 1951, the Passes Road was the only route between the two towns. Beyond the turnoff to Millwood, the road meanders along the Homtini Pass, finished in 1882, before passing Barrington. Because of the deep gorge of the Homtini – a Khoikhoi name meaning 'the passage' – it was initially planned to swing the route towards the coast from the Silver River. But the sandy terrain along the coast delayed progress, and in 1879 it was decided to reroute the road further inland. Still further on, the road negotiates the Karatara Pass – a Khoi name meaning 'deep and dark' – followed by the Hoogekraal Pass and the Diep River.

WOODVILLE BIG TREE This 31-m-high Outeniqua yellowwood (*Podocarpus falcatus*) is one of several yellowwoods in the Knysna and Tsitsikamma forests that qualifies for the title of Big Tree. With a circumference of 9 m, it is estimated to be more than 800 years old. Beyond Woodville, the Passes Road crosses the Touw, Silver, Kaaimans and Swart rivers.

WILDERNESS Nestling on the banks of the Touw River Estuary below hills draped in indigenous forests, the sparkling white beaches, lakes and rivers of Wilderness ④ have drawn visitors for over a century. Not to be missed is a drive to the Map of Africa viewpoint, which overlooks a near-perfect outline of Africa, or a leisurely walk along the Boardwalk, which forms part of the Pied Kingfisher Trail.

WILDERNESS NATIONAL PARK was proclaimed in 1987 to manage and conserve the delicate Wilderness lakes area. The park consists of four lakes, five rivers, two estuaries and 28 km of coastline, and is surrounded by a National Lake Area of 10 000 ha. The wetlands are an important habitat for waterbirds, and support 72 of a possible total of 95 waterbird species. Total bird numbers range between 5 000 and 15 000, although at times the wetlands support up to 24 000 birds a month. The lakes are not only popular with waterbirds, but are also ideally suited for a variety of water sports. To ensure that sensitive areas are not disturbed, the lakes have been zoned for various activities. Canoes and rowing boats, for example, may be used throughout the area, while motor boats are subject to certain restrictions. The Wilderness-Sedgefield Lakes Complex consists of three separate systems: the Wilderness Lakes System in the west, the Swartvlei System in the centre and the Groenvlei in the east.

WILDERNESS LAKES The Touw River and its estuary are linked to three interconnected lakes, a system known as the

Wilderness Lakes. The river is connected to the first lake, Eilandvlei, by a meandering channel, the 5,5-km-long Serpentine. Also known as Lower Langvlei, the 150-ha Eilandvlei owes its name to Drommedaris Island which lies at its centre. To the east, the lake is linked by a channel to Langvlei, which was formed when the sea level was much higher than it is today and the lowlands between the dunes were inundated. Langvlei, in turn, is linked by an 800-m-long channel to Rondevlei ③, the easternmost of the Wilderness Lakes. Covering 143 ha, Rondevlei was formed some 7 000 years ago when a deflation basin formed by wind was inundated by rising sea levels. The lake is an important habitat for several waterbird species, such as greater crested and blacknecked grebes and redknobbed coot. For birding enthusiasts, there is a hide at the lake's northeastern edge.

SWARTVLEI Covering 1 085 ha, Swartvlei is the largest and deepest of the Wilderness-Sedgefield Lakes Complex. It owes its name to the dark colour of the water, which is produced by plant colloid and certain acids. The lake is an example of a river valley that was drowned when sea levels rose due to warmer climatic conditions approximately 6 000 years ago. Swartvlei is connected to the sea by a channel which is blocked by a sand bar for more than half the year. The sheltered waters are home to the Knysna seahorse, and the lake is a popular destination for yachting, powerboat, water-skiing and windsurfing enthusiasts. It also offers excellent angling and birding opportunities.

GROENVLEI was formed some 3 000 years ago when its channel to the sea was cut off. Situated about 3 m above sea level, it is the only freshwater lake in the system. Because it is not linked to any rivers, it is recharged by rainwater seeping through the dunes and the freshwater springs at its eastern end. Groenvlei owes its name and its colour to the algae that flourish in the water.

GOUKAMMA NATURE RESERVE This scenic reserve ① covers 2 500 ha of coastal fynbos, coastal forest, 14 km of coastline and Groenvlei. The marine reserve adjoining the coast extends for 1,85 km seawards. Visitors can explore this scenic reserve along several day walks, canoe or sail on the Goukamma River and try their luck at angling, either along the coast, in the river or in the vlei. Accommodation is limited to a rustic bush camp on the shores of Groenvlei and a thatched rondavel overlooking the Buffalo River.

BELVIDERE The Holy Trinity Church ⑤ on Belvidere was built by Thomas Duthie, owner of the estate between 1833 and 1857. Consecrated on 5 October 1855, the church is a miniature of the Norman style of the 11th and 12th centuries. Sandstone was quarried at a nearby site, while stinkwood and yellowwood timber came from the Knysna forests. Except for the parapet, the pulpit was carved from a solid block of sandstone. The magnificent stained glass rose window was made in England from pieces of glass obtained from churches bombed during World War II.

2

3

4

5

1

24
165 KM

2

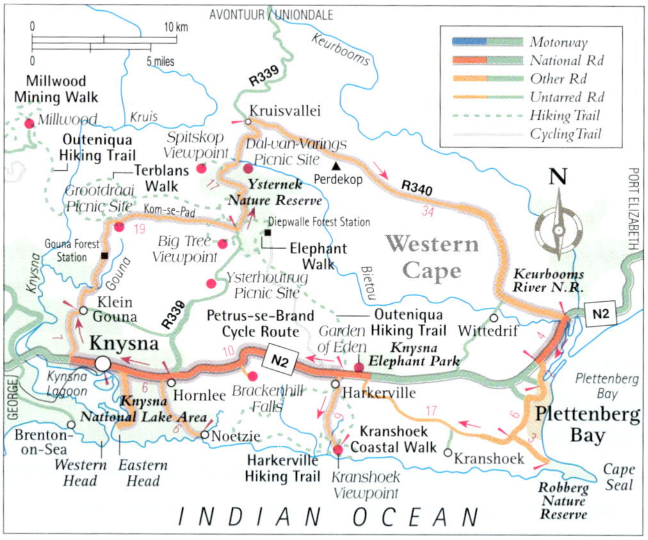

KNYSNA See Tour 22, page 58.

KNYSNA FORESTS Stretching from Mossel Bay in the west to Harkerville in the east, the indigenous forests of Knysna ① cover about 45 000 ha of state and private land. Together with the Tsitsikamma forests to the east, this is the largest natural forest complex in South Africa. Towering forest giants draped with strings of hanging lichens, monkeyrope (*Rhoicissus tomentosa*), colourful mosses, glades of ferns and tranquil streams create a wonderland inhabited by bright forest birds such as the Knysna lourie (*Tauraco corythaix*) ②. Among the 125 species of trees are Outeniqua and real yellowwoods, stinkwood, red and white alders, ironwood, white pear and assegai, while tree ferns and dense undergrowth give the forest a fairy-tale aura.

KNYSNA ELEPHANTS Gouna, together with the adjoining Diepwalle, Buffelsnek and Kransbos forests, forms part of the area that was inhabited by the last remaining Knysna elephants. In the 1870s the forests were home to an estimated 400 to 500 elephants, but by 1913 their numbers had dropped to a mere 13. A survey conducted in 1968 and 1969 found only 10 elephants, but no steps were taken to safeguard their future, and by 1979 the population had dwindled to three: a cow, calf and an old bull. In December 1988 the tracks of a newly born calf were discovered, but it was not until June 1994 that an attempt was made to revive the Knysna population by relocating three young elephant cows from the Kruger National Park. However, an extended search turned up only one elephant, the old matriarch. After being kept in a boma at Diepwalle for nearly two months, the trio were released in September 1994. The youngest calf died of pneumonia about two weeks after release, while the remaining two cows failed to adapt to their forest home. After causing damage to private property, it was decided to relocate the two surviving elephants to the Shamwari Game Reserve, near Port Elizabeth. Then, in September 2000, a young bull was unexpectedly sighted in the Gouna forest.

PERDEKOP The 20-minute walk to the summit of the 729-m-high Perdekop rewards visitors with spectacular views over the Keurbooms River valley and the Langkloof Mountains to the north. Looking south, the plantations and indigenous forests extend to where the coastal plateau meets the sea.

PLETTENBERG BAY Originally named Bahia Formosa (Beautiful Bay) by the Portuguese navigator Manuel de Mesquita Petrestrélo, Plettenberg Bay was renamed after Dutch Governor Joachim van Plettenberg in 1779. The town developed around a woodcutters' post established in 1787, and the ruins of the timber store built in that year can still be seen. With 20 km of beaches stretching from Robberg Peninsula to the mouth of the Keurbooms River, Plettenberg Bay, with its luxurious Beacon Isle Hotel ③, is one of the most fashionable holiday destinations along the Southern Cape coast. The brisk winds in the bay make it ideal for sailing, boardsailing, and surfing, while the Keurbooms River offers good water-skiing and canoeing opportunities, and numerous good rock angling sites. Among the town's historic attractions are a replica of the beacon erected by Governor van Plettenberg in 1787 and St Peter's Church (1881). The quaint St Andrew's Chapel was built entirely from yellowwood as a family school and chapel in 1849.

ROBBERG NATURE RESERVE At the southwestern end of Plettenberg Bay, the white sandy beach gives way to a peninsula jutting into the ocean for 4 km and ranging in width from 1 km to just 250 m at The Gap. Robberg features a rugged coastline with high sea cliffs, patches of drift sand and spectacular rock formations, among them the

Blaasbank (Blowhole) and Brugklip (Bridge Rock). Archaeological excavations at Nelson's Bay Cave have produced evidence that the cave was inhabited for more than 100 000 years. The earliest inhabitants were Middle Stone Age people who occupied the cave from about 120 000 to 50 000 years ago. They were followed by Later Stone Age people, who lived in the cave from about 18 000 to 2 000 years ago, and finally by Khoikhoi pastoralists. The peninsula can be explored along three trails, ranging in duration from 30 minutes to three hours.

KNYSNA ELEPHANT PARK is home to three young elephants: Harry, Sally and Duma. Harry and Sally were orphans from an elephant cull in the Kruger National Park and were relocated to their new home in 1994. They were joined three years later by Duma, brought from a game farm. Visitors are taken on a guided safari into the 50-ha camp where the elephants roam, and will gain a fascinating insight into the habits and other aspects of elephants. Once the elephants have been located, visitors can touch and feed them. There is also a 25-ha private nature reserve and a 2,5-km walk, the Bushpig Trail.

GARDEN OF EDEN ④ is an apt name for this pristine tract of indigenous forest with its towering yellowwoods, stinkwoods and lush undergrowth. This is an excellent example of the wet forest type, in which the trees attain heights of about 15 m. There are picnic facilities, and visitors can experience the atmosphere and tranquillity of the forest by setting off on a 30-minute walking trail.

KRANSHOEK The Kranshoek viewpoint offers expansive vistas over the rugged coastline, with its numerous rocky bays, some 200 m below. Picnic facilities are provided here, as well as at the picturesque waterfall where the Kranshoek River plunges into a deep gorge. The Kranshoek Walk, a 9,4-km route that leads through indigenous forest down to the coast and back up to the plateau, can be hiked in about 4 hours.

BRACKENHILL FALLS lie in the upper reaches of the Noetzie River. After a few gentle leaps over rocky ledges, the river plunges over a sheer cliff into a deep gorge carved into the coastal plain. The name Noetzie is Khoikhoi in origin and means 'black' – a reference to the colour of the water. Picnic facilities are provided. The falls and nearby Brackenhill are named after the bracken fern (*Pteridium aquilinum*), a rambling fern which forms dense communities in clearings and is especially abundant after fires.

NOETZIE has a delightful beach and a small lagoon set against a backdrop of indigenous forest. To the east of the beach is a cluster of holiday homes reminiscent of medieval castles ⑤. The history of the stone-built castles dates back to 1913, when Mr HS Henderson bought several plots along the coast. The first house was built in 1932; it incorporated a water tower that made it look like a castle, so crenellated battlements were added. In keeping with the original building, the neighbouring houses were built in the same style. Dominating the complex is Pezula (a Shona name meaning 'high up'), which features an imposing corner tower. For a number of years, it was the holiday home of Garfield Todd, former Prime Minister of Southern Rhodesia, but was re-acquired by the Henderson family in 1970.

KNYSNA HEADS Guarding the entrance to the Knysna Lagoon, the sheer cliffs of The Heads stand astride the narrow passage that has been cut into an ancient marine terrace. Early attempts to persuade the authorities to ship timber through The Heads were unsuccessful because of the dangers posed by submerged rocks in the narrows. In 1817 the *Emu*, a Royal Navy brig sent to determine the feasibility of establishing a harbour, struck a rock and ran aground in the entrance. Over the next 79 years, numerous ships were wrecked or damaged while negotiating the treacherous passage, the last being the Norwegian whaler, *Pisang*, which capsized in 1914. From below ⑥ and from the summit of the Eastern Head are views over the lagoon, while the Featherbed Nature Reserve on the slopes of the Western Head is accessible only by joining a cruise on the lagoon.

3

4

5

6

1 

25
175 KM

 2

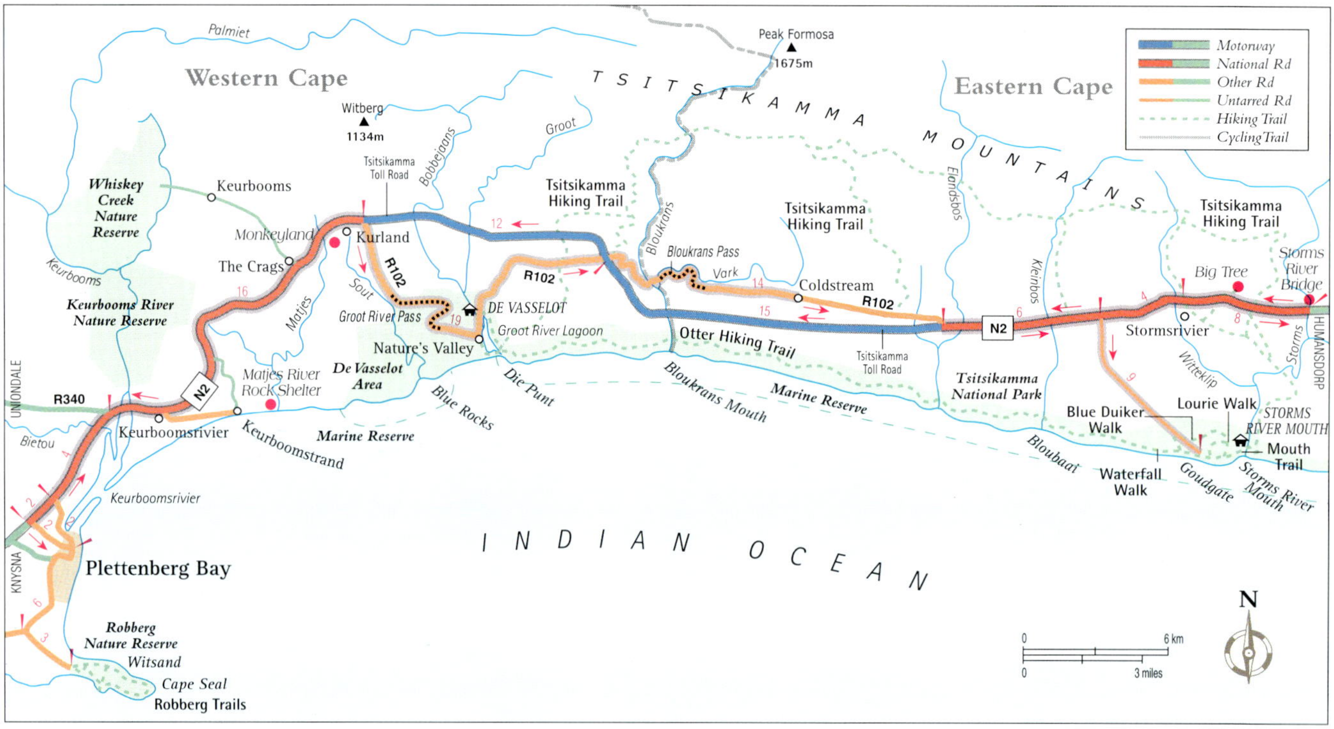

PLETTENBERG BAY See Tour 24, page 62.

THE KEURBOOMS RIVER NATURE RESERVE Both the river and the reserve take their names from the keurboom (*Virgilia divaricata*), which grows in profusion along the river banks. Rising in the Outeniqua Mountains, the Keurbooms River flows south-eastwards and then swings south, forming a magnificent lagoon before entering the sea just east of Lookout Beach. The river is popular with anglers, as well as water-skiing, boardsailing and canoeing enthusiasts. To the north of the bridge that crosses the river, an area of 780 ha has been set aside as the Keurbooms River Nature Reserve to protect the forests and fynbos vegetation. Not to be missed is a cruise up the river, which includes an optional 30-minute walk through the indigenous forests.

MATJES RIVER ROCK SHELTER This cave was formed by waves pounding against the coastal cliffs at a time when sea levels were much higher than today. When sea levels fell, the cave provided a convenient home to Later Stone Age people who exploited the marine environment. Human habitation of Matjes River rock shelter dates back some 11 000 years. The cave has one of the largest known shell middens in the world and was also used as a burial site. Stone tools, ornaments and other artefacts recovered from the cave have enabled archaeologists to gain an insight into the way of life of the cave's inhabitants. Situated on the western bank of the Matjes River, the cave is accessible from Keurboomstrand by walking along the beach at low tide.

GROOT RIVER PASS With its near-impenetrable vegetation and precipitous ravines, the Tsitsikamma forest presented a formidable barrier until well into the 19th century. Early travellers were forced to cross the Tsitsikamma Mountains near Plettenberg Bay and follow the Langkloof to Humansdorp. It was not until 1867-68 that Christopher Harison and Thomas Bain surveyed the forest, but it was the Great Fire of 1869 that opened the way for the construction of a road. Using convict labour, Bain set about building the Groot River Pass, which descends 220 m in just 4 km, reaching the Groot River in 1881.

NATURE'S VALLEY is a picturesque holiday village nestling between the Groot River lagoon and a headland draped in magnificent indigenous forest. Stretching for 2 km from Die Punt to Blue Rocks, the sandy beach ③ is popular with sunbathers, while the De Vasselot section of the Tsitsikamma National Park offers a variety of day walks.

DE VASSELOT Covering 1 645 ha of indigenous forest and 916 ha of fynbos, the De Vasselot Nature Reserve was incorporated into the Tsitsikamma National Park in 1987. The rest camp on the banks of the Groot River offers accommodation in two-bedded huts and camping facilities. Visitors can explore the area along a network of six nature trails, while boardsailing, sailing and canoeing are permitted on the lagoon and the river.

BLOUKRANS PASS Beyond Nature's Valley, the road clings to the wooded precipices as its zigzags up to the coastal plateau. Just before reaching the summit, there is a viewpoint with stunning views over the Groot River lagoon and Nature's Valley. Just over 6 km further on is the second of the Tsitsikamma passes built by Bain. A convict station was built here during the construction of the pass. In a report written in 1881 by the chief roads inspector, the work on Bloukrans Pass was described as 'heavy, involving some deep scarping and high retaining walls'. Shortly after crossing the Bloukrans River there is a magnificent view of the toll road bridge over the river.

TSITSIKAMMA NATIONAL PARK The core of this park was proclaimed in 1964 as the Tsitsikamma Coastal National Park – Africa's first marine park. Stretching for 65 km between Oubosstrand in the east and the Groot River estuary at Nature's Valley, the landward boundary of the park generally follows the 200-m contour. The park originally stretched seawards for 800 m, but this was subsequently extended to 5,5 km. Its main attractions are the rugged coastline, sheer wave-cut cliffs and the beautiful indigenous forests. The rest camp near Storms River Mouth offers a wide range of accommodation options and recreational activities. In addition to the famous 42-km-long Otter Trail, which takes five days to complete, there are several day walks. Especially popular is the Mouth Walk, which meanders to the suspension bridge ① spanning the Storms River Mouth ④ Visitors can get close-up views of the awesome gorge, with its 150-m-high cliffs, by taking a boat cruise up the river. The numerous small bays and coves are ideally suited to snorkelling, while scuba divers can explore the offshore world by following an underwater trail.

BIG TREE About 5 km east of the turnoff to the Storms River Mouth rest camp, a signpost indicates a parking area near one of several 'Big Trees' along the Garden Route. A short walk from the parking area leads to a mighty Outeniqua yellowwood (*Podocarpus falcatus*), which towers 36,6 m above the forest floor and has a crown spread of 32,5 m. Its circumference at chest height is 8,5 m, while the trunk is 18,3 m long with an estimated volume of almost 51 m^3. A boardwalk has been built to prevent compacting of the forest floor by the large number of visitors.

STORMS RIVER GORGE The road bridge spanning the Storm's River was built in the mid-1950s at a cost of £100 000 to replace the historic Storms River Pass built by Thomas Bain. Designed by the renowned Italian architect, Professor Ricardo Morandi, the 192-m-long bridge consists of two arched sections which met perfectly when they were lowered from opposite sides of the ravine. In recent years, the deep gorge has become a major destination for adventure-seekers. Blackwater tubing trips are conducted in the gorge, while the Stormsriver Gorge Challenge involves a 110-m abseil, a two-hour blackwater tubing trip and mountain biking.

TSITSIKAMMA TOLL ROAD Built at a cost of R58 million, the 27-km toll road between the Elandsbos River and Ladywood was officially opened in June 1984. Its main attraction is, without doubt, the three spectacular bridges spanning deep river gorges. With a height of 216 m, the 451-m-long Bloukrans Bridge offers adrenalin junkies the highest commercial bungi jump in the world: a seven-second freefall of 180 m. The impressive Groot River is crossed by a bridge with a span of 301 m, 172 m above the river bed, while the nearby bridge over the Bobbejaans River has a span of 286 m and is 170 m high.

MONKEYLAND This sanctuary is home to some 16 primate species ②, among them black and white ruffed lemurs from Madagascar, squirrel monkeys from South America, hooded capuchin, goldenhanded tamarin and blackeared marmoset. The sanctuary consists of 12 ha of indigenous forest which has been enclosed by a 6-m-high fence. Within the sanctuary, the primates – previously kept in zoos, as pets or bred in captivity – are able to roam freely. Visitors are taken on a guided walk through the forest to water holes, hides, viewing platforms and a canopy walk, from where the primates and a variety of forest birds can be viewed at close range. The remaining 38 ha of Monkeyland serves as a green belt for animals such as bushpig, bushbuck, blue duiker, baboon and vervet monkey.

3

4

OPPOSITE TOP: HEALING PLACE OF CREDO MUTWA (P.71); BOTTOM: CAPE RECIFE LIGHTHOUSE (P.68). **THIS PAGE** TOP LEFT: GRAAFF-REINET WINDMILL (P.78); TOP RIGHT: SCULPTURE AT OWL HOUSE, NIEU-BETHESDA (P.78); CENTRE LEFT: SPOTTED EAGLE OWL AT SEAVIEW (P.69); ABOVE: PORT ELIZABETH REGATTA (P.68); LEFT: SUNDAYS RIVER (P.70).

EASTERN CAPE

26
150 KM

1

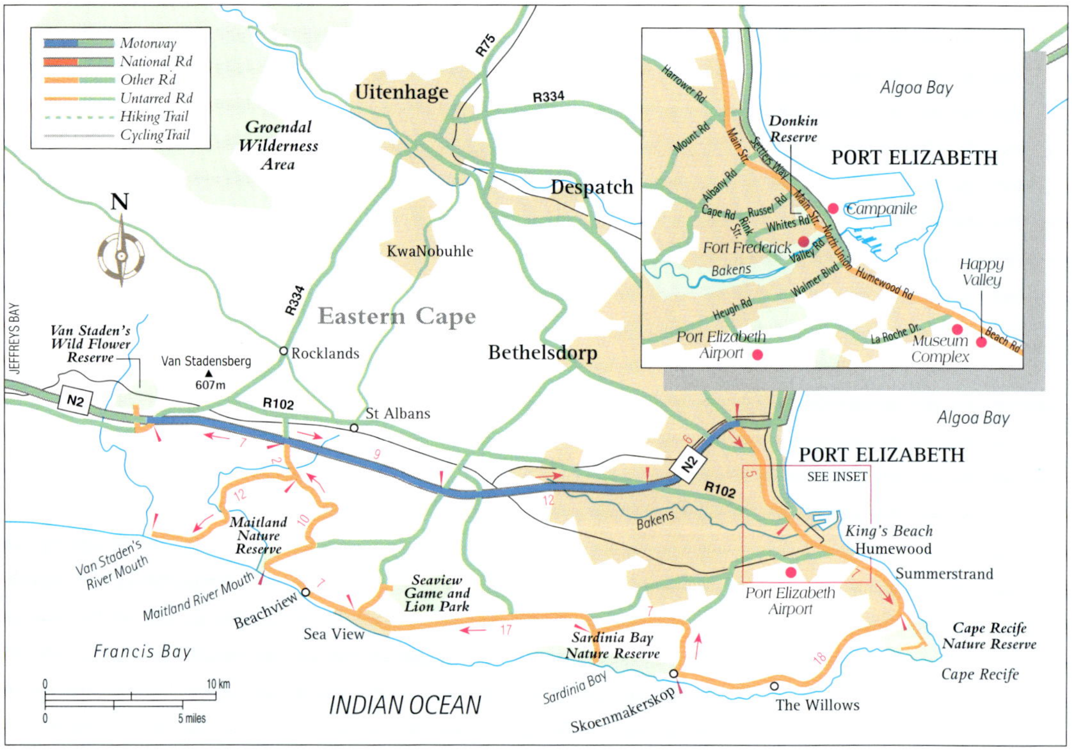

PORT ELIZABETH lies on the shores of the sweeping bay originally named Baia da Lagoa (Bay of the Lagoon) by Manuel de Mesquita Perestrêlo in 1576, a reference to the lagoon at the mouth of the Baakens River. A small settlement developed around Fort Frederick, built on the heights above the Baakens River in 1799 to prevent a possible landing by French troops. The history of Port Elizabeth is inextricably linked to the arrival of the 1820 Settlers – 4 000 emigrants who left Britain for the Eastern Cape in 21 ships between December 1819 and March 1820. Sir Rufane Donkin, the Acting Governor of the Cape, visited the settlement on 6 June 1820; at his request, it was renamed Port Elizabeth in memory of his wife, who had died of fever in India two years earlier. An important city landmark is the 51,8-m-high Campanile, which was erected in 1923 to commemorate the landing of the 1820 Settlers.

Among the many other historical buildings and sites are the row of double-storey terraced houses in Donkin Street ③, built between 1860 and 1880; the Pyramid in the Donkin Reserve, dedicated to Elizabeth Donkin; and the row of townhouses in Cora Terrace, built in the Regency style from about 1856 onwards. The complex of Settler houses in Castle Hill is an interesting example of early Eastern Cape townhouses. No 7 Castle Hill, built in 1830, is the oldest house in the city and appropriately serves as a period-house museum. Facing the Market Square ② are the historic Library (1848), the statue of Queen Victoria and the City Hall (1862). An excellent way to appreciate the city's many historic buildings is to follow the Donkin Heritage Trail, linking 43 places of interest.

SOUTHERN BEACHES Many visitors are attracted to Port Elizabeth by its sandy beaches. King's Beach stretches for 1,6 km from the harbour breakwater to Humewood Beach and offers safe swimming and sunbathing. The city's best-known beach, Humewood, features a promenade and attracts large crowds of sunbathers. About 2 km beyond Humewood lies Port Elizabeth's third sandy beach, Summerstrand. Hobie Beach is a popular venue with boardsailing and hobie cat enthusiasts, while the adjacent Pollock Beach offers excellent surfing.

BAYWORLD in Humewood comprises the Oceanarium, Snake Park, Tropical House and Museum. The Oceanarium is famous for its performing bottlenose dolphins and seals, while two large aquaria provide fascinating views of colourful fish, sharks and other forms of marine life. An extensive collection of snakes, including python, black mamba, cobra and puff adder, as well as crocodile and other reptiles, can be seen at the Snake Park, and regular demonstrations are given by snake handlers. In the Tropical House, with its 7-m-high artificial outcrop, streams, waterfalls and bridges, visitors can follow a winding path through lush tropical vegetation. The Museum contains fascinating displays on marine biology and the history of Port Elizabeth, a collection of period costumes, beadwork and genealogies of the Xhosa-speaking people of the Eastern Cape, and a life-size replica of an *Algoasaurus* dinosaur.

CAPE RECIFE is a promontory that forms the southernmost extremity of Algoa Bay. The name is a corruption of the earlier Portuguese name Cabo de Recife, which means 'cape of the reef', a reference to dangers such as Recife Point and Thunderbolt Reef not far offshore. An area of 336 ha has been set aside as the Cape Recife Nature Reserve to preserve the shoreline, coastal dunes and vegetation. Visitors can explore the reserve on foot by following the 7-km-long Roseate Tern Trail, or do birding from a hide. The 24-m-high octagonal lighthouse at Cape Recife ④ is the third oldest along the South African coast. Designed by the Surveyor General of the Cape Colony, Colonel Charles Michell, it came into service on 1 April 1851. The remains of a World War II military observation post can be seen on the heights behind the lighthouse.

WESTERN BEACHES Several popular holiday resorts nestle along the coast west of Cape Recife. Set amid green lawns, the Willows Holiday Resort lies in a sheltered rocky bay with two tidal pools. Schoenmakerskop village lies along a rocky stretch of coast, with numerous pools and gullies offering excellent opportunities for swimming. It has been suggested that the hill after which the village was named owes its name to Johannes Schumacher, a soldier and artist who accompanied Colonel Robert Gordon when he explored the area in 1778. A cannon points to the site where the Portuguese galleon, *Sacramento*, ran aground in July 1647.

Continuing further west, Sardinia Bay is a small rocky bay with a sandy beach. Fishing is prohibited in the marine reserve, which extends 2 km out to sea. The Sardinia Bay Nature Reserve provides protection for 320 ha of coastal dune fynbos. Still further west, the residential village of Sea View lies along a stretch of rocky coast, but visitors can swim in the tidal pool. A landmark in the village is the hotel, formerly the HMS *Good Hope*, which served as a training 'ship' for officers of the Royal Navy during World War II.

2

SEAVIEW GAME AND LION PARK is home to some 40 species of African wildlife, including lion, cheetah, giraffe, zebra and a variety of antelope such as springbok, kudu, wildebeest and blesbok. Visitors can do self-drive game-viewing in the 46-ha park, and get close-up views of two of Africa's large cat species in the cheetah and lion enclosures. A programme to breed the rare white lion was introduced in 1999. Night game drives offer visitors an opportunity to see nocturnal animals and birds.

3

MAITLAND RIVER MOUTH Flanked by rocky coastline to the east and kilometres of sandy beach to the west, this resort at the mouth of the Maitland River is a popular destination for both rock and surf anglers. A short distance inland from the river mouth, the scenery is dominated by towering sand dunes, while the Maitland Nature Reserve covers 127 ha of coastal forest and scrub. There are two nature trails along which visitors can explore the forest's Cape chestnut, white stinkwood, forest elder and candlewood trees. An old wagon road leads to a long-abandoned lead mine in the reserve. The river and the nature reserve were named after Lieutenant-General Sir Peregrine Maitland, Governor of the Cape from March 1844 to January 1847.

VAN STADENS RIVER MOUTH is a popular coastal resort with a magnificent setting at the mouth of the Van Stadens River. Its 6-km stretch of unspoilt beach is popular with sunbathers and anglers, while the beautiful lagoon offers safe swimming, boardsailing and canoeing. The high dunes along the western shores of the lagoon provide exciting opportunities for sandboarding.

VAN STADENS WILD FLOWER RESERVE lies on the coastal plateau at the foot of the Van Stadens Mountain. Bounded by the Van Stadens River Gorge ① in the west, the reserve covers 500 ha of fynbos, indigenous forest and cultivated gardens. A profusion of proteas, ericas, pincushions, ground orchids and other fynbos species cover the gentle slopes to the north of the N2. Among the reserve's botanical rarities are the Van Stadens conebush (*Leucadendron orientale*) and a fire lily (*Cyrtanthus stadensis*). The southern plateau slopes and the banks of the river are draped in indigenous forest, consisting of species such as white pear, kooboo berry, Cape plane and cheesewood. The mountain and the river owe their name to Marthinus van Staden, who was awarded a loan farm in the area around 1744.

4

1

27
283 KM

2

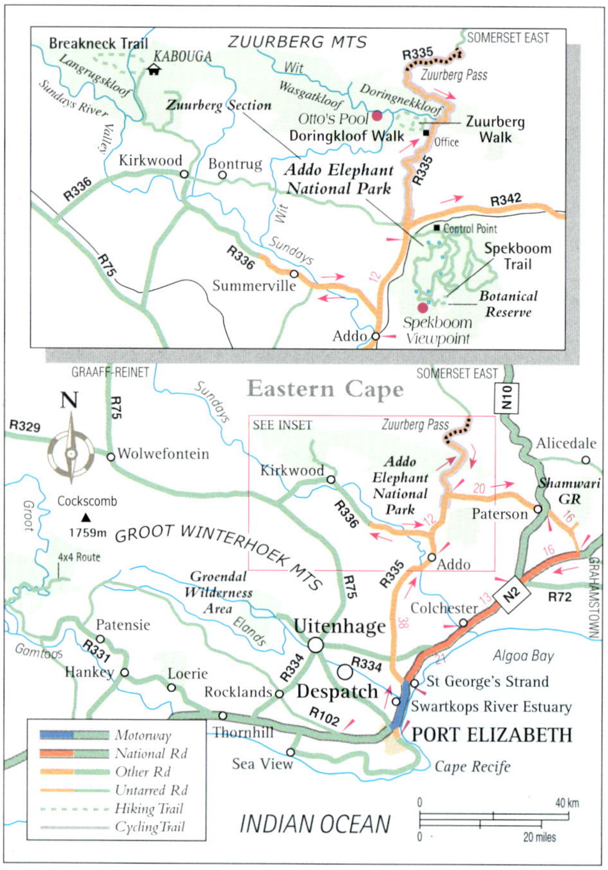

3

4

PORT ELIZABETH See Tour 26, page 68.

SWARTKOPS RIVER ESTUARY The Swartkops River rises in the Groot Winterhoek Mountains and flows for about 80 km before reaching the sea at Algoa Bay, 15 km north of Port Elizabeth. Over the last 16 km it forms a magnificent estuary, characterised by intertidal mudflats and salt marshes. The Afrikaans name means 'black hills', a reference to the dark colour of the vegetation and the shadows cast by the escarpment along the estuary's northern edge and the nearby hills. The estuary is a popular recreational area with yachting, power-boating, boardsailing and canoeing enthusiasts, as well as anglers. It is also the most important estuary for waterbirds between Knysna Lagoon and Durban harbour, supporting up to 20 000 waterbirds a year. Among these are the rare African black oystercatcher, Caspian tern, greater and lesser flamingos and the bobtailed godwit. Amsterdamhoek is a popular holiday resort situated picturesquely between the dunes and the estuary, and has numerous jetties jutting into the water ⑤. It was named after the *Amsterdam* which ran aground nearby on 15 December 1817.

NORTHERN BEACHES Beyond the Swartkops River estuary lies a vast stretch of unspoilt sandy beaches and dunes, known as Port Elizabeth's 'northern beaches'. Three beach resorts, Bluewater Bay, Brighton Beach and St George's Strand, offer superb swimming, angling and surfing.

ADDO is a small settlement which developed around the railway junction where the line branches off to the Sundays River Valley. The Khoikhoi name is said to mean 'euphorbia ravine', a reference to the abundance of tree euphorbias growing in the area.

SUNDAYS RIVER VALLEY The Sundays River Valley stretches for 64 km from Korhaansdrifpoort, where the river flows through the Zuurberge, to its mouth at Algoa Bay and varies in width from 1,6 to 6,4 km. The first farm in the valley was awarded in 1812, but it was James Kirkwood who realised the area's potential by irrigating the fertile alluvial soil. Between 1877 and 1883, he bought 21 farms, totalling 302 883 ha, and formed the Sundays River Land and Irrigation Company. After his death, the land was divided into smaller farms and an irrigation channel built. In 1910, the Strathsomers Estate Company took over all the irrigation interests in the valley, and a few years later Sir Percy Fitzpatrick's company, the Sundays River Settlements Company, bought up a substantial part of the valley. Following appeals to the government for assistance to build a dam, the Darlington (formerly Mentz) Dam was completed in 1922, providing a supply of water more reliable than relying on flood irrigation. The valley is today one of the country's main citrus-producing regions, with lucerne being another important crop.

ADDO ELEPHANT NATIONAL PARK ① was established in 1931 as a sanctuary for the eastern Cape's last surviving elephants. From a nucleus of 11 animals, the population has grown steadily and today the park is home to over 300 elephants ③. It is also a sanctuary for the East African subspecies of the black rhino, which was introduced in 1962 before the importance of genetic purity became accepted. These rhino could in future play an important role in the repopulation of game parks in East Africa. In 1995, seven black rhino of the western subspecies were introduced into the park, but they are kept separate to prevent genetic contamination. Other large mammals to be seen include eland, red hartebeest and Cape buffalo – at one time, this was the only population of foot-and-mouth-free buffalo in South Africa. The park has played an important role in the reintroduction of this species elsewhere in South Africa and in Namibia. Dungbeetles ② are some of the park's smaller residents.

GREATER ADDO NATIONAL PARK The protection enjoyed by the elephants in Addo has led to the need to expand the park. From its original size of 6 852 ha, the park has been increased to over 100 000 ha, and the planned Greater Addo Elephant National Park will eventually cover an area of 400 000 ha, stretching right down to the coast, including the Alexandria dunefields. The park will be able to support more than 2 500 elephants and will also offer visitors the opportunity to see whales and dolphins offshore.

ZUURBERG PASS Before the construction of the Olifantskop Pass north of Paterson, the route from Port Elizabeth into the interior took travellers over the Zuurberg Pass. The historic Zuurberg Inn, built in 1861 as a coaching inn, was badly damaged by a fire in 1902, but was subsequently rebuilt. From the summit, there are sweeping views northwards over the Great Karoo, with the vast expanses of Addo bush stretching to the south.

ZUURBERG SECTION OF THE ADDO ELEPHANT NATIONAL PARK Originally a state forest, the 21 121-ha Zuurberg was proclaimed a national park in 1985. It was amalgamated with the Addo National Park ten years later, and has since been enlarged through further land acquisitions. It is a rugged wilderness ④ characterised by spectacular folded mountains, deep forested kloofs and a diversity of vegetation types. Visitors can explore the area on foot by following self-guided day walks or set off on an overnight horse trail. Along the way, visitors may chance upon kudu, bushbuck, mountain reedbuck, grey rhebok, common and blue duikers and Cape mountain zebra. A family of hippo from the Kruger National Park was reintroduced into the Sundays River in 1992.

PATERSON Established in 1879, the country village of Paterson was named after its founder, John Paterson. A prominent Eastern Cape personality, Paterson founded the *Eastern Cape Herald* newspaper in 1845 and played a major role in establishing the Grey Institute in Port Elizabeth.

SHAMWARI GAME RESERVE is the only privately owned Big Five reserve in South Africa that is located in a malaria-free area. Covering 18 000 ha, the reserve was opened in 1992 and has won several international awards for its conservation vision. The reserve has been stocked with over 5 000 animals; in addition to the Big Five, there are 18 antelope species and a large diversity of smaller mammals. Also of interest is Credo Mutwa's Kaya Lendaba (the house of stories), a traditional African arts and culture village depicting the culture and lifestyles of the Xhosa and other southern African peoples.

The programme for day visitors starts at noon with lunch on the game-viewing deck of the Conservation Centre. Designed in partnership with the Born Free Foundation, founded by actress and conservationist Virginia McKenna, the centre consists of a museum and educational facility. Lunch is followed by an hour-long visit to Kaya Lendaba, and visitors are then taken on a game drive ⑥ under the guidance of an experienced game ranger. The programme concludes at around 18:30.

5

6

INTO THE BAVIAANSKLOOF

1

28

440 KM

2

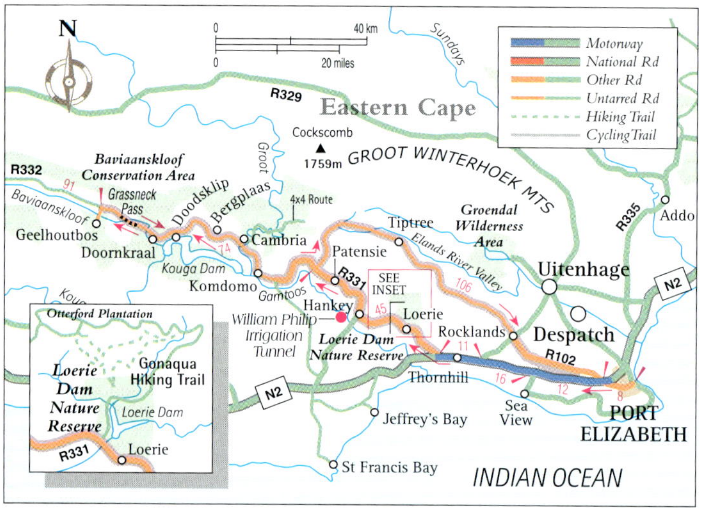

WILLIAM PHILIP IRRIGATION TUNNEL South Africa's first irrigation tunnel was built to water land in a wide horseshoe bend of the Gamtoos River. The 94-m tunnel runs through a ridge that forces the river to swing northwards. Construction began from opposite ends in 1842 under the supervision of William Philip, son of Dr John Philip. Labourers recruited from the mission station used hammers, chisels and pick-axes to tunnel through 88 m of solid rock. The tunnel was completed on 13 August 1844, but a year later William Philip drowned in the Klein River. The tunnel was extensively damaged when the Gamtoos River came down in flood three years later, and again in 1867, but it was repaired both times. Close to the tunnel there is a short, but steep, path to the Bergvenster, a natural rock window eroded through a ridge. Those who tackle the scramble will be rewarded with spectacular views of the mosaic of farmlands in the Gamtoos River Valley framed by the 'window'.

PORT ELIZABETH See Tour 26, page 68.

GAMTOOS RIVER VALLEY stretches in a southeasterly direction from the confluence of the Groot and Kouga rivers. The Khoikhoi named the valley Xami – 'lion' and 'the roaring lion' – but it is possible that it was named after a Khoikhoi chief. With its abundance of water and fertile alluvial soil, the valley is a major producer of citrus fruit, while vegetables, lucerne, tobacco and potatoes are grown under irrigation.

LOERIE, a small settlement situated in the foothills of the Elands and Groot Winterhoek Mountains, owes its name to the Loerie River. The river, in turn, was named after the Knysna lourie, which inhabits the indigenous forests along the river banks. The name was already in use when the explorer William Paterson visited the eastern Cape in the late 1780s. Limestone mined at the Limebank quarry is transported in cocopans along an 8-km overhead cableway, said to be the second longest in the country, to Loerie station for shipment by rail to Port Elizabeth. The Loerie Dam Nature Reserve covers 1 000 ha of valley bushveld, indigenous forest and fynbos. The reserve serves as an environmental education centre, and activities for day visitors include angling and boating on the dam, and a 7-km-long day walk. Loerie is also the end of the unique 72,86-km Great Train Race, an annual competition between a steam locomotive and 10-member relay teams.

HANKEY developed around the mission station established on 1 619 ha of the farm Wagendrift, bought in 1822 by Dr John Philip, Superintendent of the London Missionary Society (LMS). The decision to establish the mission station here was taken when the Bethelsdorp mission near Port Elizabeth, founded in 1803 for remnants of the Gonaqua Khoikhoi, became too small. Situated at the foot of a ridge along the Klein River, a tributary of the Groot River, the mission was named after William Hankey, Treasurer of the London Missionary Society.

PATENSIE is the western terminus of the branch line of the Avontuur narrow-gauge railway line and an important commercial centre for the citrus, tobacco and vegetable farms in the area. The name is a corruption of a Khoikhoi name which is said to mean 'resting place for the cattle'. About 16 km beyond Patensie the road passes a striking rock resembling the profile of Queen Victoria. The geological strata of this area, known as the Enon Conglomerates, were formed when boulders, pebbles, sand and clay were deposited in an early basin of the Gamtoos some 100 million ears ago. The material was subsequently cemented together to form conglomerate.

KOUGA DAM was completed in 1976 to provide a reliable source of water for the metropolitan area of Port Elizabeth and the Gamtoos irrigation scheme. When full, the dam has a capacity of 128 million m^3 and the water backs up 28 km behind the 365-m-long dam wall. The 94-m-high double-arch wall was the first of its kind in South Africa. Picnic facilities are provided.

BAVIAANSKLOOF Bounded by the Baviaanskloofberge to the north and the Kouga Mountains to the south, this wild kloof stretches from Die Poort westwards for some 150 km. It owes its Dutch name to the many baboons encountered by early explorers and farmers, who began settling in the valley early in the 18th century. Here they raised angora goats, and cultivated citrus fruit, wheat and a variety of vegetables, and pure vegetable seed. Aloe nectar ② is also eaten here. Die Poort, the eastern entry to the Baviaanskloof, is a spectacular natural gateway carved by the Groot River through the Coutomietberg and the Komdoberg.

After meandering for 10 km through Die Poort, the road passes Cambria, famous for its sweet citrus. Cambria is the Gaelic name for Wales, and was probably bestowed on the area by one of the early farmers because the scenery reminded him of his homeland. The road then snakes out of the valley along Combrink's Pass to Bergplaas, a large grassland plateau. Just before meandering down the Holgat

Pass, the route passes Waterpoort. For many years, the deep gorge was a formidable obstacle between the farming communities of Enkeldoorn and Bergplaas, but in the early 1960s a cableway was built to transport livestock and agricultural produce across the gorge. Still further on is the turnoff to Doodsklip, allegedly named after people died there under mysterious circumstances. About 5 km on comes the turnoff to Rooihoek, with its tranquil mountain pool set against a backdrop of a stark quartzite ridge.

From the Kouga Valley the road hugs the valley slopes as it meanders steeply out of the gorge carved by the Baviaanskloof River to the summit of the Grassneck Pass where a viewsite affords spectacular vistas over the rugged countryside. Continuing further west, the road descends more gently and then crosses the Baviaans River several times before reaching Geelhoutbos.

BAVIAANSKLOOF CONSERVATION AREA ① The Baviaanskloof forms the core of this conservation area, which covers 174 000 ha of deep valleys, rocky plateaux, wild rivers and spectacular mountain peaks ④. Complementing the wild scenery is an astonishing diversity of vegetation, ranging from lush indigenous forest and valley bushveld, dominated by tree euphorbias, to grassy fynbos and spekboomveld. Among its more than 1 100 plant species are no fewer than 17 members of the protea family and botanical treasures such as the endemic Willowmore cedar and the rare Karoo cycad (*Encephalartos lehmanii*). Since 1985, several farms have been purchased and incorporated into the conservation area, and Cape mountain zebra, eland, buffalo and red hartebeest have been reintroduced. The area has been managed by the conservation department of the Eastern Cape since 1994, and there are plans to extend it substantially. Basic camping facilities are given at Komdomo, Doodsklip, Rooihoek, Akkerendal and Apieskloof while Geelhoutbos has self-catering chalets. Donkey carts ③ are common forms of transport.

ELANDS RIVER VALLEY Between the Elandsberge to the south and the Groot Winterhoek range to the north, the Elands River has carved a beautiful valley. Dominating the scenery at the western end of the Groot Winterhoek range is the 1 758-m-high Cockscomb, so named because the five crests resemble the comb of a rooster. With its fertile alluvial soil and numerous streams draining the mountain slopes, the valley contains many farms on which a variety of crops are grown. The lush valley and the mountain with its arid fynbos slopes owe their name to the abundance of eland (*Taurotragus oryx*) that roamed the area until it became settled.

3

4

1

29
255 KM

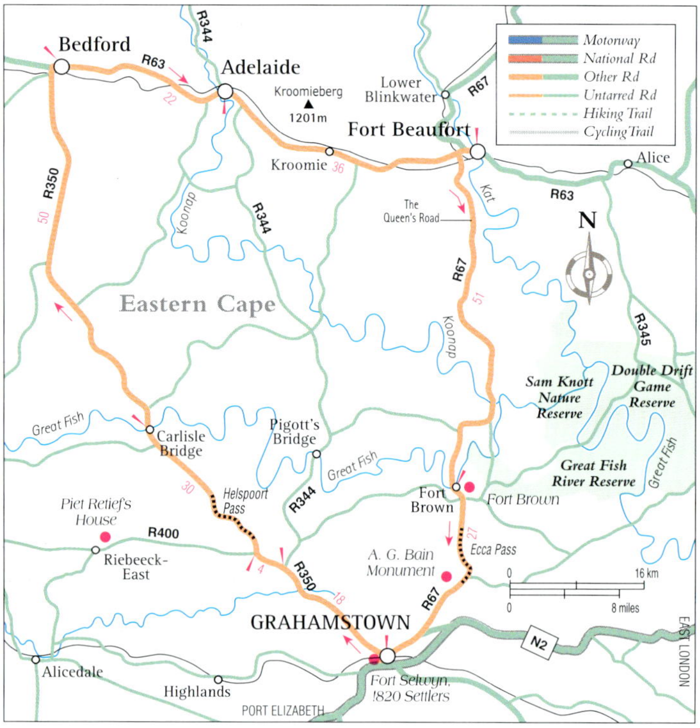

2

3

GRAHAMSTOWN was established in 1812 by Colonel John Graham as the military headquarters for a line of forts built along the Fish River, recognised in 1780 as the eastern boundary of the Cape Colony. The first erven were sold in 1815, and four years later the town consisted of between 25 and 30 'solid' houses. It grew considerably with the arrival of a number of the 1820 Settlers – mainly skilled artisans and craftsmen who were allowed to leave their failing farms. As a result, Grahamstown rapidly changed from a military settlement into a bustling trading town and a centre for the Settlers. In and around Artificer's Square is a well-preserved complex of quaint Settler cottages, dating back to around 1823. Prominent among the city's churches are the Gothic-style Cathedral of St Michael and St George ②, which took 128 years to complete, and the Commemoration Church (1850). Other historic buildings include Retreat Number 1, where the Voortrekker leader Piet Retief lived; Shaw Hall (1832); Woodville, built in the 1860s; and the City Hall (1882).

Grahamstown is an important educational centre and is home to three of South Africa's leading schools and to Rhodes University. The JLB Smith Institute of Rhodes University has a fascinating display telling the story of the famous coelacanth. The Albany Museum complex consists of the Albany Museum, with its fine ethnographic displays; the Observatory (1850); the Provost, built in 1838 as a gaol; Fort Selwyn; and the History Museum, which focuses on the 1820 Settlers. An important event on South Africa's arts calendar is the annual Grahamstown Festival ①.

1820 SETTLERS MONUMENT ③ Overlooking the city from Gunfire Hill, the 1820 Settlers Monument was built as a living and functional memorial to the courage and endeavours of the 1820 Settlers and other English-speaking pioneers who came to South Africa. Opened in 1974, the complex consists of a 900-seat theatre and several conference halls, and is also the centre of the 1820 Foundation. In July each year, the complex is host to the country's premier cultural event, the National Arts Festival. Also on Gunfire Hill is Fort Selwyn, built in the mid-1830s as a residence for Captain CJ Selwyn, commander of the Royal Engineers in Grahamstown from 1835 to 1851.

BEDFORD The history of Bedford is closely linked to the Scottish party of the 1820 Settlers, led by Thomas Pringle. They were not located with the English settlers in the Albany district, but were initially allocated land in the Baviaans River valley and later in the valleys of the Mankazana and Koonap rivers. North of Bedford, in the Baviaans River valley, is the Glen Lyden Church, built in 1828 under the leadership of Thomas Pringle to serve both the Presbyterian and Dutch Reformed Church congregations of the valley. Still higher up the Baviaans River valley is the farm Eildon, where Pringle himself settled. A shepherd's tree marks the nearby site of his Emigrant's Cabin, a beehive-shaped hut where he wrote the poems *The Emigrant's Cabin* and *Evening Rambles* and his account of life on the frontier, *Narrative of a Residence in South Africa.*

ADELAIDE Situated against the backdrop of the Winterberg mountains, the picturesque country town of Adelaide serves the surrounding sheep and cattle farms. It has its origins in a military post established on the banks of the Koonap River in 1834, and was named after Queen Adelaide, the wife of William IV. The first town erven were sold in 1849 by the newly formed congregation of the Dutch Reformed Church. The town's Our Heritage Museum is housed in a magnificent double-storey house which served as a Dutch Reformed parsonage between 1860 and 1964. It depicts the rural lifestyle of the mid-19th century, and has a valuable collection of old silver, glass and porcelain. Adelaide's history is closely linked to the 1820 Settlers, and numerous place names serve as reminders of the Scottish party of Settlers who settled here under Thomas Pringle. Among them was his brother John, who was awarded the farm Glen Thorn in the Mankazana valley, to the north of Adelaide, in 1824. Of historical interest on the farm is the stone Presbyterian church, built in 1840.

FORT BEAUFORT developed around a military post established in 1822 in a bend of the Kat River by Colonel M Scott to counter raids by the Xhosa chief, Maqoma. It was named after the Duke of Beaufort, the father of Lord Charles Somerset. At the end of the Sixth Xhosa War (1834–35) the British Governor, Sir Benjamin D'Urban, ordered the construction of strong fortifications in the border region. The circular Martello Tower ④, built in 1837 of dressed stone, provided a formidable defence against any attack, and at times also served as a safe haven. A small swivel cannon was mounted on the open observation area at the top of the tower. In the old officers' quarters, which date back to 1839, are maps, documents, photographs and equipment relating to the history of the area. Fort Beaufort was at the centre of the War of the Axe, which started when an axe was stolen from a shop in the town in March 1846. The Victorian Bridge ⑤ was built in about 1840.

FORT BROWN was established in 1817 as a military post along the Fish River as part of Lord Charles Somerset's plan to protect the frontier of the Cape Colony. On the instructions of Sir Benjamin D'Urban, Somerset's successor, the fort was converted in 1835 into one of the largest strongholds along the Fish River. A high stone wall enclosed the living quarters and stables, and in one corner a 3,5-m-high gun tower was built. A stone stairway in the gun tower led up to a room with loopholes to fire from, while a three-pounder mountain gun, which could be swivelled, was mounted on the roof. The powder magazine was built underneath the floor of the gun tower. The fort was manned until 1861, and was later used as a police post.

QUEEN'S ROAD This was the first of many roads built by Andrew Geddes Bain after he was appointed to build roads in the eastern border areas in 1837. Linking Grahamstown to Fort Beaufort and Balfour, the road was completed around 1842 and was named after Queen Victoria, who ascended the throne in 1837. Bain was the road engineer, while the construction was supervised by Major Charles Selwyn of the Royal Engineers.

ECCA PASS The heights about 15 km north of Grahamstown were the most challenging obstacle faced by Andrew Geddes Bain when he built the Queen's Road. Bain named the heights and the pass after the Ecca River – a tributary of the Fish – whose Khoikhoi name is said to mean 'salty' or 'brackish river'. As well as being a brilliant road engineer, Bain was also a keen geologist. While building the Queen's Road, he studied the composition of the rock formations along the route and named the 225–270-million-year-old sedimentary blue shales and mudstones at the foot of the pass the Ecca Group. A monument at the summit of the pass honours this great road engineer, whose many achievements include Michell's Pass near Ceres, Bain's Kloof Pass over the Klein Drakenstein Mountains near Wellington and the Katberg Pass.

4

5

1

30
175 KM

3

2

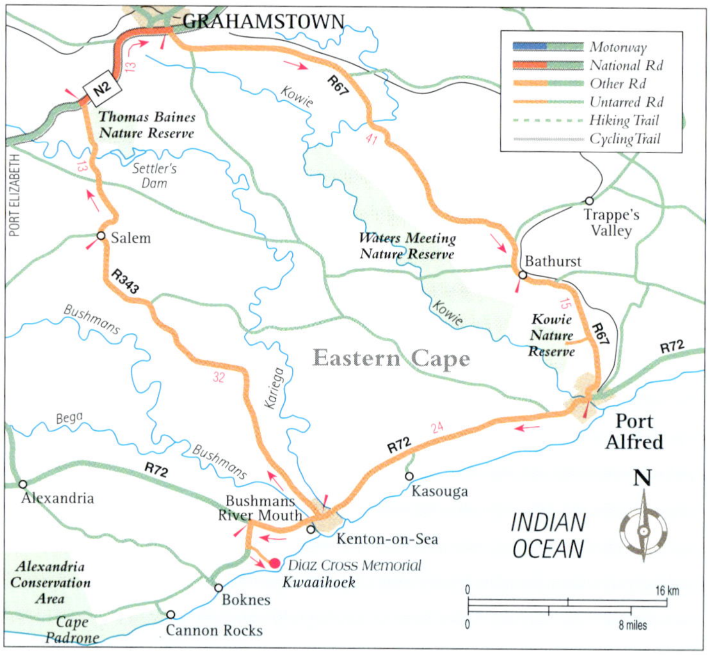

GRAHAMSTOWN See Tour 29, page 74.

BATHURST owes its distinctive English atmosphere to its origin as the first administrative centre for the 1820 Settlers. The name honours Lord Bathurst, the British Secretary of State for the Colonies at the time. Bailey's Beacon, about 1 km northeast of the town, marks the spot from where the various parties of the Settlers were directed to the farms that had been allocated to them. Among the town's historic buildings are the Methodist Church (1832) ① and St John's Church, built by the Church of England parish. At the outbreak of the Sixth Frontier War in December 1834, the half-built church served as a refuge for settler women and children until they could be evacuated to Grahamstown. After British troops reoccupied Bathurst in January 1835, the church was fortified, and it was consecrated on New Year's Day 1838. During the War of the Axe (1846–47) and the Eighth Frontier War (1850–53), it again served as a place of refuge. Also of interest is the water-driven wool mill built by Samuel Bradshaw, a weaver who led a party of 64 Settlers from Gloucestershire. The first of its kind to be built in South Africa, the mill was completed around 1826 and produced blankets and rough cloth for the settlers. One of the country's most extensive collections of early agricultural implements can be seen in the Bathurst Agricultural Museum. The Bathurst district is noted for its pineapple farms, and the 16 m-high giant pineapple on Summerhill Farm is a well-known landmark. The structure offers fine views of the farm, while an audiovisual presentation provides information on the history and cultivation of this fruit. Children in the area are often seen selling hand-made windmills ②.

PORT ALFRED is a popular seaside resort on the banks of the Kowie River, with its trademark arched bridge, and is affectionately referred to by residents as The Kowie. With its expanses of sandy beach and the river – navigable by small craft for 25 km – water-sport enthusiasts are attracted by the marina ④ and excellent opportunities for swimming, angling, water-skiing, surfing and scuba diving. The town developed on the eastern bank of the river around the harbour established in the 1820s to provide a port for the 1820 Settlers. It was originally named Port Frances, after the daughter-in-law of Lord Charles Somerset. A treacherous sandbank at the river mouth, however, hampered the development of the port, and contributed to its closure towards the end of the 1800s. The town was renamed after Prince Alfred, the second son of Queen Victoria, when he visited the Eastern Cape in 1867. Among the town's many historic reminders are the original sneezewood bollard where ships tied up, the old mill on the western bank of the river, the drift where the 1820 Settlers crossed the Kowie River and the Methodist Church, built in 1823.

KOWIE NATURE RESERVE protects 20 ha of dense valley bushveld on the eastern banks of the Kowie River, the name of which comes from a Khoikhoi word meaning 'pipe river'. The best way to reach the reserve is by taking a boat trip along the meandering Kowie River. Facilities include picnic places and a two-hour nature trail along the banks of the river.

WATERS MEETING NATURE RESERVE The Kowie Canoe Trail offers an exciting way of appreciating the scenic beauty of the river, which is lined by tall tree euphorbias. On the first day, canoeists paddle upstream on the incoming tide from Port Alfred to the Waters Meeting Nature Reserve. Situated on the eastern bank of the river, the 4 259-ha reserve offers basic overnight facilities for canoeists and an optional hiking trail. A viewpoint offers magnificent views over the wide Horseshoe Bend in the river. Trailists return to Port Alfred the following day, preferably on the outgoing tide.

BUSHMANS RIVER MOUTH is a popular holiday resort on the western bank of the Bushman's River estuary. The river, navigable for 27 km, is popular with water sport enthusiasts, while the white, sandy beaches attract sunbathers and anglers.

KENTON-ON-SEA lies on the eastern bank of the Bushman's River and stretches 2 km eastwards to the Kariega River, which is navigable for 17 km. Holiday-makers are drawn by the excellent opportunities for water sports and sunbathing. The scenic coastline is characterised by Dune Rock, which has been eroded into fascinating shapes, protected coves and rocky headlands. The Mermaid and Whalerock pools are popular swimming and snorkelling spots.

KWAAIHOEK Originally named Penedo das Fontes (rock of the fountain) by the Portuguese, Kwaaihoek marks the spot where Batholomeu Dias planted a padrão (cross) dedicated to St Gregory on 12 March 1488. Having reached the Keiskamma River a few days earlier, Dias was forced by his reluctant crew to turn back, and erected the cross on the 30-m-high headland. (The promontory is also known as Cape Padrone, a corruption of the 18th-century Portuguese name Ponta do Padrão.) With a height of about 2 m, the limestone cross served as a landmark for over a century, but there are no references to it after the 16th century. After a thorough search by the historian, Professor Eric Axelson, fragments of the cross were discovered early in 1938. The fragments were taken to the University of the Witwatersrand where the cross was reconstructed. A replica was erected at Kwaaihoek in June 1940.

SALEM was established along the banks of the Kowie River by the party of 1820 Settlers led by Hesekiah Sephton. They were accompanied by a Methodist minister, Rev William Shaw, and on 1 January 1822 the foundation stone of a church was laid. A carpenter, Richard Gush, supervised the construction of the church, which was built from mud blocks and thatch. The church was consecrated on 31 December 1824, but in 1832 it was replaced by a rectangular structure built from stone and somewhat resembling a house. During the Frontier Wars, the church often served as a refuge for women and children. Richard Gush, a Quaker pacifist, gained fame during the Sixth Frontier War when he dissuaded the Xhosa from attacking the town. Like a typical English village, Salem has a village green and several well-preserved Settler houses built in the Georgian style. Prominent among these is Upper Crofts, a double-storey house with a façade of whitewashed stonework.

THOMAS BAINES NATURE RESERVE
This reserve covers 1 003 ha of undulating valleys and plains covered mainly in valley bushveld vegetation. The reserve is named after the explorer and artist, Thomas Baines, who came to the Cape in 1842 and lived for some time in Grahamstown. The reserve contains several fine specimens of the tree aloe. For many years, the species name, *Aloe bainesii*, honoured Baines, but it was renamed *Aloe barberae* ③ a few years ago as this was the first scientific name to be published. Visitors can explore the reserve by following 15 km of game-viewing roads; among the species to be seen are white rhino, buffalo, eland, red hartebeest, black wildebeest and mountain reedbuck. Picnic facilities are provided in the southern corner of the park at the Settlers Dam – a popular destination with angling, yachting, boardsailing and canoeing enthusiasts.

4

1 

31
515 KM

 2

GRAAFF-REINET was laid out in the foothills of the Sneeuberg, where the Sundays River makes a wide, horseshoe bend. Established in 1786 and named after Governor Cornelis van der Graaff and his wife, Reinet, it is the fourth-oldest town in South Africa. With its water furrows and period architecture, Graaff Reinet has largely retained the character of a 19th-century rural town, and has the largest number of proclaimed national monuments of any town in South Africa, such as the powder magazine ③. Lining the streets are magnificent Cape Dutch mansions, Victorian cottages with decorative 'broekie-lace' woodwork, a few Georgian houses and flat-roofed Karoo cottages. Among the most outstanding buildings are the H-plan Cape Dutch Reinet House, built in 1812 as a parsonage and now a museum; the Residency (an annex of the museum); and the Drostdy, designed by Louis-Michel Thibault and completed in 1806. Immediately behind the Drostdy is Stretch's Court, a mall lined with quaint mid-19th-century cottages.

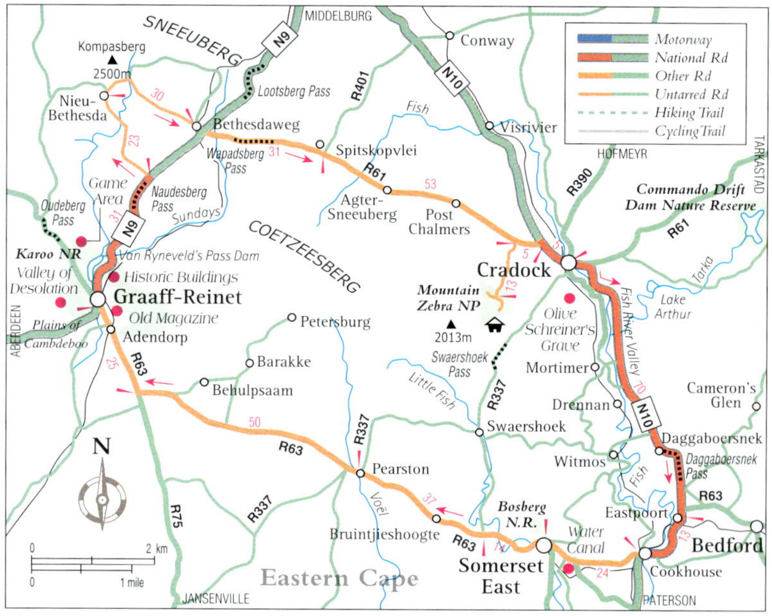

VALLEY OF DESOLATION This scenic natural attraction lies within the Karoo Nature Reserve, which virtually encircles Graaff-Reinet. The 16 500-ha reserve became a reality in 1979 after Dr Anton Rupert, President of the Southern African Nature Foundation (now WWF South Africa), proposed the establishment of a reserve to protect a representative example of Karoo veld. The reserve's most spectacular feature is the Valley of Desolation ④, where erosion has exposed a dolerite dyke which intruded into the softer sedimentary rocks of the Beaufort Series about 150 million years ago. Dolerite is more resistant than sedimentary rock, and deep weathering along the cracks and seams has produced jointed dolerite pillars reaching heights of 90–120 m. From the car park, a 1,5-km walk leads to viewpoints overlooking this spectacle and the Karoo plains far below. Also conspicuous is Spandaukop, a conical hill capped with dolerite.

NIEU-BETHESDA lies in the fertile valley of the Gats River, a tributary of the Sundays River, in the foothills of the Compassberg. The main street is lined with pear trees and quince hedges, which form the boundaries of the plots. Founded by the Reverend Andrew Murray, minister of the Dutch Reformed Church in Graaff-Reinet, it was named after the biblical Bethesda, but later became known as Nu Bethesda and still later as Nieu-Bethesda. Its main attraction is the Owl House ⑤, where artist Helen Martins lived as a recluse until her death in 1976. Considered an eccentric by many, Miss Helen – as she was known – devoted much of her life to the 'search for light and enlightenment'. This search is reflected in the finely ground glass of different colours that covers the walls and ceilings of the house, while numerous mirrors reflect light from candles and lamps in the rooms. Outside in the Camel Yard are hundreds of cement sculptures of owls, camels, lambs, sphinxes, serpents and figures of naked men and women fashioned by Martins and her assistant, Koos Malgas. Also of interest in the village are the water mills dating back to 1860, and the Dutch Reformed Church, consecrated on 11 February 1905.

MOUNTAIN ZEBRA NATIONAL PARK Situated below the Bankberg, this 8 400-ha park was proclaimed in 1937 to save the Cape mountain zebra ① from extinction. The park was established with a nucleus of five stallions and one mare, none of which were still alive by 1960. Fortunately, a neighbouring farmer, Mr JH Lombard, had donated 11 animals to the park in 1950, and their numbers increased to such an extent that mountain zebra could even be translocated to other parks and nature reserves. In addition to the mountain zebra, the park is also a sanctuary to a healthy population of mountain reedbuck, grey rhebok, black wildebeest, red hartebeest, eland, blesbok and kudu. Smaller mammals include klipspringer, common duiker and steenbok, while the carnivores are represented by caracal, Cape and bat-eared foxes and aardwolf. A 42-km circular road leads to Rooiplaat, an area much favoured by game, and along the wooded valley of the Wilgeboom River. Despite its small size, the diversity of game and the spectacular scenery make this park one of the Eastern Cape's top attractions. There are short nature trails, a 25,6-km three-day hiking trail and comfortable accommodation ②.

CRADOCK is the main town in the Eastern Cape Midlands and the centre for the surrounding farms, which are well known for the production of mohair, wool and red meat. The town developed around the fort erected on the farm Buffelshoek in 1813 on the instructions of the British Governor, Sir John Cradock. It was officially named in honour of Cradock on 21 January 1814. One of the town's landmarks is the Dutch Reformed Mother Church, which was completed in 1868. Built from local sandstone, the neoclassical church, with its Doric pillared portico and imposing steeple, is similar in design to the church of St Martin-in-the Fields in London.

One of South Africa's greatest authors, Olive Schreiner, lived in Cradock between 1867 and 1870 in a flat-roofed cottage which has been turned into a museum devoted to her life. Her grave lies on Buffelskop to the south of the town, and can be reached along a 17-km drive. Another attraction is the Karoo Sulphur Spring on the western outskirts of the town. Water from the mineral-rich spring, which has a flow of 4 500 litres of water per hour and a temperature of 31° C, is fed into a swimming pool.

COOKHOUSE lies on the western bank of the Great Fish River, which demarcated the eastern boundary of the Cape Colony until 1819. One explanation of its name is that it referred to a small stone house used as a shelter for the preparation of meals by British troops stationed along the river. Another interpretation is that the name refers to the hot conditions endured by the soldiers.

SOMERSET EAST, a charming country town with oak-lined trees, was laid out on the banks of the Little Fish River in 1825 and named after Governor Lord Charles Somerset. Situated below the Bosberg, the town lies at the centre of a productive sheep and angora farming district. It has several fine examples of Eastern Province Georgian buildings, among them the Old Officers' Mess, built in 1815 by Somerset himself. As a tribute to the South African artist, Walter Batiss, who grew up in Somerset East, the building houses a permanent collection of his art. Also of interest is the Somerset East Museum, with its splendid rose garden and oak trees. Built in 1818, the stately house served as a residence, a *drostdy* (magistrate's court) and as a parsonage. The museum, furnished in the style of a late-19th-century clergyman's home, depicts the history of the town and surrounding district as far back as 1770.

PLAINS OF CAMDEBOO Beyond the Bruintjieshoogte Mountains, the vast Plains of Camdeboo stretch westwards to the Camdeboo Mountains which lie northwest of Aberdeen. It has been suggested that the Khoikhoi name means 'green hollow' or 'green hole', a reference to a hippo pool surrounded by lush greenery. The first loan farms in the Camdeboo were given out in 1770, and in 1785 it was incorporated into the newly proclaimed district of Graaff-Reinet. The author, Eve Palmer, gave a vivid description of life in the Camdeboo in her book, *The Plains of Camdeboo* (1966).

3

4

5

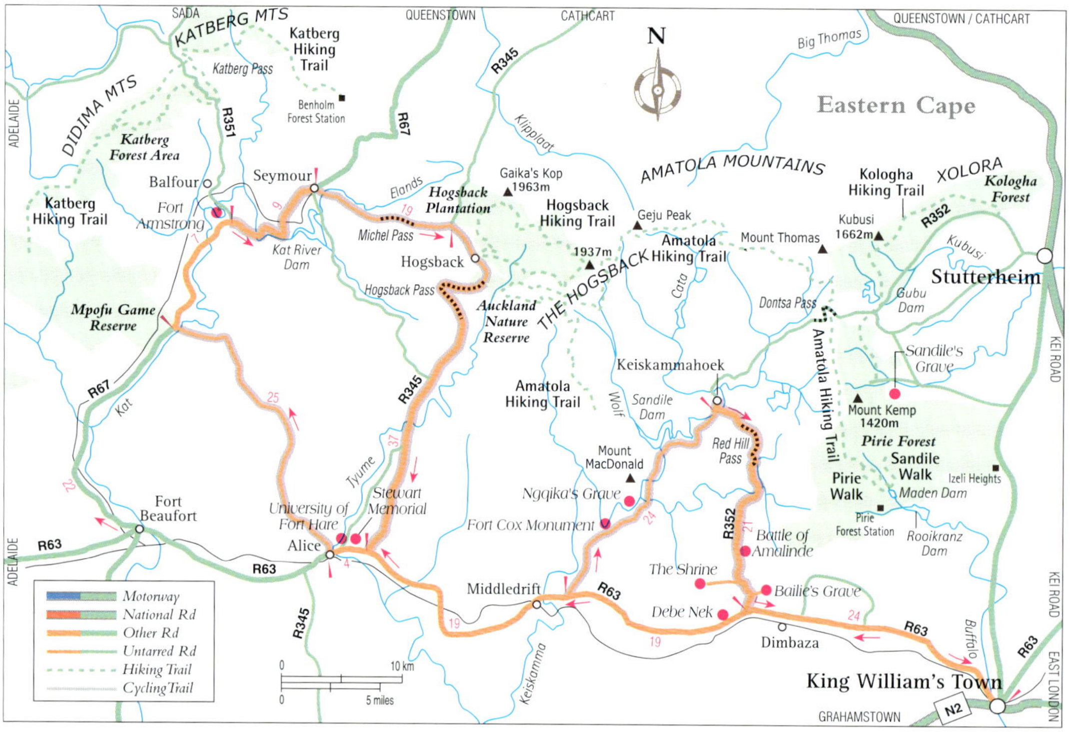

32
275 KM

1

ALICE lies on the western bank of the Tyume River and was founded in 1847 at the end of the War of the Axe (1846–47). The town of Alice was named after one of Queen Victoria's daughters, and was once the administrative centre of the Victoria East District.

On the outskirts of Alice is the University of Fort Hare, named after the fort built along the east bank of the Tyume River in 1847. The largest fort in the Eastern Cape, it was named after Lieutenant-Colonel John Hare, acting Lieutenant-General of the Eastern Province in 1838. The university was established in 1916 as the South African Native College on land donated by the Church of Scotland; among its many distinguished alumni are Nelson Mandela, Oliver Tambo and Seretse Khama. In terms of apartheid South Africa's policy of Bantu education, it became an ethnic university for Xhosa-speaking students in 1959. Throughout the 1960s, Fort Hare was one of the main centres of the Black Consciousness Movement, and in the 1970s and 1980s its students participated actively in class boycotts and student unrest.

KING WILLIAM'S TOWN has its origins in the Buffalo Mission Station established on the east bank of the Buffalo River by the Reverend John Brownlee of the London Missionary Society in 1825. Following the Sixth Frontier War (1834–35), the British Governor, Sir Benjamin D'Urban, annexed the land between the Keiskamma and the Kei rivers, naming it the Province of Queen Adelaide. A fort was built near the ruins of the mission station (destroyed during the war) and on 24 May 1835 the site was proclaimed the capital of the new province. It was named after the reigning monarch, William IV. The British government, however, refused to ratify the annexation, and barely seven months later the province was abolished. At the outbreak of the Seventh Frontier War (1846–47) the frontier territory was reoccupied by British forces, and on 23 December 1847 the Crown Colony of Kaffraria was proclaimed, with King William's Town as its capital.

The Amathole Museum (formerly known as the Kaffrarian Museum) has interesting displays on the region's German settlers, as well as a world-famous collection of over 40 000 mammals. Its most celebrated exhibit is Huberta, a hippopotamus that wandered approximately 700 km from Zululand to the Keiskamma River between 1928 and 1931. The SA Missionary Museum is appropriately housed in the Gothic Revival-style Wesleyan Church, built in 1855. Among King William's Town's many historic buildings are Grey Hospital (1859), Town Hall (1867), the Old Court House and Post Office (1877), British Kaffrarian Savings Bank (1908) and the Old Residency.

DIMBAZA was established in the late 1960s as a 'resettlement village', a euphemism for the dumping grounds for black people moved out of white areas in apartheid South Africa. Between 1970 and 1980, the population of Dimbaza grew from 3 600 to 18 700 and Dimbaza became synonymous with abject poverty, overpopulation and environmental degradation. Industrial development only began in 1973. Five years later some 18 factories, employing just over 1 000 people, had been established, focussing mainly on textiles, clothing, leather products and furniture. Following Ciskei's 'independence' from South Africa in 1982, Dimbaza was identified as Ciskei's industrial capital. Like the other homelands, Ciskei was reintegrated into South Africa in 1994.

DEBE NEK marks the western extremity of the Kommetjies Flats, a plain pitted with ring-like mounds, or *kommetjies*, each about a metre in diameter and with a central bowl 30–100 cm deep. Stretching from about 10 km west of King William's Town, the flats extend for about 16 km^2 around Debe Nek. The *kommetjies* are said to be composed of the casts of the world's largest known earthworms, the giant *Microchaetus*, which are reputed to attain a length of up to 7 m.

SEYMOUR ③, a small rural village at the foot of the Katberg, also owes its origin to a military post established in 1846 at what was originally known as Elands Post. A fort was built on the plateau next to the village, and when the town was laid out seven years later it was named after Lieutenant-Colonel Charles Seymour, military secretary to Sir George Cathcart. In the late 1800s, part of the fort was converted into a residence for the magistrate. A sandstone sundial erected on the site of Elands Post in 1839 can be seen in the garden of the Residence. Another relic of the village's military past is the Seymour Hotel, which served as a mess and recreation centre for the garrison in 1852.

HOGSBACK is a tranquil village set amid indigenous forests ②, pine plantations, streams and waterfalls on the slopes of the Amatola Mountains. The English country gardens, with their azaleas, rhododendrons and hydrangeas, as well as peach, apple and plum trees and berry bushes, are the legacy of Thomas Summerton, who settled at Hogsback in the 1880s. The village is famous for its berries, among them wild blackberries, blackcurrants, strawberries, raspberries and gooseberries. Unlikely to escape attention are the tunnel-like avenues of hazel trees, while the Oak Avenue is a popular short walk. Visitors can explore the magnificent indigenous forests by following a network of trails ①. Attractions include the Big Tree, a 34-m-high yellowwood, and waterfalls with descriptive names such as Madonna and Child, Kettlespout, Swallowtail, Bridal Veil and Thirty-Nine Steps. Another attraction is St Patrick-on-the-Hill, a small circular memorial chapel built of dressed stone by the Houghton family in 1935. In October each year, Hogsback hosts an arts festival featuring cabaret, piano recitals, jazz and classical guitar music, as well as songs and dance.

KEISKAMMAHOEK The R63 road to Keiskammahoek leads past several historic sites relating to the Frontier Wars. Heading in a northwesterly direction, the road passes the site of Fort Cox, one of the many military posts established during the Frontier Wars and named after Major William Cox of the Gordon Highlanders. Built in 1847, the fort was further strengthened in 1850 and served as a central staging point. A short way on is Burnshill, where British forces suffered defeat during the War of the Axe (1846–47). The Burnshill Mission, established in 1830, was named after John Burns, one of the founders of the Glasgow Missionary Society. A short way on lies the turnoff to the grave of Chief Ngqika Gaika, father of Sandile. He died on 13 November 1829, and was buried on the site of his kraal. At Boma Pass, at the top end of Sandile Dam, a 700-strong British force that had set off from Fort Cox was ambushed in a narrow gorge on Christmas Eve in 1850. Twenty-three British soldiers were killed in the attack, which became a prelude to the Eighth Frontier War (1850–53), also known as the War of Mlanjeni.

Keiskammahoek lies in a basin at the confluence of the Keiskamma and Gxulu rivers below the Amatola Mountains. Established as one of a chain of military outposts, it played an important role in the Frontier Wars between 1846 and 1853. Castle Eyre, on the western outskirts of the settlement, was built in 1852. The town is an important commercial centre for the timber and agricultural (livestock and tobacco) industries.

From Keiskammahoek, the R63 leads over Red Hill Pass in a southerly direction. Amalinde marks the site of the bloodiest battle in the history of the Xhosa-speaking people west of the Kei River. The battle was precipitated by the claim of Chief Ngqika Gaika to chieftainship over the Rharabe Xhosa, which led to a quarrel with his uncle, Ndlambe. In 1818 Chief Ngqika's son, Maqoma, was defeated by Ndlambe at the Battle of Amalinde, but a British force came to the assistance of Ngqika and defeated Ndlambe. A short way further on is the turnoff to the Ntaba ka Ndoda National Shrine. Situated at the foot of the mountain of the same name, the shrine was built in honour of the Xhosa chiefs who fought against British rule. Continuing further, there is a memorial on the left of the road marking the spot where Lieutenant Bailey and his men were killed in action during the Frontier War of 1834–35. The name Keiskamma is of Khoekhoen origin, meaning either 'puffadder river' or 'glittering water'.

2

3

1

33
400 KM

2

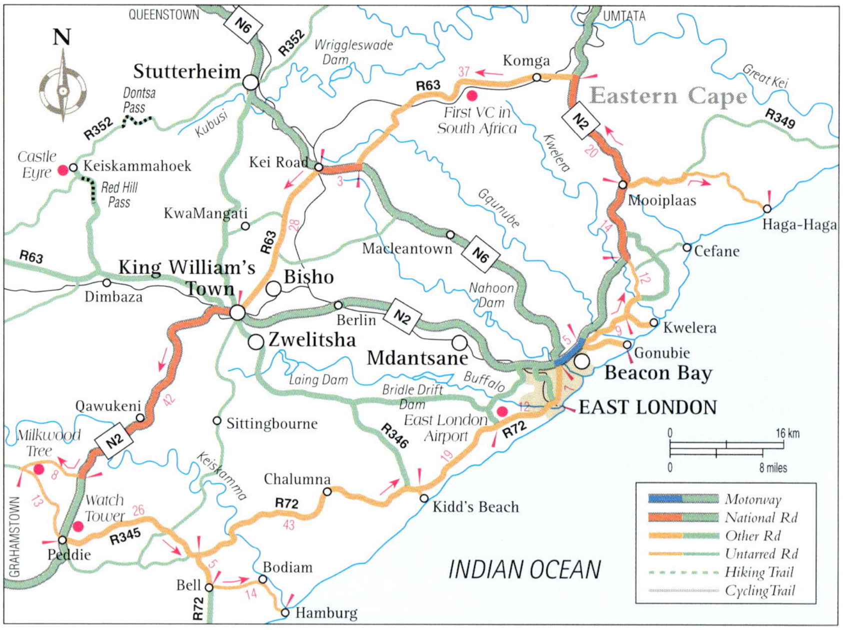

EAST LONDON developed around the port established in 1847 as a landing place for British troops and supplies destined for the eastern Cape frontier. Situated at the mouth of the Buffalo River, the settlement was first named Port Rex but was renamed East London in 1848. The city is famed for its long stretches of beach ③ which attract numerous sunbathers, anglers and surfers. Eastern, Orient and Nahoon beaches are popular with sunbathers; Bonza Bay and Nahoon offer ideal conditions for boardsailing while Nahoon Reef is an internationally noted surfing destination.

Among the city's historical links with the turbulent period of the Frontier Wars is the old powder magazine on the site of Fort Glamorgan, built in 1849 against a hill on the western bank of the Buffalo River. Gately House, built in 1878, is an excellent example of a period townhouse. It contains a fine collection of Victorian furnishings and serves as the city's Town House Museum. The Ann Bryant Art Gallery has a valuable collection of works by English and South African artists.

Among the other historic buildings are the City Hall (1899), Public Library (1906) and Cuthberts Building. The East London Museum focuses on the natural and cultural history of the Border area. Among its displays are a gallery devoted to the coelacanth, comprehensive collections of South African fish and seashells and ethnographic collections focusing on the Xhosa-speaking people. East London's Steve Biko Memorial commemorates the death of the father of the Black Consciousness Movement, who died in police custody from injuries he sustained during interrogation in Port Elizabeth in 1977.

GONUBIE Set against a backdrop of forested dunes, the coastal town of Gonubie lies alongside a tranquil lagoon at the mouth of the Gqunube River. The river – navigable for 5 km upstream – coastline and open ocean offer excellent angling possibilities. Visitors can enjoy swimming ①, sunbathing, surfing and a walk on the boardwalk ②, while several sporting facilities are available in the town. The name is said to be Khoikhoi in origin, meaning 'bramble river'.

KWELERA This holiday towns owes its name to the Kwelera River, a corruption of the Khoikhoi name Goerecha, meaning 'many aloes'. The rocky beach here is a longstanding favourite with anglers.

HAGA-HAGA ④ is a beautiful seaside village flanked by sandy beaches at the foot of green hills. The lagoon and beach offer safe swimming, while the rocks extending along the seafront present good angling opportunities.

KOMGA Lying amid rolling green grasslands, Komga was established as an agricultural centre in 1877 on the site of a military camp established 23 years earlier. The Khoikhoi name is said to mean 'lots of clay', or 'clayish'. A monument in the town recalls the epic 1842 journey of Dick King, who covered the 960-km distance between Port Natal (now Durban) and Grahamstown on horseback in ten days.

VICTORIA CROSS MEMORIAL About 20 km west of Komga, a stone monument honours Major Hans Garett Moore, the first recipient of the Victoria Cross in South Africa. During the Battle of Draaibosch, fought here on 29 and 30 December 1877, Moore and three others went to the assistance of a comrade named Giese who had been overtaken by the Xhosa. Their heroic attempt failed to save Giese, and Moore was stabbed in the forearm. The following day, a patrol led by Moore was attacked by a Xhosa force of 1 000 warriors on foot and 600 mounted men. Moore and his men held off the attackers, who eventually fled.

BISHO, a Xhosa name meaning 'buffalo', lies to the east of King William's Town. It was built by the South African government as the capital of the Ciskei homeland after the apartheid government refused to incorporate King William's Town into the Ciskei, which became 'independent' in 1982. Following the reintegration of Ciskei into South Africa in 1994, Bisho became the capital of the Eastern Cape province. Among the sites relating to the struggle against apartheid is the grave of Steve Biko, who was born in Ginsberg township on the outskirts of King William's Town. Also of interest is the site of the Bisho Massacre, where 28 people were killed and 200 injured when Ciskei soldiers opened fire on thousands of ANC marchers on 7 September 1992.

KING WILLIAM'S TOWN See Tour 32, page 80.

MILKWOOD TREE This famous milkwood, known as the Umqwashu tree, is a symbol of the Mfengu people's release from subservience to the Gcaleka people. Their decision to seek British protection during the Sixth Frontier War (1834–35) incurred the wrath of Chief Hintsa. To create a buffer against Xhosa attacks, the British Governor, Sir Benjamin D'Urban, ordered the resettlement of the Mfengu south of Fort Peddie. Protected by troops of the 2nd Division, some 17 000 Mfengu men, women and children moved westwards across the Kei and the Keiskamma rivers. Having finally reached safety, the Mfengu affirmed their loyalty to God and the British monarch at this spot.

PEDDIE was once one of the most important military posts on the eastern frontier of the old Cape Colony. In 1835 a fort shaped like an eight-pointed star was built at Peddie as part of a defence line west of the Keiskamma River. It played an important role in protecting the Mfengu against attacks by the Xhosa and in the defence of the eastern frontier. The sturdy stone-built watch tower dates back to 1841, when the fort was strengthened. To protect those inside, the entrance to the double-storey building was placed 3 m above the ground, with a retractable entry ladder. A cannon could be fired from the roof. Just outside Peddie, on the road to Hamburg, are the church and residence of the Reverend John Ayliff, who accompanied the Mfengu to Peddie, and the Durban or Ayliff Methodist mission station.

HAMBURG was one of the villages in British Kaffraria where over 2 900 German immigrants were settled in 1857 in yet another attempt to stabilise the volatile eastern frontier. The emigration scheme was funded by the British government and the emigrants were recruited from members of the King's German Legion, a military unit disbanded after the Crimean War. The village was named after Hamburg in Germany. Situated on the southern bank of the Keiskamma River, the village is a popular holiday destination, offering excellent river boating and surf angling, and sweeping white beaches.

KIDD'S BEACH lies on the southern shores of the lagoon formed by the Mcantsi River. The lagoon, sandy beach at the mouth of the Mcantsi River and tidal pool offer safe swimming, while the outstanding waves are popular with surfing and boardsailing enthusiasts. Anglers are attracted by the excellent fishing opportunities along the rocky coastline. The village was named after Charles Kidd, who was mayor of East London in the 1860s.

3

4

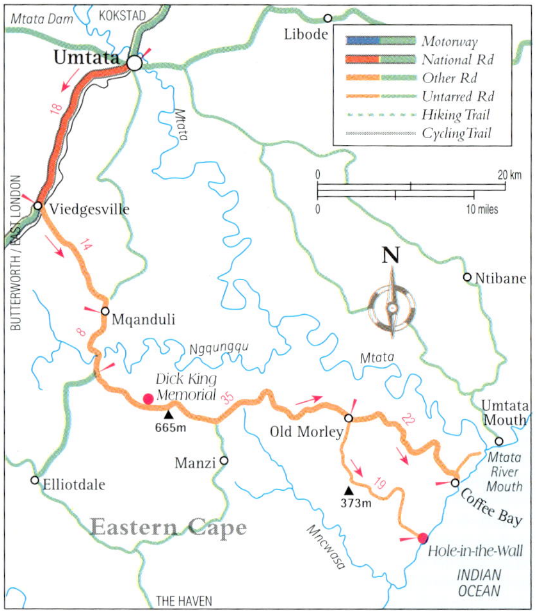

34
275 KM

1

UMTATA lies on the banks of the Mtata River, after which it has been named. Although the name was already in existence in 1688, there are several explanations for its origin. Among these is the abundance of umThathi trees, or sneezewood, growing along the river. Another explanation is that the name is derived from the custom of the Thembu people to place their dead in the river. The bodies were cast into the river with the words 'mThathe Bawo' (take them, Father), and it has been suggested that the noun 'Umtata' was evolved to name the river.

Situated in Thembuland, Umtata developed around the settlement founded on the river's south bank in 1871. The Paramount Chief of the Thembu, Ngangelizwe, granted land to a group of white settlers to act as a buffer against attacks by the Pondo living north of the river. The settlement expanded steadily after the Anglican Church founded a mission, and an influx of traders and a group of Voortrekkers also swelled the number of inhabitants. Umtata became the administrative centre of the General Council for the Transkeian Territories, established in 1902 to combine the various territorial councils under a single authority. When Transkei became 'independent' from South Africa on 26 October 1976, Umtata became the capital. Among the places of interest are the dome-shaped Bunga, which served as the Transkeian 'parliament' for over 50 years, and the sandstone Town Hall, built in 1908. The mounted cannon in front of the Town Hall is one of several salvaged from the famed wreck of the *Grosvenor*, which ran aground south of the Msikaba River on the night of 2 August 1782.

BOMVANALAND The coastal area between the Mtata and the Mbashe rivers is mainly inhabited by the Bomvana people, one of 12 clusters or complexes of the Southern Nguni or Xhosa-speaking people of the Eastern Cape. Bomvanaland was ceded to the British government in February 1878, and became known as the Elliotdale District. In December the same year it was incorporated into Thembuland. From Viedgesville the road to Hole-in-the-Wall and Coffee Bay meanders across an undulating landscape characterised by round mud and thatch homesteads ⑤ perched on grassy hill slopes and crests. The homes generally face east and often only the east-facing aspect is painted white, while the remainder of the house is left a natural grey colour. In the early mornings, smoke from wood fires drifts into the air and cattle bellow in their wooden stockades as villagers prepare to go about their daily tasks: tending to small patches of maize, grazing their herds and fetching water and firewood. At bus stops, groups of people engage in conversation while waiting patiently for transport, while women balancing heavy loads on their heads are a familiar sight outside trading stores, as are Xhosa initiates ①. Stray animals are a constant threat, and motorists are thus cautioned to be alert at all times.

MQANDULI was proclaimed a magistracy in 1876, and was once an important administrative and commercial centre of Bomvanaland. The village owes its name to a nearby hill, and the name is said to mean 'grindstone-maker' – a reference to a craftsman who once lived there.

DICK KING MEMORIAL This memorial is one of several erected on the route taken by Richard Philip King, better known as Dick King, during his epic ride from Port Natal (now Durban) to Grahamstown. Following the second British occupation of Natal in May 1842, a 250-strong British force under Captain TC Smith was besieged by the Natal Voortrekkers. Realising their desperate situation, King and his attendant made the 960 km journey in ten days to summon help. The siege of Port Natal was lifted in late June when a relief force arrived by sea.

HOLE-IN-THE-WALL ③ is one of the most impressive landmarks along the Wild Coast. Standing at the mouth of the Mpako River, the cliff consists of dark-blue shales, mudstones and sandstones of the Ecca Group, dating back some 260 million years. These rocks were subsequently intruded by a dolerite sheet, and the 'hole' was created over millions of years by the buffeting waves, which eroded away the softer rocks underneath the dolerite to form an arch. The same process also eventually separated the cliff from the mainland. Hole-in-the-Wall was named by Captain Vidal of the vessel *Barracouta*, sent by the British Admiralty in 1823 to survey the coastline between the Keiskamma River and Lourenço Marques (now Maputo). Vidal took his ship to within 800 m of the coast, '... where two ponderous black rocks above the water's edge, upwards of 80 feet above its surface, exhibiting through the phenomenon of a natural archway', prompting him to name it the Hole-in-the-Wall. The local Bomvana people named the formation 'EsiKhaleni', or the Place of the Sound. Many ships, such as the *Jacaranda* ④ near Qolora Mouth, have been wrecked along this treacherous coastline.

Local legend has it that the Mpako River once formed a landlocked lagoon as its access to the sea was blocked by the cliff. When one of the 'sea people' fell in love with a beautiful girl living in a village on the edge of the lagoon, the girl's father forbade her to see her lover. At high tide one night, the sea people came to the cliff and, with the help of a huge fish, rammed a hole through the centre of the cliff. As they swam into the lagoon they shouted and sang, causing the villagers to hide in fear. In the commotion the girl and her lover were reunited and disappeared into the sea. On certain nights, it is said, the singing and shouting of the sea people can still be heard.

COFFEE BAY is a well-known Wild Coast holiday resort nestling below grassy hills and coastal dunes at the mouths of the Nenga and Mbomvu rivers. The rocky coastline ② here is popular with rock and surf anglers, while sunbathers are attracted to the 1-km-long stretch of sheltered beach. Coffee Bay is said to owe its name to a cargo of coffee beans that was washed ashore after a ship ran aground nearby. Some of the beans were washed into the lagoon of the Nenga River where they took root and stuggled for many years to grow. The date and name of the ship are obscure, but it has been suggested that it could have been the *Hercules*, which was wrecked near the mouth of the Mtata River in 1852, or a vessel which ran aground in the bay in 1863.

MTATA RIVER MOUTH is typical of the magnificent coastal scenery of the Wild Coast. Here, a large sandbar forces the Mtata River into a narrow channel overlooked by a rocky outcrop with a profusion of tree euphorbias. On the river's eastern bank, the rocky coastline gives way to a 2-km stretch of white sandy beach. Before setting off on this detour, motorists are advised to enquire about the condition of the track.

2

3

4

5

35
320 KM

1

2

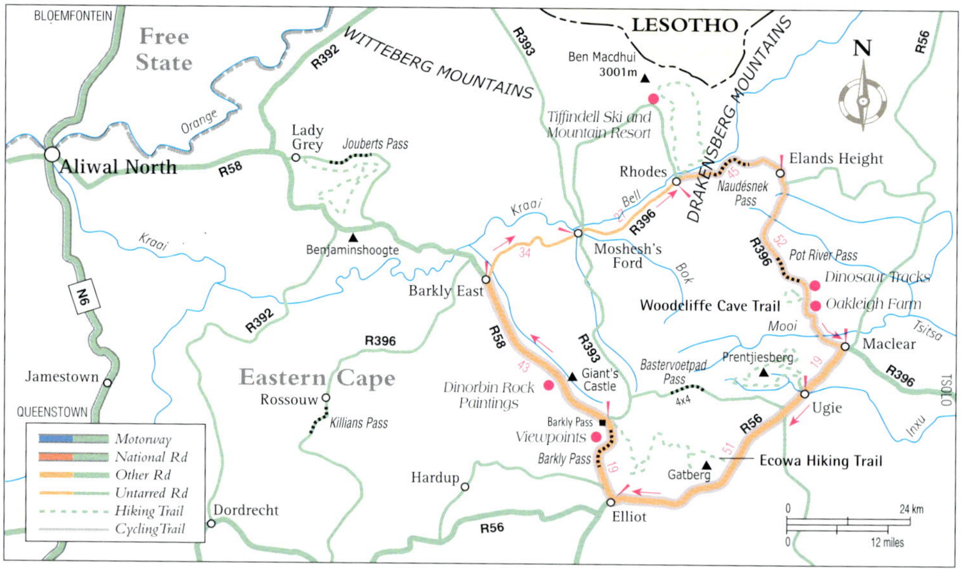

NAUDÉSNEK PASS At the foot of the Naudésnek Pass (1 920 m) ②, the road passes a monument to the intrepid Naudé brothers, who built a rough track across the mountains in 1896. Using picks, shovels and a horse cart, they followed the route that their horses instinctively took when they were driven up the mountain. Following much of the original route, road engineer George Mandy constructed a military road linking Maclear with Lundin's Nek in 1911. From the foot of the pass, the road climbs steeply out of the Bell River valley in a series of switchbacks to the 2 500-m-high summit of the pass, from where there are spectacular views over the undulating countryside to the south.

BARKLY EAST Nestling in the foothills of the Cape Drakensberg at 1 813 m, Barkly East ① is one of the highest, coldest towns in the country. In winter, the high mountain peaks are often snowcapped, while snow sometimes blankets the town and surrounding grasslands, creating scenes more reminiscent of Europe than of the northeastern Cape – hence the town's claim to being the Switzerland of South Africa. Barkly East was established in 1874 and named after Sir Henry Barkly, Governor of the Cape from 1870 to 1877. It is the commercial centre for the surrounding merino sheep farms, and the district is also well known for its cattle studs, dairy produce, grain and potatoes. The town cemetery contains the grave of Lord Kitchener's horse, which was buried during the South African War.

There are several beautiful sandstone buildings, among them the Dutch Reformed Church and the local museum, which focuses on early forms of transportation and the town's history. Also of interest is the unique railway linking Barkly East with Lady Grey to the northwest. Owing to the mountainous terrain, a system of eight 'reverses' was incorporated into the line, which has a gradient of 1 in 36, one of only two such systems in the world. The Class 19D steam locomotive that stands in the town's square is a reminder of the early days of rail transport.

RHODES lies in the tranquil valley of the Bell River, dominated by the high peaks of the Drakensberg. Founded in 1893, the settlement was originally named Rossville after Reverend David Ross, the Dutch Reformed minister of Lady Grey. In 1900, it was renamed after Cecil John Rhodes, Prime Minister of the Cape, who, as a gesture of appreciation, sent a wagon-load of stone pine trees, which still dominate the village centre. The Rhodes Hotel, with its Victorian architecture and small-town charm, was originally known as The Horseshoe. The old stone-built school and hostel were designed by the renowned architect Sir Herbert Baker, and accommodated 250 children during the village's heyday. Over the years, though, the population of this once-thriving farming community dwindled; the school was closed in the 1970s when there were only 11 pupils.

Today, Rhodes is a popular winter destination when the slopes of 3 001-m-high Ben MacDhui (the Eastern Cape Drakensberg's highest point) are covered in snow, creating ideal skiing conditions. At Tiffindell, 25 km north of Rhodes, winter snowfalls are supplemented by snow-making machines. In summer, the mountain streams offer fine trout angling opportunities. Other popular activities are horse-riding, hiking and birding.

OAKLEIGH FARM DINOSAUR TRACKS Imprinted in the rock along the banks of the Pot River are the tracks of a large, four-footed dinosaur and a smaller, two-legged one. Although southern Africa has an abundance of dinosaur fossils, these tracks are of particular interest as they are preserved in the Molteno Formation, the lowest formation of the Stormberg Series. This places the tracks among the earliest evidence of dinosaurs in the subcontinent, dating back some 180 million years. The four-footed dinosaur, which also left behind the mark of its dragging tail, was probably a member of the Prosauropoda, one of the most primitive groups of plant-eating dinosaurs. The two-legged tracks were made by a small theropod, a fast carnivorous dinosaur that moved on its hind legs and appears to have hunted in packs. There are tracks of at least seven theropods, formed when these primitive reptiles walked across the muddy bed of an ancient river. As the water subsided, the mud dried out, preserving the tracks and forming mud cracks – still visible on the surface.

MACLEAR lies in the valley of the Mooi River amid white sandstone outcrops, rolling grasslands where sheep graze, and maize fields. The town grew up around the military camp established in 1876 for troops travelling to Matatiele and was named after Sir Thomas Maclear, the Astronomer Royal at the Cape from 1833 to 1870. As the terminal of the branch railway line from Sterkstroom, the town serves the district's sheep and cattle farms, while dairy products, wheat and maize are also produced. Places of interest include the historic dressed-stone Sivewright Bridge, built in 1890 and named after the first member elected to represent the area in the House of Assembly in 1888. Also worth visiting is the 26-m-high Tsitsa Falls, situated a few kilometres outside the town. The clear mountain streams around Maclear are a popular drawcard with trout anglers.

UGIE developed around the mission station established in 1863 on the banks of the Inxu River by the Reverend William Murray. The mission was named after a river of the same name in Aberdeenshire, Scotland, near Murray's place of birth. The town was founded in 1885 when land was sold, and it remains an agricultural centre today. An extensive collection of agricultural implements and equipment can be seen in the town's Tractor Museum. To the northwest of Ugie lies the picturesque Prentjiesberg ('picture mountain'), with its interesting crenellated spires and rocky turrets. The mountain was named after the numerous rock paintings (attributed to the San) found in the caves and overhangs. The streams in the area are well stocked with trout.

ELLIOT Laid out in a valley of the Slang River, the farming town of Elliot ③ is set against a backdrop of rugged mountains with magnificent sandstone formations. The town was established in 1885, and its name honours Sir Henry George Elliot, Chief Magistrate of the Transkeian territories from 1891 to 1902. Its Xhosa name, Ekowa, means 'mushroom', a reference to the fungi growing in the area in summer. To the northeast of Elliot, the scenery is dominated by the Gatberg, which rises 440 m above the valley below. This landmark owes its Afrikaans name (meaning 'hole mountain') to the hole that has been eroded through the softer strata near its summit. The Xhosa name, uNtunjinkala, means 'crab's opening'. The majestic 80-m-high Gillie Cullem Waterfall lies 18 km south of the town.

BARKLY PASS ④ meanders for 10 km from Elliot over the southern Drakensberg. From the 2 012-m-high summit there are magnificent vistas of the rolling grasslands, deep ravines and valleys lying more than 600 m below, and on a clear day the Indian Ocean can be seen some 80 km away. Interesting natural rock sculptures, such as Camel Rock, Vulture's Roost and the Castle, can be viewed from several vantage points to the west of the summit.

DINORBIN ROCK PAINTINGS Although many of the caves and overhangs in the Eastern Cape Drakensberg are adorned with beautiful rock paintings, the Dinorbin site ⑤ features one of the longest known galleries in South Africa. Stretching over a distance of 32 m, the paintings (attributed to the San) include rhebok, human figures in various postures, therianthropes (partly animal, partly human forms) and large eland.

3

4

5

KWAZULU-NATAL COAST, MIDLANDS & DRAKENSBERG

OPPOSITE TOP LEFT UMHLANGA LIGHTHOUSE (P.93); TOP RIGHT: DURBAN FISHERMEN (P.92); BOTTOM: DURBAN RICKSHA DRIVER (P.92); **THIS PAGE** TOP LEFT: ZULU CRAFTS (P.92).; TOP RIGHT: UMGENI RIVER BIRD PARK (P.92); CENTRE: DURBAN (P.92). ABOVE LEFT: INDIAN SARIS, DURBAN (P.92); ABOVE CENTRE: DRAKENSBERG SKIING (P.99); ABOVE RIGHT: ORIBI (P.91).

1

36
180 KM

2

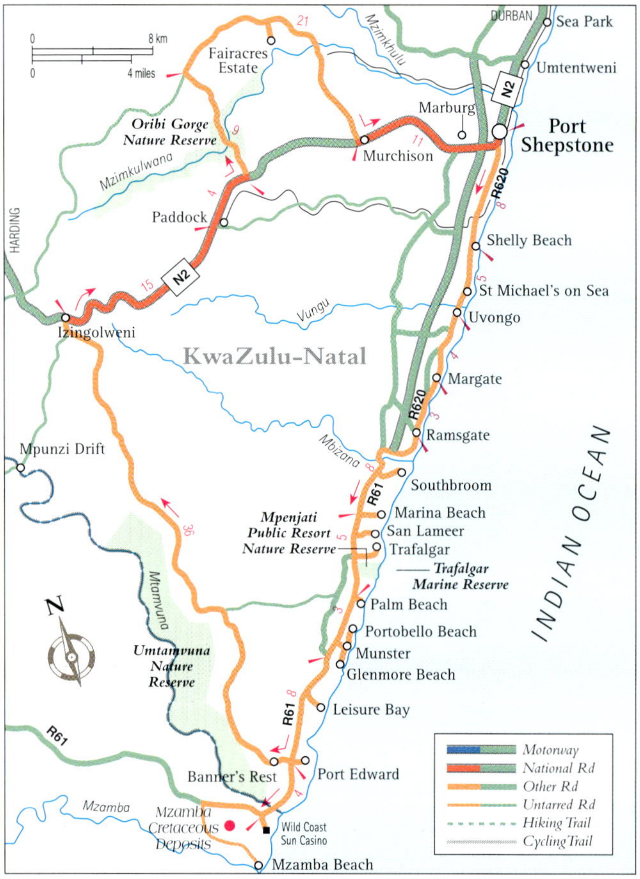

PORT SHEPSTONE lies along KwaZulu-Natal's Hibiscus Coast – known for its many hibiscus flowers ① – which stretches from Scottburgh to Port Edward. Situated at the mouth of the Mzimkhulu River (a Zulu name meaning 'place of the great kraal'), it was the discovery of marble deposits on the bank of the river in 1867 that first attracted settlers to the area. The town was established four years later and named after Sir Theophilus Shepstone, Administrator of Native Affairs in the Natal government. The river mouth soon became a port for the export of marble, lime and sugar. The harbour was developed following the arrival of a party of 246 Norwegian immigrants in 1886, but the port fell into disuse after the railway line reached the town in 1901.

The largest town along the South Coast, Port Shepstone is a popular resort, offering safe bathing in a tidal pool and a lighthouse as a landmark ②. The coast and estuary offer good angling opportunities, while boating is possible on the river. The history of the town is depicted in the Port Shepstone Museum, which has a maritime focus. One of the largest collections of seashells in South Africa can be seen at the Sea Shell Museum at Shelly Beach, a few kilometres south of Port Shepstone.

BANANA EXPRESS The only remaining narrow-gauge (610 mm) passenger train in KwaZulu-Natal, the Banana Express operates regular tourist excursions between Port Shepstone and Paddock. Construction of the 122-km-long rail line between Port Shepstone and Harding dates back to the early 1900s. By 1911, the first 40 km was completed as far as Paddock Station and the line was subsequently extended to Harding. For many years, sugar cane, timber, cement and fertiliser were hauled along the line, but in 1986 the line was closed as it had become uneconomical. It was reopened in December the following year, and is operated by the Port Shepstone and Alfred County Railway Company. The passenger coaches are hauled by a narrow-gauge Garratt 16A locomotive. Numbers 155 and 156, which are owned by the Alfred County Railway, were the last Garratt-class locomotives built in the world. The 60-tonne locomotives can pull a load of 150 tonnes on 14 trucks up a gradient of 1 in 37. Paddock Station, a national monument, marks the end of the excursion. Here, passengers can enjoy lunch under the trees in the tranquil grounds of the stationmaster's house.

UVONGO is a picturesque seaside resort with an attractive garden layout and a beautiful lagoon. The name is a corruption of the Zulu word *ivungu*, which means 'the place of a low, rumbling sound' – a reference to the sound made by the 23-m-high waterfall which plunges into the lagoon near the beach. The resort, together with nearby St Michael's-on-Sea and Manaba Beach, offers tidal swimming pools, safe bathing, boating on the Vungu Lagoon and good angling opportunities. St Michael's-on-Sea is a popular destination for surfing enthusiasts, and is renowned for the excellent waves to be found when southwesterly winds blow. A large variety of colourful exotic and indigenous birds can be seen at the Uvongo Bird Park, which features a walk-in aviary.

MARGATE is one of the most popular coastal resorts ③ along the Hibiscus Coast. Proclaimed a township in 1941, it was named after the seaside resort of the same name in England. Its beachfront features a magnificent palm-lined beach (popular with sun-worshippers and bathers), grassy terraces, an amusement park and a wide range of sporting and entertainment facilities. The Nkhongweni River forms a magnificent lagoon at its mouth, which can be explored in canoes or paddle boats. The coast is popular with rock and surf anglers – especially in winter when schools of shad follow the Sardine Run – as well as with ski-boat anglers. Strung along the coast south of Margate are the seaside resorts of Ramsgate, Southbroom, Marina Beach, San Lameer, Trafalgar, Palm Beach and Munster.

PORT EDWARD, the most southerly resort along the KwaZulu-Natal coast, has a fine stretch of sandy beach as its main attraction. Situated 4 km north of the Mtamvuna River near the CH Mitchell Bridge ④, the town was established in 1924 on the farm Bannerman's Rest and named after the Prince of Wales (later King Edward VIII). Tragedy Hill, overlooking Silver Beach, marks the spot where a party led by the well-known trader, Henry Francis Fynn, was murdered in 1831 after they were suspected of being in possession of cattle stolen from the Zulu king, Dingane. Fynn escaped the massacre, but the others were less fortunate.

MZAMBA CRETACEOUS DEPOSITS These famous marine fossil beds are exposed in a 10-m-high cliff that forms a prominent headland about 2,5 km south of the Mtamvuna River, a Xhosa name meaning 'the reaper of mouthfuls'. The deposits consist of greyish-brown sandstone, and limestone rich in fossil material dating back some 80 million years to the Upper Cretaceous period. The lower layers contain numerous tree trunks that have been silicified (converted into silica). Many of these were penetrated by marine worms before silicification was completed. There is also an abundance of marine shells, among them spirally coiled cephalopod ammonites, echinoids (sea urchins) and bivalve shells. When the formation was brought to the attention of the scientific world in 1855, it provided the first evidence of fossils from the Upper Cretaceous.

ORIBI GORGE NATURE RESERVE covers 1 837 ha of spectacular scenery created over aeons by the Mzimkhulwana River, which has carved a 20-km-long gorge – up to 350 m deep in places – through the sandstones and granites of the Oribi Flats. The densely forested slopes of the gorge are another outstanding feature of the reserve. Among the rich variety of trees growing here are tarwood, red-stem corkwood, Natal wild banana, rock ash, mountain fig, Outeniqua and real yellowwoods, large-leaved dragon tree and forest bushwillow. The forests are home to leopard, bushbuck, blue duiker and samango monkey, while the grasslands are the habitat of the oribi, a small antelope for which the reserve is named. To date, over 220 bird species have been recorded, including the Knysna lourie, Narina trogon, crowned and trumpeter hornbills, cinnamon dove, brown robin and the bluemantled flycatcher. Visitors can explore the reserve along a network of six nature walks, ranging from 1 km to 9 km. There are two delightful picnic sites along the pass that meanders through the reserve.

FAIRACRES ESTATE This area has long been popular with visitors, and the original hotel on the Fairacres Estate dates back to 1860. From vantage points along the cliff edge, visitors can enjoy spectacular views of the Oribi Gorge far below. Not to be missed is the viewsite overlooking the Horseshoe Bend in the Mzimkhulwana River, while there are also splendid panoramas of the Mzimkhulu Valley to the east. There are also numerous fascinating rock formations with imaginative names like the Overhanging Rock, Sphinx, Pulpit, Leaning Tower and Baboon's Castle – the latter a rocky citadel rising from the slopes of the gorge. Another popular feature is Lehr's Waterfall, which plunges over a sheer cliff in a tributary of the Mzimkhulwana River. The adventurous can tackle a 101-m abseil down a sheer rockface overlooking the waterfall.

3

4

1

37
210 KM

2

3

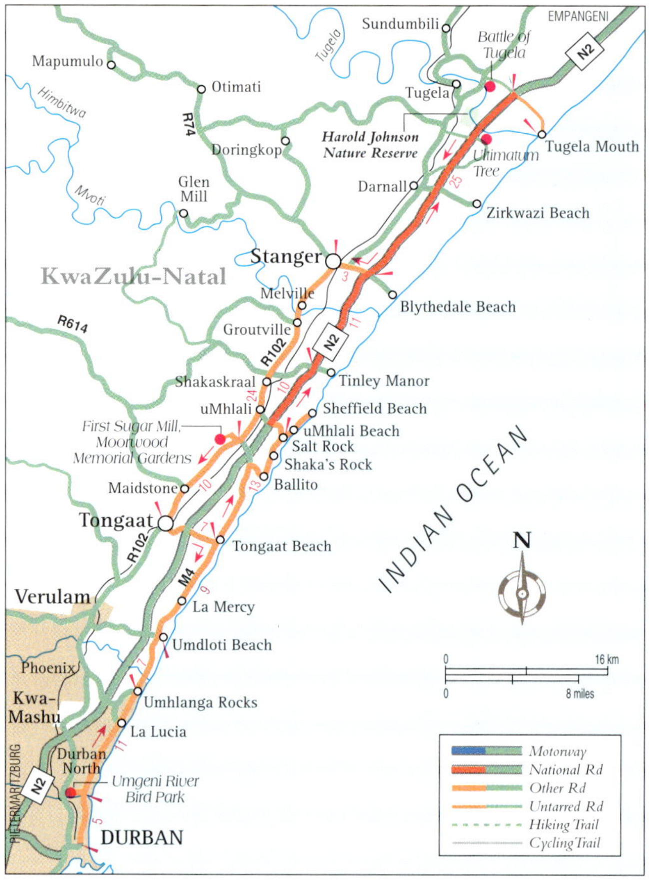

4

DURBAN, with its long stretch of golden beaches, has long been one of South Africa's premier holiday playgrounds. The focal point of the beachfront ③ is the Golden Mile, a 6-km-long strip of beachfront ⑤ lined with beaches, lawns, promenades, luxury hotels and restaurants. Stretching from Blue Lagoon to Addington Beach, the safe bathing beaches attract throngs of sun-seekers, while the Bay of Plenty is famous as a top surfing spot. Among the Golden Mile's many attractions are Funworld, which features dodgems, an aerial cableway, swing-boat and other hair-raising rides, while Waterworld offers river rides, water slides and aquatic action. Seaworld is famed for its dolphin and seal demonstrations, its shark tank – where visitors can enjoy close-up views of a variety of sharks – and the reef tank, with its rich diversity of tropical fish. The FitzSimons Snake Park has a large collection of indigenous and exotic snakes and other reptiles, and gives regular informative, entertaining demonstrations.

There is no better place to experience Durban's distinctive Asian atmosphere than at the lively Victoria Market, where anything from aromatic spices ② and oriental curios to engraved brasses and ebony ornaments can be bought. In addition to the nearby Jumma Musjid Mosque, the largest in the southern hemisphere, there are several Hindu temples and numerous excellent Indian restaurants. Adding colour to Durban's cosmopolitan atmosphere are the elaborately garbed rickshaw pullers.

The Durban Botanic Gardens, established in 1849, cover 14,5 ha of landscaped gardens and include collections of indigenous and exotic cycads, palms, orchids and exotic bromeliads.

Among Durban's many museums are the KwaMuhle Museum, which portrays the city's history from an African perspective, while the Durban Cultural and Documentation Centre focuses on the history and culture of South Africans of Indian origin. Other collections may be seen at the Natural Science Museum, Local History Museum, Old House Museum, Campbell Collection and the Natal Maritime Museum. A wide variety of Zulu and Xhosa handicrafts and artworks are sold at the African Art Centre, while the BAT Centre and the Durban Art Gallery are popular venues for art-lovers.

UMGENI RIVER BIRD PARK lies in a scenic setting of waterfalls, lush tropical vegetation and 30-m-high cliffs along the Mgeni River. With a collection of over 3 000 exotic and indigenous birds, it ranks among the top bird parks in the world. Many of the park's 400 species are rare and endangered birds that form part of an extensive captive breeding programme. Among the park's inhabitants are brightly coloured parrots, macaws, Asian hornbills, flamingoes and colourful pheasants. Visitors can walk among the birds in large walk-through aviaries, although some species are kept in individual enclosures. One of the highlights of a visit to the park is the bird show, during which a fish eagle, vulture, parrots and hornbills soar past visitors in full flight and react to signals whistled by their handler.

UMHLANGA ROCKS features kilometres of sandy and rocky beaches, a 5-km promenade offering splendid vistas of the Indian Ocean and excellent accommodation and recreational facilities. The 21-m-high lighthouse, built in 1945, is a well-known landmark. The coastline north of the lighthouse offers safe swimming, and the superb waves are popular with surfers and paddle-skiers. The resort owes its name to the Mhlanga River, a Zulu name meaning 'river of reeds', a reference to the reeds that flourish in the river's lower reaches.

Umhlanga Rocks is the headquarters of the famous Natal Sharks Board, the only institution of its kind in the world. Visitors can learn more about sharks by watching a fascinating audiovisual presentation on the board's activities, and can even watch a shark being dissected. The display hall contains a large variety of life-size replicas of sharks, rays and other fish.

SUGAR COAST This section of the coast stretches from Umhlanga Rocks northwards to Zimbali and inland to Mount Edgecombe, Verulam and Hambanathi. The coastal hills are dominated by vast fields of sugar cane ④, the origins of which can be traced back to 1847, when the first plantings took place. The foundation of the South African sugar industry was, however, laid by a British immigrant, Edmund Morewood (see Tongaat). Spread out along the coast are several popular holiday resorts. Best known among these is Umdloti Beach, named after the Mdloti River to the north. It has a magnificent beach which is popular with sunbathers, surfers and ski-boat anglers.

DOLPHIN COAST This scenic stretch of coast, extending from Ballito northwards to Zinkwazi Beach, is named after the many bottlenose dolphins ① to be seen offshore. With its fine sandy beaches and popular resorts, the Dolphin Coast has for many years been a favoured holiday destination. Ballito, named after an Italian brand of stockings, has two small bays and a tidal pool offering safe swimming. Thompson's Bay has a magnificent semi-natural tidal pool, and is bounded to the north by a rocky promontory known as Shaka's Rock. Still further north is Salt Rock, once a farm belonging to the Hulett family (a name synonymous with the sugar industry) and Umhlali Beach. Salt Rock was named after the rocky pools where Zulu women used to collect salt; the two tidal pools in front of the landmark Salt Rock Hotel are famous. Zinkwazi, the northernmost resort along the Dolphin Coast, lies on the shores of a lagoon surrounded by emerald-green fields of sugar cane.

HAROLD JOHNSON NATURE RESERVE This small provincial nature reserve covers 104 ha of coastal bush and grassland on the southern bank of the Tugela River. It has an interesting variety of epiphytic orchids and ferns, while mammals to be seen include impala, bushbuck, blue, common and red duiker, bushpig, zebra and a variety of smaller mammals.

Of historic interest is a remnant of the Ultimatum Tree, an old sycamore fig under which the British delivered an ultimatum to clan leaders of the Zulu king, Cetshwayo, on 11 December 1878. The ultimatum, among other things, defined the boundaries between Zululand and the Transvaal and demanded the immediate disbanding of the Zulu army. The Zulu rejected the ultimatum, which expired on 10 January 1879. British troops invaded Zululand the following day, signalling the start of the Anglo-Zulu War. Another site of historic interest is the remains of Fort Pearson, built in 1878 as part of a system of forts to protect the northern border of Natal. It was one of the launching points for the British invasion of Zululand in 1879, and at one stage as many as 5 000 troops were garrisoned here.

STANGER lies about 8 km inland amid vast sugar-cane plantations. The town was established in 1873 on the site where the Zulu king, Shaka, built his second capital, Dukuza, in 1825. A memorial set in an attractive garden marks the grain pit into which his body was thrown after he was assassinated by his half-brothers in 1828. Another reminder of the Zulu king is the Indaba Tree, a large Natal mahogany under which Shaka held meetings and where he was killed. Stanger is home to the Sappi Fine Paper Mill, a unique facility producing high-quality gloss-coated paper from bagasse (cane pulp).

TONGAAT is synonymous with the South African sugar industry. A few kilometres north of the town, at Compensation, an attractive memorial garden marks the site where the first sugar mill in South Africa was erected. It was here that Edmund Morewood began the large-scale planting of sugar cane after a consignment was imported from the Indian Ocean island of Réunion in 1847. Four years later, Morewood built his own sugar mill, and in January 1852 exhibited his sugar at the offices of the *Natal Witness*. Also at Compensation is Crocodile Creek, home to some 7 000 crocodiles, alligators and pythons. Of interest in Tongaat is the Juggernath Puri, the tallest and oldest (1901) Hindu temple in South Africa.

5

38
225 KM

1

2

3

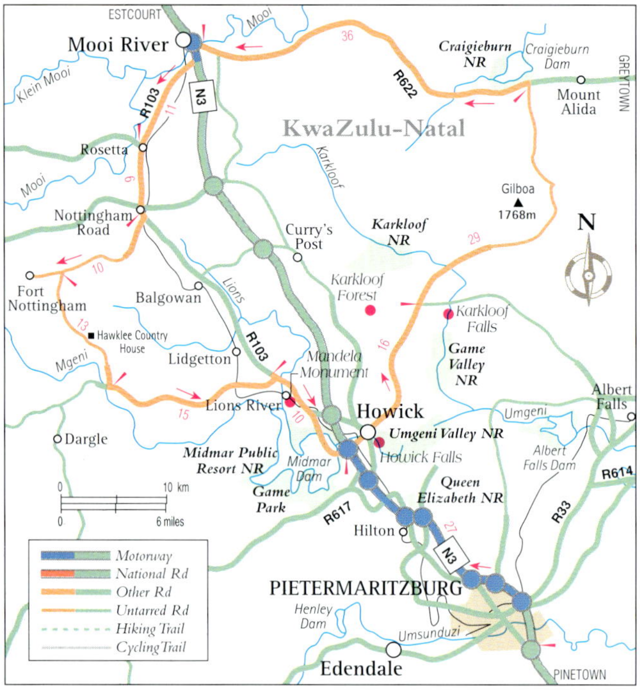

PIETERMARITZBURG, also known as The Heritage City, owes its special character to its rich architectural heritage. Laid out on a grid plan, with a market square as the focal point, part of the city's unique atmosphere and charm comes from the network of quaint, narrow pedestrian lanes linking Church and Longmarket streets. Regarded as one of the finest Victorian cities in the world, Pietermaritzburg's numerous historic treasures include the imposing City Hall (1900) ② – the largest all-brick building in the southern hemisphere – the Legislative Assembly (1889) and Legislative Council (1899) buildings, Government House (late 1860s), Publicity House (1884) and the late-19th-century railway station.

Despite its overwhelmingly British colonial character, the city's history is intimately linked to that of the Voortrekkers, who settled here in 1838. They named the settlement Pietermauritzburg after Pieter Mauritz Retief, who led the first trek into Natal. In 1938, it was decided to honour the leader of the second trek, Gert Maritz, as well and the name was changed to Pietermaritzburg. Among the buildings relating to the trekkers are the Voortrekker Museum, Voortrekker House (the only surviving double-storey Voortrekker house in Pietermaritzburg, dating back to 1846) and Welverdient, the house of trek leader Andries Pretorius.

Of more recent historic interest is the statue in Church Street Mall honouring Mahatma Gandhi, who developed the philosophy of satyagraha, or non-violent resistance, to achieve social and political reform in South Africa. Other major attractions include the Natal Museum, the Macrorie House Museum (furnished with Victorian period pieces) and Comrades Marathon House, headquarters of one of the world's most famous ultra marathons. The Tatham Art Gallery has an extensive collection of South African art, as well as collections of 19th and 20th-century British and French painting. An interesting pastime is hunting down the more than 2 000 elephants that are depicted on buildings, arches, poles and windows in the city. The Natal National Botanic Garden covers 49 ha of landscaped and natural gardens focusing on the indigenous flora of KwaZulu-Natal. Outdoor enthusiasts can explore the city's Green Belt along several well-marked walks.

MIDLANDS MEANDER The route described here mainly follows the Midlands Meander, stretching from Hilton northwards to Mooi River and from Rietvlei in the east to the Dargle Valley in the west. Formed in 1985, when six artists and craftspeople ① opened their studios and workshops ③ to the public, it is the original arts and crafts route in South Africa and has since developed into the largest route of its kind in the country. The Midlands Meander consists of four routes linking over 120 art studios, country hotels and pubs, guest houses, and herb and flower gardens.

HOWICK Situated in the centre of a thriving agricultural district, the small town of Howick is also known as the Heart of Waterfall Country. Here, the Mgeni River plunges 94 m over sheer dolerite cliffs into a narrow gorge as it makes its way downstream to the Albert Falls Dam. Howick Falls ④, together with 32 ha of land around it, was proclaimed a national monument in 1951. A viewing platform provides fine views over the falls, but the more adventurous can set off on the Gorge Walk, a two-hour hike to the pools at the base of the falls and back. In addition to the Howick Falls, there are four other waterfalls in and around Howick.

UMGENI VALLEY NATURE RESERVE covers 700 ha of land along a 10-km stretch of the Umgeni Valley immediately below Howick Falls. Owned by the Wildlife and Environment Society of Southern Africa, the reserve was established in 1976 and serves as an environmental education centre for school children, teachers and adults. The diversity of habitats, ranging from acacia thornveld to grassland, can be explored along a network of trails. Game to be seen includes giraffe, eland, wildebeest, zebra, impala, nyala, mountain reedbuck and oribi, while some 213 bird species have been recorded to date.

KARKLOOF FALLS After winding through grasslands and pine plantations, the Karkloof River tumbles over the Woodhouse Falls before plunging 88 m over a sheer cliff into the 50-km-long forested Karkloof Valley. Situated on a plantation owned by forest products company Sappi, picnic facilities are provided, but the area is closed to the public during the fire season. Keep an eye out for the Karkloof blue butterfly (*Orachrysops ariadne*) which is endemic to the area and which is also the emblem of the Midlands Meander. At one time, the valley was the main route between Natal and the Transvaal; the Afrikaans name means 'horse cart ravine', and refers to an incident in 1845 when a horse cart overturned after the horses took fright. The Karkloof River is a tributary of the Mgeni River, and its Zulu name, Mlambomunye, means 'one stream' or 'another stream'.

MOOI RIVER, the northern gateway to the Midlands, is a busy agricultural centre for the surrounding cattle and dairy farms, as well as several racehorse studs. The town was named after the Mooi River (Afrikaans for 'beautiful river'), a tributary of the Thukela, which rises high in the Drakensberg. The Rhode Museum contains photographic displays and a collection of dairy implements. The upper reaches of the Mooi River offer some of the finest brown trout angling in the country.

FORT NOTTINGHAM Surrounded by undulating hills and plains, the quiet agricultural settlement of Nottingham Road was founded in 1905. It owes its name to the Nottingham Regiment, which was stationed here in the early 19th century in anticipation of incursions by the Basotho. Situated some 10 km south, Fort Nottingham is the third-oldest fort in KwaZulu-Natal. It was built in 1856 to discourage cattle raiding by the San. During the Langalibalele Rebellion of 1873, the fort served as a base for military operations against Chief Langalibalele.

LION'S RIVER Between Lion's River and Tweedie, a commemorative plinth marks the site where South Africa's first democratically elected President, Nelson Mandela, was arrested on 5 August 1962, while driving with Umkhonto we Sizwe (MK) member Cecil Williams. Following his arrest, Mandela was tried with ten others in what became known as the Rivonia Trial, which began in October 1963 and ended in June 1964. He was sentenced to life imprisonment, many years of which were spent on Robben Island, and was released on 11 February 1990.

MIDMAR DAM is one of the major components of the Midmar Scheme, which provides water to millions of urban and rural households from Pietermaritzburg to Durban. Situated on the Mgeni River, the dam has a capacity of 178 million m^3 and covers 15,6 km^3 when full. It consists of a 140-m-long concrete overspill section flanked by earth embankments, with a total length of 1 310 m. Construction began in 1961 and was completed four years later.

A popular venue for yachting ⑤, water-skiing and windsurfing enthusiasts, Midmar also offers excellent opportunities for bass and carp fishing. The dam and certain designated areas are managed as a resort, offering accommodation, camping, children's playgrounds and picnic spots. The adjoining Midmar Nature Reserve is managed by KZN Wildlife, and has been stocked with white rhino, reedbuck, red hartebeest, Burchell's zebra, blesbok and blue wildebeest.

4

5

1

39
240 KM

2

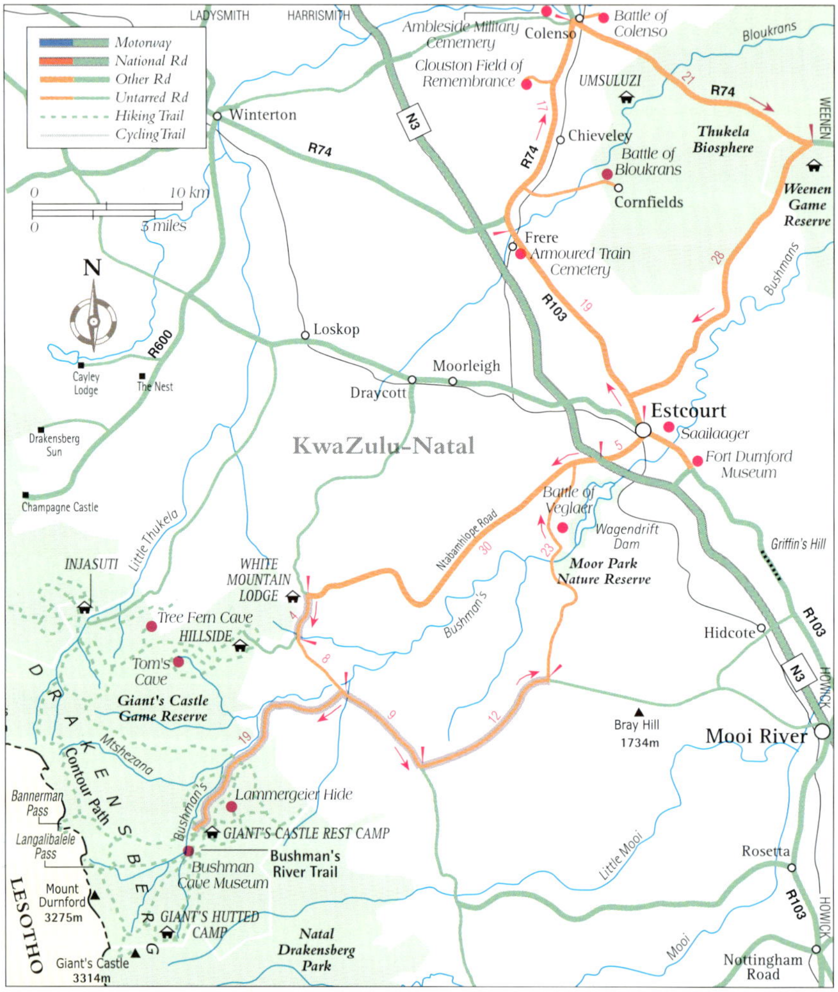

ESTCOURT, an important industrial town, also serves a prosperous stock breeding and agricultural area. It is a convenient gateway to some of the Battlefields Route sites. Estcourt , on the banks of the Bushman's River, was first named Bushmans River Post, or Bushmans Drift. In 1863, it was renamed after Thomas HS Estcourt, who had sponsored a number of British settlers under the Byrne immigration scheme. The town's historic buildings include the Powder Magazine (1859), first Government School (1876) and Railway Bridge (1885).

GIANT'S CASTLE GAME RESERVE ⑤ lies on a grassy plateau amid the deep valleys of the Bushman's and Little Thukela rivers, with the Drakensberg forming an impressive backdrop. Proclaimed in 1904, the 34 000-ha reserve forms part of the Natal Drakensberg Park, and is home to herds of eland, as well as grey rhebok, mountain reedbuck, common duiker and oribi. It is also a sanctuary for the endangered bearded vulture (*Gypaetus barbatus*) ②, which can be seen gliding overhead or from the hide where carcasses are put during the winter months to supplement the birds' diet.

Giant's Castle is renowned for its rock paintings ③, and these can be viewed on a guided tour of the Main Caves, which contain over 540 individual paintings. Visitors can explore the valleys and undulating grassy hills along a network of trails covering 285 km. These range from under 2 km to self-guided overnight trails and guided wilderness trails in the reserve's Injasuti section. The Hillside section of the reserve is the base for daily horse rides ④ and overnight horseback trails. A variety of accommodation types are available for overnight visitors.

THE MOOR PARK NATURE RESERVE covers 264 ha of grassland, thornveld, valley bushveld and sandstone cliffs at the head of the Wagendrift Dam. Among the species of game to be seen are black wildebeest, blesbok, Burchell's zebra, mountain reedbuck and impala, while some 190 bird species have been recorded to date. Picnic facilities are provided and visitors can set off on the Old Furrow Trail, a 6-km-long self-guided interpretive trail. Veglaer, where the Voortrekkers fought a three-day battle against a large Zulu force from 13 to 15 August 1838, has been inundated by the Wagendrift Dam. The dam is a popular destination with boating, yachting, canoeing and angling enthusiasts.

FORT DURNFORD Situated on the crest of a hill overlooking the Bushman's River, Fort Durnford was built on the site of a post established in 1847 against San raiders. Originally named the Ordnance Reserve, the post provided an excellent vantage point over the area and the two drifts over the river. A detachment of the 45th Regiment was stationed here, and various rough walls were built. Following the Langalibalele Rebellion of 1873, a sturdy stone fort was built in 1874–75 to protect the town from a possible attack by the Zulu.

It was named after Major Anthony Durnford who commanded the Natal Carbineers during the ill-fated attack on Langalibalele in which three carbineers and two black auxiliaries were killed. Durnford, who commanded the Number 2 Column when British forces invaded Zululand, was killed during the heroic last stand at Isandlwana. The fort is now a museum, with interesting defence mechanisms and a reconstructed Amangwane homestead in the grounds.

SAAILAAGER was the site where Voortrekker leader Gert Maritz formed a laager on the banks of the Bushman's River in early 1838 to guard against a possible Zulu attack. While the trekkers were encamped here, plots were laid out for cultivation and irrigated with water from the river. Following the murder of Piet Retief on 6 February 1838, Zulu forces attacked the Voortrekker laagers and camps in the Bloukrans and Bushman's river valleys on 16 and 17 February. Since Saailaager was off the line of attack of the main force, it was not attacked until later in the day, giving Maritz time to prepare. Another factor in the trekkers' favour was that the Bushman's River was in flood, and the Zulu strategy of crossing the river by forming a human chain could be thwarted by shooting the anchor men on the banks. As a result, Maritz and his party were able to repel the attack successfully.

ARMOURED TRAIN CEMETERY AND MEMORIAL A plaque and the graves of four British soldiers mark the site where Winston Churchill, war correspondent for the *London Morning Post*, was captured on 15 November 1899. The 25-year-old Churchill was one of 164 people aboard an armoured train that came under Boer fire as it approached a bend in the railway line near the Bloukrans River. The driver increased speed, and as the train rounded a bend it crashed into rocks which had been placed on the line. The three trucks were derailed, but the locomotive managed to break through and continue on to Frere. Losses to the British totalled seven dead (three died of wounds), 45 wounded and 74 taken prisoner.

COLENSO, on the banks of the Thukela River in the foothills of the Drakensberg, was originally known as Commando Drift. On 15 December 1899, the town made headlines when British forces under General Sir Redvers Buller made a disastrous attempt to cross the Thukela River in order to relieve Ladysmith. Mistaking the position of a ford where they intended to cross, the 5th Brigade came under heavy fire from the Boers in a loop of the river, forcing Buller to order the evacuation of the troops. Meanwhile, Colonel CJ Long had moved twelve 15-pounder guns forward to within rifle range of the Boer positions across the river. The marksmanship of the Boers eventually forced the gunners to abandon the guns, ten of which subsequently fell into Boer hands. British casualties totalled 214 killed or died of wounds, 693 wounded and 199 taken prisoner or reported missing, against 8 Boers killed or died of wounds and 30 wounded. Reminders of the battle may be seen at the Clouston Garden of Remembrance ① and the Ambleside cemetery, where the remains of most of the 5th Brigade soldiers killed on 15 December were buried in a mass grave.

THUKELA BIOSPHERE This reserve of about 100 000 ha consists of the 6 500-ha Weenen Game Reserve and several privately owned conservation areas and farms. Established in terms of the criteria laid down by UNESCO, the biosphere aims at promoting conservation and community upliftment through the sustainable development of natural resources and the development of tourism. There is a variety of accommodation facilities, ranging from tented camps to thatched stone cottages. Activities include wilderness walks, game-viewing and night drives, horse trails, river-rafting, mountain biking, fishing and birding.

WEENEN GAME RESERVE forms the core area of the Thukela Biosphere. Visitors can explore the 6 500-ha reserve along the 47-km network of roads, or follow a fairly easy 4x4 route. Game to be seen includes giraffe, black and white rhino, buffalo, zebra and a variety of antelope, including roan, eland and red hartebeest. The reserve's bird list stands at 279 species, among them black stork, bald ibis, blue crane, whitethroated robin and redbilled oxpecker. There are three picnic sites, and overnight visitors can either camp in the campsite, opt for the tented camp or book a five-bedded cottage.

3

4

5

40

275 KM

1

2

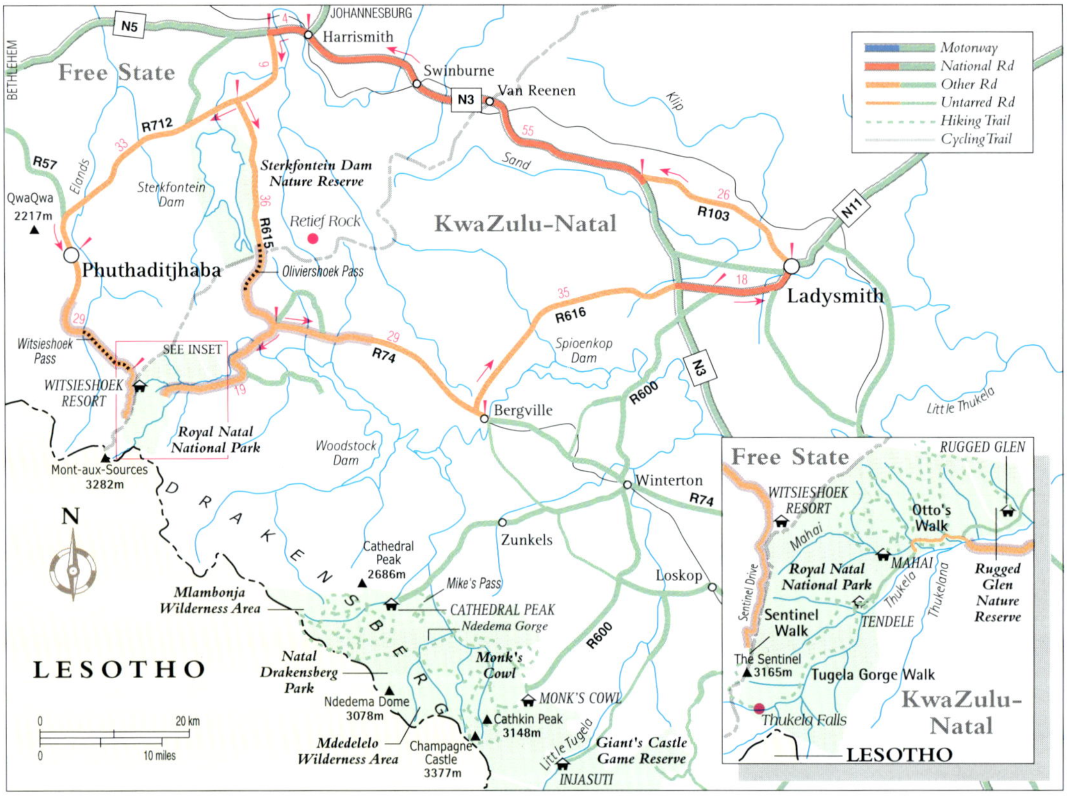

HARRISMITH, on the banks of the Wilge River, is dominated by 600-m-high Platberg to the northeast of town. Horse-drawn carts are still a common mode of transport among the local rural people (1). Established in 1849, Harrismith was named after the British Governor of the Cape, Sir Harry Smith. In addition to its central location midway between Gauteng and the KwaZulu-Natal coast, the town is also an important agricultural centre. The 5 000-ha Platberg Nature Reserve, extending from the edge of the town to the summit of the flat-topped mountain, is stocked with a variety of game including blesbok, black wildebeest, eland, springbok and red hartebeest. The blockhouse on the slopes of Platberg was built by the British in 1901 as part of their strategy to isolate and capture the Boer forces during the South African War. Also of interest is a 150-million-year-old, 33-m-long petrified tree trunk in the Harrismith Town Hall garden. The imposing light-brown sandstone building, with its towered façade, was completed in 1908.

PHUTHADITHJABA, a name translated as 'meeting place of the nations', is the main centre of QwaQwa. It was formerly known as Witsieshoek, a name given in honour of a Kholokwe chief, Wetsi, who lived in the area between 1839 and 1856. Chief Wetsi and his tribe fled to a large cave to the southwest of Witsieshoek in 1856 to escape a large Boer commando, which seized 1 700 head of cattle and 400 horses. A smaller commando later invaded Witsieshoek and burnt down the kraals, forcing Wetsi and his followers to flee to Basotholand. The Mopeli statue, erected 7 km south of Phuhadithjaba, honours Paulus Mopeli, a brother of Basotho leader Moshweshwe, who settled in Witsieshoek in 1867. The sprawling residential and industrial town was developed in the early 1970s as the 'capital' of the bantustan of QwaQwa, created for the Bakwena of Chief Mopeli and the Batlokwa, two South Sotho groups living outside of Lesotho.

SENTINEL DRIVE From Phuthaditjhaba the road winds along the Witsieshoek Pass, with its 1 in 7 gradient, to the Witsieshoek Mountain Resort, perched on the edge of the Escarpment. The resort opened in 1972 and is situated at an altitude of 2 200 m, making it one of the highest holiday resorts in South Africa. From here, the mountain road snakes past Breakfast Rock, The Dome, The Pudding and Witches to reach the car park at the base of the 3 165-m-high Sentinel, after a drive of 6 km. Terminating at an altitude of 2 540 m, the Sentinel Drive is the highest gravel road in Southern Africa that can be undertaken in a sedan car. The car park is the starting point for the three-hour hike to the top of the Amphitheatre and the 3 282 m-high Mont-aux-Sources. However, a short walk from the car park to the Escarpment edge will reveal dramatic views of the Royal Natal National Park far below, as well as Eastern Buttress and the Devil's Tooth at the eastern end of the Amphitheatre.

STERKFONTEIN DAM lies in the upper reaches of the Nuwejaarspruit and forms part of the Drakensberg Pumped Storage Scheme, which supplements the water supply of the Vaal Dam. Commissioned in 1977, the 2 290-m-long earthfill embankment was extended to 3 060 m in 1980, while the height was increased from 69 m to 93 m. Up to 630 million m^3 of water a year is pumped from the Woodstock Dam on the Thukela River up the Escarpment to the Sterkfontein Dam. The water is stored here and is released into the Wilge River, a tributary of the Vaal, only when there is a need to augment the water level in the Vaal Dam. The rationale for this is that, being very deep, the Sterkfontein Dam loses much less water through evaporation than the much shallower Vaal Dam. The dam wall contains 17 million m^3 of material, making it the largest dam wall in South Africa in terms of volume. With a surface area of nearly 70 km^2 when full and a capacity of 2 656 million m^3, Sterkfontein is the third-largest reservoir in South Africa. It is popular with anglers, and windsurfing and boating enthusiasts. The dam is the focal point of the 18 000-ha Sterkfontein Dam Nature Reserve, which is dominated by grasslands and cream-coloured sandstone outcrops.

THE RETIEF ROCK is one of the best-known landmarks on the routes followed by the Voortrekkers. Here, Voortrekker leader Piet Retief made camp at the foot of the Kerkenberg on 2 October 1837. Three days later, Retief set off with 14 men to visit the Zulu king, Dingane. A fortnight later, when Retief had not returned, the chief laager under Abraham Greyling was moved to a spring higher up the slopes of the Kerkenberg. When Retief had not returned from Dingane's camp by his birthday, his daughter Deborah wrote 'P Retief Den 12 Novr. 1837' in green paint on the overhanging rock. The following day, Greyling broke up camp and descended into Natal along the Retief Pass. Around Retief's name can be seen the names of several members of the Bethlehem Commando, who occupied the Oliviershoek Pass on 10 October 1899, on the eve of the Boer invasion of Natal at the outbreak of the South African War.

ROYAL NATAL NATIONAL PARK provides protection to some of the most dramatic scenery in the Natal Drakensberg Park, including the awe-inspiring Amphitheatre ③. Stretching between the Sentinel in the west and Eastern Buttress and the Devil's Tooth in the east, the sheer basalt wall rises over 700 m above the Little Berg, while the Thukela Falls plunge more than 600 m in five leaps over the Escarpment edge. The park's main attraction is its spectacular mountain scenery, which visitors can explore along a 100-km network of 25 footpaths, ranging from 3 km to a full-day hike of 25 km. By far the most picturesque route is the Gorge Walk, which leads past the conspicuous Policeman's Helmet rock formation to the 50-m-long tunnel carved by the Thukela River. Visitors can also see the highlands protea ② ride horses and try their hand at trout fishing in the river or the dam. Established in 1916, the park was given the name of Royal Natal National Park following the British Royal Family's visit to the park in May 1947. Accommodation ranges from camping at Mahai and Rugged Glen to the Tendele Hutted Camp and the historic Royal Natal National Park Hotel.

BERGVILLE Established in 1897 by a retired mariner, Captain Wales, the tranquil village of Bergville has developed into an agricultural and trading centre. Of historical interest in the town is the Upper Thukela Blockhouse, built by the British forces during the South African War. The Spioenkop and iNtabamnyama battlefields, where Boer and British forces met in battle from 20 to 24 January 1900, lie about half-an-hour's drive to the northeast of Bergville.

LADYSMITH See Tour 41, page 102.

3

BATTLEFIELDS & ZULULAND

OPPOSITE TOP LEFT: RURAL ZULU SCENE (P.104); TOP RIGHT: LOGGERHEAD TURTLE HATCHLINGS (P.106); BOTTOM: KOSI BAY (P.108).**THIS PAGE** TOP LEFT: ZULU BASKETS (P.104); TOP RIGHT: ZULU WOMEN NEAR UMFOLOZI (P.106); CENTRE: ZULU HOMESTEADS (P.104); LEFT: KOSI BAY FISH TRAPS (P.108); ABOVE: WHITE RHINO CALF, HLUHLUWE-UMFOLOZI PARK (P.106).

KWAZULU-NATAL

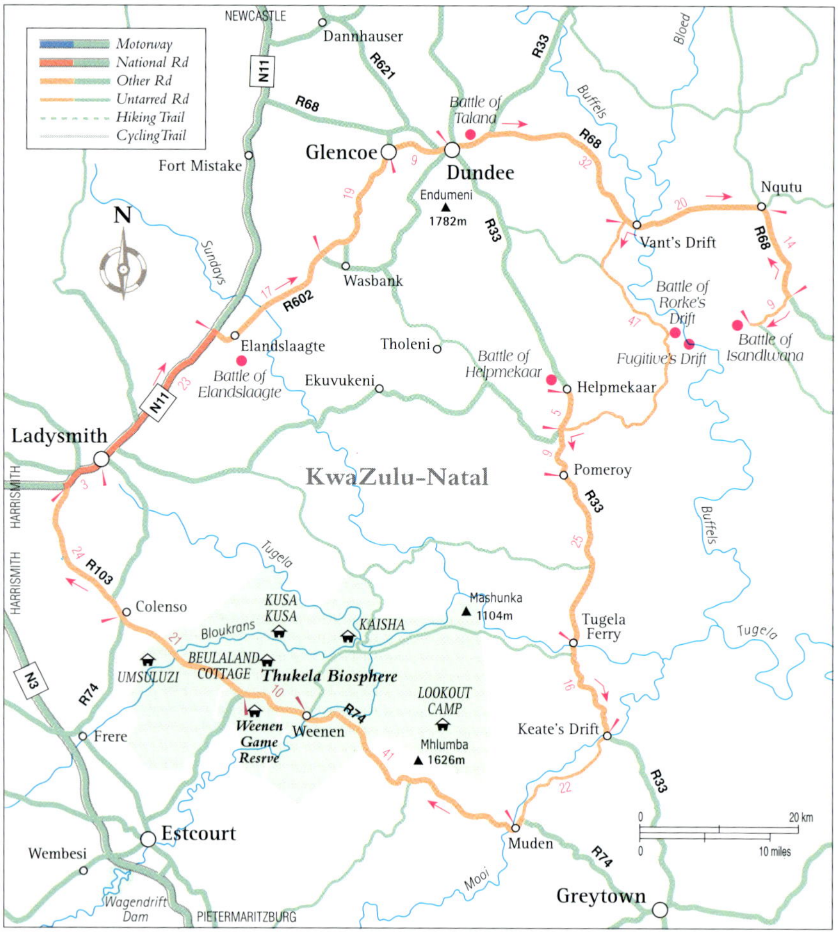

41

455 KM

1

BATTLEFIELDS ROUTE Situated in the northern part of KwaZulu-Natal, this region has the largest concentration of battlefields in South Africa. The route links 17 key towns to over 50 historical sites, embracing the struggles between Voortrekker and Zulu, the Anglo-Zulu War of 1879, the First War of Independence (1880–81), the South African War (1899–1902) and the Bambatha Rebellion of 1906. In addition to the numerous battle sites, the route also offers visitors opportunities to experience Zulu culture and to enjoy hiking, fishing, game-viewing and birding.

LADYSMITH On 30 October 1899 (a day that became known as Mournful Monday), British forces were humiliated at the Battle of Modderspruit. The battle, conceived by General Sir George White as a knock-out blow to the Boer forces, turned into a rout after the Boers changed position during the night and forced the British to retreat into Ladysmith. The town came under siege on 2 November 1899 when Boer forces occupied all the encircling hills, except Platrand which formed part of the British forward defence line. Situated 5 km southwest of the town, Platrand (also known as Wagon Hill) was the key to the capture of Ladysmith, but two Boer attacks on the flat-topped hill were beaten back. On 27 February 1900, General Buller's forces crossed the Tukhela River and advanced on Ladysmith, causing the Boers to abandon their positions. The siege was relieved the following day, 118 days after it began. British casualties were high; 563 soldiers died of disease, 211 were killed in action, 59 died of wounds and 10 were reported missing. It is not known how many Boers were killed in action, but an estimated 60 died of wounds. The story of the siege is depicted in the town's Siege Museum.

ELANDSLAAGTE saw battle on 21 October 1899 when a 3 500-strong force under the command of Major-General JDP French recaptured the railway station, occupied two days earlier by Boer forces. After heavy fighting, the Boers were compelled to retire, but 290 (including 105 wounded) were taken prisoner. There are several monuments and war graves ③ in the vicinity.

DUNDEE Situated in the foothills of the Biggarsberg, Dundee was established in 1882 on the farm owned by a Scottish immigrant named Peter Smith. Named after Dundee in Scotland, the town lies in a prosperous livestock farming and coal-mining area. After winning the Battle of Talana, British forces found themselves surrounded by 10 000 Boers and short of artillery ammunition. Unable to send reinforcements, General Sir George White ordered the British forces under Brigadier-General James Yule to fall back on Ladysmith. On 22 October, the British withdrew from Dundee under cover of darkness, taking only what they could carry and abandoning the garrison's food supply and stores, as well as their wounded, to the Boers. The town and the military camp surrendered without resistance the following day.

TALANA Following the declaration of war on 11 October 1899, Boer forces from the Orange Free State and Transvaal invaded northern Natal. The first shots of the South African War were fired at Talana, 2 km from Dundee, on 20 October 1899. After an artillery attack on Talana Hill, seized by Boer forces early in the morning, the British launched a concentrated infantry attack, forcing the Boers to retreat. Misfortune struck, though, when fire from two of the British batteries inflicted casualties on their own troops. Although the British captured the hill, it was at considerable cost: 66 men killed or died of injuries, 185 wounded and 246 taken prisoner, or reported missing. The Boers lost 35 killed or died of wounds, 91 wounded and 30 taken prisoner, or reported missing. The Talana Museum has displays on the battle at Talana and on the Anglo-Zulu War, and also includes the Iscor Hall of Mining, Chamber of Mines Coal Museum, Consol Glass Collection and the Brick Heritage display.

HELPMEKAAR was one of the British garrisons along the supply line of the Centre Column which invaded Zululand at Rorke's Drift on 11 January 1879 during the Anglo-Zulu War. During the South African War, General Buller's forces broke through the Boer defence lines in the Biggarsberg at Helpmekaar on 13 May 1900, opening the way for the recapture of Dundee. The remains of a Boer fort on the crest of the hill and a British military cemetery with a single grave are reminders of this battle.

ISANDLWANA ranks among the worst defeats suffered by the British Army in Africa. Following the start of the Anglo-Zulu War on 11 January 1879, the British commander-in-chief, Lord Chelmsford, invaded Zululand with a force of 4 659 men at Rorke's Drift. On 20 January, the British set up camp to the south of Isandlwana ①, a prominent hill, unaware of the fact that the main Zulu army of about 20 000 men was concentrated only about 5 km away, at Nqutu Hills. The following day Chelmsford sent out a reconnaissance patrol, which was lured further away from the camp by an apparently retreating Zulu force.

On 22 January Chelmsford and 800 men went to the assistance of the patrol, leaving Colonel H Pulleine in charge of the camp. Around mid-morning, Pulleine's force of about 1 774 was reinforced by 500 men who arrived with Colonel Durnford, who soon left to defend Chelmsford against a possible Zulu attack from the rear. Using the traditional ox-horn formation, the 20 000-strong main Zulu army attacked the camp, but the attack of the central force was stalled. The attack resumed at 13:00, and within half an hour the camp was overrun by the Zulu warriors. Most of those who managed to flee were pursued and killed, with only a few surviving. Over 1 000 Zulu were killed in the battle of Isandlwana, while the British lost 52 officers and 1 277 men, including 471 black troops.

FUGITIVE'S DRIFT A few men managed to escape from Islandlwana, but on finding the road to Rorke's Drift blocked they tried to escape in a more southerly direction towards the Buffalo River. But most of them were pursued and overtaken by the Zulu; among those killed were Lieutenants N Coghill and T Melville, who had tried to save the Queen's Colours. They were buried where they fell ②.

RORKE'S DRIFT ④ was attacked late on the afternoon of 22 January by the reserve of the Zulu forces that had not taken part in the Islandlwana assault. The British force consisted of 8 officers and 131 men, of whom 35 were ill, while the Zulu force numbered between 3 000 and 4 000. After being driven from the hospital building, the redcoats took cover behind a line of biscuit boxes and eventually retreated to a redoubt of mealie bags. The Zulu attack continued until after midnight and repeatedly penetrated the British defences, necessitating hand-to-hand combat. The assault was abandoned only in the early hours of the morning. On the British side, 17 men were killed, while one officer and seven men were wounded. The Zulu casualties are estimated at over 500. The defenders of Rorke's Drift received 11 Victoria Crosses – the highest number ever awarded for a single engagement.

2

3

4

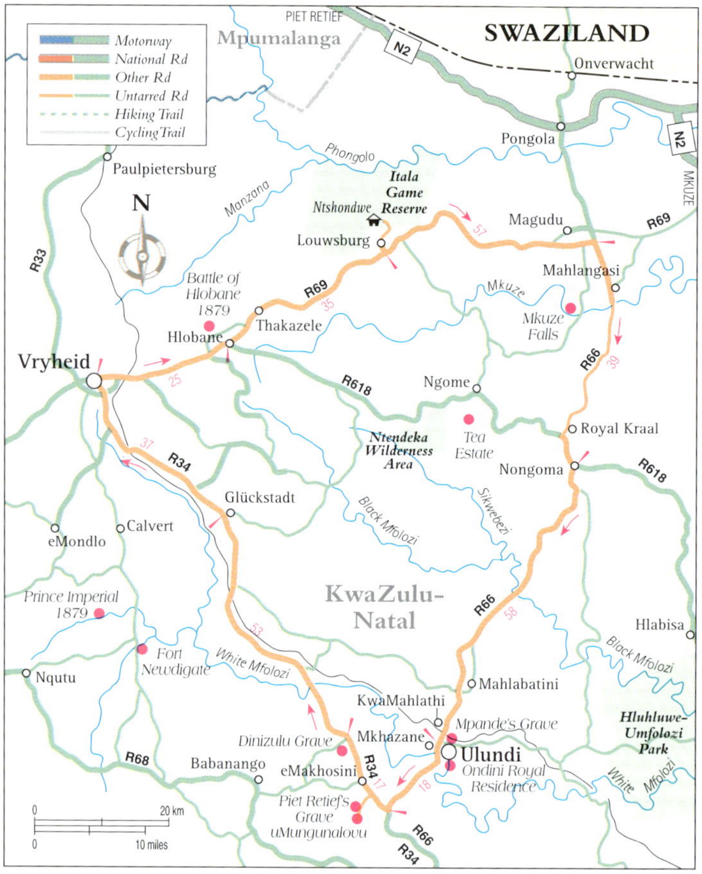

1

42
450 KM

2

ZULULAND takes its name from the Zulu people ①. The name belonged to an early chief and translates as 'heaven'. The largest cultural group in South Africa, the Zulu belong to the northern Nguni group of Bantu-speaking people inhabiting southeastern Africa. A fiercely independent and proud nation, the Zulu are popularly known for their beehive-shaped homesteads ③, *iklwa* (a short spear often called an assegaai), crafts ② and fear-inspiring dances. Zululand covers the area from the mouth of the Thukela River northwards to the border with Mozambique and to the north of the Phongolo River. The western boundary more or less follows the course of the Mzinyati or Buffalo River from its confluence with the Thukela River to its source in the Drakensberg.

In January 1879, British troops invaded Zululand after the Zulu King Cetshwayo refused to meet the terms of a British ultimatum. After the war, Zululand was divided into six districts, and was formally declared a British possession on 19 May 1887. The territory was incorporated into Natal ten years later. In terms of South Africa's policy of creating bantustans, KwaZulu became self-governing in 1977, but unlike Transkei, Ciskei and Bophuthatswana it did not opt for 'independence'.

VRYHEID, an Afrikaans name meaning 'freedom', was established in 1884 as the capital of a Voortrekker republic proclaimed on 16 August of that year. The settlement of a group of Transvaal Voortrekkers in the upper reaches of the White Mfolozi River came after a commando led by Lucas Meyer helped Dinizulu (son of Cetshwayo) to defeat Zibhebhu, a headman who drove Cetshwayo out of power. The 'Nieuwe Republiek' (New Republic) was incorporated into the Zuid-Afrikaansche Republiek (ZAR) on 20 July 1888 and at the end of the South African War it was transferred to Natal. Among Vryheid's places of interest are the Old Raadsaal (Council Chamber), dating back to 1885 and now a museum, and the Old Fort at the rear of the Raadsaal, which accommodated a prison and the house of President Meyer. Other noteworthy buildings are the imposing dressed-stone Dutch Reformed Church and the Carnegie Library, built in 1908.

HLOBANE, a Zulu name for 'beautiful place', is a coal-mining centre that witnessed the defeat of British forces by a Zulu *impi* (regiment) on 28 March 1879 during the Anglo-Zulu War. Ascending Hlobane Mountain from the east under cover of darkness, a 675-strong British force was eventually forced to retreat along the Devil's Pass down the Ntendeka Mountain. The British lost 15 officers and 79 men killed, while over 100 irregular troops led by Colonel E Wood as well as followers of Hamu – Cetshwayo's brother, who had joined Wood earlier in March – were also killed. The number of Zulu casualties is unknown.

LOUWSBURG, a small rural town, serves the surrounding cattle ranching and maize farms. It was proclaimed a township in 1920 and is named after David Louw, an early pioneer of the area.

ITALA GAME RESERVE covers nearly 30 000 ha of undulating grassy hills, deep valleys and magnificent bushveld vegetation. Bounded by the Phongolo River in the north, the reserve is home to some 80 mammal species, including white and black rhino, the only tsessebe population in KwaZulu-Natal, eland, blue wildebeest, red hartebeest, Burchell's zebra and giraffe. Among the more than 320 bird species recorded in Itala are bald ibis, black, martial and crowned eagle, yellowthroated longclaw and yellowspotted nicator. Visitors can follow the Nghubu Loop Auto Trail, a 30-km self-drive interpretive route, or join guided morning or afternoon game drives ④. Other options include guided early morning and afternoon game-viewing walks, or the four self-guided walks from Ntshondwe Camp. Set against a backdrop of impressive cliffs, Ntshondwe has been well integrated into the natural landscape, and its chalets and other facilities have been built with minimum impact to the environment. A variety of accommodation options, ranging from camping sites and chalets to a bush lodge and bush camps, are available.

NONGOMA, originally known as Ndwandwe after a southern Nguni clan of that name, was later named after a Ndwandwe chief's village, KwaNongoma, which means 'the place of the witchdoctor'. Today, Nongoma is a busy commercial centre in the heart of Zululand.

ULUNDI, the legislative capital of KwaZulu-Natal, lies on the northern banks of the White Mfolozi River and its Zulu name is translated as 'the high place'. Site of the royal village of the Zulu kingdom, Ulundi is inextricably linked to the history of the Zulu people and their resistance to British colonialism. To the north of the town is the grave of Mpande, who ruled Zululand as king from 1840 to 1872 and established his royal village at Nodwengu, just north of Ulundi, around 1845. Following Mpande's death, Cetshwayo established his military capital at Ondini, about 5 km southeast of Nodwengu. The village was burned by the British after the Battle of Ulundi, but has been partially reconstructed. The KwaZulu Cultural Museum in the Ondini Historic Reserve has a fascinating collection of beads and other craftwork, weapons and other items depicting Zulu culture.

A monument about 3 km west of Ondini marks the site of the final battle of the Anglo-Zulu War, fought on 4 July 1879. Here, a force of 2 281 British regulars and 465 black troops under the command of Lieutenant-General Lord Chelmsford, inflicted a decisive defeat on the 15 000 to 20 000-strong Zulu force. The Zulu losses have been estimated at between 950 and 1 500 killed, while three British officers and 10 men were killed and 69 wounded.

eMAKHOSINI, or the Valley of the Kings, is the birthplace of the Zulu nation. Among its numerous historic sites are Mthonjaneni Spring, from where water was brought for the personal use of King Dingane, and the graves of Voortrekker leader Piet Retief and 69 of his followers. They were killed at KwaMatiwane near uMgungundhlovu on 6 February 1838 on the instructions of Dingane after concluding a land treaty. In the nearby Mkhumbane Valley is the royal village established by Dingane, who became king after the assassination of Shaka by two of his brothers in 1828. Named uMgungundhlovu ('the secret meeting place of the elephant'), the Zulu capital consisted of between 1 700 and 2 000 beehive-shaped homesteads, and had a population of between 10 000 and 12 000 people. Eight regiments, each consisting of about 1 000 soldiers, also lived in the royal village. The village has been partially reconstructed and the site museum provides a fascinating insight into the life of its people. As well as occupying a central place in Zulu culture, the Valley of the Kings is also the burial place of Zulu kings, and contains the graves of Senzangakhona, father of Shaka, Dingane and Mpande, and Dinizulu, who ruled as king from 1884 to 1888 and 1898 to 1907.

3

4

1

43
355 KM

3

2

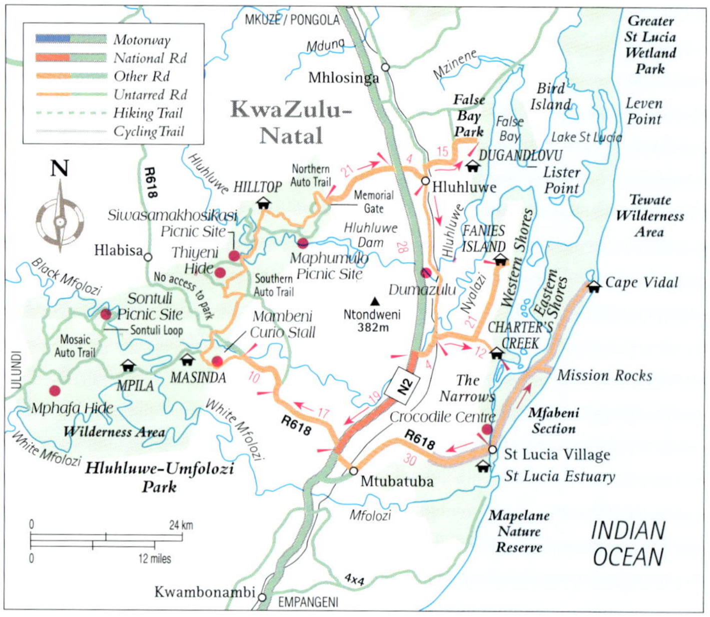

GREATER ST LUCIA WETLAND PARK Declared a World Heritage Site in 1999, the Greater St Lucia Wetland Park ⑤ presents an ever-changing kaleidoscope of lake, marshland, forested coastal dunes and grasslands. The nucleus of the park is Lake St Lucia, which was proclaimed a game reserve in 1897 – making it one of Africa's oldest conservation areas. It is also the third largest in area in South Africa. To the early Zulu and Thonga inhabitants the lake was known as Cwebeni las Entlengeni, or 'the lagoon of the rafts'. About 70 km in length and 18 km at its widest, the lake is home to large populations of hippo and crocodile and is considered a wetland of international importance. Over 350 bird species have been recorded in the park's rich diversity of habitats and ecosystems, and at times the lake attracts large numbers of Palaearctic waders, pinkbacked and white pelicans ④, greater flamingo and other waterfowl. The park was created by amalgamating various conservation areas and former state forests to form a total area of 260 000 ha. Stretching from Mapelane northwards, the park incorporates the St Lucia Game Reserve and Marine Reserve, False Bay Park, Sodwana Bay (where loggerhead turtles ③ breed), Mkuzi Game Reserve and the Maputaland Marine Reserve.

ST LUCIA VILLAGE Nestling along the shores of the St Lucia estuary, the village of St Lucia is a popular holiday resort, attracting large numbers of anglers and those seeking to relax in its peaceful surroundings. The village takes its name from Cape St Lucia, named by the Portuguese navigator Manuel de Mesquita Perestrêlo, when he passed the headland on 13 December 1575, the feast day of Saint Lucy. The best way to see the estuary is to take a two-hour trip on board the *Santa Lucia*, an 80-seater launch equipped with a viewing deck. At the St Lucia Crocodile Centre, visitors can get close-up views of Nile crocodile ⑥, as well as two other African species – dwarf and long-snouted – and American alligator. The centre aims to educate people about the importance of crocodiles in nature and offers interesting displays about various aspects of the biology and way of life of these forbidding reptiles. Visitors can explore the St Lucia Game Park along several short self-guided trails, including one to the mangrove community along the estuary's shore.

MTUBATUBA lies amid vast sugar cane plantations on the floodplains of the Mfolozi River. An important commercial centre for the surrounding farms, it was established in 1903. Its name honours a former chief of the Mtetwa clan and is said to mean 'creator of opportunities'.

HLUHLUWE-UMFOLOZI PARK covers 96 000 ha of deep wooded valleys, grassy hillsides and thornveld. Originally proclaimed on 27 April 1897 as two separate reserves, Hluhluwe and Umfolozi – together with the St Lucia Game Reserve – are the oldest conservation areas in Africa. The two reserves were consolidated after the Corridor, a stock-free area created to prevent the spread of nangana (sleeping sickness) to the cattle of tribespeople living in the area, was proclaimed a game reserve in 1989. Umfolozi is famed for its role in saving the white rhinoceros from extinction and today it is a sanctuary to one of southern Africa's largest populations of white and black rhinos. It was at Umfolozi, too, where Africa's first wilderness area was set aside and where, in the 1950s, conservationist Dr Ian Player pioneered the first wilderness trails.

Visitors can explore the park on more than 200 km of game-viewing roads; in addition to white and black rhino, there is always a possibility of chancing upon the other members of the Big Five: elephant, buffalo, lion and leopard. Among the other large mammals to be seen are giraffe, kudu, nyala, waterbuck, impala, blue wildebeest and Burchell's zebra. With a bird checklist of over 400 species, the park is a delight to birding enthusiasts. Noteworthy species include African finfoot, Delegorgue's pigeon, cinnamon dove, white-eared barbet, yellowspotted nicator, Rudd's apalis, yellowbilled and redbilled oxpeckers. Activities for visitors include interpretive auto trails, guided early morning and night drives, guided walks and overnight wilderness trails in Umfolozi. A variety of accommodation options is available.

HLUHLUWE VILLAGE ① owes its name to the Hluhluwe River, itself derived from the Zulu name (umHluhluwe) for the thorny or monkey rope (*Dalbergia armata*) which grows in profusion along the river bank. The village is the centre of an intensive agricultural area where sugar cane, pineapples and timber are harvested.

DUMAZULU, a name meaning 'the thundering Zulu', is devoted to the history, culture and customs of the Zulu nation. This traditional village consists of over 50 Zulu people living in a homestead where they perform daily tasks and manufacture crafts much as the Zulu people did a century ago. Visitors can watch the women making clay pots, weaving baskets and doing beadwork, while the men are involved in tasks like making spears and shields – the traditional weapons of Zulu warriors. The highlight of a visit to Dumazulu is watching the spectacular dances ②, while in the evening guests can watch Zulu plays over dinner. Other attractions include a snake park with over 100 species of indigenous snakes, and a crocodile park.

FALSE BAY PARK lies on the western shores of Lake St Lucia, where the lake is roughly shaped like an H. It is a popular destination with anglers, but the presence of species such as African broadbill, crested guineafowl, yellowspotted nicator and pinkthroated twinspot make it an excellent spot for birders. For those who wish to explore their surroundings on foot there are two self-guided interpretive walks. The Dugandlovu Hiking Trail meanders for 8 km through bush and along the lake shore to a rustic overnight camp overlooking Hluhluwe River. Also of interest are the marine fossils to be found along the lake shore, among them fossil corals and ammonites. The patches of sand forest are home to the rare suni and several interesting tree species, while reedbuck, waterbuck, nyala, impala, bushbuck and Burchell's zebra are among the animals to be encountered on foot. Facilities are limited to camp sites and a swimming pool.

FANIES ISLAND, on the western shores of Lake St Lucia, overlooks a maze of reed-covered islands, and was named after an early Zulu headman. Situated among magnificent coastal forest, the tranquil rest camp has a long-standing reputation for superb fishing, but also offers excellent birding possibilities – the Narina trogon and trumpeter hornbill can be seen here. Along two self-guided trails, visitors might chance upon red duiker, bushbuck and reedbuck, while the lake is home to hippo. Facilities include rest huts, a seven-bed cottage and a swimming pool.

CHARTER'S CREEK, on the western shores of Lake St Lucia, is a popular base for angling, bird-watching, or simply relaxing in the peaceful atmosphere. It was named after AE Charter, a former provincial secretary who was a keen conservationist. Visitors can explore the rest-camp surroundings by setting off on the two self-guided trails, or experience the tranquillity of the lake on a luxury boat cruise. Tours last between 1,5 and 2 hours; in addition to hippopotamus, crocodile and African fish eagle, there is also a chance of seeing buffalo, waterbuck, reedbuck and kudu along the lakeshore. Accommodation ranges from a seven-bed cottage to rest huts.

4

5

6

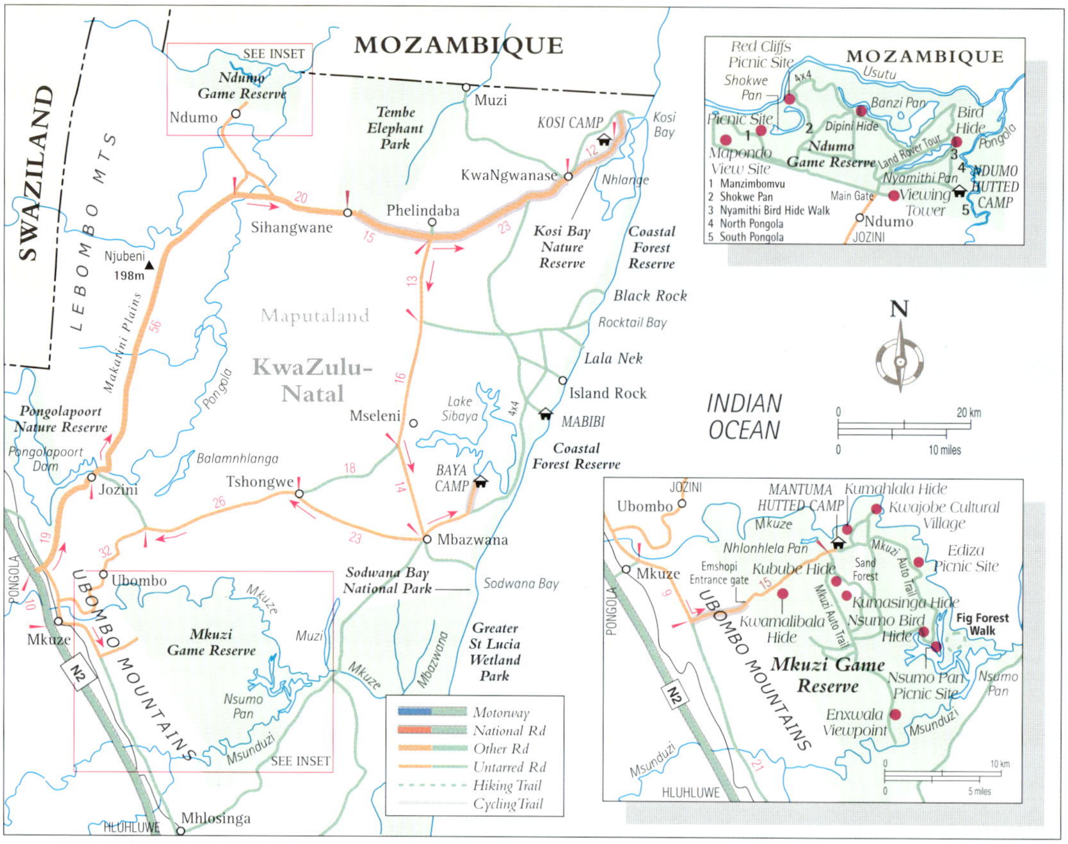

44
440 KM

1

MAPUTALAND Bounded by the Ubombo and Lebombo mountains in the west, Maputaland covers the vast coastal plain extending eastwards to the shores of the Indian Ocean and from just south of the Mfolozi River northwards to Mozambique. Its landscape is a mosaic of white beaches, lakes, marshlands, sand forest and mangroves. The coastline is the main southern Indian Ocean breeding ground of the leatherback turtle, while the Kosi palms fringing Lake Amanzimyama are home to of one of South Africa's rarest breeding birds, the palmnut vulture (*Gypohierax angolensis*). Situated at the southern limit of distribution of several bird species and with a rich diversity of ecosystems, Maputaland is a popular destination with birders.

MKUZE VILLAGE takes its name from the Mkuze River, a name which possibly might be derived from the Zulu name for the lavender tree (*Heteropoxis natalensis*). Situated alongside the N2 highway linking Ermelo and Durban, the small community is an important trade and transport centre.

NDUMO GAME RESERVE Covering 12 420 ha, the landscape of Ndumo alternates from tranquil pans lined by fever trees and magnificent riverine forests to floodplains, patches of sand forest and woodlands. Several of Ndumo's 420 bird species reach the southern limit of their distribution in southern Africa here, making the reserve one of the region's birding hotspots. Noteworthy species include yellowspotted nicator, Neergaard's sunbird, Rudd's apalis, pinkthroated twinspot and Stierling's barred warbler. Ndumo is home to probably the highest concentration of nyala in South Africa, and also has large hippo ② and crocodile populations. Other species of game to be seen include suni, black and white rhino, buffalo, giraffe, reedbuck, impala, Burchell's zebra and red duiker. Visitors can explore the park by taking one of several guided walks, or book a guided tour in a 4x4 vehicle to the pans in the eastern section of the reserve. In the western section, there is a 47-km network of game-viewing roads, a viewpoint, game-viewing hide and picnic places. Accommodation is available in Ndumo Camp, or in the upmarket Ndumo Wilderness Camp overlooking the backwaters of Banzi Pan.

TEMBE ELEPHANT PARK Fears that the last herds of free-ranging elephants in South Africa would be wiped out by poachers during the civil war in Mozambique prompted the proclamation of this park in 1983. These elephants used to migrate seasonally from the much larger Maputo Elephant Reserve in Mozambique along the Futi Channel to the Tembe area, but by 1989 their numbers had declined from an estimated 400 to a mere 120. The population in Tembe Elephant Park now numbers about 150, while the population in the Maputo Elephant Reserve is over 200 strong. Although the elephants are Tembe's major drawcard, the park also provides protection to the country's largest tracts of sand forest. This is the habitat of several rare bird species (among them yellowspotted nicator, Rudd's apalis and Neergaard's sunbird), and is home to the only viable population of suni in South Africa. Also associated with the sand forest are the red squirrel (also referred to as the Tonga squirrel) and the four-toed elephant shrew.

Other mammals to be seen are white and black rhino, giraffe, nyala, waterbuck, reedbuck, impala, blue wildebeest and red duiker. The southern part of the park is accessible by a network of sandy tracks negotiable by 4x4 vehicles only. Facilities include a luxury tented camp and two game-viewing hides, one overlooking Mahlasela Pan and the other the Muzi Swamp. Two short self-guided trails have been laid out in a fenced 2-km² area at Ngobozana at the entrance gate.

KOSI BAY is one of the most unique and fascinating areas in southern Africa. Despite its name, it is not a bay, but consists of four interconnected, roughly circular lakes linked to the sea by an estuary with a narrow mouth. Amanzimnyama, the southernmost lake, is fringed by stands of Kosi palms that provide nesting sites for the rare palmnut vulture. A narrow channel links it to Nhlange (Third Lake), the largest of the four lakes and covering an area of up to 37 km². The narrow Mtando Channel links Nhlange to Mpungwini (Second Lake) which, in turn, is linked to Makhawulani (First Lake) and the estuary, where Thonga fish traps form intricate criss-cross patterns. The mangrove community near the estuary mouth is unique, as it is the only such community in South Africa to feature five species of mangrove.

Visitors to Kosi Bay Nature Reserve can take guided walks to various places, such as Lake Amanzimnyama, while guided walks to the fishing kraals start from the community campsite at the entrance gate to Kosi Mouth. The rock pools near Kosi Mouth offer superb snorkelling opportunities, and boat angling on the lakes (Amanzimnyama excluded) is another popular pastime. Campsites and three fully furnished thatched lodges are available on the shores of Lake Nhlange.

LAKE SIBAYA Covering up to 77 km², Sibaya ③ is the largest freshwater lake in South Africa and an important wetland for waterbirds, attracting up to 20 000 waterfowl at times. Among the nearly 300 bird species recorded to date are yellowspotted nicator, brown robin, Woodward's batis, pinkthroated longclaw, gorgeous bush shrike, purplebanded sunbird and African spoonbill ①. The lake is home to hippo, crocodile and a variety of fish. But because of low nutrient levels the fish are small in size and angling is not a major attraction. Sibaya is, however, situated conveniently close to Nine Mile Beach, a popular coastal angling spot. Among the smaller mammals to be seen in the coastal dune forest are red and common duiker, samango and vervet monkeys, thicktailed bushbaby, red squirrel and bushpig, while reedbuck favour the open grassland areas. Visitors can explore the surroundings of Baya Camp, a rustic bush camp on the lake's southern shores, by following a 3,4-km trail, or book a boat trip on the lake. Accommodation is also available in the upmarket Sibaya Lake Lodge.

MKUZI GAME RESERVE Covering some 36 000 ha of bushveld, Mkuzi Game Reserve forms part of the Greater St Lucia Wetland Park, to which it is linked by the Mkuzi Swamps ④. The reserve offers visitors a superb game-viewing experience, with black and white rhino, leopard, hippo, giraffe, nyala, impala, blue wildebeest and Burchell's zebra among the species to be seen. There are several hides overlooking water holes and Nsumo Pan and a 41-km self-drive interpretive trail. There are guided birding and game-viewing walks, as well as night drives. Not to be missed is a guided walk along the Mkuze River, with its enormous sycamore fig trees, or the Fig Forest Walk, a 3-km self-guided route through a magnificent forest of sycamore fig and fever trees. Also worth visiting is the Kwajobe cultural village, with several beehive homesteads, reconstructed in the area where the Kwajobe people lived until they were resettled outside the reserve in 1947. Various accommodation options are available to visitors.

2

3

4

FREE STATE & LESOTHO

OPPOSITE TOP LEFT: ORANGE THROATED LONG-CLAW, FREE STATE; TOP RIGHT: LESOTHO ROAD (PP.115&116); BOTTOM: FREE STATE SUNFLOWERS. **THIS PAGE** ABOVE: LESOTHO SCENIC (PP.115&116); LEFT: PONY TREKKING, LESOTHO (P.117); BELOW: FREE STATE VISTA BETWEEN CLARENS AND FOURIESBURG (P.112).

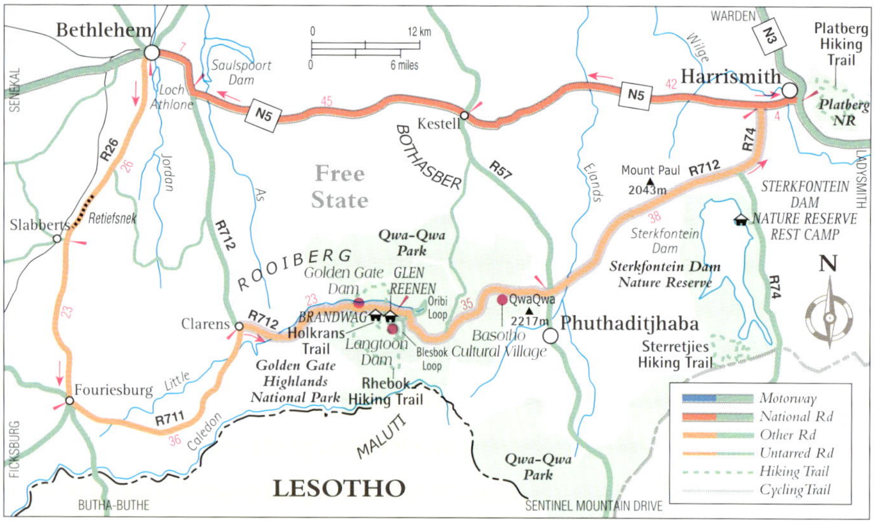

45

335 KM

1

BETHLEHEM, the oldest and largest town in the region, is the commercial centre of the eastern Free State. Established in 1860 on the banks of the Jordaan River (named after the River Jordan which flows into the Sea of Galilee), the town was likewise given a biblical name. The favourable conditions for the cultivation of wheat induced the first white settlers to name the settlement after the biblical Bethlehem, a name meaning 'house of bread'. The town has numerous beautiful sandstone buildings, while the Wolhuterskop Nature Reserve will appeal to nature lovers. Covering 1 200 ha, the reserve has been stocked with springbok, red hartebeest, eland and zebra, among other species. Adjoining the reserve, higher up the Jordaan River, Loch Athlone is a popular holiday resort offering boating, water-skiing, angling and recreational facilities such as a swimming pool, floodlit tennis courts and a water slide.

FOURIESBURG lies within the territory disputed by the Basotho under Moshoeshoe I, resulting in the Basotho wars of 1858, 1865 and 1867. In terms of the Treaty of Thaba Bosiu, signed in 1866 by Chief Paulus Mopeli (Moshoeshoe's brother), the areas of Fouriesburg, Clarens, the Little Caledon River and Witsieshoek were awarded to the Orange Free State. Fouriesburg also figured in the South African War: following the occupation of Bloemfontein by British forces in March 1900, the Boer forces fell back to the Brandwater Basin, establishing a provisional government at Fouriesburg and making the town their headquarters. The British sealed off five of the six passes giving access to the basin and encountered little resistance from the Boers when they attacked Slabbert's Nek on 23 July. The only remaining exit, the Golden Gate, was sealed off on 28 July and the following day General Marthinus Prinsloo and 4 300 men surrendered. About 20 km east of Fouriesburg, a memorial to the British and Boer forces killed in battle marks the site of Surrender Hill, where the Boers laid down their arms. General JH Olivier, however, refused to recognise the surrender and escaped with 1 500 men through the Golden Gate. In Fouriesburg itself is the house where President Marthinus Steyn lived during the town's brief tenure as a capital city.

CLARENS The picturesque highland village of Clarens lies in a pastoral setting ② of spectacular sandstone outcrops and streams lined by willow and poplar trees. Established in 1912, Clarens was once a retirement village, holiday retreat and home of the Sotho ①, but has become popular with artists, whose work can be viewed at several art galleries, workshops and gift shops. The streets of the village are lined by fine sandstone dwellings, two beautiful sandstone churches and an old mill which is still in working order. Children delight in visiting Cinderella Castle, built from 37 000 beer bottles. There are several rock painting sites on farms in the area, and visitors can also undertake guided fossil-hunting trips.

Clarens owes its name to the Swiss town where President Paul Kruger died in exile on 14 July 1904. The Zuid-Afrikaansche Republiek (ZAR) President's historical links with the area date back to 1866, when five men of his Transvaal Commando were killed in a skirmish against the Basotho at Noupoortsnek. The name has also been given to the Clarens Formation, the distinctive cream or beige sandstones of the Little Berg.

GOLDEN GATE HIGHLANDS NATIONAL PARK is renowned for its mountain scenery, dominated by impressive sandstone formations and expanses of grassveld. Among the well-known landmarks are the twin bluffs after which the park has been named, the Sentinel (or Brandwag) ③, Mushroom Rocks and Gladstone's Nose which resembles the profile of the former British prime minister. Visitors can explore the vicinity of the two rest camps along several short nature trails ranging from one to five hours in duration. Especially rewarding is the Holkrans Trail, a self-guided trail featuring spectacular caves and sections which have to be negotiated by wooden ladders. Not to be missed, though, is a guided walk to Cathedral Cave, where a stream plunges some 30 m through a narrow opening in the cave roof resembling the domed roof of a cathedral. As the cave is used as a roosting and nesting site for a bald ibis colony, walks are only conducted outside the breeding season. Other options include horse-riding and leisurely drives along the two game-viewing loops. Among the game to be seen are grey rhebok, black wildebeest, blesbok, red hartebeest, klipspringer and zebra, while oribi can be seen on the short loop named after this species. The bald ibis is a standout among the park's 150-odd bird species, while a variety of birds of prey, including the occasional bearded vulture, can be seen from the vulture restaurant.

QWAQWA NATIONAL PARK was proclaimed in 1991 as a nature conservation area of the QwaQwa homeland. Covering 22 000 ha of highland mountain scenery, the horseshoe-shaped park borders the Golden Gate Highlands National Park to the north, east and the south, where it also borders Lesotho. The park's main attraction is the imposing outcrops of Clarens sandstone. QwaQwa, the flat-topped mountain after which the area is named, is a prominent landmark in the east of the park. It has been suggested that the Khoikhoi name means 'vulture', a reference to the Cape vulture colony living on the cliffs. A variety of outdoor activities are offered and 4x4 enthusiasts have a choice of three routes which can be completed in three to four hours. Accomplished equestrians can explore the park by joining two-day horse rides conducted over weekends, while hikers can tackle the two-day Avondrus Hiking Trail, which covers 27 km.

BASOTHO CULTURAL VILLAGE ④
Situated within the QwaQwa National Park, the Basotho Cultural Village consists of a collection of homesteads ranging from reed-and-stick beehive structures to more modern constructions featuring colourful geometric patterns. Cultural activities are staged at an amphitheatre, and there is also a shop and restaurant. The village is a living museum where visitors can learn about the history and culture of the South Sotho people by participating in traditional games and watching clay pot-making, weaving and the grinding of maize. A tour of the village takes about an hour, but visitors can also join the Ngaka (traditional healer) on a two-hour guided walk focusing on the medicinal and customary uses of plants. Well-preserved rock paintings along the route provide an added dimension to the trail. At the restaurant visitors can sample a traditional Sotho meal of maize meal, meat, wild spinach and pumpkin.

STERKFONTEIN DAM See Tour 40, page 98.

HARRISMITH See Tour 40, page 98.

KESTELL lies amidst a patchwork of maize-lands and cattle farms typical of the eastern Free State. The town was established in 1905 and named after a Dutch Reformed minister, Reverend John Daniel Kestell. Kestell is noted for its beautiful sandstone buildings, dominated by the Dutch Reformed Church, which was commissioned in 1909 and consecrated on 31 March 1928. During the South African War, the town saw fighting at nearby Groenkop, when a Boer force under the command of General Christiaan de Wet launched a surprise attack. Leaving their horses at the base of Groenkop, the Boers ascended the mountain under cover of darkness and attacked the British forces on Christmas Day 1900. British casualties were 58 killed, 84 wounded and 206 captured, while the Boers lost 14 men.

2

3

4

1

46
320 KM

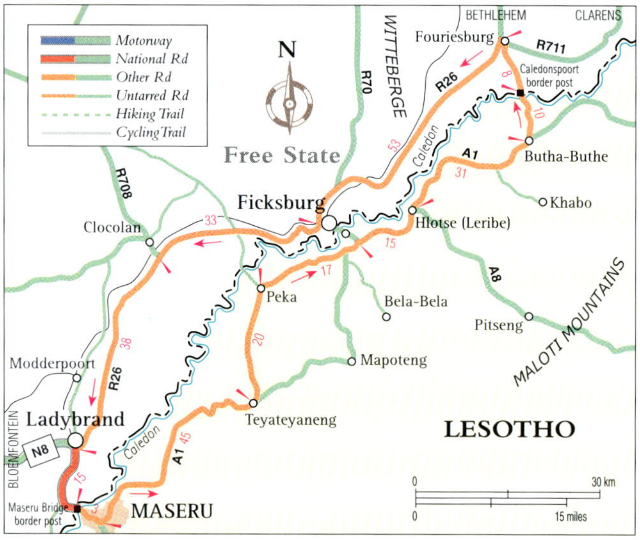

2

3

FOURIESBURG See Tour 45, page 112.

FICKSBURG lies in a magnificent setting between the Mpharane (Imperani) Mountains and the western banks of the Caledon River. Founded in 1867, the town was named after Commandant-General Johan Fick, who commanded the Boer forces in the Third Basotho War. The town is centred around a nucleus of three sandstone buildings: the old Magistrate's Court, built in the late 19th century, the Town Hall (1897) and the Post Office (1907). The Magistrate's Court now serves as a museum devoted to the town's history and the cherry industry.

The fertile valley of the Caledon River here is covered with wheatlands, fields of asparagus and cherry orchards, and is especially attractive during the first three weeks of September when the white cherry blossoms transform the valley into a fairy-tale landscape. The cool, mild winter temperatures are ideally suited to growing cherries, and the Ficksburg region has become the largest producer of this fruit in South Africa. Twelve cultivars are grown, with yellow cherries being produced for the glacé industry and 'red' cherries sold for fresh consumption. In November the town hosts the annual Cherry Festival.

CLOCOLAN takes its name from the Sesotho word *hlohloloane*, which is translated as 'bump and fight' – a reference to a dispute over a basket of wheat. Situated to the west of Prynn's Mountain, the town was laid out on two farms in 1906. The cherry industry of the eastern Free State originated in the Clocolan district, where the first trees were planted by Henry Pickstone in 1904. The surrounding farms are also important producers of wheat, maize and potatoes. Handwoven carpets, rugs, jerseys and other articles are produced by Lethoteng Weavers, a community project, at an informal factory in the town.

MODDERPOORT ranks as one of South Africa's top cultural attractions and features San rock art, Iron Age remains and the well-known Cave Church. The 6 000-ha farm Modderpoort was bought for the Society of St Augustine by Bishop Twells in 1869. The first place of worship was a rock shelter, which was ingeniously converted into a church by building a wall, incorporating a door and window, across the entrance. The priory was built in 1871 and the sandstone church was completed in 1902. The graves of missionaries who worked here can still be seen, as well as the grave of the Basotho prophetess, Mantsopa Makheta. Fearing that she would become too powerful, Moshoeshoe sent her into exile to Modderpoort in the late 1860s, where she converted to Christianity. Following her conversion, it appears that she practised a combination of traditional ancestor worship and Christianity. Pilgrims still visit her grave.

LADYBRAND lies at the foot of the amphitheatre formed by the Platberg amid picturesque sandstone outcrops and grasslands. Established as a frontier post in 1867 in territory conquered from the Basotho, the settlement was named after Lady Catherina Brand, wife of Sir Christoffel Brand, the first Speaker of the Cape Legislative Assembly, and the mother of Johannes Brand, President of the Free State. Situated close to Maseru, Ladybrand is the main gateway to Lesotho and is also an important agricultural and trading centre. In common with other eastern Free State towns, the town has several splendid sandstone buildings, among them the Dutch Reformed Church, the old Magistrate's Court and the secondary school (1905). Overlooking the town is The Stables, a 30-m-high rock crevice used by the Boers to stable their horses during the Basotho War of 1858. There are also numerous rock painting sites in and around the town, among them Tripolitania in the Tandjiesberg. The Catherina Brand Museum contains the fossil remains of a dinosaur known as *Euskelosaurus* and a display on the printing industry in the Free State.

LESOTHO See Tour 47, page 116.

MASERU See Tour 47, page 116.

TEYATEYANENG Also known simply as TY, Teyateyaneng owes its name to the Teja-Tejane River, a name variously interpreted as meaning 'the winding little river', or 'quicksands'. Prior to becoming the headquarters of the Berea district of Basotholand (Lesotho), it was preceded by two earlier settlements, both known as Advanced Post. A site for a new district headquarters was agreed on between the Resident Commissioner, Sir Godfrey Lagden, and Chief Masopha in February 1886. The deal was struck after the Chief indicated that he was willing to pay taxes on condition that he had his own district headquarters. A further condition was that he could recruit police from his own people. TY is famous for its weaving industry, and there are two weaving workshops where fine rugs and tapestries ⑥ are produced from pure mohair sheared from angora goats ⑦ in the Maloti Mountains ④.

HLOTSE was founded in 1876 when Major Charles Bell, one of four magistrates of Basotholand, moved the seat of his magistracy to this spot. The town is the headquarters of the Leribe district, but, confusingly, Hlotse was often called Leribe in the past. In the years following its establishment, the town was besieged during the Gun War (1880–81). Of historic interest is a tower, the only remaining part of the fort built by Bell, and the Anglican Church built by the Reverend John Widdicombe in 1877. A few kilometres north is the Leribe Mission, founded in 1859 by the French missionary, François Coillard. Not to be missed are the dinosaur tracks in the bed of the Subeng River, north of Hlotse, where two rows of about 23 tracks made by a five-toed dinosaur are imprinted in the rock.

BUTHA-BUTHE is named after the sandstone plateau 2 km east of the town where Moshoeshoe established a stronghold in 1820 before moving to Thaba Bosiu in 1824. The name means 'place of lying down', or 'place of reclining', and has been interpreted as referring either to three nearby hills that resemble reclining lions, or to the fact that Moshoeshoe rested here. Butha-Buthe was founded in 1884 so that the Basotho people ①, ② and ③ could pay their taxes at the town instead of travelling to Hlotse (Leribe), and serves as the headquarters of the country's smallest and northernmost district. It is also the gateway to Oxbow (site of a ski resort) and the Roof of Africa road – the oldest trans-Lesotho route – which links Butha-Buthe and the Sani Pass ⑤.

4

5

6

7

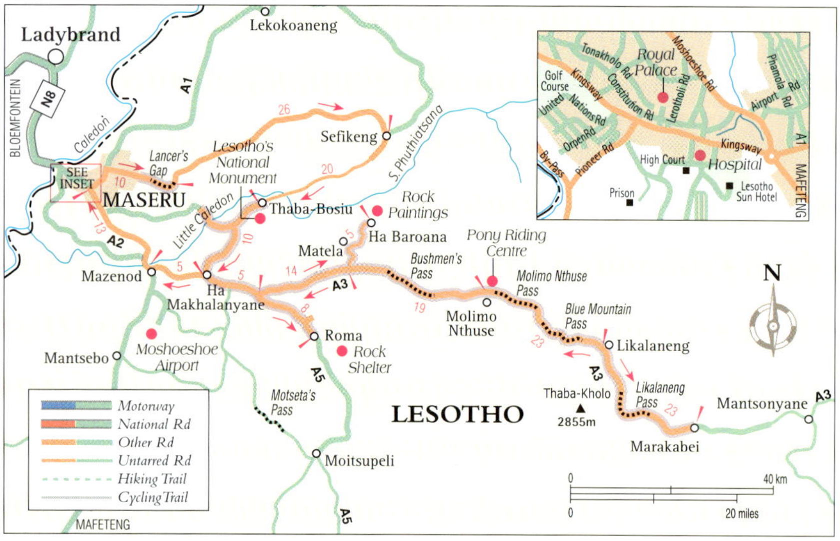

47

305 KM

LESOTHO Also known as the Mountain Kingdom and the Kingdom in the Sky, Lesotho ① is the only country in the world with all its territory above 1 000 m. Except for the Lowlands in the west, it is an extremely rugged land, characterised by high mountains dissected by deep river valleys. Lesotho is home to the Basotho people, who emerged as a nation between 1815 and 1820 when Moshoeshoe united the remnants of various Sesotho-speaking tribes dispersed by the Mfecane. Disputes with the Voortrekkers over land led to three wars between 1858 and 1867, and in March 1868 Basotholand was annexed by the British. When the territory's borders were demarcated, the area west of the Caledon River, referred to by the Basotho as the Conquered Territory, was excluded. In 1884 Basotholand became a High Commission territory, and at independence, on 4 October 1966, changed its name to Lesotho. Blankets were first imported into Basotholand in the 1860s, and still form an integral part of Basotho life. During ceremonies such as the circumcision of boys, a blanket indicates whether a man is married or not, and blankets are also worn on special occasions. Another hallmark of the Basotho is the distinctive conical straw hat, known variously as *tlhoro*, *mokorotlo* or *molianyeo*. It has been suggested that the hat owes its shape to Qiloane, a cone-shaped mountain near Moshoeshoe's stronghold of Thaba Bosiu. Although Lesotho's road network has improved considerably during the last 20 years, the Basotho pony is still an important means of transport ② in the remote mountain villages. Small-stock farming with angora goats and sheep is the main economic activity, while maize and vegetables are cultivated in river valleys. Much of the country's income is, however, derived from migrant labour, although the massive Lesotho Highlands Water Project, which began in 1991, has provided a much-needed economic boost to this poor and landlocked country.

MASERU, the capital of Lesotho, lies on the eastern bank of the Mohokare, or Caledon River, and its Sesotho name is translated as 'the place of red sandstone'. The city developed around a police camp that was established in 1869 by Commandant JH Bowker, Agent of the British High Commissioner for South Africa. Situated at a ford across the river, a bustling trading centre soon sprung up. During the Gun War (1880–81), the settlement came under frequent attack, and several outlying buildings were set alight when Maseru was attacked in October 1880. In 1884, when the first Resident Commissioner, Colonel Marshall Clarke, was appointed, Maseru became the administrative centre for Basotholand. The town's development accelerated with the opening of a railway line and a road bridge across the Caledon River in December 1905. In the 1960s, many South Africans were attracted to Maseru when casinos – prohibited in South Africa at that time – opened in the capital. However, tourist numbers dropped dramatically following the introduction of legal gambling in the 'independent' homelands. Political instability in the latter half of 1998 resulted in the burning of several buildings in Maseru.

LANCERS' GAP A short way out of Maseru the road ascends along a pass through Lancers' Gap, a natural sandstone gateway giving access to the Berea Plateau. The name is somewhat misleading, though, as the route was apparently never used by the 12th Royal Lancers, commanded by Sir George Cathcart, who were defeated by the Basotho at Seliba-sa-Masole in 1852. From the summit of the pass, there are fine views over Maseru and the Conquered Territory. The Sesotho name of the pass, Khalong-la-Ratsosane, honours a headman who lived in the area in the 1830s.

THABA BOSIU is the most important historic site in Lesotho. It was here that the Basotho nation was consolidated by its founder, Moshoeshoe. After establishing his first stronghold at Butha-Buthe, Moshoeshoe moved south and occupied a flat-topped mountain on the Berea Plateau in 1824. This impregnable natural fortress became known as Thaba Bosiu (Mountain of Night), and from here Moshoeshoe united various scattered groups of Sotho into a new nation.

Thaba Bosiu withstood attacks by the Ngwane, Tlokwa, the army of Mzilikazi and Boer forces of the Orange Free State Republic. On 8 August 1865, during the Seqiti War, the Boer forces made an unsuccessful attempt to storm the mountain. In the second attack, on 15 August, Commandant Louw Wepener was shot dead while leading a group of men up the mountain slopes. The Boers were eventually forced to abandon their attempt, with the loss of 11 men killed, and a fruitless month-long siege followed. During the third Basotho War of 1867, when the Free State forces conquered virtually the entire Lowlands, Thaba Bosiu was the only fortress that remained invincible. Guides are available for walks to the summit, where Moshoeshoe's two-roomed house and grave can be seen.

HA BAROANA, a name meaning 'place of the little Bushmen', is one of the best-known and most accessible rock painting sites in Lesotho. Depicted on the walls of the sandstone overhang are finely executed paintings of groups of dancers, hunters, human figures with decorative patterns on their legs, eland, hartebeest and a variety of other animals and birds. The site is often also referred to as Ha Khotso.

MOUNTAIN ROAD ③ Until the 1950s, access to the interior of Lesotho across the centre of the Maloti Mountains was limited to horseback. Construction of the Mountain Road linking Maseru to eastern Lesotho began in the 1950s, and by 1959 the road reached Mantsonyane, 127 km east of Maseru. The 47-km section of road to Thaba-Tseka was opened in 1969, and two years later the first trans-Maloti crossing became possible. The Front Range of the Maloti Mountains forms a formidable barrier, and the Bushman's Pass is the first of several passes that have to be negotiated along the Mountain Road.

MOLIMO NTHUSE, a Sesotho name meaning 'God help me', is the second major pass along the Mountain Road. Nestling among a grove of poplar, plane and willow trees alongside a mountain stream near the base of the pass is the Molimo Nthuse Hotel. About 2 km further on is the Basotho Pony Trekking Centre, established in the 1980s by the Irish government and the Lesotho Tourist Board to promote pony trekking in Lesotho.

BEYOND MOLIMO NTHUSE the road winds across the Blue Mountain Pass (2 620 m) and then passes the turnoff to Likalaneng, where the Mohale Dam is being built. The dam forms part of the massive Lesotho Highlands Water Project, which is designed to meet the water needs of South Africa's densely populated and heavily industrialised Gauteng region. Still further on the road winds across the Likalaneng Pass and then reaches Marakabei, a small village deep in the mountains.

ROMA Originally known as Mohale at Tloutle, Roma developed around the mission station established here in 1862 by the Roman Catholic Church. In time, the mission became known as Ba-Roma, or 'the place of Roman Catholics'. Roma is an important educational centre and home to the National University of Lesotho, which had its beginnings as a Catholic college. Opened in April 1945 in a converted primary school, the institution later became known as the Pius XII College. In 1964 it was transformed into the University of Botswana, Lesotho and Swaziland. Eleven years later, legislation was passed to convert the Roma campus into the National University of Lesotho.

1

2

3

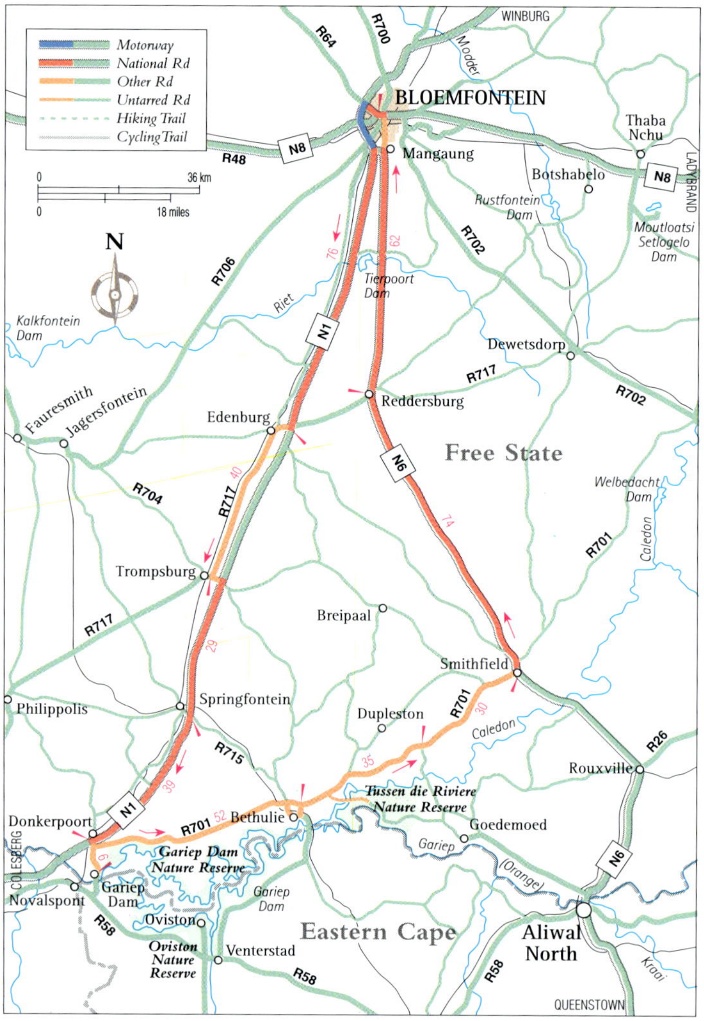

1

48
530 KM

2

BLOEMFONTEIN, the capital of the Free State, was originally known to the Sotho people as Mangaung, a name meaning 'place of the cheetahs'. Founded in 1846 by Major Henry Warden, the British Resident in Griqua territory, the settlement was named after the abundance of flowers that grew around a spring. Since 1910, as the seat of the Court of Appeal, the city has been the judicial capital of South Africa. Bloemfontein ③ occupies an important place in the country's history: here, in 1912, the South African Native National Congress (renamed in 1923 as the African National Congress) was formed.

One of the best ways to appreciate the city's many historic treasures is to follow the Rose Walk, which consists of two routes. Among the places of interest are the Tweetoringkerk (1880), the only twin-spired Dutch Reformed Church in the country, the Presidency (1886) – the official residence of the last three presidents of the Free State – and the First Raadsaal ②. Built in 1849 as a school, the modest building, with its thatched roof and floor of smeared dung, became the first meeting chamber of the Free State Volksraad, or Parliament. The Fourth Raadsaal, completed in 1893, is a magnificent sandstone and red brick building with an entrance porch resembling a Greek temple. Also of interest is the Edwardian-style Supreme Court (1906), the National Women's Memorial, erected in memory of the Boer women and children who died in the South African War, and the adjoining War Museum. Highlights of the National Museum are a reconstruction of an early 1900s Bloemfontein street scene, an extensive archaeological collection – including the 250 000-year-old Florisbad skull – and the country's largest collection of fossil ammonites.

The Free State National Botanical Garden north of the city covers 7 ha of cultivated gardens, lawns and walkways, while the natural highveld vegetation in the remaining 63 ha has been left undisturbed.

EDENBURG is an important centre for the cattle and sheep farms of the surrounding district. The town was established on the farm Rietfontein, bought in February 1862 to build a church. The Free State Volksraad (Parliament) turned down the first application for the town's recognition, but permission was, however, given in March the following year. The town's name is variously said to be a corruption of Edinburgh, the Scottish capital and birthplace of the Reverend Andrew Murray – for many years the only minister in the Free State – or a reference to the biblical Garden of Eden.

TROMPSBURG It was initially named Jagersfontein Road and Hamilton, after the British Governor of the Orange River Colony from 1902 to 1910. Trompsburg was laid out on the farm Middelwater, owned by the brothers Jan and Bastiaan Tromp, when the railway line reached here in 1891. It subsequently became known as Trompsburg.

SPRINGFONTEIN is an important railway centre at the junction of the lines from the Eastern Cape and Gauteng and the branch line to Koffiefontein. The town was established in 1904 on part of the farm Springfontein, named after a strong artesian spring that surfaces here. The town's history is closely linked to the South African War, and among the reminders of the war are the concentration camp (704 people, mainly children, died here), the camp cemetery and the separate cemetery where unbaptised children who died in the concentration camp were buried. Several blockhouses erected by the British along the railway line can still be seen.

GARIEP DAM The town of Gariep Dam dates back to the 1960s when it was built to house the 3 500 people involved in the construction of South Africa's largest dam. Originally named Oranjekrag, it was redeveloped into a holiday resort when the dam ④ was completed in 1969.

Covering a surface area of 374 km^2 when full, the dam has a capacity of 5 346 million m^3. Spanning 914 m across the course of the Gariep (Orange) River, the water backs up for 100 km behind the 88-m-high dam wall and reaches a width of up to 24 km in places. The dam forms part of the Orange River Development Scheme, which includes the Vanderkloof Dam downstream and an 82,5-km-long tunnel linking the Gariep River with the Fish River in the Eastern Cape.

The dam ① is popular with anglers and water-sport enthusiasts, while the Gariep Nature Reserve along the dam's northern shores can be explored along a 25-km network of game-viewing roads. The 13 500-ha reserve consists predominantly of grassland, and is habitat for black wildebeest, blesbok, red hartebeest, springbok, mountain reedbuck and grey rhebok.

BETHULIE may hold the distinction of having had the most names of any South African town. It had its origins in a mission station established by the London Missionary Society in 1829 at Moordenaarsgat to work among the San. After the mission was taken over by the Paris Evangelical Missionary Society in 1835 it was named Caledon, presumably after the river of that name. To avoid confusion with Caledon in the Cape, it was subsequently renamed Verheullpolis, Bethulia (a biblical name referred to in Judith 4:6 and 7) and Heidelberg, before the name eventually reverted to Bethulie. Proclaimed in March 1863, the town is located in a sheep and cattle farming area that also enjoys distinction for its saddle horse stud farms. Among the places of interest in and around the town is Pellissier House, built in 1835 by the Reverend Jean-Pierre Pellissier, a missionary of the Paris Evangelical Missionary Society. One of the oldest surviving buildings in the Free State, it now houses a museum dedicated to local history. Also of interest is the Horse Monument, the stately Dutch Reformed Church dating back to 1887 and the graveyard and monument marking the site of the largest British concentration camp used during the South African War.

TUSSEN-DIE-RIVIERE NATURE RESERVE, a few kilometres east of Bethulie, covers 22 000 ha of land at the confluence of the Caledon and Gariep (Orange) Rivers. The reserve's network of roads and three trails allow visitors to see white rhino, eland, gemsbok, red hartebeest, blesbok, black wildebeest, springbok, impala and Burchell's zebra. Because the reserve also caters for hunters, it is closed to non-hunters during the hunting season, which usually runs from May to August. Among the 225 species of birds recorded in the reserve are no less than 26 raptors, as well as several lark and chat species. One of the reserve's special attractions is a field of eroded dolerite blocks balancing precariously on top of each other. Also known as the Klipstapels (Rock Piles), these intrusions were exposed millions of years ago when the softer sedimentary rocks of the Beaufort Series were eroded away.

SMITHFIELD The laying of the foundation stone of a church by Sir Harry Smith, Governor of the Cape Colony, on the farm Waterval in 1848 did little to boost the growth of this town. When erven were placed on the auction block in December 1848, buyers were deterred by the scarcity of water in the area, and in the following year the town was moved to the farm Rietpoort, 24 km northeast of the original site. The Basotho War Memorial in front of the City Hall serves as a reminder of the turbulent frontier wars in which the town also played a role. The Caledon Museum contains a display on the life of Christiaan De Wet, the famed Boer general of the South African War, as well as Grietjie, a ship's cannon used in the Free State wars against the Basotho, and an 18th-century kitchen. Outside Smithfield is the farm Leeukop, where De Wet was born in 1854, the remains of the Traacha Wool Washing Works, established in 1874, and the farm Beersheba, the site of a former French mission station.

REDDERSBURG developed around the Dutch Reformed Church built on the farm Vlakfontein, purchased in 1859. The Afrikaans name means 'Saviour's town' and the town is said to have been named in honour of Jesus Christ. The village contains beautiful sandstone churches of the Reformed and Dutch Reformed churches and a memorial to men from the district killed during the South African War. The obelisk in the main street is a memorial to General De Wet, who attacked a British garrison of about 600 men on 3 April, forcing them to surrender after a 24-hour engagement.

3

4

THIS PAGE LEFT AND BELOW: SOWETO STREET SCENES (P.122). **OPPOSITE** TOP LEFT AND RIGHT: NDEBELE CRAFTS AND MURALS (P.128); CENTRE: JOHANNESBURG SKYLINE (P.122); BOTTOM LEFT: NDEBELE HOMESTEAD (P.128); BOTTOM RIGHT: SUIKERBOSRAND ZEBRA (P.124).

GAUTENG, SUN CITY & THE PILANESBERG

GAUTENG & NORTH-WEST

49
225 KM

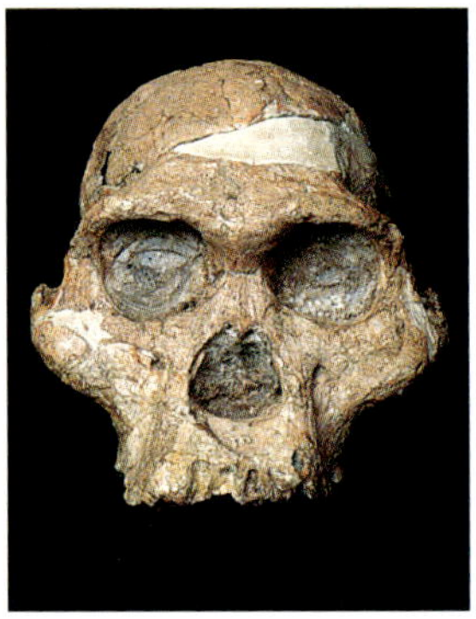
1

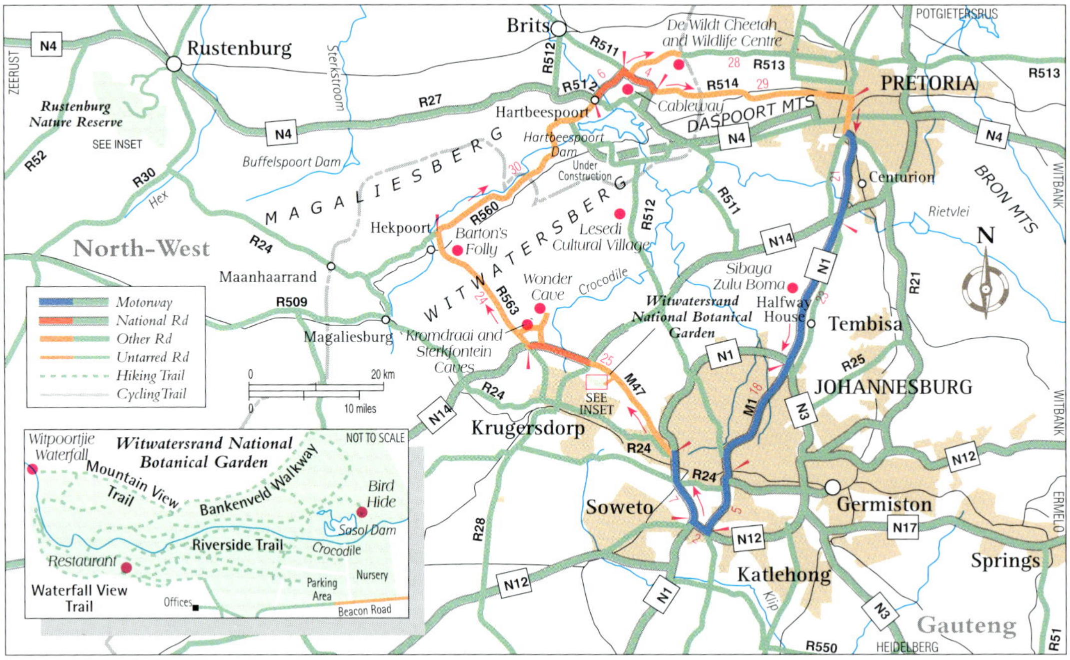

JOHANNESBURG, the business and financial capital of South Africa, developed after the discovery of the Main Reef by George Harrison and George Walker on the farm Langlaagte in March 1886. The site of this significant discovery can be seen in George Harrison Park, about 11 km west of the city centre. The discovery of gold resulted in a rush of fortune-seekers, and a shanty town of over 2 000 inhabitants sprung up. Laid out on the farm Randjieslaagte, the settlement was named after Johann Rissik, an official in the office of the Surveyor-General of the Transvaal Republic, and Christiaan Johannes Joubert, chief of mining and a member of the Volksraad (Parliament).

Also known as eGoli, a Sotho name meaning 'city of gold', Johannesburg ③ is a vibrant, cosmopolitan city, and its attractions are many and varied. Among the most important are Gold Reef City (see Tour 50, page 125) and Soweto, South Africa's most famous black city – comprising 27 townships and 30-odd informal settlements. Tours of Soweto have become popular, and a number of outfits offer such excursions. MuseumAfrika, in the city centre, focuses on the peoples of southern Africa, and incorporates the Geological Museum, Museum of South African Rock Art and the Bensusan Museum of Photography. Johannesburg's other museums focus on themes as diverse as the history of the dynamite industry and music to Judaism, period costumes and military history. Popular outdoor attractions include the 100-ha Herman Eckstein Park, with its zoological gardens, Melville Koppies, an important archaeological site, Delta Park and Melrose Bird Sanctuary. There are several cultural villages in close proximity to the city centre, among them Phumangena Zulu Kraal, Lesedi Cultural Village and Sibaya Zulu Kraal. Also of cultural interest is the Gertrude Poset Gallery with its fine collection of beadwork, masks, headdresses and other forms of African art from southern, central and western Africa. The city also has a wide range of galleries, jazz clubs, restaurants and theatres to choose from.

WITWATERSRAND NATIONAL BOTANICAL GARDEN is one of eight National Botanical Gardens run by the National Botanical Institute. Covering 225 ha of landscaped gardens, lawns and natural vegetation, the garden is set against the backdrop of the impressive 70-m-high Witpoortjie Waterfall. In addition to protecting one of the few remaining patches of undisturbed highveld vegetation, the gardens contain an arboretum of indigenous trees, a marsh garden, collections of indigenous shrubs, cycads and succulents and a garden devoted to ferns and shade-loving plants. The cliffs of the waterfall are home to a famous breeding pair of black eagles. In addition to the walkways there is a geological trail, a bird hide overlooking Sasol Lake, an interpretive centre and a restaurant.

CRADLE OF HUMANKIND is the collective name for the fossil hominid sites of Sterkfontein, Swartkrans, Kromdraai and environs which were declared a World Heritage Site in 1999. Situated in the dolomite hills north of Krugersdorp, Sterkfontein ② is one of the richest early hominid (early human) sites in the world. Significant finds made here include Mrs Ples ①, the first complete hominid skull (discovered in 1947), and the fossil skeleton of Little Foot, a 3,3-million-year-old human-like primate unearthed in 1998. To date, over 600 hominid fossils, thousands of animal fossils, fragments of fossil wood and over 9 000 stone tools have been uncovered in 12 sites within the area since archaeological excavations began here in the 1920s. At Sterkfontein are also a number of underground chambers with magnificent stalagmites, stalactites and other flowstone formations. There are guided tours of the caves, and the adjoining Robert Broom Museum has displays on human evolution and background on the origins and archaeological work carried out at the cave.

Also in the Sterkfontein area is the Wonder Cave, a huge subterranean cavern featuring stalactites and stalagmites up to 15 m high, and the Old Kromdraai gold mine. The gold reef was discovered in 1881 and was proclaimed a public digging in December 1885, the first such proclamation on the Witwatersrand.

BARTON'S FOLLY was built during the South African War in 1901 to guard the entrance to Hekpoort, a narrow kloof through the southern slopes of the Magaliesberg, and formed part of a line of blockhouses in the Magaliesberg. Built under the supervision of Major-General Geoffrey Barton, Commanding Officer of the 6th (Fusilier) Brigade, its unusual shape – which differed from the typical two-storey blockhouses of the time – earned it the name Barton's Folly.

MAGALIESBERG Rising 330 m above the surrounding plains, the Magaliesberg is the most conspicuous of the three parallel quartzite ridges dominating the landscape north of Johannesburg. With a length of about 170 km it stretches in an arc from just south of Rustenburg to Pretoria and then eastwards to the Bronkhorspruit Dam, forming a natural divide between the highveld and the bushveld. Originally named the Cashan Mountains, the Voortrekkers named the range after Mogale, a Tswana chief, and corrupted it to Magaliesberg. Dissected by numerous kloofs with crystal-clear streams, waterfalls and pools, the range is home to over 150 bird species, including three breeding colonies of the Cape vulture and a variety of other raptors, kingfishers, crimsonbreasted shrike, the elusive African finfoot and the Marico flycatcher. Animals occurring here include leopard, brown hyaena, mountain reedbuck, bushbuck, klipspringer and baboon. Although the Magaliesberg is almost entirely private property, most of the range was declared a Natural Area in 1977 and a Protected Natural Environment in 1993.

HARTBEESPOORT DAM ④ was built in 1923 to provide water for an irrigation scheme downstream. Water from the dam, which has a maximum depth of 45 m and a capacity of 186 million m^3 when full, is fed into a network of irrigation canals totalling 547 km in length. With a height of 59 m, the 149,5-m-long dam wall spans the narrow gorge cut between Kommandonek and Silkaatsnek by the Crocodile River, a tributary of the Limpopo River. A single-lane road passes through a short tunnel and then runs along the dam wall, which is decorated with a Roman-style triumphal arch. Covering nearly 19 km^2 when full, the dam has long been a popular playground with powerboating, water-skiing, yachting and freshwater angling enthusiasts. In the villages nestling along the shore may be found a profusion of art and craft shops, art galleries and studios, farm stalls and restaurants. Visitors can ascend by cable car to the summit of the Magaliesberg (a popular hang-gliding venue). The Hartbeespoort Aquarium is one of the largest freshwater aquariums in Africa.

DE WILDT CHEETAH AND WILDLIFE CENTRE Since its establishment in 1971 by Anne van Dyk and her brother Godfrey, the centre has received international acclaim for its work in the breeding of endangered animals. Starting off with nine cheetah, the centre's breakthrough came in March 1975 when the first cubs were born in captivity. Although notoriously difficult to breed, nearly 500 cheetah cubs have been born at De Wildt since then. In 1978, a wild dog breeding project was initiated and also proved to be successful, followed by the birth of the first ever captive-bred king cheetah. This enabled zoologists to prove that the king cheetah was an abnormally marked variant and not a subspecies of the cheetah. Several king cheetah have since been bred at De Wildt. Another milestone in the centre's history was the release in the Karoo National Park in 1994 of six riverine rabbits bred in captivity, nine years after a breeding programme started in 1985 at De Wildt. One of South Africa's most endangered mammals, a specimen was caught near Victoria West in 1979, 32 years after the last one was captured. Among the other species bred at De Wildt are brown hyaena, black-footed cat, suni and Egyptian vulture – a species which has become extinct in South Africa. Two-hour guided tours enable visitors to see the animals, which are kept in large enclosures, in near-natural surroundings.

2

3

4

1

50

365 KM

2

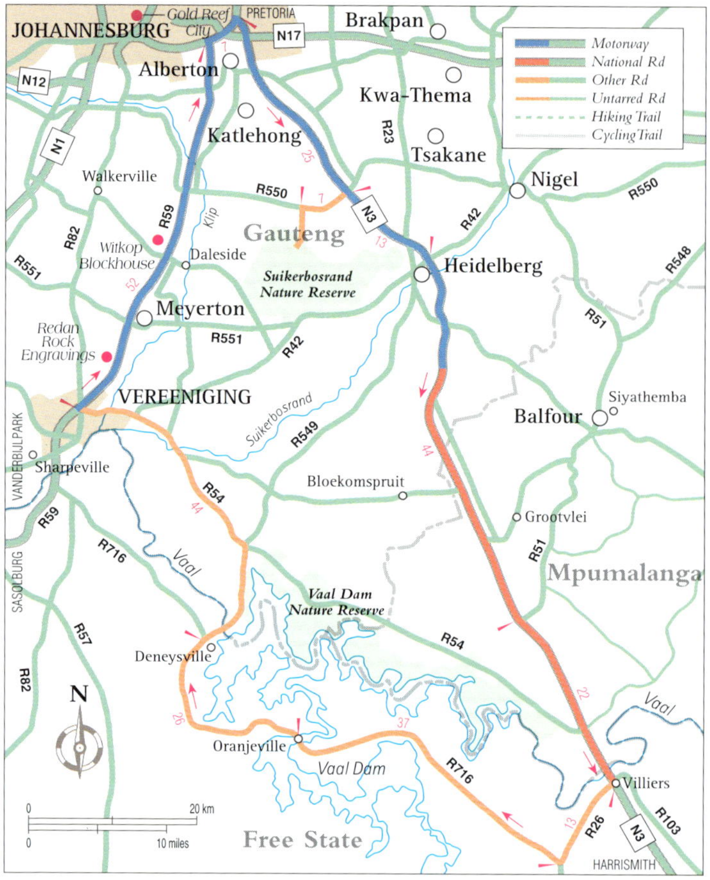

JOHANNESBURG See Tour 49, page 122.

HEIDELBERG lies in a region originally named Suikerbosrand by the Voortrekker party that explored the area in June 1836. The name, meaning 'sugarbush ridge', refers to the common sugarbush (*Protea caffra*) which is abundant on the ridges in the area. Attracted by good grazing and water, a Voortrekker group under Commandant PD Jacobs settled in the area during 1839–40. Situated alongside a busy ox-wagon road, the town developed around a trading store established on the farm Langlaagte by a German shopkeeper, Heinrich Ueckermann, in 1860. When the town was established in 1866, it was named after Heidelberg in Germany, where Ueckermann had been trained. At the outbreak of the War of Independence (1880–81), on 16 December 1880, Heidelberg became the capital of the Zuid-Afrikaansche Republiek (ZAR).

An obelisk featuring busts of Paul Kruger, Piet Joubert and MW Pretorius, the triumvirate who headed the reconstituted republican government, is a reminder of this chapter of the country's history. Heidelberg also has a beautiful sandstone Dutch Reformed Church, built in the Early Norman style and completed in 1891. The town's famous 'bakoond' resembles a large outdoor baking oven, and was built to conceal Heidelberg's water supply during the War of Independence. The Heidelberg Motor Museum, housed in the goods sheds of the railway station, has a fascinating collection of early bicycles (including penny farthings), motorcycles, veteran cars, racing cars and a Class 16 steam locomotive. Built in Dutch-Flemish Renaissance style, the old railway station building dates back to 1895.

SUIKERBOSRAND NATURE RESERVE covers 13 337 ha of grassveld, woodlands and shrublands to the west of Heidelberg. Visitors can explore the reserve along a 60-km tourist route, or follow two self-guided interpretive trails. Suikerbosrand has been stocked with 12 antelope species, including blesbok, black wildebeest, red hartebeest, reedbuck, mountain reedbuck and springbok, while Burchell's zebra also occur. Among the approximately 250 bird species recorded to date are several interesting grassland species such as greywing francolin, several lark species, Ayre's cisticola, pipits and orangethroated longclaw. The Diepkloof Farm Museum is centred on one of the oldest farmhouses north of the Vaal River, on the farm established by Jan Gabriël Marais in the 1850s.

VILLIERS was established in 1882 on the farms Pearson Valley and Grootdraai, on the southern bank of the Vaal River, and was named after Lourens de Villiers, the owner of both farms. With its beautiful gardens and willow trees lining the banks of the Vaal River, Villiers is a pretty town serving the maize farms and cattle ranches in the area and is an important rail junction.

VAAL DAM ③ Completed in 1938, the Vaal Dam was built to meet the growing need for water by the densely populated and heavily industrialised PWV (Pretoria, Witwatersrand, Vereeniging) area (now Gauteng). But by the early 1950s, it became necessary to increase the dam's capacity and the height of the wall was raised from 54,2 m to 60,3 m, increasing the dam's capacity from 994 million m^3 to 2 188 million m^3. In 1985, the dam wall was raised by another 3 m, increasing its capacity to 2 536 million m^3. An additional 663 million m^3 can be stored temporarily to reduce flooding danger. Because the dam can no longer meet Gauteng's water needs, water is transferred from the Sterkfontein Dam in northeastern Free State (see Tour 40, page 98) into the Vaal system. The dam's water supply was further augmented in 1998 when it received its first water from the Lesotho Highlands Water Project. With a surface area of 320 km^2 and situated conveniently close to Johannesburg, the Vaal Dam is a popular recreational area, especially with power-boat, water-skiing, yachting and angling enthusiasts. Several recreational resorts lie along the dam's banks.

DENEYSVILLE was established in 1936 on the farms Witpoort and Wilhelmina, near the wall of the Vaal Dam, as a recreational town. It was named in honour of Colonel Deneys Reitz, Minister of Lands when the dam was built and author of the trilogy of the South African War, *Commando*, *Trekking On* and *No Outspan*. A mecca for water-sport enthusiasts ④, Deneysville has three marinas and is the base of a yacht and aquatic water-sport club.

VEREENIGING Situated on the northern bank of the Vaal River, Vereeniging forms part of South Africa's largest industrial complex. The town owes its existence to the rich coal deposits occurring in the area and was founded on the farms Leeuwkuil and Klipplaatsdrift in 1882. It owes its Dutch name, translated as 'association', to the first coal mining company in the area, the Zuid-Afrikaansche en Oranje Vrijstaatsche Kolen-en-Mineralen-Mijn Vereeniging. The town made world headlines in May 1902 when the terms to end the South African War were negotiated here. The treaty was, however, signed at Melrose House in Pretoria (see Tour 52, page 128). The Vaal River and its willow-lined banks are popular recreational areas, drawing many people on weekends and holidays. The town's museum displays a valuable collection of photographs of the peace negotiations, and also has interesting archaeological and palaeontological exhibits, among them *Glossopteris* fossil plants occurring in the coal seams. The Vaal Technorama Industrial Museum is the only one of its kind in the country.

Three archaeological sites of interest lie in and around the town: the Duncanville Archaeological Reserve and the Klip River Quarry, 6 km out of town, have both yielded a large number of Earlier Stone Age tools, while on an outcrop at Redan, a few kilometres to the north of the town, Stone Age shamans (medicine men) carved over 240 engravings, mainly geometrical, into the rock. Prior arrangements to visit Redan must be made with the Vaal Technorama Museum.

SHARPEVILLE, a black township outside Vereeniging, has become a symbol of the struggle against apartheid. On 21 March 1960 police opened fire on a large crowd of Pan Africanist Congress (PAC) supporters demonstrating against the pass laws, killing 69 and wounding 180. A week later, a state of emergency was declared and the ANC and the PAC were banned. Today, the massacre is commemorated as Human Rights Day, set aside as a public holiday by South Africa's first democratically elected government.

WITKOP BLOCKHOUSE This sturdy stone bastion was built during the South African War as part of a line of fortifications to defend the railway line against guerrilla attacks by the Boer forces. By early 1902 an extensive system of some 8 000 blockhouses had been built across the country. One of the principal lines of blockhouses stretched from Colesberg to Kroonstad and Vereeniging along the railway line, which was patrolled by armoured trains.

GOLD REEF CITY is a re-creation of Johannesburg in its heyday, centred around No. 14 shaft of the Crown Mine. The atmosphere of the mining town as it looked between 1900 and 1920 has been captured, complete with horse-drawn carts, can-can girls and minstrels. Lining the streets are replicas of Johannesburg's first stock exchange (built in 1887), Victorian houses, saloons and corrugated-iron stores. Among Gold Reef City's numerous attractions are a casino ①, gold-pouring demonstrations ②, gumboot dancing performances, a tour of the mine's 5th level – 220 m below the surface – and an adventure park with 26 rides, ranging from a fun train to the Anaconda, and Africa's longest river ride, the Raging River Rapids.

3

4

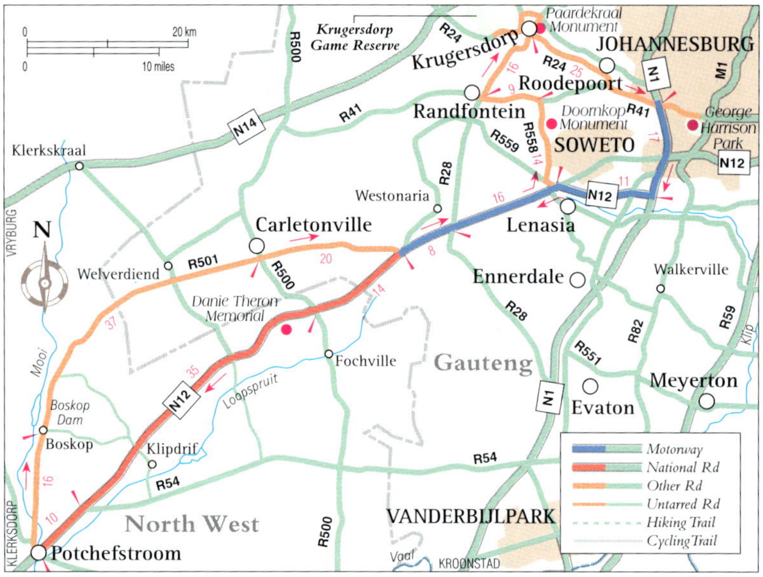

51
275 KM

1

2

JOHANNESBURG See Tour 49, page 122.

DANIE THERON MEMORIAL This memorial marks the spot where Danie Theron, one of the legendary figures of the South African War, was killed. Born at Tulbagh in the Cape, Theron settled in the Transvaal and practised as a lawyer in Krugersdorp. At the outbreak of the South African War, he joined the Boer forces as a captain in the Wielrijders Rapportgangers Corps, a unit of despatch riders that used cycles. Following the Battle of Colenso, he was placed in charge of an elite corps of scouts trained by General Christiaan De Wet and known as Theron's Verkenningscorps. Theron was killed in a skirmish against a British detachment at Elandsfontein in September 1900. In recognition of his courage, the commando training school at Kimberley was named after him in 1968.

POTCHEFSTROOM was laid out along the banks of the Mooi River in November 1838 after a Voortrekker party, led by Commandant Andries Potgieter, settled in the area. The first Voortrekker congregation north of the Vaal River was established at Potchefstroom on 25 March 1842, and the settlement also served as the capital of the Zuid-Afrikaansche Republiek (ZAR) from 1857 until it was moved to Pretoria. The opening shots of the War of Independence (1880–81) were fired at Potchefstroom on 16 December 1880, beginning a 95-day Boer siege of the town's historic Fort.

Potchefstroom's other historic buildings include the Civic Centre ⑤ cruciform-shaped Dutch Reformed Church, completed in 1866 on the site of an earlier church, and the Old Presidency (1868), a small house where the first President of the ZAR, Marthinus Pretorius, lived for many years. Other noteworthy buildings include the neo-Rennaisance-style Landdrost (Magistrate's) Offices (1895) and Totius House (1906), residence of Dr Jacob du Toit, the Afrikaans author, poet and translator of the Bible into Afrikaans. The town has three house museums: Totius House, President Pretorius Museum and Goetz/Fleischack Museum, the only surviving example of the typical townhouses built around the town's market square in the 1850s. Potchefstroom Museum focuses on the history and development of the area and has a valuable collection of paintings by Otto Landsberg. Among the town's other attractions is a 7-km-long avenue of oak trees – the longest such avenue in the southern hemisphere – with more than 700 trees. Potchefstroom is today the centre of a rich agricultural district, as well as a university town.

CARLETONVILLE, like other West Rand towns, owes its existence to the rich gold deposits occurring here. Mining in the area dates back to the 1930s after two geologists, Dr Leopold Reinecke and Dr Rudolf Krahmann, confirmed the presence of gold under a thick sheet of lava and dolomite. Meanwhile, options had secretly been taken on farms in the area, and a new gold rush began after Reinecke and Krahmann made their announcement in October 1932.

Situated in one of the richest gold-producing areas in the world, the landscape to the south of Carletonville is dotted with the hea gears of numerous mines. Among these are the Western Deep Levels, whose main shaft reaches down 3 581 m below the surface. The town was laid out on the farm Twyfelvlakte and proclaimed in January 1948. It was named after Carleton Jones, one of the directors of the Consolidated Gold Fields company. In addition to serving the mining industry, Carletonville is also a centre for the district's maize farms.

Underground caves in the dolomite, along with the effects of mining, have from time to time produced gaping sinkholes in the area. In 1962, 29 people were disasterously killed at the West Driefontein Mine when a large chunk of earth was swallowed by a sinkhole.

WESTONARIA was proclaimed a town in 1938, its name a homophone of 'western areas' – the name of the company that developed the town. The main point of interest in the area is the Pullinger Shaft, named after the Pullinger brothers, who sank the first deep-level shaft. The town is a popular destination with the sky-diving fraternity.

RANDFONTEIN, meaning 'ridge fountain', was laid out on the farm of that name in 1890, four years after the mining magnate Joseph Benjamin Robinson bought several farms in the area. In 1889, Robinson founded the Randfontein Estates Gold Mining Company and developed the mine into the largest in the world. It had a mighty 600-stamp main battery for crushing ore, a large private power station and, for its time, the largest mine dump ever created.

DOORNKOP, on the farm Vlakfontein, marks the site where the invading force led by Dr Leander Starr Jameson surrendered to the Boer forces on 2 January 1896. The expedition, known as the Jameson Raid, was planned by Cecil John Rhodes, Jameson and leaders of the Uitlanders (expatriate whites) to seize the Transvaal by force. The plan called for Jameson to invade the Transvaal from Bechuanaland (modern Botswana) and to join up with the Uitlanders near Krugersdorp, from where they would continue to Pretoria to overthrow the government. Jameson assembled a 500-strong force in Pitsane (Botswana), and on the evening of 29 December 1895 he crossed into the ZAR. A planned Uitlander rising in Johannesburg never materialised, and after advancing some 250 km into the Transvaal in three days, Jameson's force was attacked by the Boers on 1 January 1896. After being surrounded, and with a large number of his men killed or wounded, Jameson was forced to surrender.

KRUGERSDORP now falls within the new municipal area of Mogale City, created in 2001. The name of the new municipality honours the Tswana chief, Mogale, for whom the Magaliesberg is named (see Tour 49, page 123). Under its former name, Krugersdorp played a pivotal role in the events leading up to the War of Independence. In December 1880 a meeting was called on the farm Paardekraal where it was decided to restore the Zuid-Afrikaansche Republiek (ZAR) as it had existed before the British annexation of the territory in 1877. On 14 December, the burghers built a cairn nearly 3 m high, topped with the Vierkleur (the flag of the ZAR), to symbolise their determination to restore the independence of the republic. An obelisk was built on a platform over the cairn in 1891. During the South African War, the British removed the rocks from the Paardekraal Monument and dumped them in the Vaal River near Vereeniging in 1900. The town was established to the west and southwest of the Paardekraal Monument in 1887 and named after the ZAR President, Paul Kruger. Noteworthy buildings include the City Hall ④, Government Buildings (1890), comprising a Magistrate's Court and offices and the old railway station. To the west of the town lies the Krugersdorp Game Reserve, which covers about 1 500 ha. It has been stocked with about 1 000 head of game of 30 species, among them white rhino, giraffe, kudu, gemsbok, roan and sable antelope, red hartebeest, black wildebeest, springbok, impala and blesbok. For many visitors, though, the lion enclosure is the reserve's main attraction.

ROODEPOORT developed around a mining camp established by the Struben brothers on the farm Wilgespruit following the discovery of gold there in 1884. Gold-diggers and fortune-seekers rushed in, and numerous other camps soon sprung up. Roodepoort has since developed into a large residential and industrial area. Points of interest in and around the town include the Roodepoort Museum ②, the Witwatersrand National Botanical Garden (see Tour 49, page 122) and the Kloofendal Nature Reserve, where the Struben brothers discovered the Confidence Reef in September 1884. The National Railway Museum has a fascinating collection of over 100 steam, diesel and underground electric locomotives, steam cranes, steam rollers, old passenger coaches and other items from to the era of steam. Roodepoort is host to the biennial Roodepoort International Eisteddfod, at Florida Lake ①. Formerly a marshy area, the lake is a popular recreation area, especially with water-sport enthusiasts ③, while the western part is an important breeding area for a variety of waterfowl.

3

4

5

1

52
510 KM

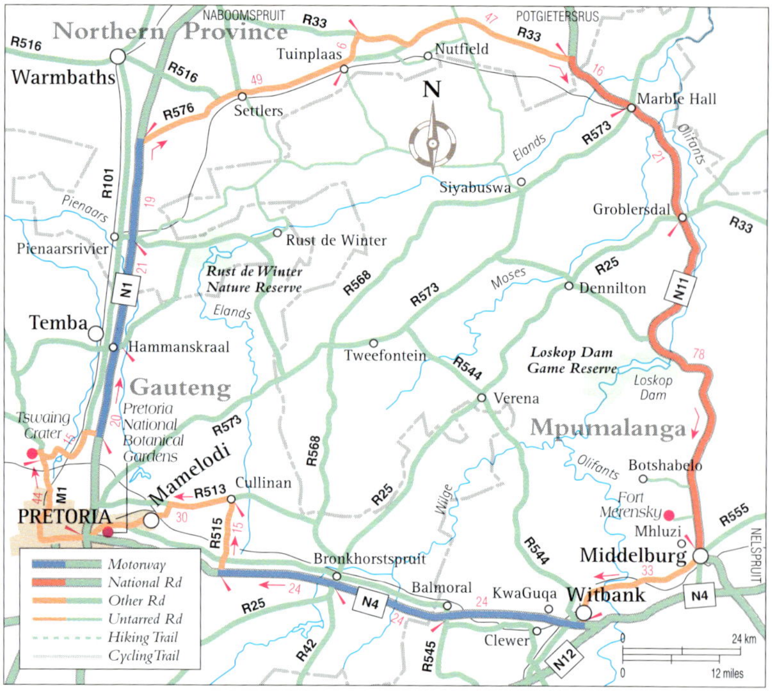

2

PRETORIA, the administrative capital of South Africa, was established in 1855 and became the capital of the Zuid-Afrikaansche Republiek (ZAR) five years later. The city's name honours the Voortrekker leader, Andries Pretorius. Also known as the Jacaranda City because of the profusion of these exotic trees, there is much to do and see in this city, which was the bastion of apartheid until the first democratic elections in 1994. In the heart of the city is Church Square, with its statue of Paul Kruger ③. Clustered around the square are several historic buildings built in the late 1880s and 1890s, among them the imposing Palace of Justice, the Raadsaal, or House of Parliament, the Grootkerk and the State Bank and Mint.

Other noteworthy buildings include the Sammy Marks Fountain ①, Paul Kruger Church (1897), Railway Station (designed by Sir Herbert Baker; extensively damaged by fire in February 2001), the City Hall ④ and Government House (1906). Dominating the skyline of the ridge to the southwest of the city centre is the Voortrekker Monument, opened in 1949 to commemorate the Great Trek, while the Herbert Baker-designed Union Buildings, with its imposing colonnades, occupy a commanding position on Meintjieskop. Fort Schanskop (1897) and Fort Klapperkop (1898) are two of the eight forts built around Pretoria to defend the Boer capital.

Among the city's numerous museums are the Transvaal Museum, a natural history museum housing, among others, a fascinating archaeological display, and the Austin Roberts Bird Hall, with its extensive bird collection; the cottage-style Paul Kruger House; and Melrose House, where the Treaty of Vereeniging was signed on 31 May 1902. The city's National Zoological Gardens are rated among the world's ten best zoos. Covering 600 ha of landscaped gardens, the zoo is home to over 600 species of animals which are kept in enclosures resembling as far as possible their natural habitats. There is also a Reptile Park and Aquarium, the latter with the largest collection of freshwater fish in Africa, as well as marine fish in artificial sea water. The focal point of the Wonderboom Nature Reserve, just north of the city centre, is a massive wild fig tree with a crown spead over 55 m. With a height of 23 m, the tree is estimated to be over 1 000 years old.

TSWAING CRATER, a Tswana name meaning 'place of salt', is one of the best-preserved meteorite impact craters in the world, and one of four in South Africa. With a diameter of just over 1 km and a depth of about 120 m, the roughly circular crater was formed about 220 000 years ago. At the centre of the crater lies a brine lake which was mined for soda during the early 1900s. Visitors can explore the crater by taking a guided tour, or by following the Crater Trail. Displays on the natural and cultural history of the crater can be seen on site, or in the Tswaing Crater Museum, the first enviro-museum in South Africa. The Mapoch Ndebele Village, a living village devoted to Ndebele culture, also forms part of the museum.

WARMBATHS ② was laid out on four farms in 1882 and originally named Hartingsburg, but was renamed Warmbad (warm bath) in 1920, after the hot spring surfacing on one of the farms, named Het Bad (the bath). The town's main attraction is the hot spring resort, with its hydro spa, outdoor pool complex, water slides, wave pool and river ride. Cable water-skiing is one of many leisure and recreational activities on offer. Adjoining the resort is a small nature reserve, which can be seen by taking a guided game drive. A wide choice of accommodation is available. During the South African War, the British built a blockhouse near the railway station to protect the line against attack by Boer commandos.

BOTSHABELO was established as a mission station by Alexander Merensky of the Berlin Missionary Society in 1865 as a refuge for subjects of Sekhukhune who were being persecuted for adopting Christianity. In the same year, a sturdy stone fort (later known as Fort Merensky) was built to protect the mission. The Sotho name, Botshabelo, appropriately means 'place of refuge', and the mission station soon developed into a sizable village with a Gothic-style church, parsonage, school, trading store, water mill and a teacher's training school. Merensky also opened a printing press, where a Sesotho version of the Bible, hymn books and school books were printed, and a book bindery.

The main attraction of Botshabelo is the South Ndebele open-air museum, which offers a vivid picture of Ndebele history and culture. A living museum, it depicts the development of Ndebele architecture from the early dome-shaped grass homesteads to mud-walled homes with their famous mural decorations. Guided tours are available. The area surrounding the mission has been set aside as a nature reserve which can be explored along day walks. Trailists might chance upon eland, black wildebeest, blesbok, red hartebeest, springbok and Burchell's zebra. Accommodation is available.

MIDDELBURG was established in 1866 after it was decided to subdivide the Lydenburg congregation of the Dutch Reformed Church. Originally given the biblical name of Nazareth, it was renamed Middelburg in 1874 on account of its position midway between Pretoria and Lydenburg. The town lies in an area rich in coal deposits and has developed into a major industrial and agricultural centre, serving the coal mines, power stations, stainless steel factory and surrounding farms. Places of interest include the White Church, built for the Dutch Reformed Church congregation in 1890, the concentration camp cemeteries south of the town and on Kanonkop, and the sandstone Meyer Bridge, built over the Little Olifants River in 1895.

WITBANK owes its existence to the region's rich coal deposits. The first shaft was sunk by Samuel Stanford in 1896, and the town was laid out seven years later by the mining company, Witbank Colliery. Its Afrikaans name, meaning 'white ridge' is derived from the light-coloured outcrop near the railway station. Since its establishment in 1903, Witbank has developed into a major centre for the area's 20-odd collieries, smelters and other industries. Of historic interest is the mine shaft at the Transvaal and Delagoa Bay Mine, where Winston Churchill hid after his escape from Pretoria.

CULLINAN, a charming village with terraced Victorian cottages, developed around the Premier Diamond Mine. The mine was opened following the discovery in 1902 of a rich kimberlite pipe by Sir Thomas Cullinan, in whose honour the village was named. Among the many large diamonds recovered from the mine, the most famous is the 3 106-carat Cullinan Diamond, the largest gem diamond ever found. Bought by the Transvaal government, it was presented to King Edward VII and forms part of the British Crown Jewels. The Willem Pretorius Agricultural Museum, 10 km north of Cullinan, is centred around an old farmstead dating back to 1880. It comprises the historic house, outbuildings, stables and a museum where old agricultural implements are displayed.

PRETORIA NATIONAL BOTANICAL GARDEN covers 75 ha of natural vegetation, lawns and landscaped gardens on Silverton Ridge, a quartzite outcrop to the east of Pretoria. Over 1 000 species of flowering plants and trees occur naturally in the garden which also has cultivated sections devoted to fynbos plants, succulents, cycads, aloes and forest species. Among the indoor treasures are the internationally known Desmond Cole Lithops Collection – devoted to the unusual succulents also known as 'flowering stones' – and the valuable Hardy Collection of plants from Namaqualand, Madagascar and Namibia. There are paved walkways, nature trails and an artificial waterfall in the forest adjoining the tea garden.

3

4

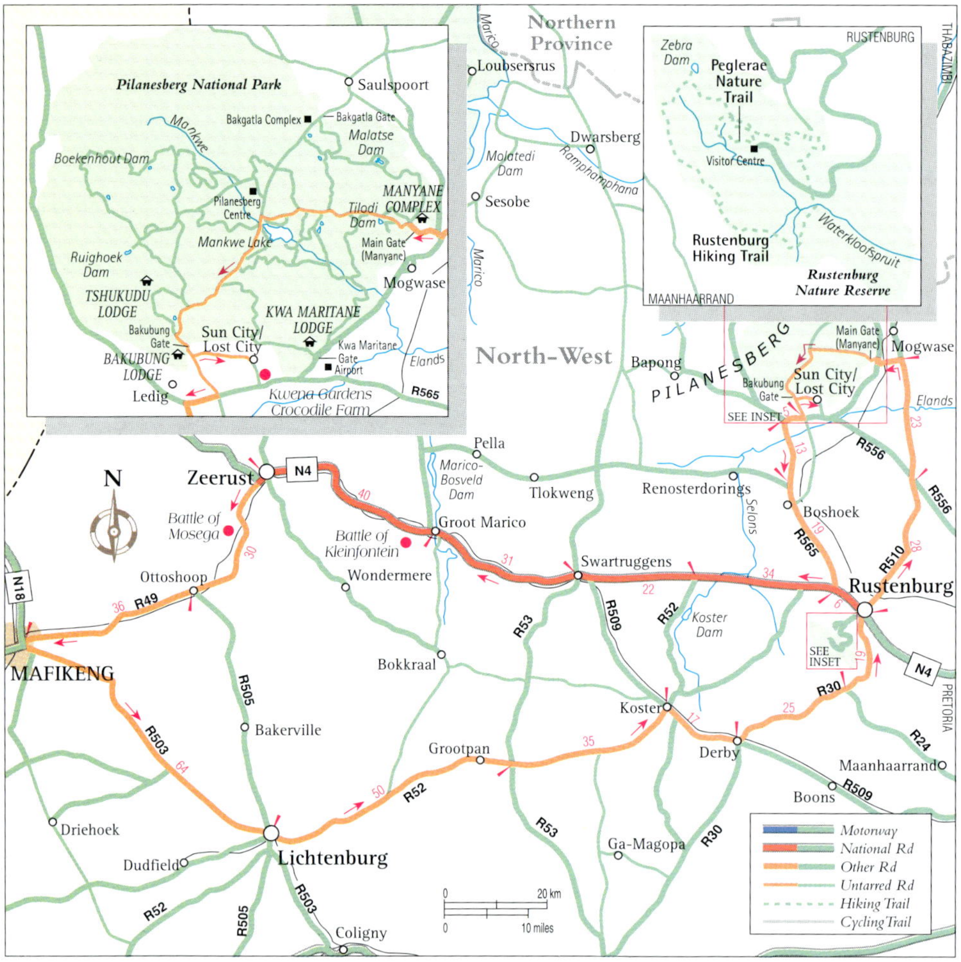

53
595 KM

13 waterfalls, numerous cascades and a water slide with a 97-m drop. In addition to the Palace Hotel, there are three other hotels and a wide range of entertainment and recreational facilities. Among the other amenities are the Entertainment Centre (consisting of the Superbowl, slot machine area, restaurants and bars), a Casino, the Sun City Lake with a variety of water sports, and the Gary Player Country Club, famous for the annual Nedbank Million Dollar Golf Tournament.

PILANESBERG NATIONAL PARK is home to the Big Five, a rich diversity of other game and over 350 bird species. Covering 580 km², Pilanesberg is home to one of the largest white rhino populations in the world, as well as sable, roan, kudu, blue wildebeest, gemsbok, springbok and impala, while hippo and crocodile inhabit the crater lake in the centre of the park. Other species to be seen include giraffe and Burchell's zebra, cheetah and brown hyaena. The park lies within one of the most fascinating geological areas in southern Africa: an alkaline complex produced by volcanic activity some 1 200 million years ago. There are nearly 200 km of game-viewing roads, numerous viewing points, picnic sites, hides and a walk-in aviary near the Manyane Gate. Accommodation ranges from three luxury lodges to chalets and campsites.

RUSTENBURG The first Voortrekker farmers settled in the Rustenburg area in 1841, following the defeat of Mzilikazi and the Ndebele during a punitive expedition two years earlier. The third-oldest town north of the Vaal River, the settlement was proclaimed in 1851 and named Rustenburg, meaning 'town of rest'. Its growth accelerated after Dr Hans Merensky discovered a seam of platinum-bearing rock near here in 1925. Today Rustenburg is an important centre for the nearby mines producing platinum-group metals and chromite, as well as an agricultural district known for its citrus fruit, tobacco, sunflower seed, maize and beef production. Places of interest include the Anglican Church(1871), Dutch Reformed Church (1903) and a replica of the stump of a seringa tree under which the Gerevormeerde Church was founded in February 1859. Also of interest is the Hervormde Church Square, where the divided Voortrekker leaders Andries Potgieter and Andries Pretorius were reconciled in 1852. West of the town is Boekenhoutsfontein farm, where Paul Kruger lived from 1873 until his election as President of the Zuid-Afrikaansche Republiek (ZAR) in 1883. A complex of farm buildings is now a museum.

RUSTENBURG NATURE RESERVE covers 4 257 ha of the Magaliesberg on the southwestern outskirts of the town. It is home to a variety of antelope, including sable, kudu, black wildebeest, red hartebeest, blesbok, springbok and reedbuck, as well as Burchell's zebra. Among the more than 230 bird species recorded to date are Cape vulture, martial eagle, 11 chat and thrush species, Meyer's parrot and the striking lilacbreasted roller. Facilities for visitors include an information centre, interpretive trail and an overnight hiking trail.

SUN CITY & LOST CITY It was the vision of one man – hotel and casino magnate Sol Kerzner – that transformed a tract of African bush into an internationally famous resort. The focal point of the Sun City complex is the magnificent Palace of the Lost City ①, conceived as a mythical kingdom destroyed by an earthquake and 'lost' until its rediscovery in 1991. Attractions of the Lost City include the Valley of Waves, which features a wave pool,

SWARTRUGGENS Named after the distinctive black ridges in the area, the village of Swartruggens is a centre for the surrounding cattle, maize and tobacco farms. It was established on the farm Brakfontein in 1875.

GROOT MARICO Were it not for mampoer and the writings of Herman Charles Bosman, Groot Marico would probably have remained a little-known backwater. Although the area was settled around 1845, the town was only established over a century later, in 1948, on the farm Wonderboom. Mampoer, a potent home-distilled spirit made from peaches and other soft fruit, is still produced in the district.

KLEINFONTEIN BATTLEFIELD is marked by a roadside memorial to the southwest of Groot Marico. By the end of 1900, the Boer strategy of guerrilla warfare was beginning to pay off, and the guerrillas of General Koos de la Rey had regained control over large areas of the southwestern Transvaal. On 24 October 1901 De la Rey's forces captured a British convoy, including 12 wagons of ammunition and many horses and mules.

ZEERUST, the main town of the Marico district, lies amid acacia bush in the valley of the Klein Marico River. It grew around the church built in 1867 on the farm of Casper Coetzee who, unfortunately, did not live to see the completion of the church. The town was named Coetzee Rust in his memory (later abbreviated to Zeerust), while the Tswana name, Sebatlani, means 'dusty place'. It is an important centre for the surrounding cattle ranches, as well as the chrome and lead mines in the area. Of interest in the town are the Church of St John the Baptist (1873), the third Anglican church built north of the Vaal River, and the Zeerust Museum, which portrays the district's history.

THE BATTLE OF MOSEGA When the Voortrekkers began settling north of the Vaal River in 1836, the Ndebele chief, Mzilikazi, became alarmed. In August 1836 two Voortrekker parties were attacked, and a month later a large Ndebele force attacked the Boer laager at Vegkop. In January 1837, a punitive expedition consisting of 107 Voortrekkers, 40 Griquas and 60 Rolong captured Mosega, Mzilikazi's stronghold, killing 400 Ndebele and capturing 7 000 head of cattle.

MAFIKENG, a Tswana name meaning 'place of rocks', was established by Sir Charles Warren as an administrative centre when Bechuanaland (modern-day Botswana) was annexed to the Cape. During the South African War, this frontier town grabbed world headlines when the British garrison, commanded by Colonel Robert Baden-Powell, was besieged by Boer forces in October 1899, a few days after the outbreak of war. The siege was only relieved 271 days later, after Lord Roberts broke through at Paardeberg. To the northwest of Mafikeng is Mmabatho, built as the capital of Bophuthatswana, a homeland that became 'independent' from South Africa in 1977 and was reintegrated in 1994.

Among Mafikeng's numerous historic sites are the cemetery, where British soldiers and members of the British South African Police killed in the siege were buried, Kanonkopjie with Warren's Fort, built in 1884, and the Mafikeng Club, which dates back to 1894. Other attractions include Maratiwa, the house where ANC founder member Sol Plaatjies wrote his account of the siege of Mafikeng, the site of his newspaper office and the Kgotla, tribal meeting place of the Barolong Boo-Ratshidi.

LICHTENBURG was founded in 1873 as a centre for the surrounding cattle farms. The town became the scene of a frantic diamond rush following the discovery of alluvial diamonds to the north in 1925. Although the frenzy died down after about ten years, claims are still being worked in the area. Today the town serves a prosperous agricultural area producing maize, sunflower seeds and groundnuts. Landmarks include the historic Dutch Reformed Church (1890), two memorials to the famous Boer General, Koos de la Rey, and the Gruisfontein Battlefield, where the Boers suffered heavy losses during the South African War. The Ampie Bosman Cultural History Museum, Andries Beyers Agricultural Museum, Lichtenburg Museum and the collection of paintings by South African artists in the William Annandale Art Gallery are among the town's other attractions. Just north of the town is the 6 000-ha game-breeding centre of the National Zoological Gardens in Pretoria, and some 25 km northwest of the town the diamond diggings at Bakerville can be seen.

1

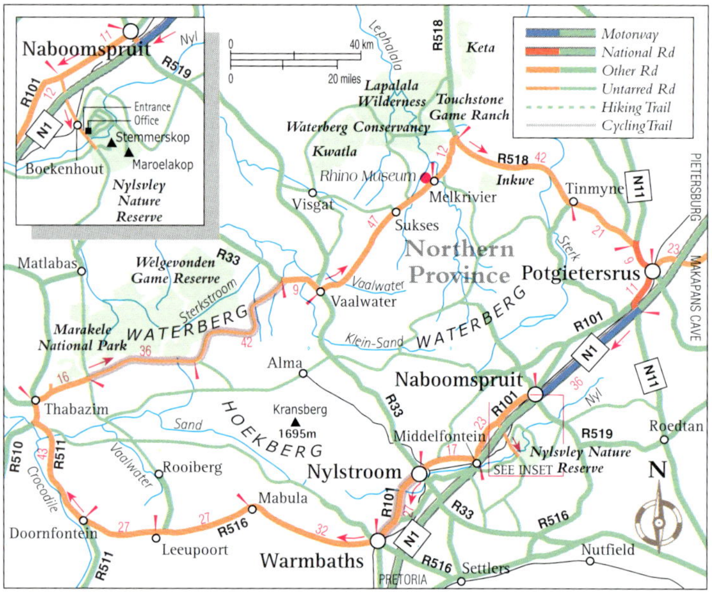

54

575 KM

1

2

NYLSTROOM When a party of Voortrekker religious zealots heading for the Holy Land first saw Kranskop, east of Nylstroom, in the 1860s they naively mistook the hill for a pyramid and the Mogalakwena River for the upper reaches of the River Nile. As a result, the town was named Nylstroom (Nile stream) when it was founded in 1866. Places of interest include the old Reformed Church (1889) – the oldest church north of Pretoria – and the site of a South African War concentration camp and the camp cemetery. Among the other attractions are an old locomotive that saw service on the line between Pretoria and Nylstroom near the end of the 1800s, the Nylstroom Museum, Waterberg Museum and JG Strijdom House, where one of South Africa's former prime ministers lived for many years. The town is a centre for the cattle ranches and citrus fruit farms of the region.

WARMBATHS See Tour 52, page 128.

THABAZIMBI, an indigenous name meaning 'mountain of iron', owes its existence to the discovery of rich iron ore deposits in the area in 1919. Exploitation of the deposits began in the 1930s and the mining town, built on the farm Kwaggashoek by Iscor, has a natural, park-like atmosphere. It was proclaimed in 1953 and has developed into an important centre for the area's cattle and game ranches.

WATERBERG Rising some 600 m above the Springbok Flats to the east, the Waterberg stretches in an arc from a few kilometres northeast of Thabazimbi west for 150 km to near Potgietersrus. Its Afrikaans name, meaning 'water mountain', is an apt one, for this pristine tract of land has numerous rivers, streams, waterfalls and springs ③ and ④. The area provided the setting for the classic *The Road to Waterberg* by well-known author Eugene Marais, who also wrote *The Soul of the White Ant*. Although this is prime cattle country, many of the landowners have switched to game-farming and the Waterberg Conservancy, established in 1982, covers over 150 000 ha. Plans are under way to register the Waterberg as a biosphere reserve under UNESCO's biosphere reserve programme. Nature reserves ② and ⑤ and game farms exist side by side. The St John the Baptist Anglican Church ⑥ near Vier-en-twinting Riviere was built in 1914.

MARAKELE NATIONAL PARK covers 44 000 ha of mountain wilderness at the western edge of the Waterberg range. The Kransberg cliffs on the park's southern boundary are home to the largest Cape vulture colony (over 700 breeding pairs) in the world, while nearly 300 other bird species have been recorded to date. Among these are peregrine and lanner falcons, red-crested korhaan, Burchell's glossy starling, Kalahari robin and whitecrowned shrike. Proclaimed in 1994, the park's Tswana name fittingly means 'place of sanctuary'. In addition to the Big Five, rare species such as tsessebe, roan and sable have been reintroduced. Among the other species roaming the park's woodlands and grassveld are giraffe, kudu, eland, waterbuck, red hartebeest, nyala and impala. Most of the game-viewing roads are suitable for sedan cars, but certain routes can only be negotiated by 4x4 vehicles. Facilities include a rustic bush camp for groups on the Apies River and a tented camp on the Matlabas River (which is accessible by 4x4 vehicle only).

LAPALALA WILDERNESS takes its name from the Lephalala River (a Tswana name meaning 'barrier'), which flows through the 24 000-ha conservation area. Lapalala is a sanctuary to rare and endangered species such as black rhino, roan and sable, as well as white rhino, hippo, giraffe, kudu, red hartebeest, blue wildebeest, impala and Burchell's zebra. The Lapalala Wilderness School, established in 1985 by well-known conservationist Clive Walker, is based at Lapalala. Since its foundation, the school has conducted environmental education programmes for thousands of children and teachers. Facilities for visitors include a fully catered luxury tented camp on the banks of the Kgogong River and ten self-catering camps. Guided walking trails are conducted over weekends and from Monday to Thursday.

Not to be missed is a visit to the Waterberg Cultural and Natural History Museum, situated close to the main access road to Lapalala Wilderness. Housed in the old Melkrivier School building, the museum's displays focus on the natural and cultural history of the Waterberg area. The museum incorporates the Rhino Museum, the only one in the country devoted entirely to this species.

POTGIETERSRUS was established by the Voortrekkers in 1852 and initially named Vredenburg (town of peace). In 1858, however, it was renamed Pietpotgietersrust, in honour of Piet Potgieter who was killed in the siege of Makapans Cave (see page 133) in 1854. Still later, the name was shortened to Potgietersrus. Malaria and animosity between the Voortrekkers and the Ndebele caused the trekkers to abandon the settlement around 1870. It was reoccupied in the 1890s, and today is an important agricultural and mining town. The Arend Dieperink Museum has an interesting exhibit on the archaeology of Makapans Cave, as well as a collection of Sotho and Voortrekker items. The game-breeding centre of the National Zoological Gardens in Pretoria, on the town's northern outskirts, breeds rare exotic and indigenous animals and birds, and black rhino and indigenous game species can be seen in the 850-ha reserve. There are picnic sites for day visitors and a walk-in aviary, and guided tours are offered.

MAKAPANS CAVE, a series of dolomite caves in the Makapans Valley, is of significant archaeological and historical interest. At the Historic Cave, the Ndebele chief Mokopane and his followers took refuge from a Boer commando in late October 1854, following the murder of 28 Voortrekkers a month earlier. The Ndebele blocked the two entrances with stone walls; since the Boers were unable to take the caves by force, they besieged Makapans Cave for 25 days. Some Ndebele, among them Mokopane, managed to escape, but when the Boers finally stormed the cave they found the bodies of at least 1 500 people who had either starved to death or died of thirst. The nearby Cave of Hearths has a long history of occupation, stretching from the Earlier Stone Age to the mid-1800s, but the most important archaeological site is the Limeworks Cave. Here, the remains of more than a dozen hominids (of the genus *Australopithecus africanus*) (1) have been unearthed from the dumps outside the cave and the sediments cemented by lime deposits inside the cave. In addition to the hominid fossils, which date back some three million years, a large number of fossilised animals have also been discovered.

MOORD DRIFT A roadside memorial is a reminder of the murder of 28 Voortrekker men, women and children at three separate localities in September 1854. Following the murders, the Boers undertook a punitive expedition against Chief Mokopane which resulted in the siege of Makapans Cave.

NABOOMSPRUIT, an Afrikaans name meaning 'stream of the euphorbia trees', owes its name to the abundance of the common tree euphorbia (*Euphorbia ingens*) growing along the river bank. Established in 1907, the town is an important agricultural and mining centre.

NYLSVLEY covers 16 000 ha of grassy floodplains – the largest wetland of its kind in the country – formed by the Nyl River. With a bird checklist of 426 species, and attracting up to 80 000 birds at times, Nylsvley is one of the top birding destinations in South Africa and an important breeding habitat of several threatened and rare species. Among these are slaty egret, bittern and rufousbellied heron, while the wetland also supports the largest breeding colonies of squacco heron and great white and black egrets in South Africa. To date, some 17 duck species have been recorded, while moorhens, herons, rails, crakes and coots are all attracted to the wetlands. The 4 300-ha Nylsvley Nature Reserve provides protection to about 800 ha of the floodplain and offers excellent birding opportunities. Picnic facilities are provided and visitors can either explore the reserve on foot or drive along the 30-km network of tracks west of the Nyl River. Animals to see include giraffe, tsessebe, roan, kudu, reedbuck, blue wildebeest and Burchell's zebra.

3

4

5

6

OPPOSITE SWAZI CRAFTS AND REED DANCE (P.142); **THIS PAGE** TOP LEFT: BERLIN FALLS (P.136); TOP RIGHT: MAC MAC FALLS (P.136); LEFT: BOURKE'S LUCK POTHOLES (P.137); CENTRE: GOLD PANNING IN PILGRIM'S REST (P.137); ABOVE: *MAMPOER,* LYDENBURG (P.138).

MPUMALANGA & SWAZILAND

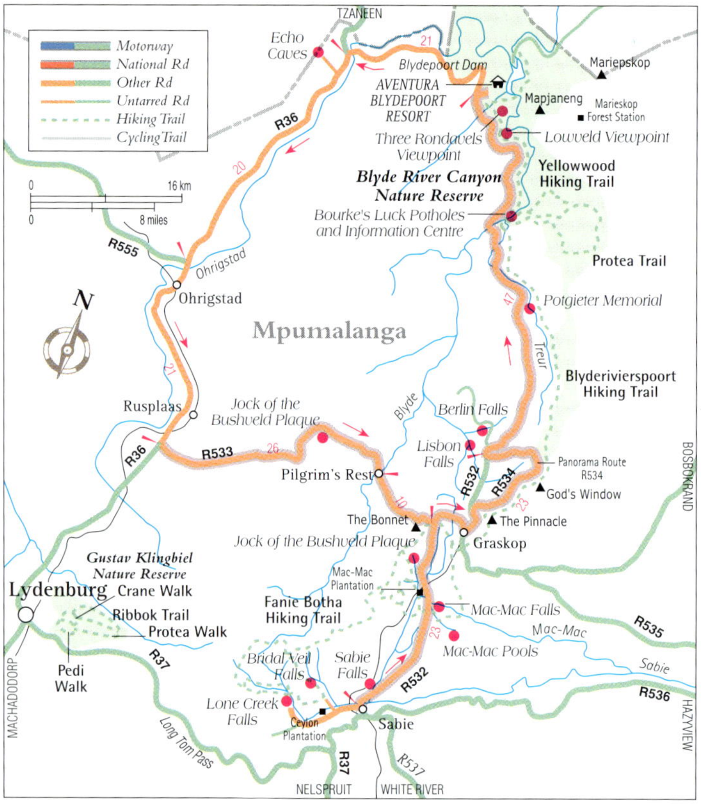

55
285 KM

1

2

SABIE Long before the first whites settled here, the area was famous with big-game hunters, adventurers and transport riders. The town's name is derived from the African name Sabielala, meaning the 'Sabie Sleeping Place'. The first farm, named Grootvantijn (Big Fountain) was awarded to CJ Badenhorst in 1846, but it was the discovery of gold – first alluvial and later reef – which attracted large numbers of diamond-miners and fortune-seekers. The gold fields were nowhere near as rich as those of the Witwatersrand, and most diggers eventually drifted away. Today, Sabie is the centre of one of the largest concentrations of commercial forest plantations in the world. Not to be missed is a visit to the SAFCOL Forestry Museum, with its interesting displays on the forest products industry. St Peter's Anglican Church (1913) was designed by the well-known architect, Sir Herbert Baker. Sabie is also an important tourist centre, and there are several magnificent waterfalls in and around the town. Among these are the 70-m-high Bridal Veil Falls, Lone Creek Falls – which leap 68 m over a sheer cliff – Horseshoe Falls and 46-m-high Sabie Falls.

MAC MAC POOLS ① were created by building a number of low cement walls in a tributary of the Mac Mac River. The pools are especially popular on hot summer days. Picnic facilities with braai places and toilets are provided.

MAC MAC FALLS Shortly before reaching the Escarpment, the spectacular Mac Mac River plunges 56 m into a deep forested gorge. Originally a single-drop waterfall, the crest was split into two during the 1870s by miners searching for gold. The large number of Scots digging for gold in the area prompted President Burghers to name the mining settlement Mac Mac during his visit in 1873. Nearby is a roadside plaque erected along the transport route followed by Sir Percy Fitzpatrick and his faithful Staffordshire terrier, Jock.

GRASKOP Also known as the Window of Mpumalanga, Graskop developed around a mining settlement which sprung up close to the Escarpment edge in the 1880s. Named after the grassy hillock on which it was laid out, Graskop is an important forestry town and tourism centre. The patches of grassland around the town are an important breeding area for the blue swallow, an endangered species in South Africa.

PINNACLE Situated at the head of the Driekop Gorge, the 30-m-high Pinnacle was created over millions of years when a column of Black Reef Quartzite became detached from the main face of the Escarpment as a result of erosion.

GOD'S WINDOW ② offers one of the most spectacular views in the country. From the viewsites perched on the very edge of the Escarpment, visitors can enjoy awesome views of the sheer drop to the Lowveld, some 700 m below. At the nearby Quartzkop visitors can meander along a boardwalk through a magnificent patch of rain forest with a lush growth of clivias, ferns, mosses and dwarf yellowwoods festooned with old man's beard.

LISBON FALLS When the forestry plantations were first named, many were given the names of European capitals such as London, Berlin and Lisbon. On its way to the Escarpment edge, the Lisbon River has formed a series of pools before it cascades into three separate falls which plunger dramatically into a deep gorge, 95 m below the lip of the falls.

BERLIN FALLS At the Berlin Falls, the Watervalspruit (waterfall stream) flows through a narrow chute carved through the sheer quartzite cliffs, plunges onto a ledge and then cascades into a deep pool. These beautiful falls are estimated to be approximately 80 m in height.

THE BLYDE RIVER CANYON NATURE RESERVE Covering 27 000 ha of grassveld, sour bushveld, eroded quartzite formations and spectacular natural features, the Blyde River Canyon Nature Reserve extends from God's Window northwards for 57 km. Within the reserve lie some of South Africa's most scenic attractions, including Bourke's Luck Potholes and the Blyde River Canyon.

BOURKE'S LUCK POTHOLES These magnificent cylindrical potholes were formed by the grinding action of boulders and pebbles caught in the swirling water at the confluence of the Blyde and the Treur rivers. The site was named after a prospector, Tom Bourke, who ironically never had any luck on his claim as the gold-bearing reef lay a short distance to the south of the river. Old pieces of mining equipment strewn about the area serve as reminders of the gold rush era of the 1870s. Not to be missed is the visitors' centre, with its displays on the natural and cultural history of the Blyde River Canyon Nature Reserve.

THE BLYDE RIVER CANYON ③ With a depth of up to 700 m and a length of 32 km, the awesome Blyde River Canyon is one of the top tourist attractions in South Africa. Viewsites along the canyon edge provide sweeping views over the landscape below, Blydepoort Dam and the outcrops known as the Three Rondavels – named for their resemblance to traditional African homes.

ECHO CAVES consist of several caves in the dolomite hills at the head of the Molopong Valley. The largest chamber is about 40 m high and 100 m long, and in some of the chambers dripstone formations can be seen. The caves were named for the echo produced by some of the stalactites when they are tapped. Excavations have revealed that the caves were inhabited by Middle and Later Stone Age people, San and Early Iron Age people.

OHRIGSTAD was founded in 1845 by the Voortrekker leader Andries Potgieter and was originally named Andries-Ohrigstad, a combination of Potgieter's first name and the surname of a Dutch merchant, Andries Ohrig, who had sent gifts to the Voortrekkers two years earlier. Malaria forced the inhabitants to abandon the settlement in 1849, with some families trekking northwards with Potgieter to the Soutpansberg, and others moving south to establish Lydenburg (see Tour 56, page 138). It was only in 1923, after malaria was brought under control in the area, that Ohrigstad was re-established southwest of the original site. Today, it is the centre of a productive fruit and maize-growing area. To the northeast of the present-day town, the ruins of the original village and the graves of those who died of malaria are still visible.

PILGRIM'S REST ④ has been preserved as an authentic gold-mining village of the late 1800s and early 1900s. In 1873, the discovery of gold in Pilgrim's Creek by a miner named Alec Patterson, and a nearby discovery by William Trafford, caused miners to flock to the new gold fields. Soon the streams, hills and valleys were being worked by over 1 500 miners, and a tent and corrugated-iron town with 21 shops, 18 bars, three bakeries and two banks sprung up. The town has several museums, including the Diggings Museum, which gives demonstrations of gold-panning; the Miner's House Museum, a re-creation of a typical miner's house between 1910 and 1920; and the Reduction Works, where the gold was extracted from the ore. In sharp contrast to the humble corrugated-iron miners' cottages is Alanglade, located to the east of the town. Designed in the early 1900s by Sir Herbert Baker in Mediterranean style, the double-storey house was built for the General Manager of Transvaal Gold Mining Estates. Also worth visiting in Pilgrim's Rest are the Royal Hotel and the Cemetery, with its well-known Robber's Grave; as punishment for robbing a tent, the miscreant was shot and buried at right angles to the other graves. Also of interest is the four-arch Joubert Bridge, spanning the Blyde River at the northern end of the town. Built in 1896 with dressed stone, it was named after the Mining Commissioner at the time, JS Joubert.

3

4

1

56
290 KM

2

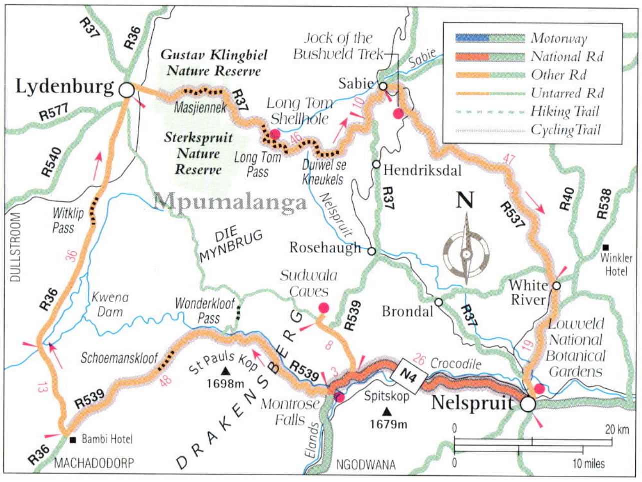

3

NELSPRUIT, capital of Mpumalanga province, lies in the fertile valley of the Crocodile River in an area known for its production of a variety of tropical fruit (pawpaws, bananas and avocados), nuts (pecan and macadamia) and citrus fruit ③. The town's development was closely linked to the building of the railway line between Pretoria and Lourenço Marques (Maputo). The section of the line from Komatipoort on the Mozambican border reached Nelspruit in 1892 and a town steadily developed around the railhead. During the final phase of the South African War, Nelspruit briefly served as the capital of the Zuid-Afrikaansche Republiek (ZAR). Proclaimed in 1905, the town's name honours the Nel brothers, who used the area for winter grazing in the 1870s and in 1890 bought the farm on which the town developed.

LOWVELD NATIONAL BOTANICAL GARDEN ④ Situated on the town's northern outskirts, the dome-shaped granite boulders and cascades at the confluence of the Crocodile and the Nels rivers form an impressive backdrop to the Lowveld National Botanical Garden. Special plantings and lawns cover 25 ha of developed gardens, while a further 135 ha have been left as natural bushveld. Highlights include a world-famous cycad collection ②, comprising all 36 southern African cycad species, 18 African species and 84 species from elsewhere in the world. There is also a complete collection of baobab species, and a comprehensive collection of Acacia trees. Visitors can follow paved walkways meandering through the garden, or take the Riverside Trail, which winds along the Crocodile River and through the African Rain Forest, with its tropical forest plants from central, east and west Africa. The garden offers good birding opportunities, while a small group of hippo can be seen in the Crocodile River. Meals are available in the restaurant.

SUDWALA CAVES are situated in the wooded valley of the Houtbosloop (wood bush stream) on the slopes of Mankelekele Mountain. The caves were formed over million of years by rainwater, charged with carbon dioxide, seeping through cracks and dissolving the limestone rock to form a maze of caverns, tunnels and passageways. Water percolating through the roof of the caverns has created a subterranean treasure chest of stalagmites and stalactites with imaginative names like the Screaming Monster, Weeping Madonna and Samson's Pillar. The main chamber, the PR Owen Hall, is roughly circular, with a diameter of 70 m and a height of up to 37 m. Visitors can take guided tours of the caves. Stone Age people lived here, and the Swazi King, Sobhuza I, took refuge in the cave when he fled from the Ndwandwe around 1818–19. In 1855, Somcuba and 3 000 of his followers were besieged in the caves by his brother Mswati.

The adjacent Dinosaur Park, with its collection of dinosaur and other prehistoric animal replicas, offers a Jurassic Park-like experience. Displayed in realistic settings is a unique collection of dinosaurs, extinct mammals and birds, evoking the vanished era when dinosaurs roamed the earth. It is said to be the biggest and most scientifically accurate collection of prehistoric animal replicas in the world. Also of interest is the Kraal Complex, a 'living' museum portraying the cultures of the Nguni people.

MONTROSE FALLS After making its way through Schoemanskloof, the Crocodile River plunges 12 m down a cliff, forming the spectacular Montrose Falls ⑤. Visitors are advised to exercise caution when exploring the area above the falls as the rocks can be treacherously slippery.

LYDENBURG Long before the Voortrekkers arrived here, the area around Lydenburg was inhabited by Iron Age people. Significant archaeological finds have been made here, notably the discovery of seven terracotta heads, later named the Lydenburg Heads, dating back some 1 500 years. The heads may have been masks, and were probably used on religions occasions or during rituals. The town of Lydenburg was established in 1850 after the Voortrekkers abandoned Ohrigstad, and was named 'town of suffering' as a reminder of those who succumbed to malaria at Ohrigstad. Reminders of the town's early days include the Voortrekker School (1851), Voortrekker Church (1852) and the Dutch Reformed Church (1894). Replicas of three of the Lydenburg Heads can be seen in the town's museum, which also has interesting displays on the Voortrekkers, gold mining and the Pedi people. The Gustav Kliengbiel Nature Reserve covers 2 200 ha to the east of the town and has been stocked with kudu, eland, blue wildebeest, blesbok, impala, grey rhebok and reedbuck. Visitors can explore the reserve along three trails, one of which meanders past the terraces and stone walls of an Iron Age settlement.

LONG TOM PASS ⑥ Winding across the Drakensberg, Long Tom Pass links Lydenburg to the towns of Sabie and Graskop on the edge of the Escarpment. This is one of the best-known and most scenic passes in the country, and is rich in history. Originally known as the Delagoosbergpad, Long Tom Pass lay on the early wagon route between Pretoria and Lourenço Marques (Maputo). A rough track was built in the early 1870s, and some of the old names of places signposted along the road – the Old Trading Post, Die Geut (chute), Staircase and Whiskeyspruit – recall those early days. Following the defeat of General Louis Botha's force at Bergendal (the last set-piece battle of the South African War) on 27 August 1900, the Boer forces split up into several groups, one of which retreated eastwards over the Drakensberg with two heavy 155-mm Creusot field guns ①, nicknamed 'Long Toms' by the British. Following the capture of Lydenburg by General Buller's forces on 7 September, several skirmishes were fought along the route over the Drakensberg between 8 and 10 December. Historic sites such as the Last Stand of the Long Toms and the Long Tom Shell Hole, a crater left by an exploding shell, have been signposted. Also to be seen is a replica of one of the guns deployed by the Boers to slow down the advancing British forces. Weighing 6 250 kg, the Long Tom had to be drawn by a span of 16 oxen and had a range of nearly 10 km.

SABIE See Tour 55, page 136.

WHITE RIVER lies amid an intensive agricultural area where tropical fruit, citrus and vegetables are produced and is also a stopover on the way to the Kruger National Park. The town was founded in 1904 by Lord Alfred Milner, administrator of the Transvaal after the South African War, as a settlement for Boer and British soldiers. It was established on the banks of the Emanzimhlope River, a Swazi name translated as 'white waters'.

4

5

6

57
345 KM

1 

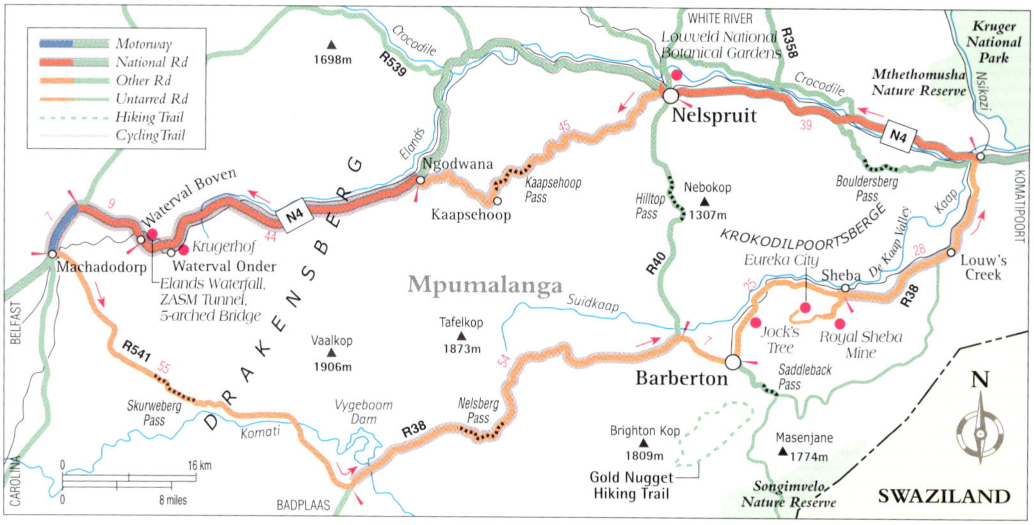

NELSPRUIT See Tour 56, page 138.

KAAPSEHOOP Situated on the edge of the Escarpment, Kaapsehoop appeared virtually overnight following the discovery of alluvial gold on the farm Berlyn (Berlin) in 1880. Originally named Duiwels Kantoor (Devil's Office), it was renamed Kaapse Hoop to reflect expectations of rich finds. By August 1882 there were 250 diggers at Kaapsehoop, and by early 1884 their numbers had swelled to some 4 000.

In its heyday, the village had two hotels, several bars, 15 shops, a school, post office and an assortment of corrugated-iron cottages and clay-brick houses. Most of the diggers abandoned the settlement when the Pioneer Reef was discovered near Barberton. After the discovery of Barber's Reef and the Sheba Reef in 1885, only a handful of diggers remained behind. Reminders of this colourful era include the remains of the old government building (1885) and the magistrate's office at the town square (known as Kommisarisplein), corrugated-iron miners' cottages, the old pear orchard with its unbelievably huge trees and the cemetery. The descriptive names of the area's many creeks and streams, such as Poverty Creek, Starvation Creek, Fool's Rush and Battery Creek, with its delightful waterfall, evoke memories of gold-rush days. The montane grassveld plain to the southeast of the village is the most important habitat of the endangered blue swallow in South Africa, while small groups of wild horses still roam the area; these are said to be the descendants of abandoned mining ponies and horses used in the South African War.

NGODWANA is infamous, rather than famous, for the pollution belched out by the factory which mills logs from the area's vast plantations for use in the production of paper.

WATERVAL ONDER owes its name to its location below the nearby waterfall on the Elands River. After evacuating Pretoria on 29 May 1900 to escape the advancing British forces, the government of the Zuid-Afrikaansche Republiek (ZAR) initially moved to Machadodorp. On 30 June, the ailing President Paul Kruger moved to Waterval Onder from where he conducted the affairs of the Republic for nearly two months. The historic presidential residence, named Krugerhof, can be seen close to the Waterval Onder railway station. Spanning the Dwaalheuwelspruit ('wandering hill stream'), a tributary of the Elands River, is the handsome Five Arch Railway Bridge ②. The stone bridge was opened to traffic in June 1894.

WATERVAL BOVEN From Waterval Onder the road ascends steeply up the slopes of the Elandsberg and about 2 km before reaching Waterval Boven passes the old Nederlandsch Zuid-Afrikaansche Spoorweg Maatschappij tunnel. In the early 1890s, the steep gradient of the Escarpment presented the biggest challenge to the engineers tasked with building the railway line ③ between Pretoria and the Mozambican port of Lourenço Marques (Maputo) to provide the ZAR with an independent outlet to the sea. To reduce the gradient, a tunnel of about 400 m was built through the Elandsberg. Drilling started from both ends in October 1892 and the two teams met in September the following year. A viewsite near the entrance of the tunnel provides a fine view over the 90-m-high Elands River Falls ④. This section of the railway line also incorporated more than 3 km of rack railway to assist the locomotives. The rack railway incorporated a middle rail fitted with a rack that engaged a pinion on the locomotive to provide extra traction. A 32-ton rack engine, capable of hauling 140 tons, was coupled behind the train to push it at a speed of 8 kph; part of the original rack system can be seen at the Waterval Boven Station. Also of interest at the station is one of the original locomotives used on this route and a monument commemorating the construction of the line.

MACHADODORP Established in 1895 on the farm Geluk, Machadodorp (Machado's town) owes its name to Joaquim Machado, who surveyed the route of the railway line between Pretoria and Lourenço Marques (Maputo) in 1883. Machado later became Governor-General of Mozambique. At the end of May 1900, the ZAR government retreated to Machadodorp where it conducted its business from a railway car. When President Kruger moved to Waterval Onder on 30 June, the Executive Committee remained in Machadodorp and travelled to Waterval Onder by train every day. Machadodorp remained the seat of government until it was moved to Nelspruit on 28 August, a day after the Battle of Bergendal.

BARBERTON Situated at the foot of the Makhonjwa Mountains in the De Kaap Valley, Barberton is a picturesque town with a profusion of jacaranda, flamboyant and indigenous trees. The town owes its existence to the discovery of gold in the hills around the present-day town in 1883. A rush of miners and fortune-hunters ensued. The town was officially named on 24 June 1884 after Graham Barber and his two cousins, Fred and Harry, who discovered a rich reef in a creek to the southeast of the town, naming it Barber's Reef. Among the town's many links with the past is the classical façade of the Kaap Gold Fields Stock Exchange building, built in 1887. Its existence was short-lived, however, as most of the brokers left Barberton following the discovery of the rich goldfields of the Witwatersrand. Other historic buildings include the Lewis and Marks Building (1887) – the town's first double-storey building – and the neogothic Masonic Lodge, built in 1884 as the Union Church and taken over by the Freemasons in 1887. The town's three house museums – Stopforth House (1886), Fernlea House (early 1890s) and Belhaven (1904) – provide a fascinating picture of life in Barberton in the gold-mining days.

Also of interest is the statue of Jock of the Bushveld, the aerial cableway (see Tour 58, page 142) and the corrugated-iron blockhouse, built in Rimer's Creek in 1901. Far less elaborate and smaller than the first double-storey stone blockhouses built in March 1900, the rectangular corrugated-iron building is the only surviving example of this type of blockhouse in South Africa. The Fortuna Mine Trail incorporates a 600-m-long tunnel built in 1907 to transport gold-bearing ore from the Fortuna Mine to the mill where the ore was crushed.

Best known among the rich diversity of flowering plants occurring in the area is the showy Barberton daisy (*Gerbera jamesonii*) ①, which has become world famous. Other noteworthy plants include the Barberton Lowveld sugarbush (*Protea curvata*) – endemic to the area – the Barberton mountain sugarbush (*Protea comptonii*), as well as several rare aloe species.

DE KAAP VALLEY The valley is said to have been named by the Voortrekker leader Marthinus Pretorius because of its resemblance to the Cape on misty days. Situated in the Lowveld, it also became known as the Valley of Death, because of the numerous miners and prospectors who died of malaria. Along the route is a plaque erected at the site of the famous Jock's Tree, where transport rider (and author) Sir Percy Fitzpatrick used to outspan under a large umbrella thorn (*Acacia tortillis*). Further along, the road passes Clutha, Joe's Luck, Sheba, Eureka and Revolver Creek – all reminders of the days when the valley was the scene of frantic gold-mining activity.

In 1885, Edwin Bray discovered the Sheba Reef, which turned out to be the richest gold-bearing formation in the world. The first 13 000 tons of ore produced an astounding 50 000 ounces of gold, and the so-called Golden Quarry became famous. A mining town called Eureka City soon developed around the Queen of Sheba Hotel, built on the plateau above the mine. Although Eureka City is now nothing more than a ghost town, the Sheba Mine is still in full operation, more than a century after the phenomenally rich reef was first discovered.

2

3

4

1

58
330 KM

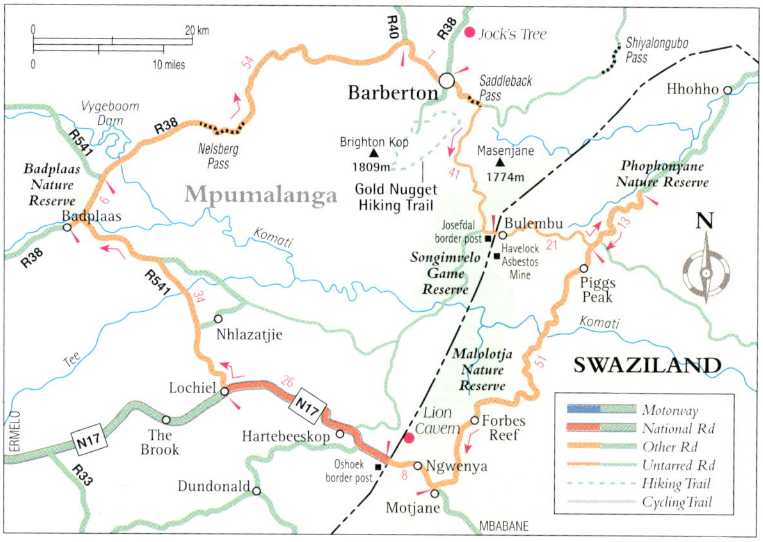

2

BARBERTON See Tour 57, page 141.

AERIAL CABLEWAY Built in 1938, the aerial cableway linking the Havelock asbestos mine in Swaziland with Barberton dominates the slopes of the Makhonjwa Mountains. The 20,36-km-long cableway is supported by 52 pylons, with the longest unsupported span being 1 207 m and the highest point above the ground being 189 m. The cableway was built to bring asbestos to the Barberton railway station and to transport coal on the returning cocopans to the Bulembu power station. Able to carry loads of up to 200 kg per pan and moving at a speed of 11 km per hour, the cableway has a capacity of 13,5 tonnes per hour.

SONGIMVELO GAME RESERVE Situated in the rugged Barberton highlands, Songimvelo covers 50 000 ha of grasslands, undulating hills, high mountain peaks, river valleys and deep gorges, and borders Swaziland's Malolotja Nature Reserve. Game roaming the reserve includes elephant, white rhino, buffalo, giraffe, Burchell's zebra and a variety of antelope – among them kudu, waterbuck, red hartebeest and impala. Grassland birds are well represented among the more than 300 bird species recorded to date. The area is rich in history, with archaeological sites dating back over 2 000 years, while relics of the Barberton gold rush of the 1880s can also be seen. Luxury and budget accommodation facilities are available in the reserve.

SWAZILAND is a landlocked country covering 17 363 km^2 of highlands, deep valleys, plains and lowlands. Along its eastern boundary, the Lebombo Mountains form a natural boundary with Mozambique and South Africa's KwaZulu-Natal province, while the western boundary with South Africa is demarcated by several high mountains. Although excavations have provided evidence that Iron Age people lived in the area some 1 600 years ago, the Swazi state was created in the early 1800s under Sobhuza I, who initially settled with his Ngwane people in the upper reaches of the Nkomati Valley after they were driven northwards by the Ndwandwe. Sobhuza later moved south-eastwards, establishing his capital in the Little Usutu Valley. After Sobhuza's death, the kingdom was ruled by a regent until 1845, when Mswati became king. He organised the Ngwane along military lines and his subjects became known as 'the people of Mswati'. Various concessions for grazing and minerals and 'friendship' treaties with the Boers saw the kingdom's territory reduced by half its original size. In 1894, Swaziland became a protectorate of the Zuid-Afrikaansche Republiek (ZAR), and in 1906 it was detached from the Transvaal and became a separate British colony. Swaziland became independent in 1968 and is ruled by a king, Mswati III, who wields both executive and legislative authority. The Swazi people ① are still deeply rooted in their culture and traditions and are known for their beautiful crafts ②, which include basketry, mats, pottery, printed cloth, jewellery and soapstone carvings, and for their reed dance ③, or *umhlanga*.

HAVELOCK, a mining town characterised by terraced miners' dwellings built against the mountain slopes, is situated near the sprawling frontier town of Bulembu. The mine came into operation in 1938 following the discovery of asbestos deposits in the valley of the Duduzi stream in 1923 and in 1928. Named after Sir Arthur Havelock, Governor of Natal, the mine was once one of the largest asbestos mines in the world. By the mid-1970s, however, production fell by nearly half, to 20 000 tonnes, when the main ore body became exhausted. The mine was closed temporarily in 1992, but subsequently resumed operation. Although production rose to nearly 27 700 tonnes in 1999, low world prices and a reduced demand due to health concerns have affected the mine's viability. The problems of transporting the asbestos from this mountainous setting were overcome by construction of the aerial cableway from the mine to Barberton.

PIGGS PEAK Following the discovery of alluvial gold in north western Swaziland in 1872, a gold-bearing reef was discovered in the hills to the west of the town by a French prospector, William Pigg, in 1884. Mining began soon afterwards, and as the mine was initially an open-cast operation, the 'Peak' soon disappeared. Later, a shaft was sunk and eight levels were mined, with the mine producing some 120 000 ounces of gold between 1889 and 1954. By the mid-1950s, however, the ore body was exhausted and the mine was closed down.

Situated amid plantations of blue gum and pine trees, Pigg's Peak ④ is the centre of the region's forestry industry, while tourists are attracted by the magnificent scenery and the many scenic drives. The area is famed for its handicrafts, ranging from mohair articles and carpets to beadwork, grass mats and baskets. The 500-ha Phophonyane Nature Reserve has as its main attraction the Phophonyane Falls, which cascade down a cliff into a series of pools. Situated a few kilometres to the northeast of the town, the reserve has a bird checklist of some 230 species.

MALOLOTJA NATURE RESERVE covers 18 000 ha of mountains, deep valleys, waterfalls, plateaux and plains in the northwest of Swaziland. Regarded as one of southern Africa's most impressive mountain parks, Malolotja is rich in history and is a sanctuary to a diverse flora and fauna. Among its outstanding features are numerous waterfalls, among them the Malolotja Falls – Swaziland's highest – and the Mahulungwane Falls, as well as two of the country's highest peaks: Ngwenya (1 829 m) and Silotwane (1 680 m). In addition to a variety of small mammals occurring naturally in the area, the park has been stocked with eland, black wildebeest, red hartebeest, blesbok, common reedbuck, impala and Burchell's zebra. To date, over 280 bird species have been recorded in the reserve, which is an important breeding ground for species such as the blue swallow, bald ibis and Stanley's bustard. Among the other noteworthy species are black-rumped buttonquail, African finfoot, grass owl and broadtailed warbler.

In the south of the reserve, the Lion Cavern in the Ngwenya Mountain is the oldest known mine in the world. Here, Middle Stone Age people excavated a 12,8-m-long tunnel into the mountainside in search of hematite and specularite; iron oxides used for ceremonial and cosmetic purposes. Research has shown that the mine, dated at between 45 000 and 41 000 years old, was used for about 20 000 years. Also of interest is the old Forbes Reef Gold Mine which lies in the reserve and is easily accessible. Visitors can explore the reserve along a 25-km road network leading to four viewpoints, but the best way to see it is on foot. There are a number of short day walks and an overnight trail network covering over 200 km. Accommodation ranges from fully equipped log cabins to campsites and backpacking camps.

FORBES REEF This wayside village owes its name to the gold reef discovered here in late 1883 or 1884 by Alec Forbes and Charles Swears. The Forbes Main Reef became the second most productive mine in Swaziland, and between 1884 and 1935 production totalled 31 037 ounces. The mine closed in 1935, but mining of some of the other reefs continued until 1966. The Forbes Reef Mine lies in the Malolotja Nature Reserve.

BADPLAAS Situated in the foothills of the Hlumuhlumu Mountains along the Seekoeispruit, Badplaas owes its name, meaning 'bathing place', to the strong thermal spring surfacing here. The spring has a temperature of 53° C at its source.

Long before the first white pioneers learnt about the spring, however, its curative powers were known to the Swazi people, who named it Emanzana, or 'the healing waters'. In 1876, a hunter named Jacob de Clerque chanced upon the spring, and it soon became a popular winter escape for people living on the Highveld.

Covering 65 ha, the Badplaas resort has 14 swimming pools, a spa, supertubes, water slides, a river ride with a 170 m drop and a host of other recreational facilities. Visitors can choose from a wide range of accommodation options. A variety of game can be seen in the adjoining 1 000-ha natue reserve.

3

4

BOTH PAGES KRUGER NATIONAL PARK (PP.146–151). **THIS PAGE** RIGHT: LION; BELOW: ZEBRA AND IMPALA AT WATERHOLE. **OPPOSITE** TOP LEFT: CARMINE BEE-EATERS; TOP RIGHT: CAPE BUFFALO; CENTRE: GIRAFFE AT WATERHOLE; BOTTOM LEFT: CAPE BUFFALO; BOTTOM RIGHT: ELEPHANT; BOTTOM: CRESTED GUINEAFOWL.

THE KRUGER NATIONAL PARK & NORTHERN PROVINCE

MPUMALANGA & NORTHERN PROVINCE

59
380 KM

1

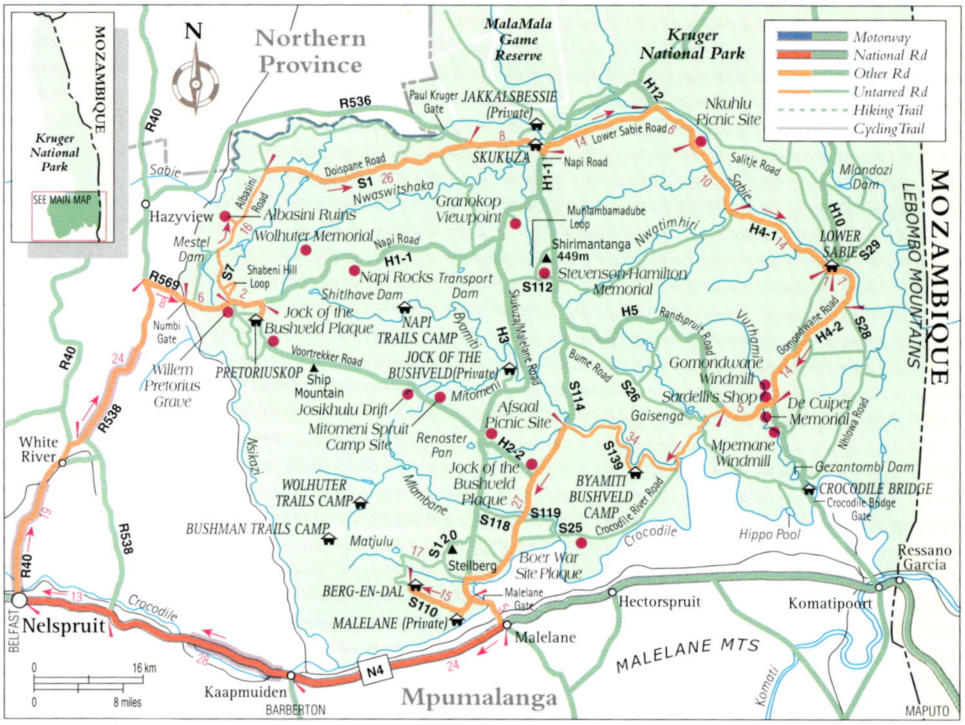

NELSPRUIT See Tour 56, page 138.

WHITE RIVER See Tour 56, page 139.

KRUGER NATIONAL PARK (KNP) Covering nearly 2 000 000 ha, the Kruger National Park is one of Africa's great game parks and ranks among the world's top conservation areas. From the Crocodile River in the south, the park stretches northwards for 350 km to the Limpopo River, and ranges in width from 25 km in the far north to 85 km in the south. This unspoilt wilderness of bushveld, woodland and thornveld is home to a rich diversity of wildlife which includes 147 mammal species. In addition to the Big Five (elephant, rhino, buffalo, lion and leopard), the park is home to a wide variety of antelope, such as sable, roan, impala, Lichtenstein's hartebeest, waterbuck, tsessebe, kudu and nyala, as well as hippo, giraffe and Burchell's zebra. It also provides protection to the only viable wild dog population in South Africa. With 490 bird species recorded to date (about 55 per cent of the total number found in southern Africa), the park is truly a birder's paradise. More than 50 raptor species have been recorded, while many of the species occurring in the north of the park have a limited distribution elsewhere in South Africa. The park is also an archaeological treasure chest, with over 250 cultural heritage sites, ranging from rock art sites (about 130 have been recorded) and Late Iron Age settlements to early transport routes. Access to Kruger is via eight gates, and accommodation ranges from rest camps with all the necessary facilities (filling station, shop, restaurant) to smaller bushveld camps without facilities, and bush lodges for groups. A vast network of roads traverses the bush, providing access to rivers, water holes, dams and viewpoints, while picnic sites in the bush allow motorists to take a break from the driving. In addition to self-drive game-viewing, the park offers a host of outdoor and adventure activities such as short, self-guided nature walks in some of the rest camps, night drives and guided walks of between three and four hours. There are also seven three-day guided wilderness trails in various remote areas of the park. Because the park lies within a malaria area, it is advisable to consult a doctor about prophylaxis, especially if visiting between December and April.

SOUTHERN KNP ① The southern portion of Kruger constitutes the historic heart of the park proclaimed in 1926. The first step to conserve the abundant wildlife of the area was taken when the Sabie Game Reserve was proclaimed between the Crocodile and Sabie rivers in 1898. The south is one of the most popular areas in the park, and is renowned for its excellent game-viewing, changing landscapes and a rich diversity of vegetation types.

PRETORIUSKOP Nestling among rocky granite outcrops on gently undulating plains, the Pretoriuskop area is rich in history. It has been suggested that the outcrop was named after Willem Pretorius, who died nearby of malaria during an expedition led by Carolus Trichardt in 1848 to find a wagon route from Lydenburg to Lourenço Marques (Maputo). Pretoriuskop was a well-known outspan on the ox-wagon route to Delagoa Bay, and was built in the mid-1870s by Alois Nellmapius. The prevalence of the tsetse fly, however, initially prevented the use of oxen on the route and goods had to be carried by porters from the Lebombo Mountains to near Pretoriuskop. The first huts were built in the late 1920s, and until malaria was brought under control in the Lowveld it was the only rest camp which remained open throughout the year. Among the camp's attractions are a swimming pool in a natural setting and an interpretive walk. The vegetation surrounding Pretoriuskop consists of tree savannah characterised by silver clusterleaf, sicklebush and bushwillow. Game occurring here includes white rhino, sable, mountain reedbuck, kudu and giraffe.

ALBASINI RUINS ④ The ruins of a shop and homestead along the Pabenispruit mark the site of what was once the trading post of legendary elephant hunter and trader, João Albasini, who settled here in 1846. Still visible are the remains of the furrow he dug to water a small orchard and a vegetable garden. Using ancient trade routes from the coast to the interior,

Albasini's porters carried supplies from Delagoa Bay to the post, from where they were taken by ox wagon to the Transvaal's interior.

SKUKUZA ② is by far the largest rest camp ③ in the Kruger National Park and also serves as the park's headquarters. The camp was named after the park's first warden, Colonel James Stevenson-Hamilton, who was given the Tsonga name of Skukuza, meaning 'the person who turned everything upside down'. Stevenson-Hamilton earned the reputation because of the many people he removed from the park and the changes he made after he became warden in 1902. In 1909, he moved the headquarters of the old Sabie Game Reserve from the Crocodile River to a new site on the banks of the Sabie River, known as Sabie Bridge, or Reserve, and later renamed Skukuza. Of interest in the rest camp is the Stevenson-Hamilton Memorial Library, where the skin of a lion killed with a knife by the legendary game ranger Harry Wolhuter in 1904, can be seen. Visitors can also see the locomotive used on the historic Selati railway line, the bridge over the Sabie River and a section of the Selati line. Skukuza lies in an area with a rich diversity of game, including big cats, wild dog, elephant, buffalo, kudu and giraffe.

LOWER SABIE takes its name from the river along which it was laid out, a name variously said to mean 'river of fear' or 'sand river'. Situated in an area known for its outstanding game-viewing, the camp was established in 1929 with three huts. The Lower Sabie Road is famous for its sightings of lion, and among the wide variety of game to be seen are elephant breeding herds, buffalo, lion, wild dog, giraffe, Burchell's zebra and antelope such as kudu, impala and bushbuck. The savannah bush in the area is dominated by marula, knob thorn and round-leaved teak trees, while the lush riverine forest is comprised of tall leadwoods, sausage trees, tamboti and ilala palms.

THE DE CUIPER MEMORIAL A memorial at Gomondwane marks the site where the expedition led by Captain Frans de Cuiper camped in July 1725 while searching for a route from Delagoa Bay to the goldfields of Monomotapa. The 31-man party left Delagoa Bay on 27 June 1725; after reaching Komatipoort, they crossed the Crocodile River and continued to Gomondwane where they camped for three days. On 12 July their camp was attacked, forcing them to retreat back into Mozambique. As a result of the attack, no further expeditions were undertaken in the area for over a century.

BERG-EN-DAL Opened in 1984, Berg-en-dal, meaning 'mountain and valley' was the first rest camp in the Kruger National Park to deviate from the traditional thatch-and-whitewashed-wall buildings that are so characteristic of the older rest camps. Instead, its face-brick buildings were designed to blend into the natural landscape, which has been disturbed as little as possible. Camp facilities include a swimming pool. Visitors can familiarise themselves with some of the trees in the area on a 1,6-km self-guided walk. Situated in the rugged Malelane Mountains, the landscape surrounding Berg-en-dal is characterised by low granitic mountains, rocky domes and valleys dominated by red bushwillow trees. Game frequenting the area includes white rhino, giraffe, kudu, mountain reedbuck, waterbuck and impala.

2

3

4

60
340 KM

1

PHALABORWA Established in 1957, the town of Phalaborwa is founded upon rich copper and other mineral deposits, which attrac-ted the attention of Iron Age people as early as the 8th century. The baPhalaborwa people dug trenches and shafts up to 6 m deep to exploit the rich copper deposits, smelted the ore and also worked iron. Important Early Iron Age sites in the area include Loolekop, Sealene and Kgopolwe.

The geological history of what is known as the Phalaborwa Complex goes back some 2 050 million years ago, when molten matter intruded into granite along three large and numerous smaller volcanic pipes. A variety of minerals were formed within these pipes, such as copper, phosphate, iron, baddeleyite and vermiculite. Over countless aeons, the overlying rock was eroded away to expose the more resistant hills that punctuate the plains around Phalaborwa. Modern mining dates back to 1938, when exploitation of vermiculite began, and today Phalaborwa is responsible for about half the annual world production of this mineral. Mining of the copper-rich central volcanic pipe began in 1956 and has created one of the largest man-made holes in Africa. With a circumference of over 5 km and a diameter of nearly 1 900 m, the near-circular open pit is 762 m deep and six times the size of Kimberley's famous Big Hole. In addition to the rich copper deposits, the mine has also been a source of phosphate (used in the fertiliser industry) and magnetite, a byproduct of copper and phosphate. As the mine has reached the maximum depth for open-cast mining, it has become necessary to switch to conventional underground mining. To appreciate the area's mining history, a visit to the Foskor Mine Museum is a must. Guided mine tours are also available. The Hans Merensky Golf Club is well known among golfers as the course is often visited by game from the adjoining Kruger National Park.

KRUGER NATIONAL PARK See Tour 59, page 146.

CENTRAL KRUGER covers a large tract of land stretching between the Sabie River in the south and the Olifants River in the north. The western half of the central area is largely a vast swathe of woodland dominated by mixed bushwillow and mopane, while the vegetation in the east is more varied. The area is noted for its breeding herds of elephant, while white rhino, buffalo, eland, sable (common in the Phalaborwa area), blue wildebeest and Burchell's zebra also occur.

MASORINI ② The earliest inhabitants of Masorini, which nestles among large boulders against a low hill, were Stone Age people. Much later, in the 19th century, it was also inhabited by Late Iron Age people who built their huts on the terraced hillside. Smelting furnaces, forges and other implements have provided evidence that the inhabitants worked iron, which they probably obtained from Phalaborwa. Artefacts such as grinding stones and potsherds are displayed in the information hut, and photographs and illustrations tell the story of the site and other aspects relating to the park's early inhabitants. Visitors can take a guided tour of the reconstructed village, which includes, among other things, the excavated remains of a smelting furnace. From the summit of the hill, there are expansive views over the surrounding landscape.

LETABA rest camp lies high above a horseshoe bend in the Letaba River, offering a grandstand view of the animals that come to quench their thirst. The Tsonga name, Letaba, means 'sand' and seemingly refers to the river's extensive sandy banks. The vegetation to the west of the rest camp is typically mixed woodland dominated by bushwillow and mopane, while the camp itself lies in a belt of mopane shrubveld, characterised by mopane and apple-leaf trees. Among the rich diversity of game to be seen are kudu, eland, tsessebe, sable, buffalo, blue wildebeest, Burchell's zebra, giraffe and the big cats (lion, leopard and cheetah). In the rest camp is the Elephant Hall, which forms part of the Goldfields Environmental Education Centre. The focal point of the hall is a display of the tusks of six of the park's largest elephants, which became known in the late 1970s as the 'Magnificent Seven'. Among these are the heaviest pair of tusks ever recorded, weighing 75 kg and 55 kg, and the 317-cm and 303,5-cm tusks of Shawu – the longest tusks on record in southern Africa. There are also highly informative displays covering all aspects of the elephant's history and biology.

OLIFANTS Situated on a cliff overlooking the Olifants (Elephant's) River ③, the Olifants rest camp was opened in 1960 to accommodate the increasing number of tourists visiting the Kruger National Park. In a departure from the usual whitewashed walls, the huts were painted dark green to blend in with the surroundings. The camp is famed for its unrivalled views of the Lebombo Mountains and the surrounding plains. Another attraction is the network of loop roads around the camp, which provide excellent game-viewing opportunities along the Olifants and Letaba rivers. The Olifants River is home to hippo and crocodile, while visitors are also likely to see elephant, buffalo, blue wildebeest, impala, kudu and Burchell's zebra. Surrounded by plains, the vegetation varies from mopane bush savanna in the north to knob thorn bush and shrub savanna to the south.

SATARA Unlike the other rest camps, Satara does not have a river, dam or mountains as an added attraction. Situated on plains dominated by marula, knob thorn and round-leafed teak savannah, it is Kruger's second-largest rest camp and its design features several large circles centred around lawns. The name Satara is said to a corruption of the Hindi word *satrah*, (seventeen). Apparently, the original farm was the seventeenth to be surveyed in this area, and the name was suggested by a Hindu labourer. Since this is one of the best grazing areas in the park, game is abundant. Large herds of Burchell's zebra and blue wildebeest occur in the area, which also supports large numbers of giraffe, kudu, elephant, impala and sable. Although there are few rivers or stretches of open water in this part of the park, there are numerous water holes along the pipeline supplying water from the Olifants River to the rest camp.

ORPEN ①, the name of the gate and the small, intimate rest camp on the park's western boundary, was named in honour of two of Kruger's biggest benefactors, James and Eileen Orpen. Between 1935 and 1944, Mrs Orpen bought seven farms totalling 24 500 ha, on the park's western boundary, and donated the land to the park. The couple also gave money for the construction of water holes, and James Orpen helped to survey and clear the western boundary line. A small rondavel, about 10 km east of the gate, marks the original entrance to the park before the incorporation of the seven farms. As a living memorial to the Orpens' contribution to the development of the park, the hut now serves as a small museum, the Rabelais Museum – named after the original farm. Good game-viewing is to be had along the Timbavati River.

2

3

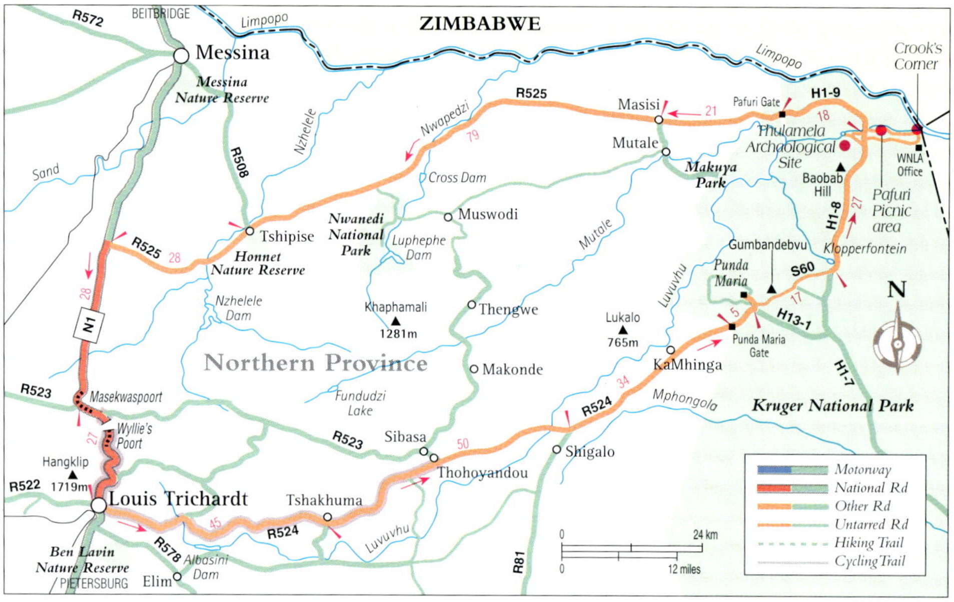

61

440 KM

1

LOUIS TRICHARDT See Tour 64, page 156.

KRUGER NATIONAL PARK See Tour 59, page 146.

NORTHERN KRUGER The northern part of the KNP lies in an ecologically unique area where nine major ecosystems meet. It is a mosaic of mopane savannah and shrubveld, baobab 'forests' ③, plains, sandstone koppies and patches of rare sand forest. This region is home to several mammal species that occur nowhere else in the park, such as Sharpe's grysbok, suni, samango monkey and yellow-spotted rock dassie, while noteworthy species as Lichtenstein's hartebeest (released in 1990 after it became extinct in South Africa) and wild dog are also found here. Other game to be seen include elephant, white rhino, buffalo, blue wildebeest, impala and Burchell's zebra. The northern Kruger is a birders' paradise, and among the rare species are Arnot's chat, Böhm's and mottled spinetails, racket-tailed roller, yellowbellied sunbird and yellowbilled oxpecker.

PUNDA MARIA, at the foot of Dimbo Hill, was originally a ranger's outpost established by Captain JJ Coetser, who was posted to the area in 1919 to put an end to ivory poaching. Apparently, the first animal Coetser saw when he entered the old Shingwedzi Reserve was a herd of zebra, and since his wife Maria was fond of black-and-white dresses he decided to call his camp Punda Maria – a combination of the Swahili name for zebra (*punda milia*) and his wife's name. The rest camp was built in 1933, and, although the original mud-and-thatch huts have been upgraded, the camp retains the rustic atmosphere of Coetser's day. Visitors can explore the camp surroundings by following a short self-guided trail.

GUMBANDEBVU, a prominent hill to the northeast of Punda Maria, is revered by the local communities as a rain hill. The Venda name, meaning 'to shave one's beard', refers to the custom which required those wanting to ascend the hill to be clean-shaven. Tradition has it that Nwakama, a daughter of a local headman and reputedly a relative of the famous Rain Queen, Modjadji, lived at the mountain. Nwakama possessed rain-making powers, and in time of drought she would take the meat of a slaughtered black cow to a certain spot on the hill where it would be offered to the rain gods. It was taboo to climb the mountain without Nwakama's permission, and only a few privileged men were allowed to accompany her when she performed her rituals.

BAOBAB HILL was for centuries a prominent landmark for travellers along the early trade routes between the coast and the interior. Between 1919 and 1927, it served as the first outspan for Mozambicans recruited by the Witwatersrand Native Labour Associ-ation (WNLA) at Pafuri to work in the gold mines on the Rand. The first roads in the north of the Kruger Park were constructed by the WNLA, and the labourers were initially transported by donkey-drawn wagons between outspans set some 40 km apart until they reached the railway line, where they continued on by train to the Witwatersrand.

WNLA OFFICE The WNLA recruitment station at Pafuri was situated at the old Mozambican border post. The post was converted into a police station when the border was closed.

CROOKS' CORNER is a triangle of land at the confluence of the Limpopo and Luvuvhu rivers which formed the northern boundary of the Shingwedzi Reserve. In the early 1900s, its remoteness and inaccessibility made it attractive to poachers and other lawless characters. It had another major advantage: situated at the boundary between South Africa, Mozambique and Zimbabwe, it was a convenient refuge for those wanting to escape from the law. In time, this spot became known as Crooks' Corner.

The Pafuri area was administered by the then Department of Native Affairs until 1968, when it was incorporated into the Kruger Park in exchange for land to the south of Punda Maria along the park's western boundary. In 1989, a historic land claim settlement was reached with the Makuleke people, when they regained 25 000 ha of land from which they were forcibly removed when the Pafuri area was incorporated into the park. In terms of the agreement the community will not be able to live permanently in the area, farm, or mine without the permission of South African National Parks, but they have rights over tourism. A variety of tourism projects are being investigated by the community for the area.

PAFURI ①, a delightful picnic spot, lies amid magnificent riverine forest of jackalberry, ana, nyala, and baobab trees fringing the Luvuvhu River ④. The river was named by the Venda people after the abundance of river bushwillow trees (*Combretum erythrophyllum*), while Pafuri owes its name to one of the early chiefs in the area. The forests are home to samango monkeys (re-introduced in 1982), nyala and a wide variety of bird species, including mottled and Böhm's spinetail, Narina trogon, broadbilled roller, wattle-eyed flycatcher and yellow white-eye, to mention but a few species.

2

THULAMELA ② is without doubt the most significant archaeological site in the Kruger National Park. Built on the plateau of Thulamela Hill, the site was inhabited by Late Iron Age people – the ancestors of the Venda – between the 15th and 17th centuries. Among the most significant artefacts found here are three small gold beads, a 1-cm-long section of a gold bracelet and two potsherds that could have been part of a crucible for gold-smelting. Chinese porcelain and perforated ornamental cowrie shells have provided evidence of contact with the east coast, while other material excavated includes clay spindle whorls, ivory and metal rings, glass beads and the remains of cattle and small stock. Further research at the site led to the excavation (with the approval of local communities) of two skeletons of inhabitants who were clearly of high status – possibly a chief, or headman, and his wife. At a ceremony attended by the local communities, the two skeletons were reburied in their original graves on 31 May 1997. The stone-walled settlement has been reconstructed and can be visited by joining a guided tour which focuses on Thulamela's history and its surrounding environment.

3

TSHIPISE Originally known as Chipise, the name of this popular spa resort is said to be a corruption of the Venda name *chia fisu*, meaning 'to be hot', a reference to the 65 °C temperature of the hot spring where it surfaces. Situated among mopane woodlands punctuated with towering baobabs, the resort's hot mineral pools are not the only attraction, and there is a wide variety of activities and recreational facilities. Game-viewing in the adjacent 2 200-ha Honnet Nature Reserve, which has been stocked with giraffe, sable, tsessebe, blue wildebeest and a variety of other species, can be enjoyed either on horseback or by joining a guided game-viewing drive. The resort offers a variety of accommodation, including the option of sleeping in a reconstructed Venda homestead.

4

WYLLIE'S POORT See Tour 64, page 157.

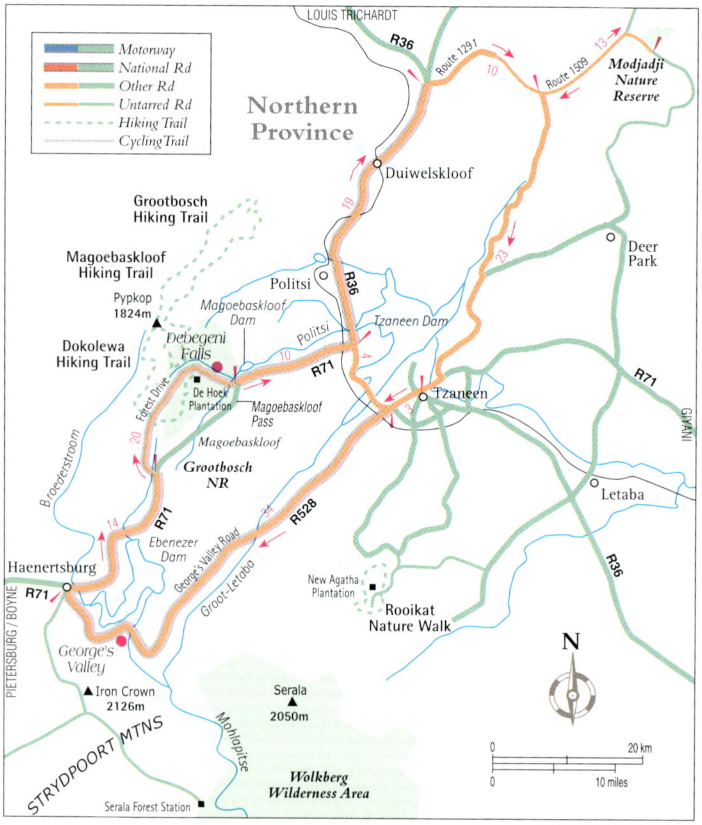

62

175 KM

1

2

TZANEEN Situated in a fertile valley at the head of Magoebaskloof, Tzaneen is the second-largest town in the Northern Province. The town was established in 1919 and its name is variously said to mean 'gathering place' (derived from the word *tsaneng*), or *tsana*, meaning 'basket of hills'. Tzaneen is the centre of one of the country's largest subtropical fruit-producing areas, and is known for its pawpaws, mangos, avocados and tea, while citrus fruit, litchis, winter vegetables and timber are other important crops. It is also a popular tourist centre and a good base for numerous scenic drives ③ through the region. The Tzaneen Museum recounts the history and culture of the region's diverse cultural groups. Among the many interesting exhibits are the royal drums of the Rain Queen, Modjadji, the largest collection of pole carvings in the country, pottery dating back 1 600 years and various ethnological artefacts. The Tzaneen Dam, on the town's outskirts, is popular with angling, water-sport and birding enthusiasts.

Since the first tea plantations ④ were established on the slopes of the Magoesbaskloof Valley in 1963, Tzaneen has become an important tea-producing area and large tracts are now covered by verdant green tea plantations. At the Sapekoe tea estate – the name is a combination of 'Sa' for South Africa and 'pekoe', the Chinese name for tea – visitors can take a guided tour of the estate and factory. The estate is located on the slopes of Magoebaskloof to the west of Tzaneen.

GEORGE'S VALLEY was named after the road-builder, George Deneys, who constructed this 35-km-long scenic road through the Great Letaba Valley to Haenertsburg. The valley is a lush paradise of banana and mango plantations, interspersed with groves of citrus and other subtropical crops. Dominating the scenery at the head of the valley is the Iron Crown (2 126 m), which lies at the junction of the Strydpoort Mountains and the Drakensberg. Ascending out of the valley, the road passes the turnoff to the Ebenezer Dam, where anglers can try their hands at reeling in bream, bass, sharptooth catfish and trout.

HAENERTSBURG got off to a promising start when gold was discovered by CF Haenert at the foot of the Iron Crown in the 1880s. Other discoveries followed in the area, and in 1887 Haenertsburg ② was established as a centre for the Woodbush Gold Fields. The reefs turned out to be disappointing, however, and most of the miners packed up and left following the opening of the Murchison fields in 1888.

MAGOEBASKLOOF ① Often shrouded in mist, Magoebaskloof is one of South Africa's most spectacular valleys, a rich tapestry of lush indigenous forest, pine plantations, streams, waterfalls, azaleas and other exotic plants. The valley and its surroundings were named after the Tlou chief, Makgoba, who resented the intrusions of prospectors, miners and woodcutters into the territory of his Sotho tribe during the 1880s. He instructed his subjects to destroy mining beacons, ordered the white intruders to leave his territory and, in another act of defiance, refused to pay tax to the Zuid-Afrikaansche Republiek (ZAR). As a result, Makgoba was arrested on 2 November 1888, but was later released. For the next few years, an uneasy peace reigned between Makgoba and the whites. However, in August 1894 a commando of nearly 800 men, with three cannons, was assembled to bring the chief to heel. Makgoba and his warriors retreated into the forest, where he defied attempts to dislodge him for several months. A series of forts was built around the forest to confine the Tlou. On one occasion the chief found himself surrounded by a commando in the vicinity of Pypnek. Under cover of darkness, however, the chief and his men evaded their pursuers. In June 1895, another attempt was made to capture Makgoba's stronghold, which was subjected to artillery bombardment. His homestead was captured on 4 June, and the chief was taken prisoner four days later by Swazi mercenaries, who beheaded him.

FOREST DRIVE, one of the most scenic routes in Magoebaskloof, meanders for 20 km through pine plantations, stands of eucalyptus and the Grootbos Forest, the largest tract of indigenous forest north of the Vaal River. Along the way, the route passes a memorial to JA O'Conner, one of the pioneers of forestry in the former northern Transvaal, the Woodbush Arboretum, which he established in 1907, and an 82,5-m-high eucalyptus – the tallest cultivated tree in South Africa. Further along can be seen plantations of tropical hardwoods such as Indian mahogany and East African mahogany, as well as yellowwoods. These trees were planted in the 1970s to meet the growing demand for wood to supply the furniture industry. The forests are home to samango monkey, bushbuck, bushpig, red duiker and leopard, and to date over 300 bird species have been recorded in the area. Among the birds to be seen are blackfronted bush shrike, chorister and starred robins, yellowthroated warbler, crowned eagle and forest buzzard.

DEBEGENI FALLS ⑤ are one of the highlights along the Forest Drive. Situated in a tributary of the Politsi River, the falls cascade for 24 m down a series of rocky steps into the deep pool for which the falls are named. A Sotho name, Debegeni is said to mean 'the place of the big pot', a reference to the pool's resemblance to a cooking pot. There are delightful picnic sites near the falls, but visitors are cautioned to be extremely careful as the rocks at the top of the falls are very slippery and several people have been killed trying to use the falls as a natural slide.

MODJADJI NATURE RESERVE The 530-ha nature reserve on the slopes of the Modjadji Valley was proclaimed to protect the largest concentration of a single cycad species in the world, the Modjadji cycad (*Encephalartos transvenosus*). Of all cycads in South Africa, this is undoubtedly the most famous, having enjoyed the royal protection of the Rain Queens for many generations. With a height of up to 13 m, the Modjadji cycad is the tallest of the 29 cycad species occurring in South Africa, although the average height is between 5 and 8 m. The golden-brown cones can weight up to 34 kg.

Picnic facilities are provided, and visitors can explore the reserve along a network of trails. The area around the reserve is inhabited by the Lobedu people whose kingdom was founded by Dzugudini, the daughter of a Shona chief who fled southwards with her followers some 400 years ago after giving birth to an illegitimate son. To put an end to the tribe's leadership struggles, a rule of female succession was instituted and King Mugodo's daughter, Modjadji, became the first Rain Queen. She became so widely known for her rain-making powers (a secret art brought along by Dzugudini) that not even Shaka would attack the Lobedu. Since Modadji I, the Lobedu have been ruled by a dynasty of Rain Queens.

3

4

5

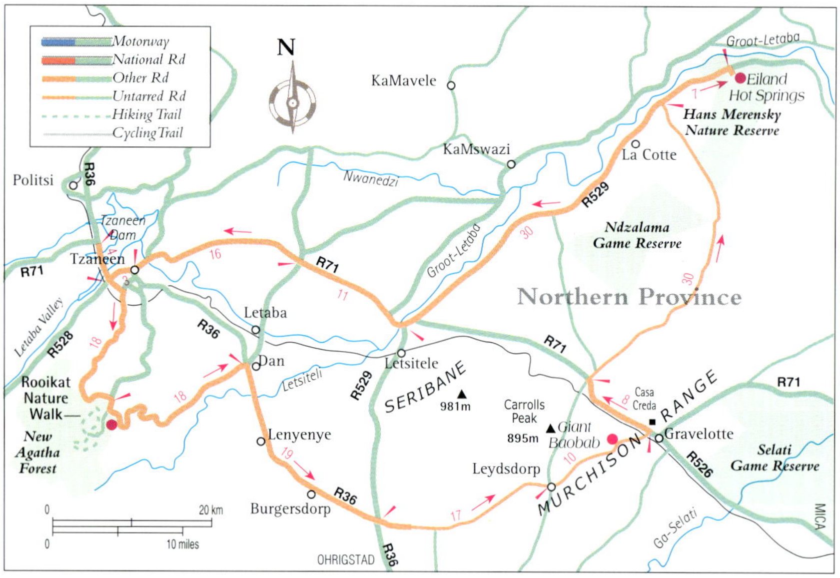

1

63
215 KM

TZANEEN See Tour 62, page 152.

NEW AGATHA In 1888, rumours of a rich gold strike in the Murchison range caused a rush of diggers to the newly discovered goldfields. Situated in the Lowveld, however, malaria and blackwater and yellow fever took a heavy toll. When the Mining Commissioner, Christian Joubert, visited the area in 1890, the miners appealed to him for a site on which to build a hospital. His choice was a spot along the Thabina River, and the hospital was named after his wife, Agatha. It was a poor choice, though, as malaria was rife here too, and the facility was later moved to higher ground in the vicinity of the homestead of Chief Mmamathola. Named New Agatha, the government building served as both administrative centre and hospital. In August 1894, the little outpost came under attack several times from the Mmamathola.

COACH HOUSE The history of New Agatha is closely linked to the days when the stage coaches operated by the Zeederburg Brothers and George Heys travelled between Pretoria and Leydsdorp, a journey which took four-and-a-half days. The weekly Zeederburg service was started in 1890, with overnight stops at Nylstroom, Agatha, Pietersburg and Haenertsburg, where Heinrich Schulte Altenroxel built a wayside inn in 1892.Known as the Kwagga Service, the Zeederburgs tried to overcome the tsetse fly problem by using tame zebras instead of mules, but the idea was abandoned as the zebras were too unpredictable. The hotel was moved to New Agatha a few years later and became a regular coaching stop until 1916, when the service was discontinued following the completion of the railway line between Tzaneen and Pietersburg.

LEYDSDORP Although traces of gold were first discovered in the foothills of the Murchison range in 1870, mining was initially not economical here. It was not until the discovery of richer deposits by Auguste Robért in 1888 that miners swarmed to the area. Two years later, a government administrative centre was established on Robért's camp and named after Dr W Leyds, the State Secretary of the Zuid-Afrikaansche Republiek (ZAR) at the time. Leydsdorp soon developed into a busy mining settlement with a police station, hospital, post office, hotel, bars, trading stores and an odd assortment of miners' cottages. The town even had its own newspaper, the *Leydsdorp Leader*.

Construction of a railway line linking what became known as the Selati Gold Fields to Komatipoort, where it joined the Eastern Line, began in 1892, but numerous problems delayed completion of the line until 1912. Leydsdorp's prosperity was short-lived, though; many miners died of fever and the village suffered from a shortage of water. So, when gold was discovered in the Sutherland range, many miners drifted further north and Leydsdorp gradually became a ghost town. In 1950, the last residents left and the village was abandoned until its restoration as a tourist attraction in the late 1990s.

MURCHISON RANGE With a length of about 140 km, the Murchison range runs from approximately 25 km south of Tzaneen westwards, to just north of Phalaborwa. It was named in 1870 after British geologist, Sir Roderick Murchison, by Edward Button and James Sutherland. Together with Tom McLachlan, Button and Sutherland made the first discovery of gold north of the Vaal River when they found traces of it in the Spekboom River in 1869. The range is rich in minerals, and zinc, copper, emeralds and antimony are mined in the area. The mining town of Gravelotte lies in the eastern foothills of the range.

GIANT BAOBAB ① In various parts of southern Africa, the hollow trunk of a baobab tree has served as a toilet, a prison and a pub – as in the case of this enormous baobab. Established by an enterprising businessman during the gold rush era, the baobab became a popular rendezvous for miners to quench their thirst and swap stories. The hollow trunk can hold 12 people standing, while many other miners used to gather around outside the gnarled trunk.

EILAND RESORT ④ was developed around the hot spring that surfaces in the bushveld just south of the Letaba River. Despite its name, the resort is not located on an island, but takes its name from the farm on which it and the adjoining Hans Merensky Nature Reserve are situated. The farm, in turn, was named after an island in the Letaba River. The hot thermal pool, swimming pools and mineral hydro spa are undoubtedly the resort's main drawcards, but there are many other activities and recreational facilities. Horse-riding excursions are available, guided game drives are conducted in the Hans Merensky Nature Reserve and motor-boating, water-skiing, sailing and canoeing can be pursued nearby. A variety of accommodation is available.

HANS MERENSKY NATURE RESERVE Bounded by the Letaba River to the north, the Hans Merensky Nature Reserve covers 5 300 ha of mainly mopane and red bushwillow woodland and scrub. The reserve was named in honour of the pioneering South African geologist, Hans Merensky, who donated a water hole to the reserve. The son of missionary Alexander Merensky (see Tour 52, page 128), the younger Merensky's prospecting skills were instrumental in the opening of several mines. Among these were Phalaborwa, the Rustenburg platinum mines and the Alexander Bay diamond fields.

The reserve has been stocked with a variety of game, but on account of the dense vegetation the animals can be difficult to spot. Hippo and crocodile inhabit the Letaba River, waterbuck are never far from the river, while giraffe, kudu, waterbuck, impala, bushbuck and Burchell's zebra are among the species to be seen in the woodlands. The visitor centre has displays on various aspects of the reserve, and there is an interpretive trail, two nature walks and an easy but delightful three-day overnight trail for visitors who prefer to explore the reserve on foot.

The reserve's checklist of about 280 birds include species such as tambourine dove, green pigeon, several kingfishers, whitethroated robin and orangebreasted bush shrike. For many birders, however, a particular highlight is ticking Arnot's chat, a species which in South Africa is restricted to mopane woodland.

TSONGA KRAAL OPEN-AIR MUSEUM Located in the Hans Merensky Nature Reserve, the museum is a reconstruction of a traditional Tsonga homestead ②. Built from natural materials, the kraal is centred around an inner court and consists of several types of shelter: sleeping huts, a sacrificial hut, cooking huts and tree, granary, cattle byre and chicken pen. Various building styles are depicted, including some no longer in use, and artisans can be seen at work on pottery, woodwork and wickerwork. As the museum is situated at the site of an ancient salt works, visitors can see how salt is produced, and demonstrations of iron forging are also given. In keeping with the concept of a 'living' museum, the Tsonga inhabitants ③ wear traditional clothing and perform music on traditional instruments.

2

3

4

64
245 KM

1

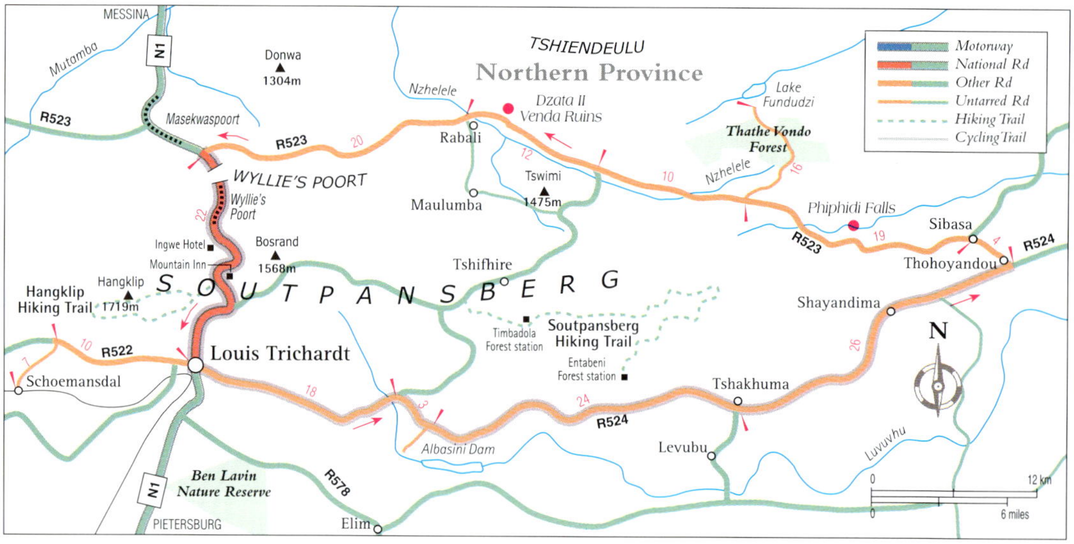

SOUTPANSBERG Rising 700 m above the surrounding plains, the Soutpansberg stretches 130 km from Vivo in the west to near Thohoyandou in the east. Dominating the scenery above Louis Trichardt is the 1 719-m-high Hanglip ('hanging lip'), a name that is probably a corruption of Hangklip ('hanging rock'). The Soutpansberg range is said to have been named by the renegade, Coenraad de Buys, who arrived in the area long before the Voortrekkers. With a price of one thousand rix dollars on his head for participating in the Graaff-Reinet rebellion of 1795, De Buys fled to the Eastern Cape and later trekked north with his half-caste wife, children and followers. In 1820, he reached a large salt pan at the base of the Soutpansberg, known in Venda as Letshoyang, or 'the place of salt'. Deeply affected by the death of his wife, De Buys abandoned his clan, who remained here and established a settlement which became known as Buysdorp. The Soutpansberg and the areas to the north and southwards to the Letaba River are home to the Venda people ①, a name meaning 'land' or 'world'.

LOUIS TRICHARDT Situated at the foot of the Soutpansberg, Louis Trichardt lies in an area rich in culture and history. The Voortrekker leader Louis Trichardt and his party stayed here from May 1836 to August 1837, before Trichardt set off on his ill-fated attempt to find a route to the sea. In October 1898, General Piet Joubert led a commando across the Doorn River in preparation for an attack on the Venda chief, Mphefu. The commando struck camp on the farm Rietvlei, where a portable iron fort was erected. In November, the Venda were subjected to a three-pronged attack in which the royal village was burnt. Mphefu and his subjects were forced to flee across the Limpopo River into Zimbabwe. A town was established the same year on the farms Rietvlei and Bergvliet and named Trichardtsdorp in honour of Louis Trichardt. The name was later changed to Louis Trichardt. The old portable fort (known as Fort Hendrina) can be seen in the town. The Church of the Vow (one of two in the country) was erected after the defeat of the Venda. The Venda people are accomplished decoraters ② and crafters, and there are many art and craft shops to tempt visitors.

SCHOEMANSDAL was established in 1836 by the Voortrekker leader Andries Potgieter and was originally named Zoutpansbergdorp. After Potgieter's death in 1852, the town came under the control of Stephanus Schoeman who named it after himself. By 1855, the population of the settlement numbered 200, and Schoemansdal had established itself as the centre of the lucrative ivory trade. To obtain ivory, white hunters supplied the Venda with arms and ammunition, but there was no control over the number of weapons in circulation. Various factors, including the introduction of taxation, strained the initially cordial relations between the Voortrekkers and the Venda. This led to the abandonment of the town in 1867 and the establishment of Pietersburg. After the Voortrekkers left, the village was destroyed by the Venda and left to the elements. The historic town has been carefully reconstructed and is now an open-air museum.

ALBASINI DAM, on the Luvuvhu River, was named after the famed Portuguese hunter and trader, João Albasini, who was buried here together with his family. Highly regarded as a hunter, Albasini would employ up to 500 men on his safaris to carry ivory to Lourenço Marques (Maputo). He opened trading routes from Mozambique into the interior and established trading posts in the Lowveld in the 1840s (see Tour 59, page 147). In 1847, Albasini moved to Ohrigstad, and when that settlement was abandoned in 1850 he moved to Lydenburg. Still later, he lived at Schoemansdal, and in 1858 was appointed Portuguese vice-consul to the Zuid-Afrikaansche Republiek (ZAR).

THOHOYANDOU was built as the capital of the South African homeland of Venda alongside the former administrative centre, Sibasa. The territory became 'independent' in 1979, but was reintegrated into South Africa in 1994. Thohoyandou was named after a legendary 19th-century Venda leader, and the name is said to mean 'the head of the elephant'.

PHIPHIDI FALLS Set amid lush forest, the Phiphidi Falls ③ cascade gently down a sloping rock face on the Mutshindudi River. In the forest above the falls is a cemetery where ancestors of the Tshivase royal family are buried. From time to time, offerings are placed on a rock above the falls.

THATHE VONDO FOREST is a magnificent tract of indigenous montane forest featuring towering common wild quince, Natal fig, knobwood, lemonwood and real yellowwood trees. Originally known as Nethathe, a name meaning 'the chaser' or 'the owner of the Thathe area', a Venda poem relates how a human-lion used to chase villagers from the forest while they were collecting wood or herding their cattle. The forest is sacred as it is the burial ground of several chiefs of the Netshisivhe family and a place of ancestral worship. Often shrouded in mist, the tangled vines and old man's beard draped over the trees lend the forest a mysterious atmosphere when the mist rolls in.

LAKE FUNDUDZI ④ From the viewpoint high up in the Soutpansberg, visitors can enjoy expansive views of Fundudzi, the Sacred Lake of the Venda. Surrounded by mountains, the lake is about 2 km long, 750 m wide and between 4 and 5 m deep. It was formed when a landslide blocked the course of the Mutale River. Lake Fundudzi has been used as a place of worship since the Venda first settled in the area and is associated with many beliefs. The water of the lake is believed to be the remains of the sea that covered the earth before the Creation, and that water from the Mutale River 'swims' over the lake, but does not mix with it. Another belief is that it is forbidden to collect water from the lake for domestic use as the container will burst open. Stories abound about Venda baskets (*mifaro*) which have been seen floating across the lake, and it is said that voices, laughter and the music from shikona dances can sometimes be heard coming from the lake. Among the explanations for the origin of the name Fundudzi is that it is derived from the words *fundu* ('to bend') and *dziba* ('large pool'), an apparent reference to the custom, among those who visit the lake, of bowing with their backs to the water and looking at the lake through their legs.

DZATA II was established as the second capital of the Vhasenzi clan of the Venda under Thohoyandou after Chief Dambanyika died near the first capital when a cave collapsed during a hunting expedition. After reputed attempts to rescue him failed, he asked to be left to die and the mountain was named Tshiendela, meaning 'grave'. Built during the late 1700s, Dzata II is characterised by a series of curvilinear walls built from flat stone around the chief's living quarters, comprising the great hut, huts for the chief's wives, the chief's kitchen and various seating places for the chief. Dzata II was abandoned by Thohoyandou's three sons after the mysterious disappearance of their father, and a new settlement was established by Mphefu at Hanglip, just north of Louis Trichardt.

WYLLIE'S POORT is a spectacular natural gateway through the Soutpansberg which was used as a passage from the north by Iron Age people. A nearby Early Iron Age site has been dated at about 1 650 years old. The poort was named after Lieutenant CH Wyllie, who surveyed it for a road in 1904.

2

3

4

THE NORTHERN CAPE

OPPOSITE TOP LEFT: QUIVER TREE (P.168); TOP RIGHT: KLIPSPRINGER, AUGRABIES (P.165); BOTTOM: SPRING FLOWERS, NAMAQUALAND (P.169); **THIS PAGE** TOP LEFT: GOUSBLOM, GOEGAP (P.168); TOP RIGHT: GARIEP RIVER (P.165); CENTRE: *MATJIESHUIS*, NAMAQUALAND (P.168); ABOVE: GROUND AGAMA, AUGRABIES (P.165).

1

65
215 KM

2

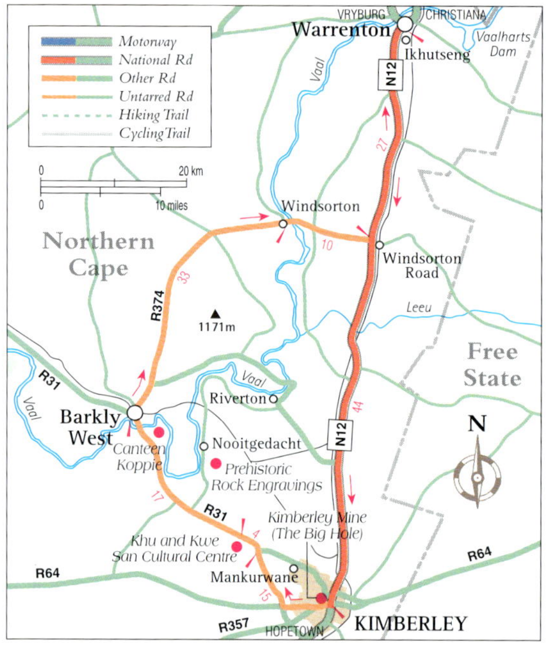

KIMBERLEY sprung up virtually overnight following the discovery of diamonds at Colesberg Kopje in 1871. Tens of thousands of fortune-hunters rushed to the scene, and soon the hillock had been replaced by a hole which was to become the largest hand-dug excavation in the world. Mined to a depth of 215 m, Kimberley Mine ③ has a circumference of 1,6 km and a surface area of about 17 ha. When the mine was closed on 14 August 1914, it had yielded 14,5 million carats (2 722 kg) worth of diamonds. Popularly known as the Big Hole ④, the mine can be viewed from a platform close to the Kimberley Mine Museum . Situated adjacent to the Big Hole, the large open-air museum consists of numerous original and reconstructed buildings, as well as other relics from the diamond-digging days, and provides a picture of life in early Kimberley. A novel way of getting around is to take the Kimberley Tram ①, which runs between the City Hall and the museum. The restored 1914 tramcar is the only one of its kind still in operation in South Africa. At the Bultfontein Mine, a working mine run by De Beers on the city's southeastern outskirts, visitors can take underground and surface tours and see the Diggers' Fountain ②.

Among the city's many architectural treasures are the City Hall, built in 1899 in Roman Corinthian style, De Beers House (the international headquarters of De Beers), and Dunluce. Dating back to 1897, the Edwardian-style Dunluce was elaborately decorated with ornate wooden decorations on the gables and wrought iron-work. The several museums are worth exploring, among them the McGregor Museum, built in 1897 by Rhodes, Dunluce (part of the McGregor Museum), Rudd House (a period museum portraying the life of the diamond magnates) and the Alexander McGregor Museum, with its extensive collection of rocks and minerals and displays on the archaeology of the Northern Cape. The William Humphreys Art Gallery houses a fine collection of South African art, while the Duggan-Cronin Gallery is an ethnographic museum with an invaluable collection of photographs chronicling the cultures of southern Africa's indigenous peoples.

The Honoured Dead Memorial is a reminder of the four-month siege of Kimberley during the South African War. The monument was commissioned by Cecil John Rhodes in memory of those who died during the siege and was designed by the renowned architect Sir Herbert Baker. Mounted on the stylobate of the monument is Long Cecil, a field gun manufactured in the De Beers workshops during the siege.

Kimberley was once home to two great South African political figures. The house where Sol Plaatjies, a founder member of the African National Congress and a distinguished journalist, lived in what was then known as the Malay Camp has been declared a national monument. Also of historic interest is the house where Robert Sobukwe, founder and first President of the Pan Africanist Congress, lived following his release from political imprisonment on Robben Island.

!KHU AND KWE SAN CULTURAL CENTRE The !Khu and Kwe peoples of Platfontein are San, but originate from Angola and Namibia rather than South Africa. In the 1970s, the men were recruited by the South African Defence Force in its struggle against Swapo in Namibia and were deployed in bases in western Caprivi and Bushmanland. When Namibia gained its independence, large numbers of the San soldiers opted to move to South Africa rather than remain in Namibia. They were resettled in military tents at Schmidtsdrift, where for nine years they endured harsh conditions, with few opportunities to earn an income. Following a land claim by the Bathlaping Tswana, the government bought the farm Platfontein where the San were moved once again. Various employment and skills development projects have been initiated, among them the production of crafts. A wide range of traditional crafts, paintings, textiles, ceramics and tinwork are for sale in the shop at Platfontein.

NOOITGEDACHT is one of several sites in southern Africa where the floor over which glaciers moved some 345 to 280 million years ago is preserved. During this period, vast ice sheets that had formed on the highlands of southern Africa and the adjoining parts of the Gondwana supercontinent began moving under their own weight. At Nooitgedacht the parallel and slightly divergent striations made by rock fragments carried in the glaciers as they moved across the Ventersdorp lavas (dating back over 2 500 million years) can clearly be seen, and are orientated in a northeast-southwest direction. These 'glacial pavements' were later used by San shamans to execute rock engravings. The Nooitgedacht engravings depict many geometric patterns, but there are also engravings of human figures, antelope, rhino and elephant.

BARKLY WEST, on the northern bank of the Vaal River, was originally known as Klipdrift. After the discovery of rich alluvial diamond-bearing gravels, thousands of hopeful diggers set up camp at what became known as Canteen Koppie. While a dispute ensued over possession of the area, the diggers declared their own republic. Attempts by ZAR President MW Pretorius to exercise jurisdiction over the area were ignored, and the dispute was only settled when Britain annexed the territory of Griqualand West on 27 October 1871. In December 1871, Sir Henry Barkly, Governor of the Cape, was also appointed Governor of Griqualand West and Canteen Koppie was later renamed in his honour. Most of the diggers left when diamonds were discovered on the farms Bultfontein, Vooruitzig and Dorstfontein in early 1871. Some diggers, however, persevered, and the search for diamonds still continues in this region, both by hand and with modern earth-moving equipment. In addition to its place in South Africa's diamond history, Canteen Koppie is also an archaeological treasure-house, and finds have included implements dating back to the Earlier Stone Age and the fossilised remains of numerous animals.

WINDSORTON, on the western bank of the Vaal River, was originally known to the Khoikhoi as Chaib, a name meaning 'place of the kudu'. The village developed around a mission station with the biblical name of Hebron, but it was the discovery of alluvial diamonds in 1869 that drew large numbers of prospectors and fortune-seekers to the area. A diamond-diggers' camp soon sprung up on land owned by a trader, PF Windsor, after whom the camp was named. Although alluvial diamonds are still mined by a few diggers, the churned-up river gravels bear testimony to more hectic days.

WARRENTON is an important railway junction, and is also the main centre for the Vaal-Harts irrigation scheme. Situated on the banks of the Vaal River, the town grew around an irrigation scheme developed by a syndicate on the western part of the farm Grasbult to supply fresh vegetables to the diggers on the diamond fields. The town itself was established in 1884 and named after Sir Charles Warren, who was appointed in 1877 to oversee the allocation of mineral rights and land in Griqualand West. The discovery of diamonds on common grazing land attracted another diamond rush and thus mining continued until 1926. Warrenton is also the main commercial centre of the Vaal-Harts irrigationscheme, which covers 36 950 ha and is one of the largest of its kind in the world. The scheme consists of a diversion weir on the Vaal River, from where water is fed into a 180-km-long canal system to water the fertile valley of the Harts River. A variety of agricultural crops such as wheat, maize, groundnuts, lucerne and cotton are grown under irrigation in the valley.

3

4

1

66
325 KM

2

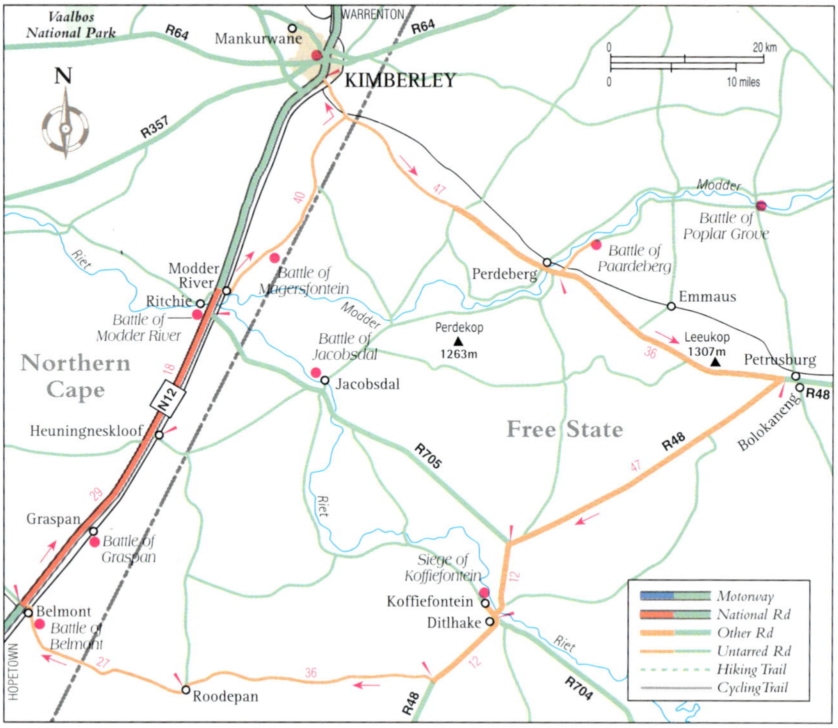

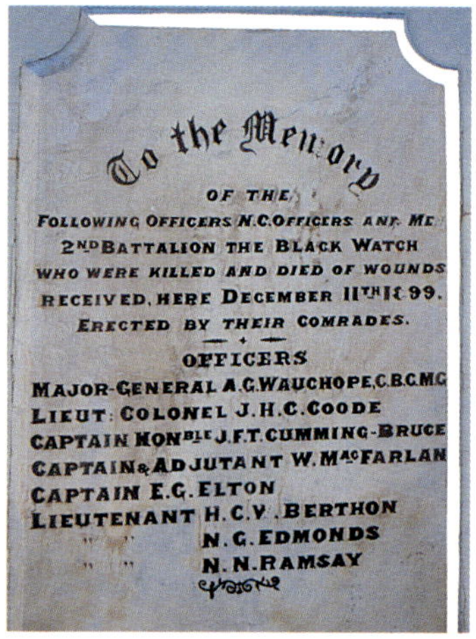

3

THE N12 BATTLEFIELDS ROUTE ① Situated on or just off the N12 , this route explores the battlefields where British and Boer forces clashed during the advance on Kimberley of Lord Metheun's Relief Column from Orange River Station. The route incorporates battlefields, cemeteries, war memorials and museums of the South African War in the Northern Cape, and also comprises wine farms and cellars, game farms and a variety of accommodation options, from cottages and bed-and-breakfasts to self-catering establishments.

KIMBERLEY Within days of the outbreak of the South African War, Boer forces laid siege to the British garrisons at Kimberley and Mafeking on the Cape border. On 14 October 1899, the Boer forces surrounded Kimberley, cutting off all outside supply lines. Contrary to expectations, the Boers did not attack, preferring the option of starving the garrison into surrender. They resorted to shelling the town, and fired 8 500 artillery rounds at Kimberley during the siege. The Honoured Dead Memorial commemorates those who lost their lives during the 124-day siege. Commissioned by Cecil John Rhodes and designed by Sir Herbert Baker, the memorial was built from sandstone quarried near the Matobos in Zimbabwe. Dominating the base is 'Long Cecil', the field gun built in the De Beers workshops during the siege. Weighing 1 625 kg, the 104,14-mm calibre Long Cecil had a range of 7 300 m and inflicted considerable damage on the Boer positions. See also Tour 65, page 160.

PAARDEBERG ⑤ was the scene of the largest and bloodiest single battle of the South African War, and culminated in the surrender of General Piet Cronje – a major blow to the morale of the Boer forces. When the Cavalry Division of General John French outflanked Cronje's positions at Magersfontein, the Boers abandoned their defences and made for Bloemfontein. But at Paardeberg, French cut off their retreat and the Boers dug in along the Modder River. On 18 February, Lord Kitchener made a concerted attack on the Boer laager, but after suffering heavy casualties the attack was called off. The Boers were reinforced when General Christiaan de Wet arrived with 300 men and seized what is today known as Kitchener's Kop, opening up a possible escape route for Cronje's men. Fearing that the lives of the Boer women and children would be endangered, Cronje remained entrenched. When Lord Roberts arrived and took over command from Kitchener, he was appalled by the British losses, cancelled all further attacks on Cronje's positions and instead resorted to shelling the Boers. De Wet withdrew when the British attacked Kitchener's Kop. With the only possible escape route closed, Cronje was forced to surrender on 27 February 1900. The British lost 258 men, 1 211 injured and 68 captured, while the Boer losses were 100 dead, 250 wounded and 4 069 taken prisoner.

PETRUSBURG, established in 1891 as a church centre and to serve as a commercial centre for this sheep farming district, was named after Petrus Albertus Venter, who left money in his will for the purchase of the farm Diepfontein where the town was laid out. Nearby is the Poplar Grove battlefield, where General Christiaan de Wet withdrew after a brief battle on 7 March 1900, opening the way for the British forces under Lord Roberts to continue their advance on Bloemfontein.

KOFFIEFONTEIN developed around a diamond-digging camp which sprung up after the discovery of a diamond by a transport rider in June 1870. A diamond rush followed and the town was officially proclaimed in 1892. The source of the diamonds, a kimberlite pipe, is mined by De Beers. The town came under siege during the South African War, but it is better known for its role as an internment camp for Nazi sympathisers during World War II. The site of the camp, at the entrance to the town, now serves as an open-air museum.

BELMONT The Kimberley Relief Column began its advance from Orange River Station, southeast of Hopetown, on 21 November 1899, but at Witput their way was blocked by a 2 000-strong Boer force under General Marthinus Prinsloo. On 22 November, the British force camped at Thomas's Farm, where an artillery battle was fought until dark. General Metheun planned to launch a dawn attack on the Boers, and at 02:00 the British force left Verner's Hill. Inaccurate intelligence and a poorly drawn map caused considerable confusion in the deployment of the British troops during the battle, but they nevertheless managed to capture the Belmont Hills, forcing the Boers to abandon their positions. The capture of the deserted hills came at a high cost to the British, who lost 75 men in the battle, and 220 injured. By comparison, the Boer losses were minimal – at least 15 dead, 30 wounded and 36 captured.

GRASPAN After retreating from Belmont, the Boer forces, under General Prinsloo, joined up with General Koos de la Rey's men and occupied the hills between Graspan and Enslin sidings. On 24 November 1899 there was a brief skirmish, but General Metheun launched his main assault early on the following morning when the artillery opened fire. Metheun's battle plan was based on intelligence reports that the hills were weakly held, but when the Naval Brigade and the infantry advanced on the hills they came under heavy fire. He then ordered the Naval Brigade and the infantry to attack the eastern koppies, which they seized only to find out that the Boers had long since withdrawn. The British cavalry, sent out to cut off a Boer retreat, was ambushed by a Boer rearguard and retired to Enslin. The engagement left 18 British soldiers killed and 143 injured, while the Boers suffered at least 19 dead, 41 wounded and 43 men taken prisoner.

MAGERSFONTEIN After abandoning their positions on the Modder River on 28 November 1899, the Boer forces occupied Spytfontein and then set up a new defence line around the Magersfontein Hills. The British artillery pounded the Boer positions on 10 December 1899 to little effect, and during the night the Boers took up positions in the 16-km-long network of trenches they had dug on the plains. At first light, they opened fire on the advancing Highland Brigade, inflicting heavy casualties on the Highlanders and pinning them down in the open. A staggering total of 948 British soldiers were killed, wounded or taken prisoner, and among the dead was Major-General Andrew Wauchope, the brigade commander (see Tour 21, page 56). Boer losses totalled about 87 killed, 168 wounded and 21 taken prisoner. Among the numerous monuments ② in the area are the Highland Regiment Memorial ④, dedicated to the 211 officers and men who were killed in the battle, or died of wounds, and the Black Watch Memorial ③.

4

5

THE PLACE OF GREAT NOISE

1

67

280 KM

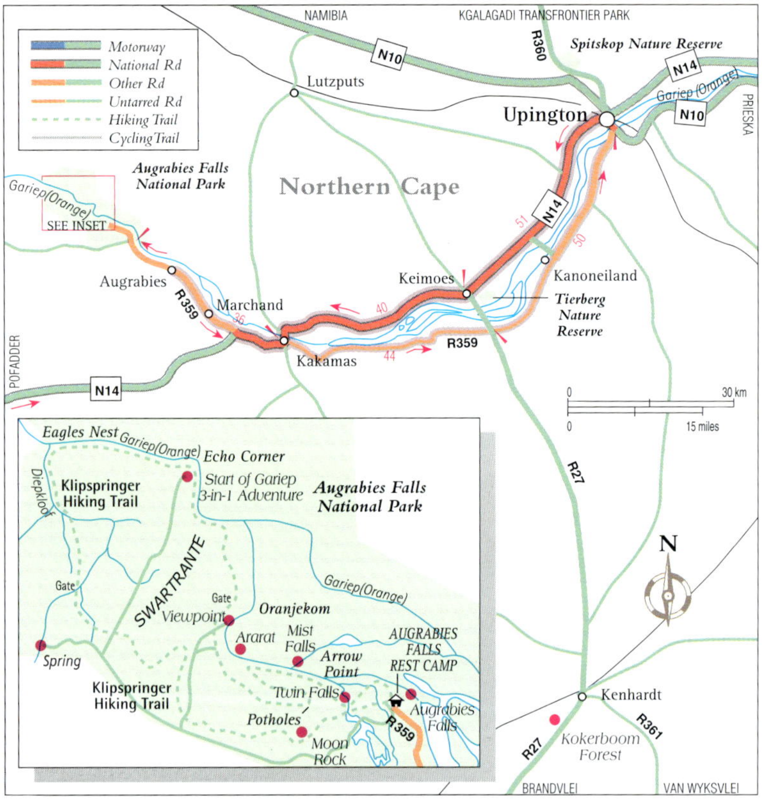

2

UPINGTON, on the northern bank of the Gariep (Orange) River, is the gateway to the Kalahari and the linear oasis formed by the river. The town developed around a mission station established by the Reverend Christiaan Schröder in 1871. Eight years later, the mission – named Olyvenhoutsdrift (fording place of the wild olive trees) – was visited by Sir Thomas Upington, the Attorney-General of the Cape, and was renamed in his honour. Today, Upington is an important commercial and agricultural centre serving the farms along the Gariep River. The Oranjerivier Wine Cellars is the largest co-operative in the country and processes up to 110 000 tonnes of grapes each season, while the town is also the centre of the country's dried fruit industry. The factory at Upington is the second largest of its kind in the world and is especially known for its sultanas, produced from the sultanina grape which has been grown along the Lower Gariep River since 1918. Other crops produced in the area include cotton, lucerne, groundnuts, peas and lentils. A prominent local landmark is the Palm Tree Avenue leading to Die Eiland resort. Planted in 1934–35, the 1 041-m-long avenue has over 220 palms ② and is the longest such avenue in the southern hemisphere.

Upington also has two unique statues, one symbolising the contribution of the donkey to the development of the area, and the other serving as a reminder of the role of the camel during the early days of policing. The Kalahari Oranje Museum is housed in the historic church built between 1873 and 1875 by the Reverend Schröder. Its theme is the history of Upington and the Lower Gariep River. The Spitskop Nature Reserve, 13 km north of the town, has a network of game-viewing roads and picnic spots. Game to be seen includes eland, gemsbok, springbok and red hartebeest.

KEIMOES lies on the northern bank of the Gariep (Orange) River in a contrasting setting of semi-desert and the lush green ribbon along the river. In the town's main street is a historic water mill ① that is still used to irrigate the farmlands along the river. The town's Khoikhoi name is translated as 'large eye', a reference to the spring around which the town developed. Tierberg Nature Reserve, 5 km southeast of the town, offers expansive views over the patchwork of irrigated fields along the Gariep River. Centred on a hill, the reserve protects a variety of succulents and a large population of the Orange River aloe, which usually flowers in July and August.

KAKAMAS was established at the end of the 1800s as an irrigation settlement for farmers who had been ruined first by a severe drought between 1895 and 1897 and then by the rinderpest epidemic of 1897. Its Khoikhoi name is said to mean 'place of drinking', a reference to its use as a watering place for stock. The town's name is synonymous with the Kakamas peach, the famous yellow cling peach (used in the canning industry) which was originally cultivated from a natural mutation found growing here.

An unusual historic site is the graves of German soldiers killed in action when a German force clashed with Union forces during World War I. Following the outbreak of war, about 6 000 Union soldiers had been assembled at Kakamas by January 1915 to invade what was then German South West Africa. On 4 February, the Union troops were attacked by a German force and a fierce battle ensued. The Germans were forced to retreat, losing seven dead, six wounded and 16 taken prisoner. Also worth seeing are the old Transformer Building, which resembles an Egyptian temple and supplied hydro-electricity to the town from 1912 to 1914, and nine original water wheels – known locally as *bakkiespompe* (bucket pumps). The first water wheels along the Gariep (Orange) River were made at Kakamas by the Craighill brothers at the end of the 1800s. Initially made from wood, these water wheels were later replaced by more durable metal ones.

MARCHAND was named after Reverend BPJ Marchand, a Dutch Reformed minister from Knysna in the Cape, who was an ardent campaigner for poor members of the Church. His campaign resulted in the establishment of nearby Kakamas in 1898.

AUGRABIES FALLS NATIONAL PARK is centred around one of the best examples in the world of a cataract waterfall ③. Here, the Gariep (Orange) River fans out into a network of islands, channels and cataracts, while the main falls plunge 56 m over a sheer granite cliff into a magnificent gorge. When the level of the river is high, there are no fewer than 19 falls, among them the Bridal Veil and Angel falls. At the main falls, several viewpoints allow visitors to gaze over one of Africa's great natural wonders and to take in the sound which earned the falls the Khoikhoi name of Aukoerebis, 'the place of great noise'. Below the falls, the Gariep (Orange) River has cut an 18-km-long gorge through the rugged moonscape of granite domes and ridges. Covering 32 000 ha, the park lies on both banks of the river, with tourist facilities provided in the southern section.

Although the falls are undoubtedly the main attraction, visitors can follow a number of short nature trails to places of interest near the rest camp. The road network gives access to viewpoints along the gorge ④, and to the Moon Rock, a large gneiss dome that dominates the surrounding plains. There is also a three-day hiking trail. Night drives are conducted, and adventurous visitors can do a one-day excursion combining canoeing, hiking and mountain-biking. Game to be seen includes springbok, klipspringer, baboon and vervet monkey, while the section to the north of the river has been stocked with black rhino. Rosyfaced lovebird, black eagle, Ludwig's bustard and a variety of larks are but a few of the 195 bird species that have been recorded. A wide choice of accommodation options are available.

KANONEILAND With a length of about 14 km and a width of 3 km, the 2 500-ha Kanoneiland is the largest of several islands in the Gariep (Orange) River. The name of the island stems from an 1878 incident in which authorities bombarded it with cannon fire for six days during a campaign to dislodge the Korana, a northern Khoikhoi group who used the island as a hideaway. In the mid-1930s a group of 52 men, known as the Old 52, occupied the island and began cultivating crops. As they had illegally seized state land, legislation had to be passed in 1939 to enable them to buy the land. Since then, a small settlement with its own school and church has developed on the island, which is intensively cultivated. A pont was used to cross to and from Kanoneiland until 1940, when a bridge was built to link the island to the southern bank of the Gariep River. The dual carriageway over the northern arm of the river was built in 1954.

3

4

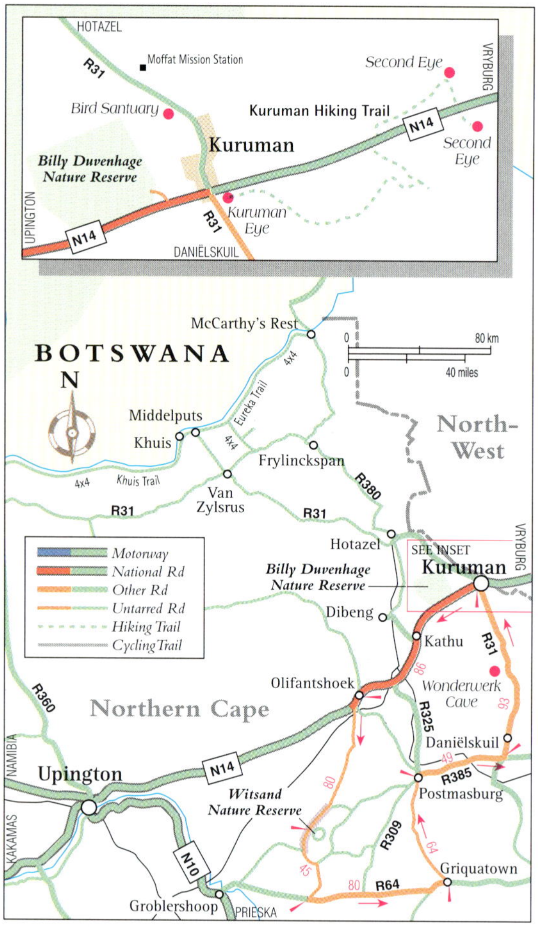

68

545 KM

1

2

KURUMAN ① The strong spring surfacing at Kuruman has attracted people for thousands of years. The early Tswana inhabitants named it Gasegonyane, or 'little water calabash'. With a daily flow of 20–30 million litres of water, Die Oog (The Eye) – as it is known locally – is the biggest natural spring in the southern hemisphere. The abundance of water produces an unexpected swathe of green amid the barren plains, and Kuruman is justly known as the Oasis of the Kalahari. The Second Eye, on the eastern outskirts of the town, has been developed into a holiday resort. To the north of the town is the Kuruman Moffat Mission ②, established by Scottish missionary, Robert Moffat, for the Bathlaping people in 1824. Within a few years, the mission ③ and ④ developed into a thriving community and became widely known among travellers and missionaries. Among the buildings to seen at the site are the 800-seat stone church (completed in 1833), the school room (1829), the Moffat homestead (1826) and the Livingstone Rooms, where famous Scottish explorer and missionary, David Livingstone, lived in 1853. Also of interest are the town's bird sanctuary, where 115 bird species have been recorded, the 1 131-ha Billy Duvenhage Nature Reserve and the Kalahari Raptor Centre, where injured and ill raptors are rehabilitated. Kuruman is the principal town of the Kalahari and the commercial centre for the surrounding stock farms and mines. Minerals and gemstones occurring in the area include iron ore, manganese and tiger's eye.

KATHU Surrounded by a dense 'forest' of camel thorn trees, Kathu owes its existence to the rich iron ore deposits which lie under the acacia woodlands. The town was established in 1972 to serve one of the five largest open-cast iron ore mines in the world, situated on the outskirts of the town.

OLIFANTSHOEK was established at the foot of the Langeberg in 1895 as a centre for the surrounding cattle farms.

WITSAND NATURE RESERVE To the west of the Langeberg range, the characteristic orange sands of the Kalahari unexpectedly give way to a field of stark white dunes and natural vleis that form the focal point of the Witsand Nature Reserve. This quirk of nature has been created by the continual leaching of the red oxide coating of the quartzite grains by water from two underground reservoirs. With a height of between 20 m and 60 m, the dunes extend over an area 9 km long and 4 km wide. Another major attraction of the reserve is the Brulsand, or Roaring Sand, at the southern edge of the white dunes. Here, the white sand overlying the red dunes makes an ominous rumbling sound when the surface is disturbed. This phenomenon has been attributed to friction between the uniform-sized sand grains and the absence of the iron oxide coating. A third requirement is dry air, as the dunes do not produce any sound when the sand is moist. Witsand Nature Reserve offers a choice of accommodation types, and facilities include swimming pools, a ground-level bird hide and nature trails.

GRIQUATOWN takes its name from the Griqua people, who settled along the Gariep (Orange) River under their leader Adam Kok in the early 1770s. Pastoralists of Garigriqua Khoi and mixed origin, they were also joined by displaced Khoisan, Basters and fugitives, and by the latter part of the 1800s they dominated the middle Gariep River area. The town began its life as a mission station established by the London Missionary Society after Cornelius Kok was persuaded to settle near a spring in 1804. Originally known as Klaarwater, the name was changed to Griquatown during an inspection of mission stations in the interior by John Campbell, a director of the society. Visitors to Griquatown can see the grave of the Griqua leader, Niklaas Waterboer, and the old mission house, now the Mary Moffat Museum. Among the exhibits is a pulpit made from local timber and packing cases by Robert Moffat.

POSTMASBURG was originally the site of a mission station named Sibilhong founded by the London Missionary Society. It later became a village of the Griquas who called it Blinklip – a reference to the numerous shiny hematite and specularite stones littering the ground. In 1892, it was founded as a religious centre for the Reformed Church congregation and named in honour of the Reverend Dirk Postma, a founder member of the church. The town lies in an area rich in minerals: diamonds were discovered near the town in 1918, and the old Posmas Mine was exploited to a depth of 45 m before the diamonds ran out, while manganese has been mined at Beeshoek, northwest of Postmasburg, since 1935.

DANIëLSKUIL, like many other South African towns, owes its existence to the presence of a spring, around which a centre for the surrounding farming community gradually developed. The Tswana inhabitants of the region knew the spring as Tlaka le Tlou, or Tlaka lo Tlou, meaning 'elephant reeds', and apparently refers to an elephant killed in the reeds near the spring. The Afrikaans name means 'Daniel's pit' and may stem from the resemblance of a 6-m-deep hole in the limestone to the biblical lion's den braved by Daniel. Following the discovery of limestone and diamond deposits in the area, Daniëlskuil has become an important centre for the nearby mines. Points of interest in and around the town are a British blockhouse built during the South African War and the Gaol, a natural limestone sinkhole erroneously said to have been used as a prison by Griqua leader, Adam Kok.

WONDERWERK CAVE was formed approximately 800 000 years ago when rainwater charged with carbon dioxide percolated along cracks in the dolomite rock, which eventually dissolved to form a cavity extending 140 m into the hillside. With a floor area of 2 000 m^2, this cave provided a perfect home for Stone Age people and is one of the few caves in South Africa to be occupied as far back as the Earlier Stone Age. Among the vast amounts of archaeological relics recovered from the site are hand axes, decorated ostrich egg shell, cleavers, and bone arrow-points. One of the most significant finds, however, was a small slab of dolomite rock decorated with an engraving, dating back some 10 200 years. Near the entrance to the cave, a variety of animals are depicted in black, yellow, ochre and white rock paintings, while a beautiful stalactite is unlikely to escape attention. The cave was not only home to early humans: from 1909 to 1911, the Bosman family lived in the cave while building their farmhouse, and in the early 1940s they exploited the cave to a depth of 35 m for bat guano. Although the archaeological material taken from the cave is displayed at the McGregor Museum in Kimberley, displays on the cave's geology and archaeology at the site museum make a visit well worthwhile.

3

4

1

2

69
440 KM

3

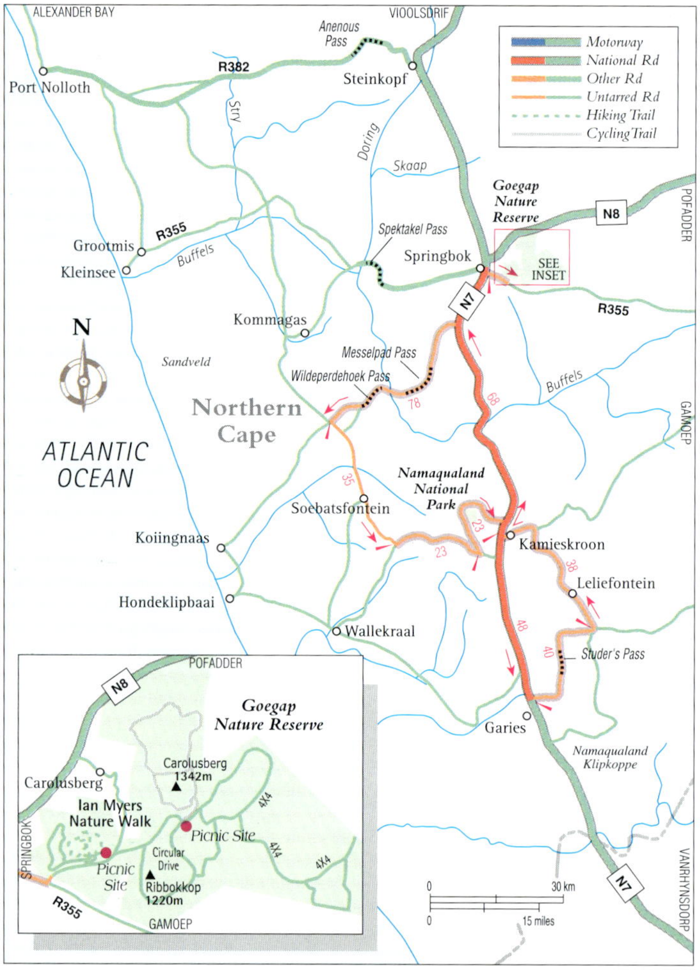

NAMAQUALAND Named after the Khoikhoi Namaqua people, who settled in the area south of the Gariep (Orange) River with their flocks of fat-tailed sheep some 2 000 years ago, Namaqualand covers 55 000 km^2 of quartz-strewn plains, undulating hills, granite outcrops and rugged mountains. Bound in the north by the Gariep River, this vast region stretches southwards to the Olifants River, and extends from the cold Atlantic Ocean in the west to Bushmanland in the east. Namaqualand is home to over 3 500 plant species, among them the dinstinctive quiver tree, the famous Namaqualand daisy (*Dimorphotheca sinuata*), bokbaai vygie (*Dorotheanthus bellidiformis*), gousblom (*Arctotis hirsuta*) and the beetle daisy (*Gorteria diffusa*). For a brief few weeks each year, the arid plains are transformed into one of nature's greatest spectacles, the annual wild flower display ① and ②. The appearance of the flowers depends upon the right amount of rain, as well as follow-up rains two or three months later. The flower season usually begins in early August in the Sandveld along the coast and in the Klipkoppe area around Springbok and Steinkopf, moving southwards and eastwards as the weather becomes warmer. The flowers are at their best between 10:00 and 16:00 on warm, windless, sunny days. Because the flowers orientate themselves towards the sun, they are best viewed from the north side (with the sun behind one's back).

SPRINGBOK, the commercial centre of Namaqualand, lies in a basin surrounded by imposing granite domes, locally referred to as *klipkoppe* (rocky outcrops). It was the copper ornaments worn by the Khoikhoi at the Cape that led Governor Simon van der Stel to mount an expedition in 1685 to find the Copper Mountains. The expedition reached the mountains on 21 October 1685; after two weeks of prospecting, three shafts were sunk at what is today known as Van der Stel's Copper Mine near Carolusberg. The low grade of the ore and logistical problems discouraged mining, and commercial exploitation of the rich ore deposits only became a reality in 1852 when the Blue Mine came into operation.

The site of the town was known to the Khoikhoi as Guchas, a name meaning 'springbok', and the early pioneers named the mining village Springbokfontein, which was later shortened to Springbok. Relics of the early mining days include the open-cast Blue Mine west of Springbok, the historic smokestack and the country's first commercial furnace, where ore was smelted between 1866 and 1871. Among the other places of interest in the town are the Anglican Church (1871) – the second oldest church in Namaqualand – the first Dutch Reformed Church, which was used until the inauguration of the Klipkerk (Stone Church) in 1921, and the Synagogue (1929) which is now a museum. The Springbok Lodge houses an extensive collection of over 900 rock, mineral and gemstone specimens. Among the specimens on display are amethyst geodes, unusual quartz crystals from a nearby mine, azurite and dioptise.

GOEGAP NATURE RESERVE lies to the southeast of Springbok and covers 15 000 ha of sandy plains interspersed with granite outcrops. Centred around the 4 600-ha Hester Malan Wildflower Garden (proclaimed in 1960), the reserve was enlarged in 1990 with the addition of the farm Goegap, a Khoikhoi name meaning 'fountain'. Many of the nearly 600 plant species recorded are annuals, and the reserve's main attraction is the annual spring flower display ⑤, when guided tours are conducted. An extensive collection of succulents can be seen at the Hester Malan Wildflower Garden, and at the nearby information centre visitors can learn more about the flora of Namaqualand. Game to be seen includes gemsbok, springbok, klipspringer, steenbok, bat-eared fox ③ and Hartmann's mountain zebra. Visitors can explore the reserve along a 17-km tourist route suitable for sedan cars, a 4x4 route and mountain bike trails. There are also two short nature walks.

OLD COPPER WAY The scenic Messelpad Pass was built between 1867 and 1869 after it became necessary to improve the original route along which copper ore was transported from Springbok to

Hondeklipbaai, where it was loaded onto ships. Named after the neat embankments of dressed stone, the pass was built by convict labourers – at times, up to 400 convicts were employed on the project. The old jail where the convicts were housed and a cemetery can be seen on the banks of the Buffels River at the foot of the pass, 48 km from Springbok. Following the completion of the railway line between Okiep and Port Nolloth in 1876, however, the pass ceased to fulfill its original purpose. Beyond the Messelpad Pass, the road winds down the Wildeperdehoek Pass (wild horse corner), presumably named after a miner or prospector's horses which ran wild.

SOEBATSFONTEIN, meaning 'spring of pleading', is said to have been named when a goatherd, Hendrik Sievert, was shot dead by a band of San, led by Barend Goeieman, in 1798, despite his pleas for mercy.

NAMAQUALAND NATIONAL PARK The nucleus of this park is the Skilpad Nature Reserve, which was originally created in 1993 to protect the unique flora of Namaqualand. When the national park was proclaimed in 1999, it was expanded by incorporating 50 000 ha of land between the Groen and the Spoeg rivers, while a further 24 000 ha is to be acquired. For most visitors, the park's main attraction is the mass display of spring flowers ④, particularly the orange daisy *Ursinia cakelifolia*, which predominates on the abandoned wheatfields of Skilpad. In the surrounding veld, however, there is a wealth of succulents and other dainty flowers often overlooked in favour of the spring flowers. Since the park is still being developed, the Skilpad section is only open during the spring flower season. Facilities include a 5-km scenic circular drive, two short nature walks, picnic places and an information centre.

LELIEFONTEIN The presence of water in an otherwise arid area and the fact that the spring attracted the pastoral Khoikhoi in summer undoubtedly influenced the decision of the Wesleyan missionary Barnabas Shaw to locate his mission station at Leliefontein. Situated east of the Khamiesberg, the mission was established on a loan farm awarded to the Namaquas by the Dutch Governor, Rijk Tulbagh. Immediately after his arrival on 23 October 1816, Shaw set about building a mission house, a small church, school and other buildings. He also established a garden which produced substantial annual crops of wheat and vegetables. The settlement was named after a member of the lily family, *Androcymbium*, which grows in profusion in the sandy soil. Of historical interest in this typical Namaqualand village are the neogothic church (1855), old parsonage and an ornamental sundial presented to Shaw.

KAMIESKROON When the Dutch Reformed Church decided to establish a seat in Namaqualand, the choice fell upon a valley on the farm Wilgehoutskloof, 8 km north of Kamieskroon. The church was inaugurated in January 1864 and became the focal point of a small village. Initially named Bowesville and later Bowesdorp in honour of Dr Henry Bowe, a well-known doctor in Namaqualand, a shortage of water and the narrow valley made expansion impossible. In July 1924 Bowesdorp was relocated to nearby Kamieskroon, and all that remains of the village today are the ruins of the old church and a few derelict buildings. Kamieskroon itself is named after the distinctive crown on the Khamies Mountains, whose Khoikhoi name means 'grassveld mountain'.

4

5

1

70
325 KM

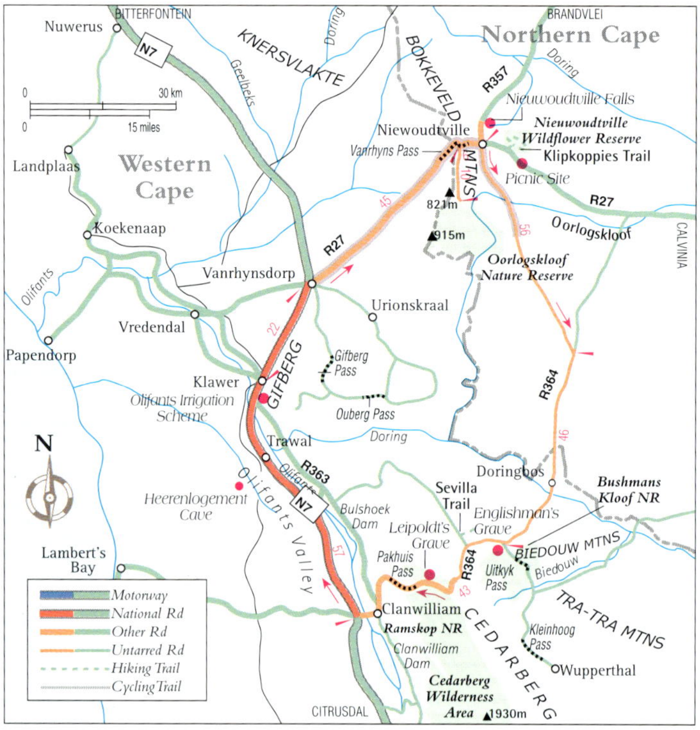

2

3

VANRHYNSDORP lies against the backdrop of the Gifberg (poison mountain), with its sheer cliffs, on the banks of the Troe-Troe River. Founded in 1887, the town was named after Petrus van Rhyn, the owner of the farm on which it was laid out. A fascinating collection of vintage radios can be viewed in the Latsky Radio Museum, while the Van Rhyn Museum focuses on the history of the area. Also of interest is the Kern Nursery, the largest nursery of indigenous succulents in South Africa. The nearby Gifberg, which owes its name to the hyaena poison-bush (*Hyaenanche globosa*), contains numerous rock painting sites and a magnificent waterfall.

BOKKEVELD MOUNTAINS From the plains northeast of Vanrhynsdorp, the road ascends to the Bokkeveld range in a series of sweeps and bends along Van Rhyn's Pass. Completed in 1962, the pass follows virtually the same route as the original road built by the famed 19th-century road engineer, Thomas Bain. The Bokkeveld range separates the coastal strip from the inland plateau, which is divided into the Koue-Bokkeveld (Cold Bokkeveld) ④, Warm-Bokkeveld and the Onder-Bokkeveld (Lower Bokkeveld). Originally known in Dutch as the Bockland, the region was named after the vast herds of springbok, blue wildebeest and zebra that used to migrate into the area in spring and early summer.

OORLOGSKLOOF NATURE RESERVE
The scenery of this 4 477-ha reserve on the Bokkeveld escarpment is dominated by the Oorlogskloof, a spectacular gorge about 500 m wide and up to 200 m deep. Its Afrikaans name, which means 'war ravine', is a reminder of a skirmish which took place in the folds of this wild tract of land in 1739 when a commando attacked a Khoisan kraal to retrieve stolen livestock. Situated in a transition zone between the fynbos and the Karoo biomes, the reserve protects a unique mixture of fynbos and succulent plants. Among the conspicuous species found here are the botterboom (*Tylecodon paniculatus*), the sprawling *Aloe mitriformis*, geelmelkbos (*Euphorbia mauritanica*) and several protea species. A variety of red-hot pokers, gladioli, watsonias and moreas provide a blaze of colour between July and September. Other attractions of the reserve are the large number of rock arches and rock paintings. Day visitors can explore the reserve along two full-day walks, while those with more time have a choice of three overnight routes, ranging between four and seven days' duration.

NIEUWOUDTVILLE Situated on the Bokkeveld Plateau, Nieuwoudtville was established in 1897 when the Dutch Reformed Church bought land from the Nieuwoudt brothers on which to build a church. The Nieuwoudtville Wild Flower Reserve is home to over 300 plant species, and its spectacular spring flower display ⑤ attracts large numbers of visitors each year. In addition to its stunning display of spring annuals, the Nieuwoudtville area is celebrated for its rich diversity of geophytes (plants with bulbs, corms or tubers), among them eight of the 17 Bulbinella species occurring in South Africa, romuleas and lachenalias. Another major attraction near the town is the spectacular Nieuwoudtville Falls ②, which plunge 90 m over a sheer cliff into a large pool. The falls are at their best during the winter months when the Doring River flows strongly. Pleasant picnic facilities are provided near the falls. Nieuwoudtville also has a number of fine old sandstone buildings and rock paintings ①.

GLACIAL PAVEMENTS About 300 million years ago, in a period known as the Dwyka Glaciation, the southern part of the Gondwana supercontinent was submerged in a shallow basin. Snow-covered highlands surrounded the basin, and, as the weather became warmer, sheets of ice began sliding down the slopes into the basin. As they moved, pebbles and boulders were dragged along, scouring the rock surfaces and in some places cutting deep grooves. A closer look at the pavement clearly shows that the ice sheets moved in a southerly and southwesterly direction.

BIEDOUW VALLEY Hemmed in by the Biedouw Mountains to the north and the Tra-Tra Mountains to the south, the valley carved by the Biedouw River is transformed into a carpet of blooms during the spring flower season. Conspicuous among the annuals are the yellow-and-white nemesias, blue heliophilas, gazanias and mauve senecios, while a variety of succulents (generally referred to as vygies) also occur.

WUPPERTHAL lies in a deep valley dominated to the north by the Tra-Tra mountains, Singkop to the south and the Cedarberg to the west. It was in this fertile valley in 1830 that the Rhenish Mission Society established its first mission station in the country. It was named by the first missionaries, Johann Gottlieb Leipoldt (grandfather of C Louis Leipoldt) and Theobald von Wurmb, after the Wupper Valley in Germany, where the society was founded in the town of Elberfeld. Tucked away in a secluded valley, with neat rows of thatched whitewashed cottages ③, Wupperthal has retained the charm of a bygone era. The thatched church, with its beautiful Cape Dutch façade, is still the focal point of village life, as it was when it was completed in 1835. Also of interest is Leipoldt House, the first mission house at Wupperthal, and the cemetery where Leipoldt and other missionaries were buried. In 1836, the missionaries introduced the craft of shoe-making to the locals, and the village is still famous today for its 'Wupperthaller' leather shoes.

ENGLISHMAN'S GRAVE A roadside memorial marks the site where Lieutenant Graham Clowes of the 6th Mounted Infantry was killed during the South African War. On 30 January 1901, Clowes was riding well ahead of his scouting party when he came under fire from a Boer commando. He was shot and killed when he courageously charged the Boers with his sword drawn, and was buried near the spot where he fell.

SEVILLA TRAIL The Pakhuis Pass area is famous for its large concentration of rock art. The Sevilla Trail, on the farm Traveller's Rest, covers 4 km and offers visitors an opportunity to view nine rock art sites. Among the paintings to be seen are elephants, handprints (including those of a child), human figures with elongated necks and zebra, or quagga.

PAKHUIS PASS was built in the 1870s by Thomas Bain to link Clanwilliam to Calvinia in the interior. The scenery along the pass is dominated by spectacular sandstone formations, rugged mountain peaks and magnificent fynbos vegetation. Visitors may choose to stop and visit the overhang where the ashes of the celebrated Afrikaans poet, author and physician, C Louis Leipoldt, were interred. In addition to his many outstanding qualities, Leipoldt was also a keen naturalist, and a member of the protea family which grows naturally here, *Serruria leipoldtii*, was named in his honour. A few faded rock paintings in the cave are a reminder of the early inhabitants of the area.

CLANWILLIAM See Tour 17, page 46.

4

5

INDEX

INDEX

Folens

AGE 6–7

Accessin

GEOGRAPH 2

CW01604100

John Corn

# Acknowledgements

Chris Affleck: 20 (top), 32 (bottom), 33, 34, 36 (all), 37 (all), 42 (America top left; Australia top left), 43 (Italy all; India top left, top right, bottom right), 44, 45 (top), 46; Alderney Government: 18 (bottom), 19 (top); Blackpool Borough Libraries: 28; John Corn: 5 (both), 6 (both), 7, 8 (both), 9 (both), 10 (both), 11 (both), 12 (both), 13 (all), 14 (both), 15 (both), 16 (both), 17 (both), 18 (top), 19 (bottom), 21, 22 (both), 23 (both), 25 (both), 26 (both), 27 (both), 30, 32 (top), 45 (bottom), 47; Bennett Dean; Eye Ubiquitous/Corbis: 42 (Australia, bottom right); Digimap/States of Guernsey: 4; Lois Ellen Frank/Corbis: 42 (America, top right); London Aerial Photo Library: 24; Richard Klune/Corbis: 29 (bottom); Bob Krist/Corbis: 42 (America bottom left, Australia bottom left); Picimpact/Corbis: 20 (bottom); Alan Schein Photography/Corbis: 35; Ted Soqui/Corbis: 42 (America, bottom right); Paul A. Souders/Corbis: 42 (Australia, top right); Paul Steel/Corbis: 29 (top); Ted Streshinsky/Corbis: 31; Brian Vikander/Corbis: 43 (India, bottom left)

© 2005 Folens Limited, on behalf of the author.

United Kingdom: Folens Publishers, Apex Business Centre, Boscombe Road, Dunstable, LU5 4RL.
Email: folens@folens.com

Ireland: Folens Publishers, Greenhills Road, Tallaght, Dublin 24.
Email: info@folens.ie

Poland: JUKA, ul. Renesansowa 38, Warsaw 01–905.

Folens publications are protected by international copyright laws. All rights are reserved. The copyright of all materials in this publication, except where otherwise stated, remains the property of the publisher and author. No part of this publication may be reproduced, stored in a retrieval system, or transmitted, in any form or by any means, for whatever purpose, without the written permission of Folens Limited.

John Corn hereby asserts his moral right to be identified as the author of this work in accordance with the Copyright, Designs and Patents Act 1988.

Editor: Chris Affleck
Layout artist: Book Matrix
Illustrations: Celia Hart
Cover design: Martin Cross
Cover image: Corbis

First published 2005 by Folens Limited.

Every effort has been made to contact copyright holders of material used in this publication. If any copyright holder has been overlooked, we should be pleased to make any necessary arrangements.
British Library Cataloguing in Publication Data. A catalogue record for this publication is available from the British Library.

ISBN 1 84303 581 2

Contents

© Folens

Where is Alderney and what is it like?

Image 1: **Aerial view of Alderney**

© Folens

Image 2: Alderney coastline

Image 3: Small islands off the Alderney coast

© Folens

Image 4: Sandy beach

Image 5: Shingle beach

© Folens

Image 6: Victoria Street

© Folens

Image 7: The airport

Image 8: The harbour

© Folens

Image 9: St. Anne's church

Image 10: The lighthouse

What type of transport is used to get to, and move around, Alderney?

Image 11: Fokker aircraft

Image 12: Passenger cabin

© Folens

Image 13: Flight crew in cockpit

Image 14: 16-seater aircraft

© Folens

Image 15: **Island taxi**

Image 16: **Island bus**

© Folens

Image 17: Train station

Image 18: Cycle hire shop

Image 19: Small boats in the harbour

© Folens

Who lives on Alderney and what work do they do?

Image 20: Special constable

Image 21: Butcher

© Folens

Image 22: **Post office staff**

Image 23: **Joiner**

© Folens

Image 24: **Tourist information staff**

Image 25: **Florist**

© Folens

How is Alderney similar to, and different from, our locality?

Image 26: Gift shop

Image 27: Tourist information centre

© Folens

Image 28: Chandler's workshop

Image 29: Bonjour guesthouse

© Folens

What do I like and dislike about Alderney? Would I like to live there?

Image 30: **New houses**

Image 31: **Older houses**

© Folens

Who has visited other places? Where are they? How far away are they? How did they get there?

Image 32: Seaside environment

Image 33: Countryside environment

© Folens

Image 34: Town environment

© Folens

What is the seaside like? Why do we like to go there?

Image 35: **Ladies on a bench in Blackpool**

Image 36: **Ice cream van**

© Folens

Image 37: Blackpool donkeys

Image 38: Postcard

How is the seaside different from our locality?

Image 39: Aerial view of Blackpool

© Folens

Image 40: Pier at Blackpool

Image 41: Shelter on the prom

© Folens

Image 42: The Golden Mile

Image 43: Coral Island

© Folens

Image 44: **Fortune teller**

Image 45: **Burger bar**

© Folens

What was the seaside like in the past?

Image 46: **Victorian Blackpool**

© Folens

Where else in the world can we have a seaside holiday?

Image 47: **Maldives**

Image 48: **Cala Gran, Majorca**

Where has Poppy Panda travelled to this week or this month?

Image 49: **Venice**

© Folens

Image 50: Disneyland

© Folens

Image 51: **Jamaican beach**

Image 52: **Birkrigg, Lake District**

© Folens

Image 53: **Dolomites**

© Folens

Image 54: Lake Windermere

© Folens

Image 55: New York

© Folens

Can we find these places on a map?

Image 56: Pyramids

Image 57: Rio de Janeiro

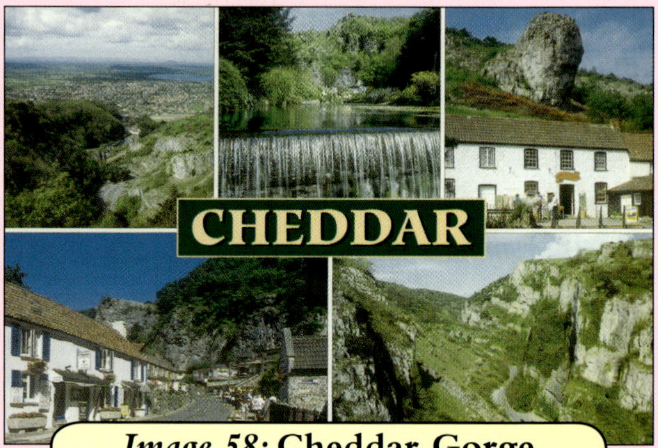

Image 58: Cheddar Gorge

Image 59: Majorca

Image 60: Colorado River

© Folens

Image 61: Tower of London

Image 62: Albufeira

Image 63: Berlin

Image 64: Mount Kilimanjaro

Image 65: Bavarian countryside

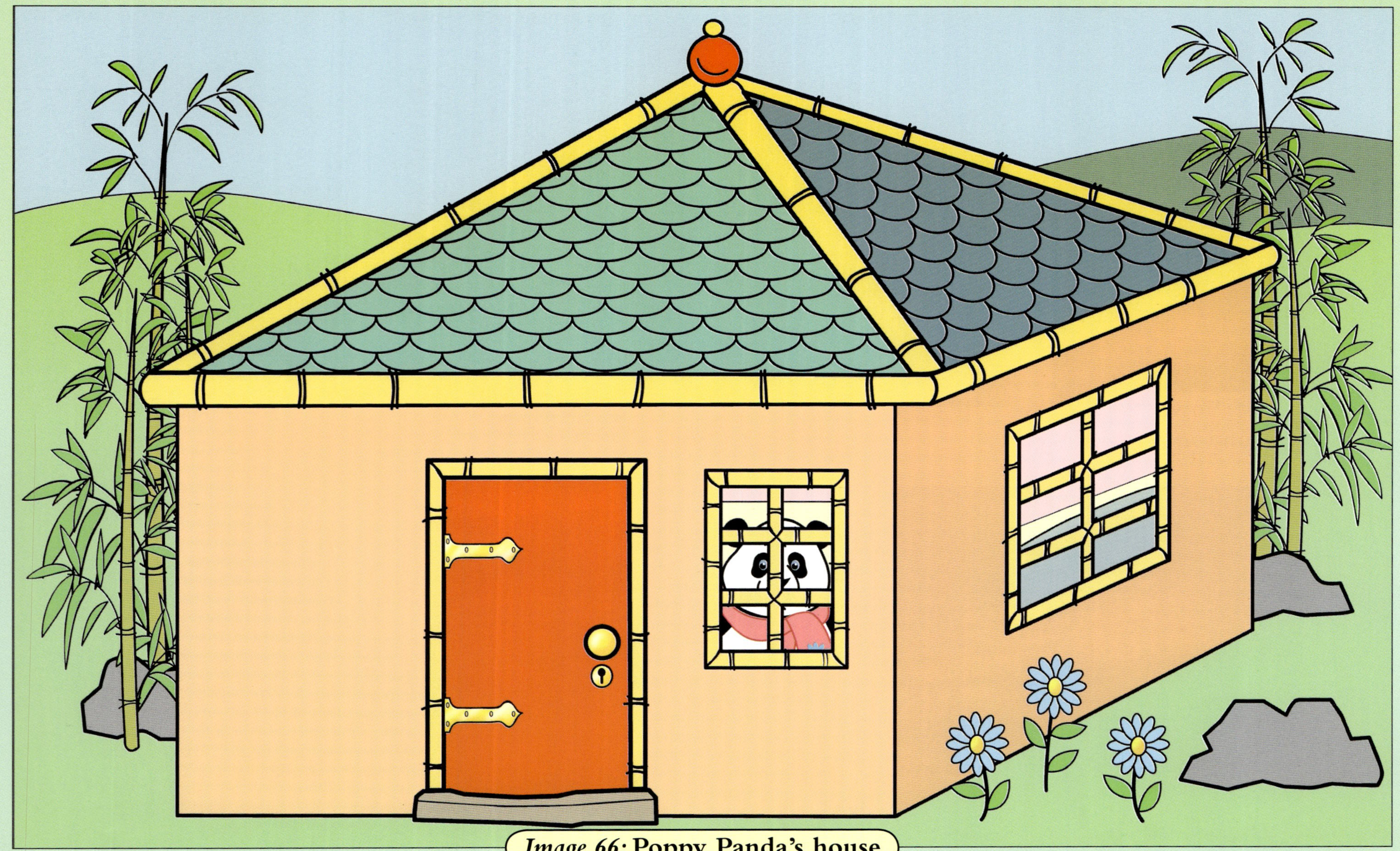

Image 66: Poppy Panda's house

© Folens

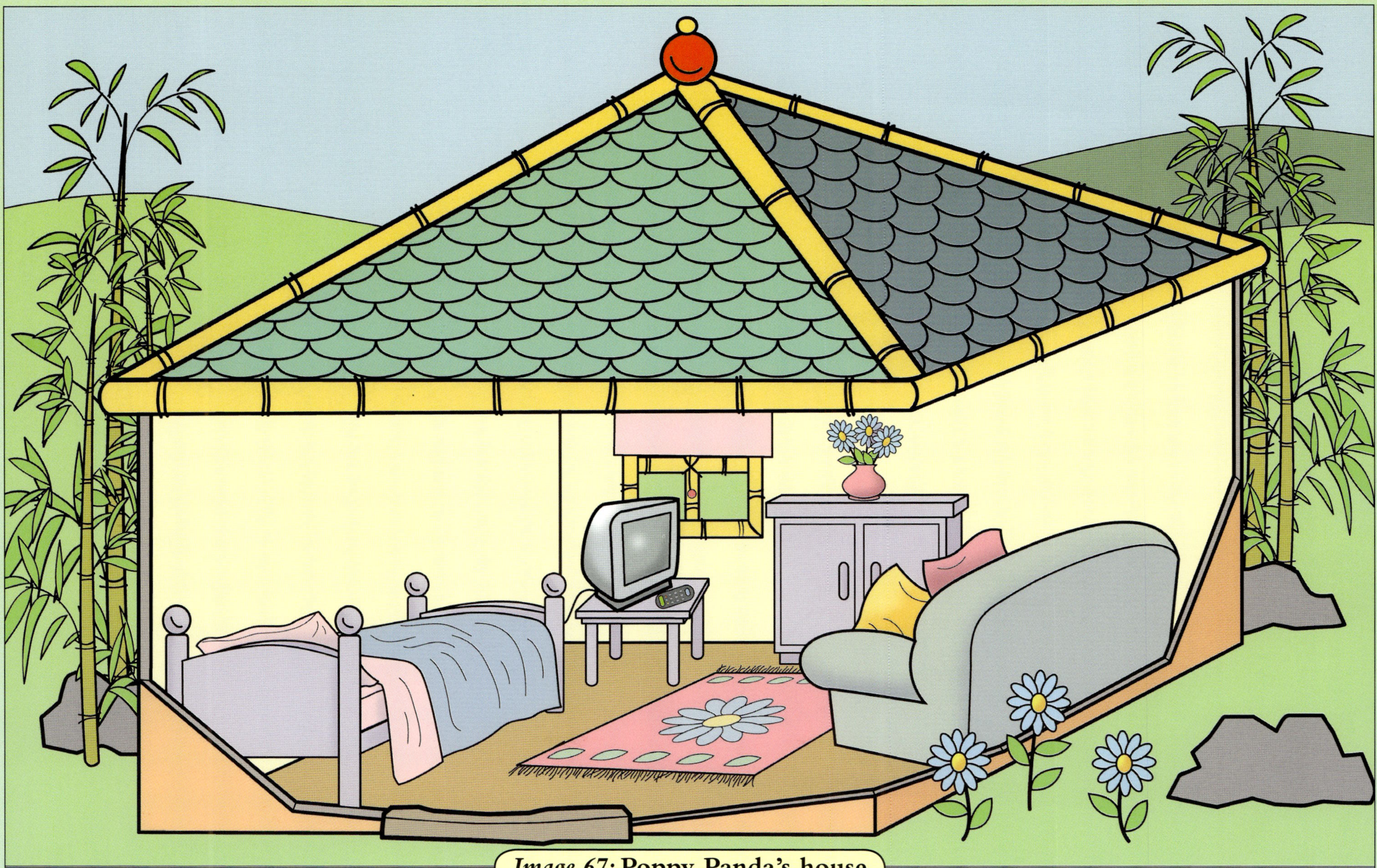

Image 67: Poppy Panda's house

© Folens

What will it be like when Poppy is there?

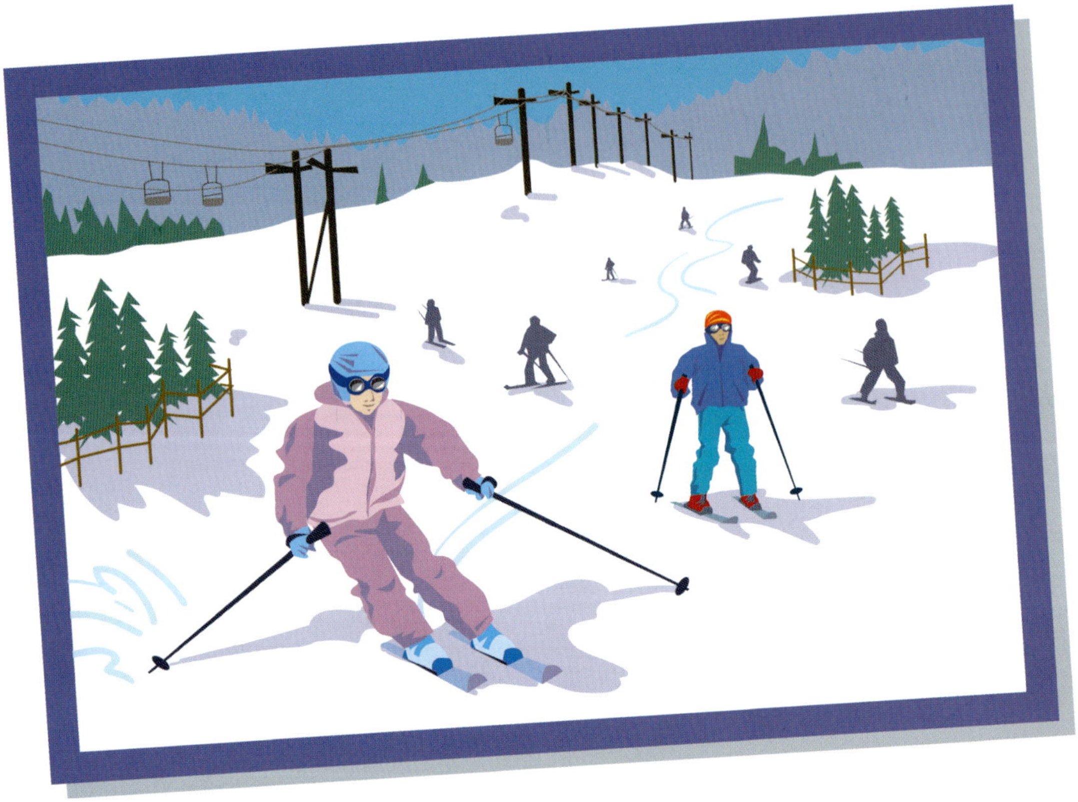

Dear all,
Having a great time, even though it's snowed every day and it's absolutely freezing!
The resort is lovely, with the snow-covered slopes and the mountain sides covered in fir trees.
We've been skiing every day and also done some sledging.
Yesterday evening we went skating on the open-air rink in the village.

Love from Poppy.

Mr B. Bear
10 High Street
Honeybury
U. K.

Image 68: **Skiing postcard**

© Folens

Dear all,
Having a great holiday. It's hot and sunny all day here. The beaches are fantastic – they seem to stretch for miles. The sea is lovely and warm and crystal clear. The resort is built between steep cliffs and there are lots of palm trees and other exotic plants everywhere. Been swimming and snorkelling every day and today I tried windsurfing. It's very difficult! See you soon.

Love from Poppy.

Mr and Mrs Panda
3 Bamboo Road
Eastfield
U.K.

Image 69: **Beach postcard**

© Folens

What will it be like when Poppy is there?

Image 70: **Artefacts from the USA**

Image 71: **Artefacts from Australia**

© Folens

Image 72: **Artefacts from Italy**

Image 73: **Artefacts from India**

© Folens

Unit 5 Where in the world is Poppy Panda?

How did Poppy travel to these places?

Image 74: **Aircraft**

© Folens

Image 75: **Car**

Image 76: **Bus**

© Folens

Unit 5 Where in the world is Poppy Panda?

Image 77: Train

© Folens

Image 78: Cruise ship

© Folens

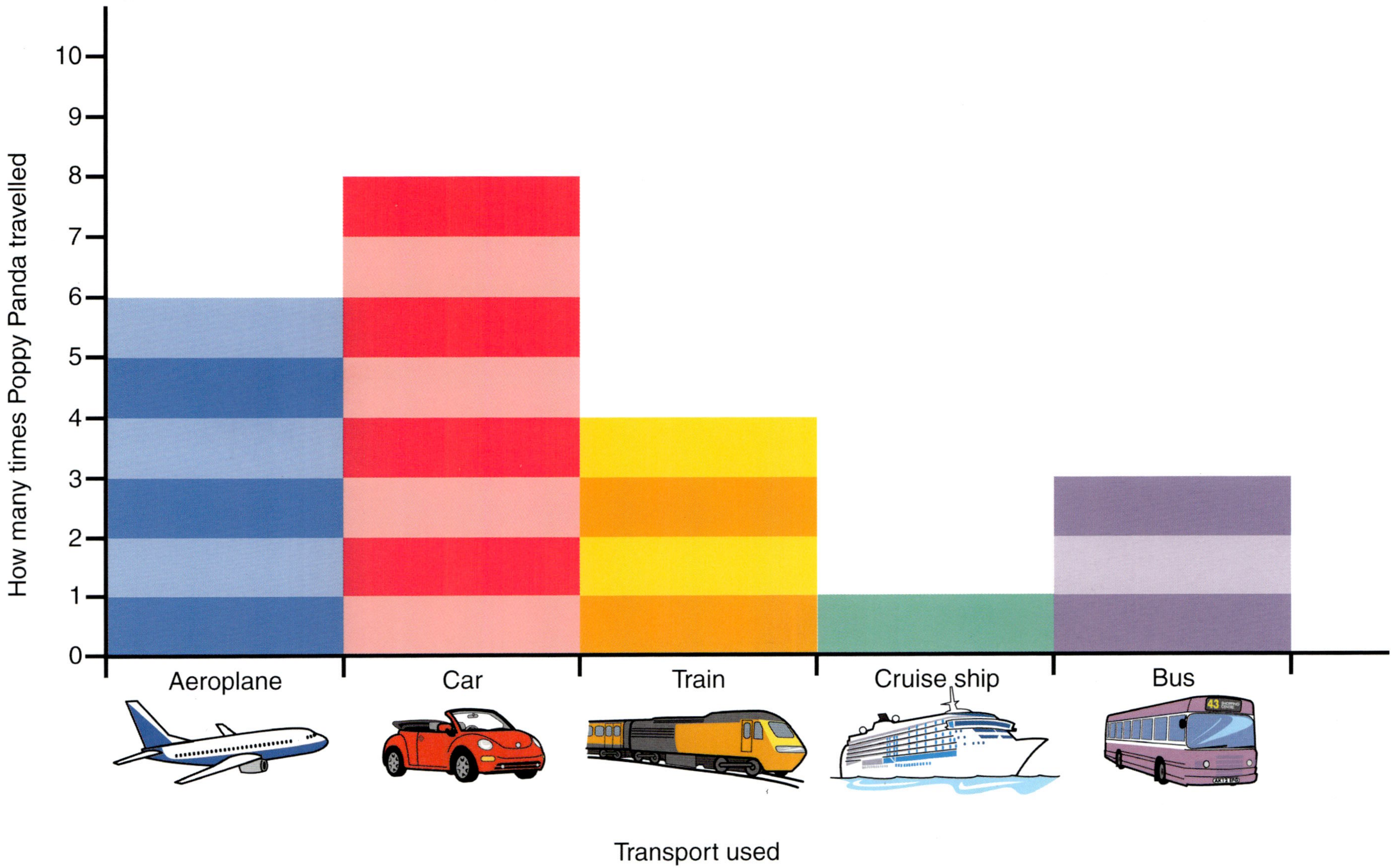

Image 79: **Bar chart**

© Folens